Backwards Game

BAKÉGYAMON

VOL. 2

Original concept by Kazuhiro Fujita

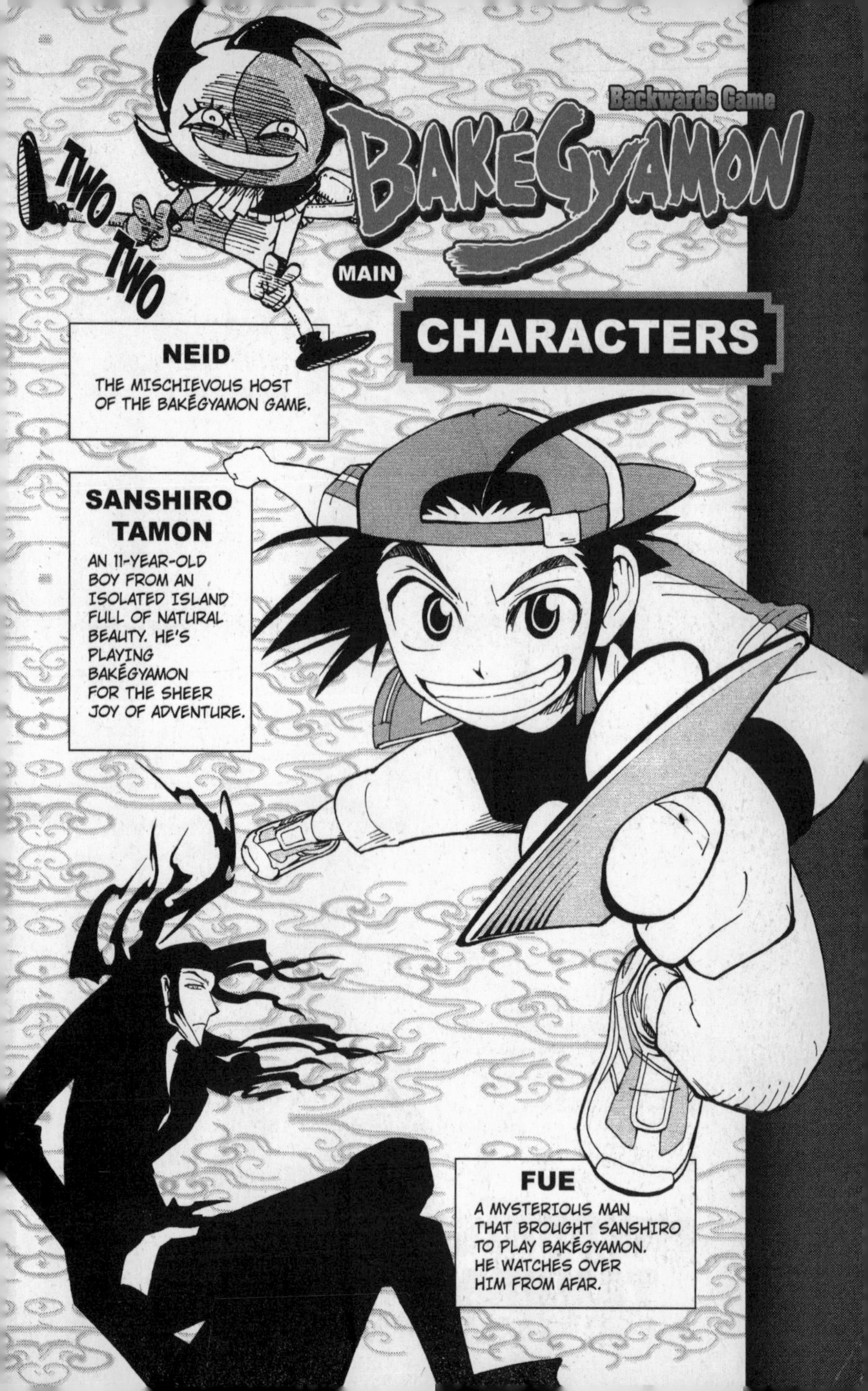
Backwards Game
BAKÉGYAMON
MAIN
CHARACTERS
TWO TWO
NEID
THE MISCHIEVOUS HOST OF THE BAKÉGYAMON GAME.
SANSHIRO TAMON
AN 11-YEAR-OLD BOY FROM AN ISOLATED ISLAND FULL OF NATURAL BEAUTY. HE'S PLAYING BAKÉGYAMON FOR THE SHEER JOY OF ADVENTURE.
FUE
A MYSTERIOUS MAN THAT BROUGHT SANSHIRO TO PLAY BAKÉGYAMON. HE WATCHES OVER HIM FROM AFAR.

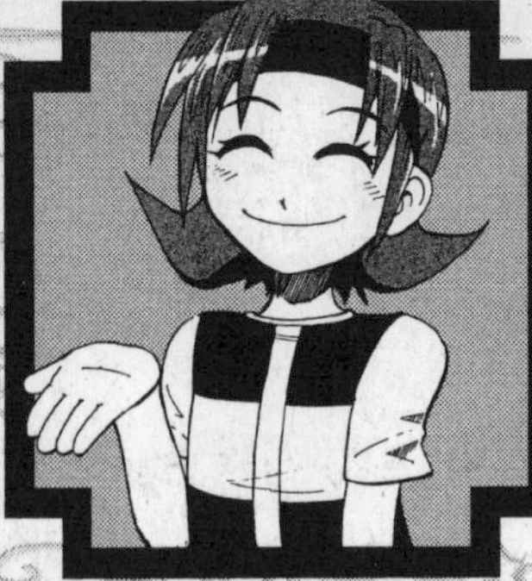

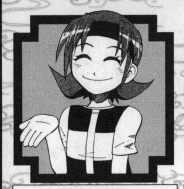

AKI HINO

A HEADSTRONG GIRL WHO'S ONE OF THE BAKÉGYAMON PLAYERS. SHE AND SANSHIRO ARE NOT THE BEST OF FRIENDS. HER WISH IS FOR MONEY.

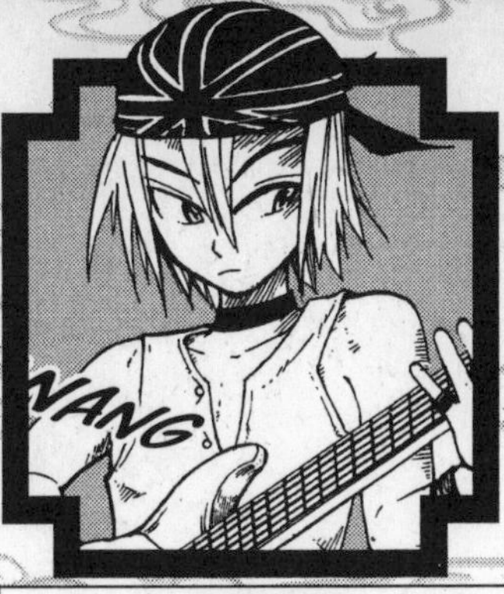
NANG

LONDON

HIS REAL NAME IS TOSHIO SAEGUSA. HE WANTS TO BECOME A MUSICIAN BUT HE'S TONE DEAF. HIS MANTRA IN LIFE IS TO BE ***COOL***.

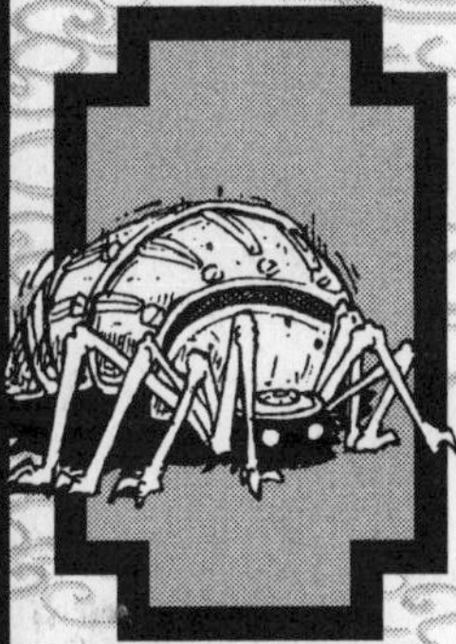

BUGUMO

A BUG-LIKE MONSTER THAT CAME FROM AKI'S GEKI FU CARD. SHE'S AFRAID OF BUGS AND HATED IT AT FIRST, BUT NOW...

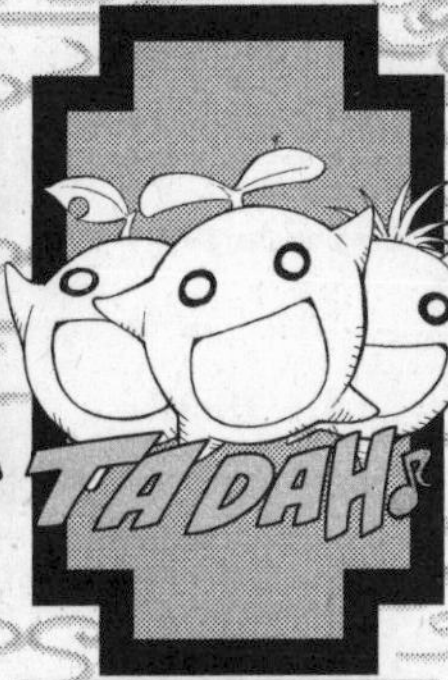
TA DAH!

DOROKOZO

A TEAM OF THREE MONSTERS THAT CAME FROM SANSHIRO'S GEKI FU CARD. THEY'RE NOT GOOD FOR BATTLES BUT THEY CAN MULTIPLY IN NUMBER.

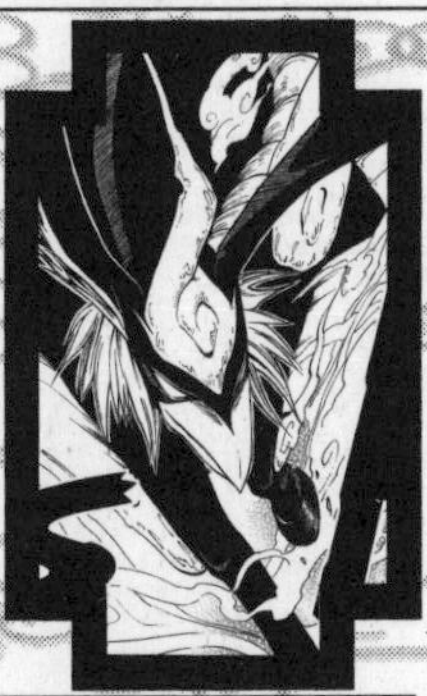

ENZAN

A MONSTER THAT CAME FROM SANSHIRO'S GEKI FU CARD. A BAD-TEMPERED CREATURE, ENZAN REFUSES TO TAKE ORDERS.

"BAKÉGYAMON" IS A GAME FOR CHILDREN CREATED BY MONSTERS. PLAYED ONCE EVERY 44 YEARS IN "BACKWARDS JAPAN," WHOEVER WINS THE GAME WILL BE GRANTED ONE WISH. ELEVEN-YEAR-OLD SANSHIRO TAMON IS EAGER TO FOLLOW IN HIS ADVENTURER FATHER'S FOOTSTEPS AND JUMPS AT THE CHANCE TO PARTICIPATE. WITH HIS BOUNDLESS OPTIMISM AND HELP FROM THE MONSTERS THAT COME FROM HIS GEKI FU CARDS, SANSHIRO HAS OVERCOME THE UNPREDICTABLE CHALLENGES SO FAR...

Contents

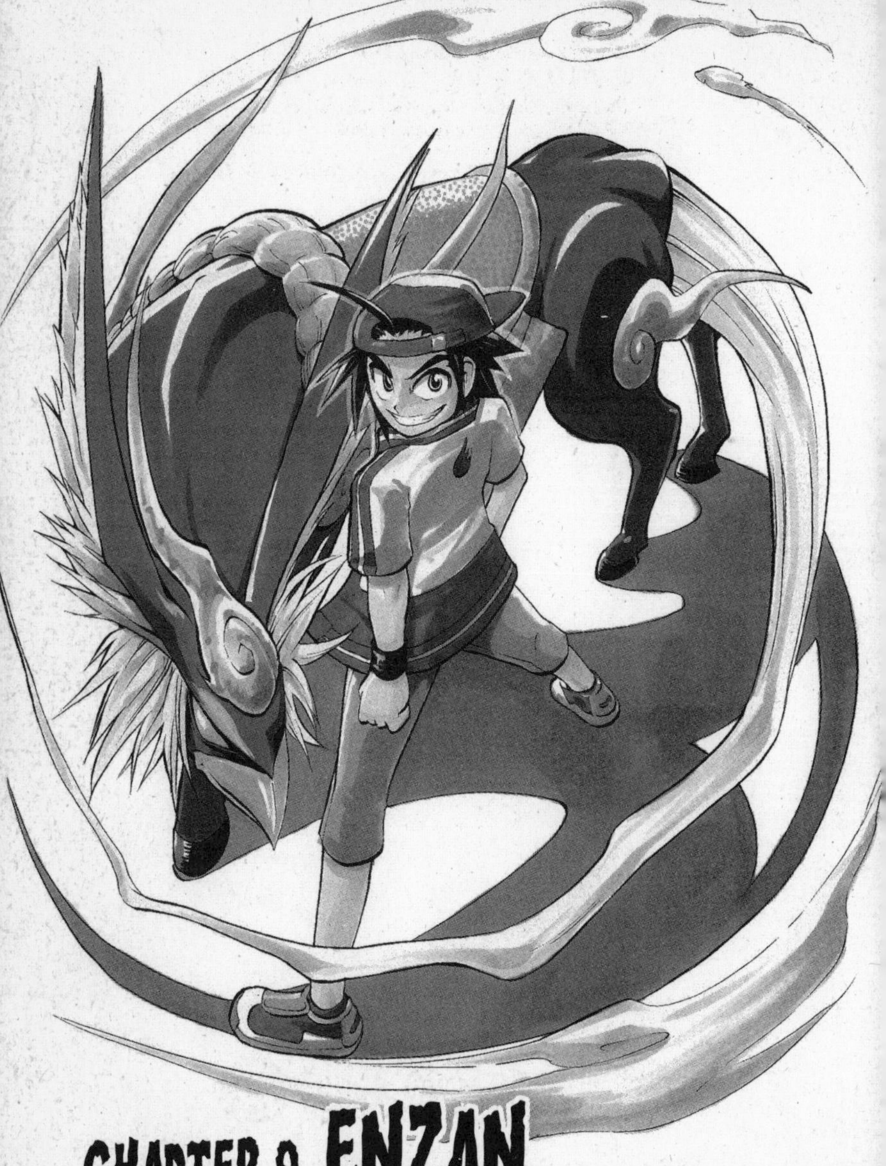

CHAPTER 9 ENZAN

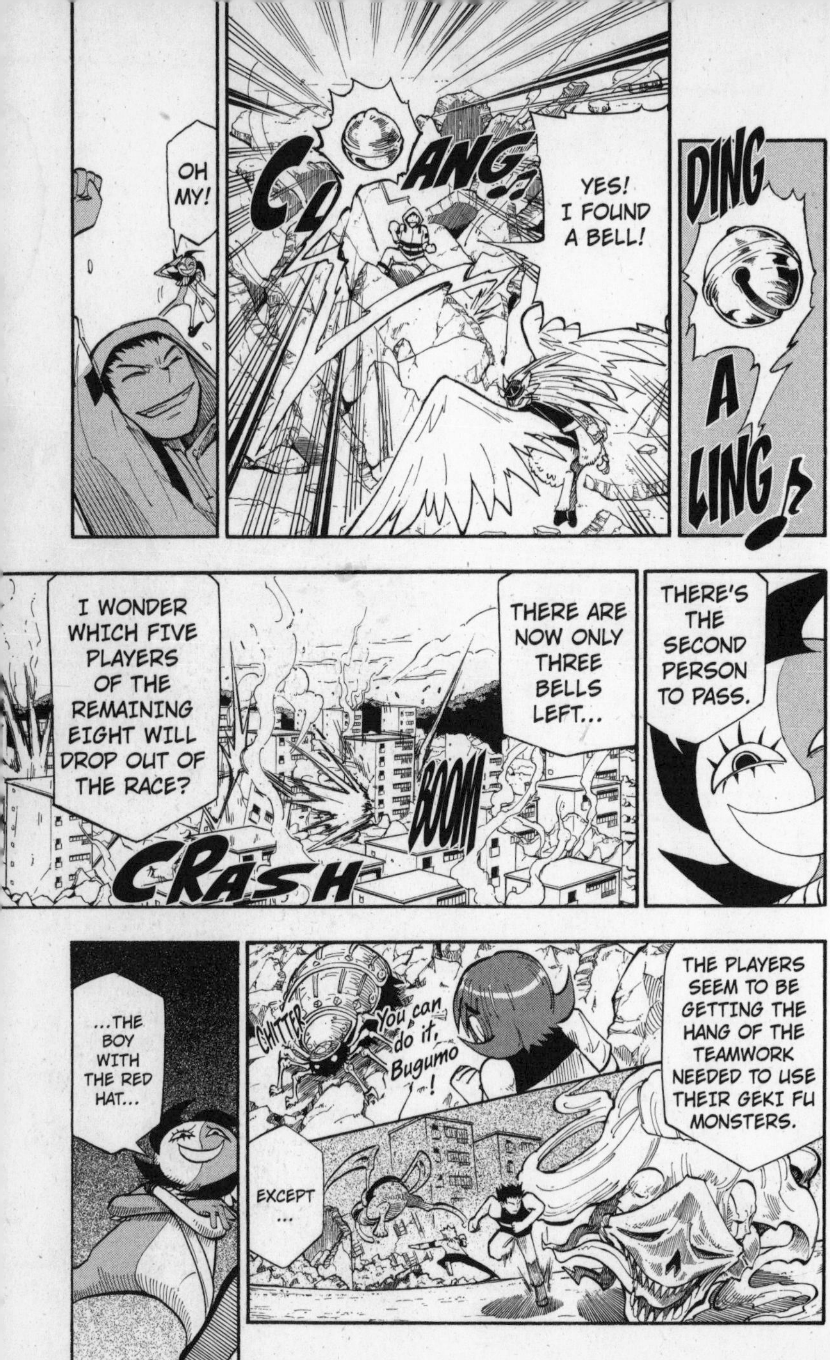
DING A LING
CLANG!!
YES! I FOUND A BELL!
OH MY!
THERE'S THE SECOND PERSON TO PASS.
THERE ARE NOW ONLY THREE BELLS LEFT...
I WONDER WHICH FIVE PLAYERS OF THE REMAINING EIGHT WILL DROP OUT OF THE RACE?
BOOM
CRASH
THE PLAYERS SEEM TO BE GETTING THE HANG OF THE TEAMWORK NEEDED TO USE THEIR GEKI FU MONSTERS.
You can do it, Bugumo!
CHITTER
EXCEPT ...
...THE BOY WITH THE RED HAT...

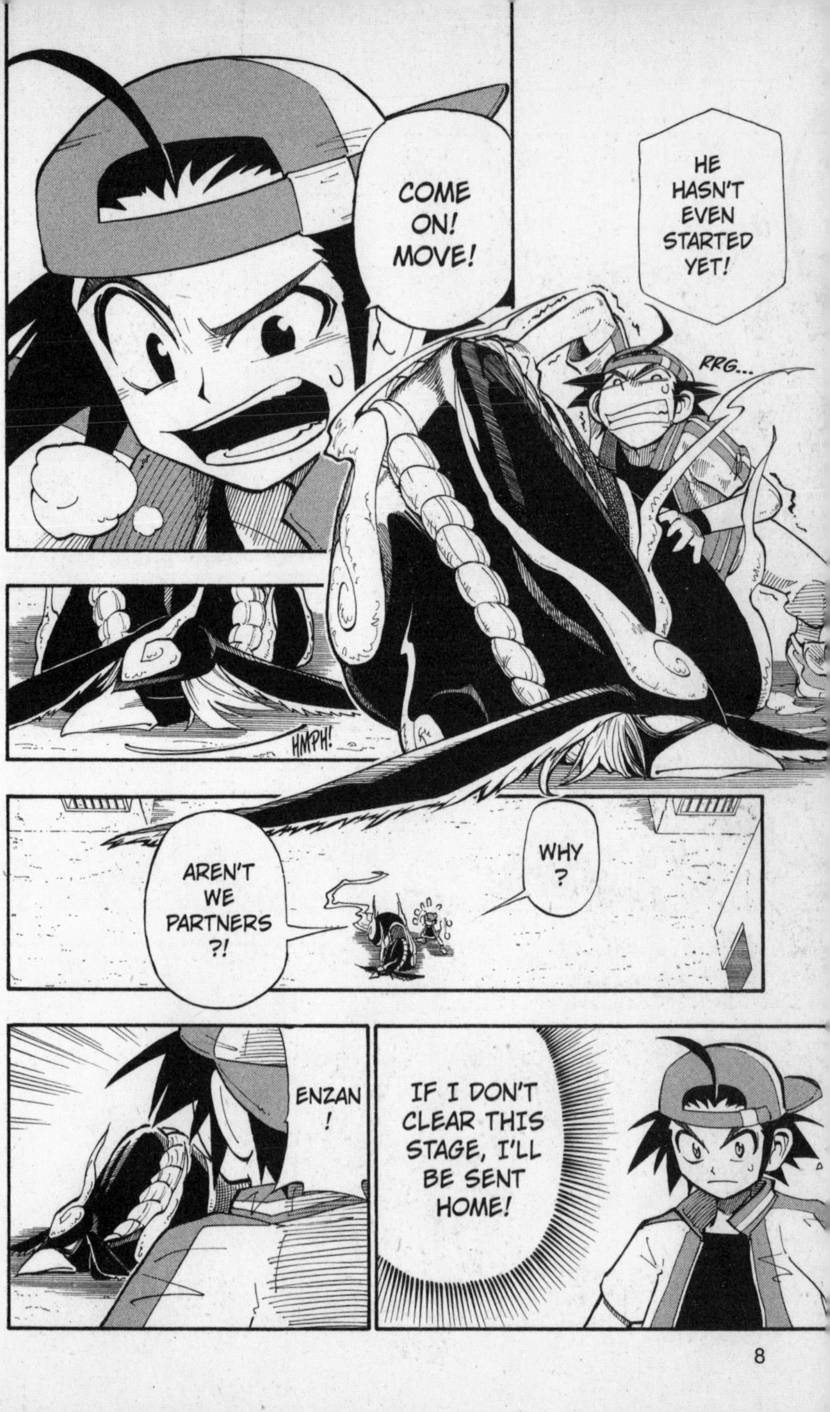
HE HASN'T EVEN STARTED YET!
RRG...
COME ON! MOVE!
HMPH!
WHY?
AREN'T WE PARTNERS?!
IF I DON'T CLEAR THIS STAGE, I'LL BE SENT HOME!
ENZAN!

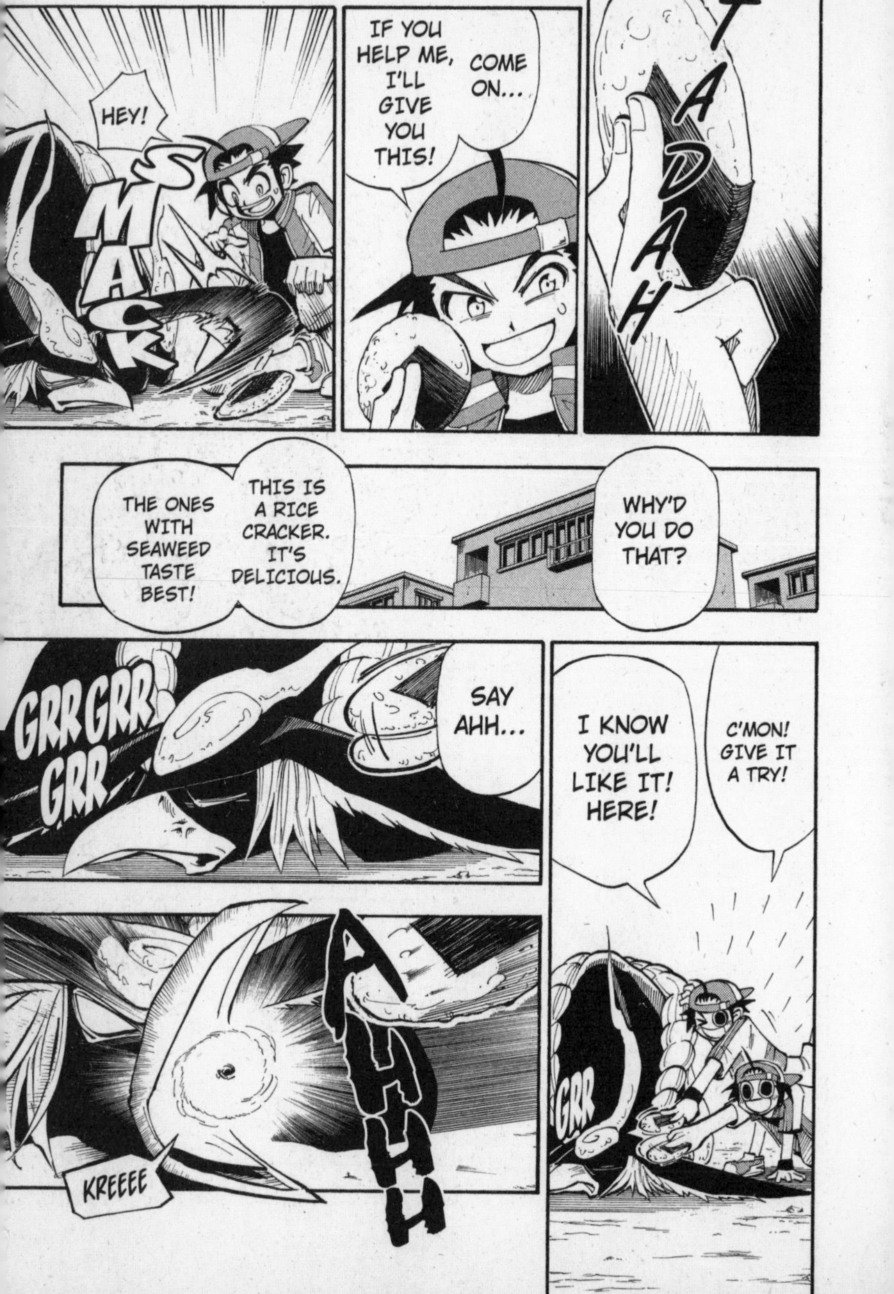
TADAH
COME ON...
IF YOU HELP ME, I'LL GIVE YOU THIS!
HEY!
SMACK
WHY'D YOU DO THAT?
THIS IS A RICE CRACKER. IT'S DELICIOUS.
THE ONES WITH SEAWEED TASTE BEST!
C'MON! GIVE IT A TRY!
I KNOW YOU'LL LIKE IT! HERE!
GRR
SAY AHH...
GRR GRR GRR
AHH
KREEEE

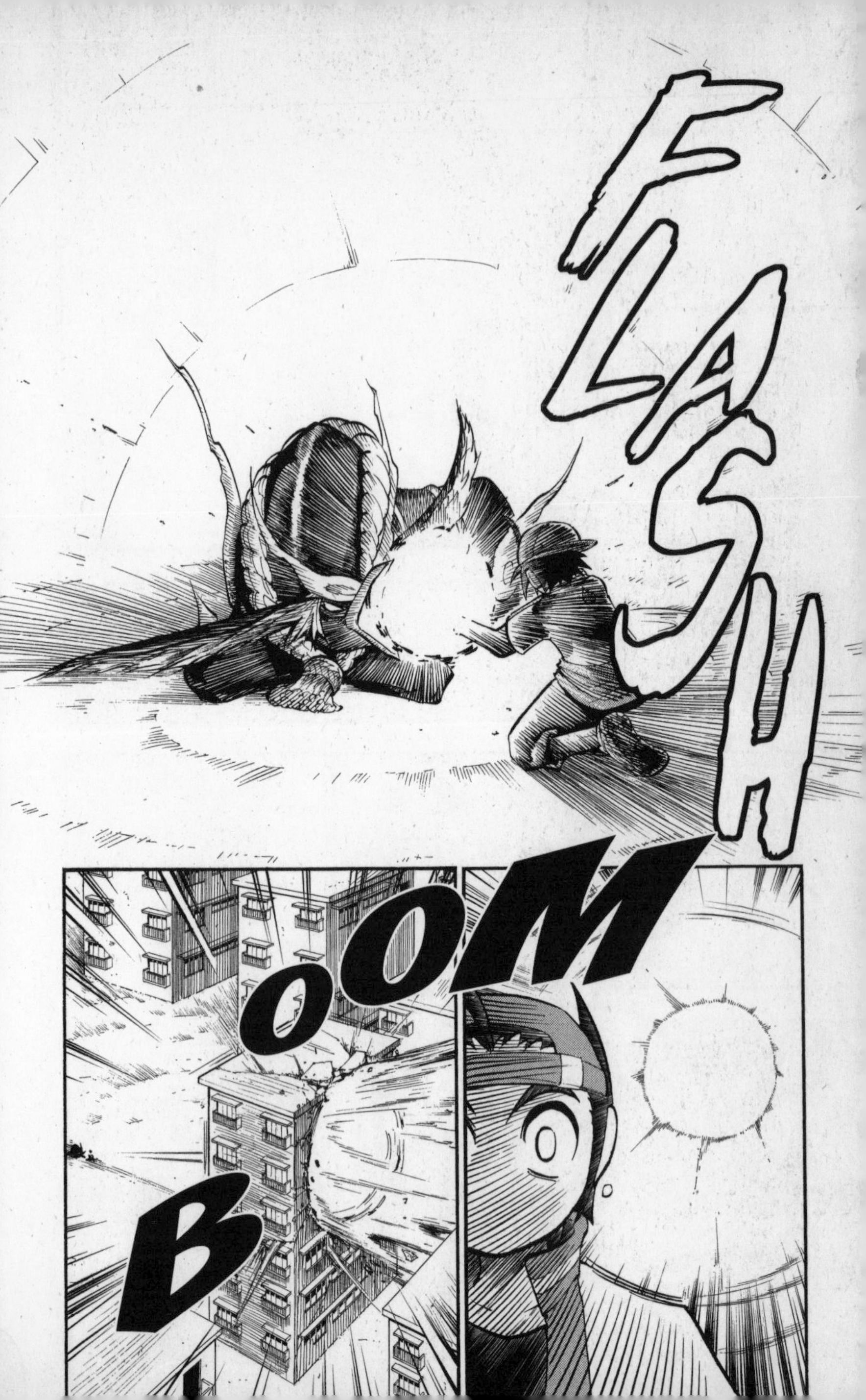
FLASH
BOOM

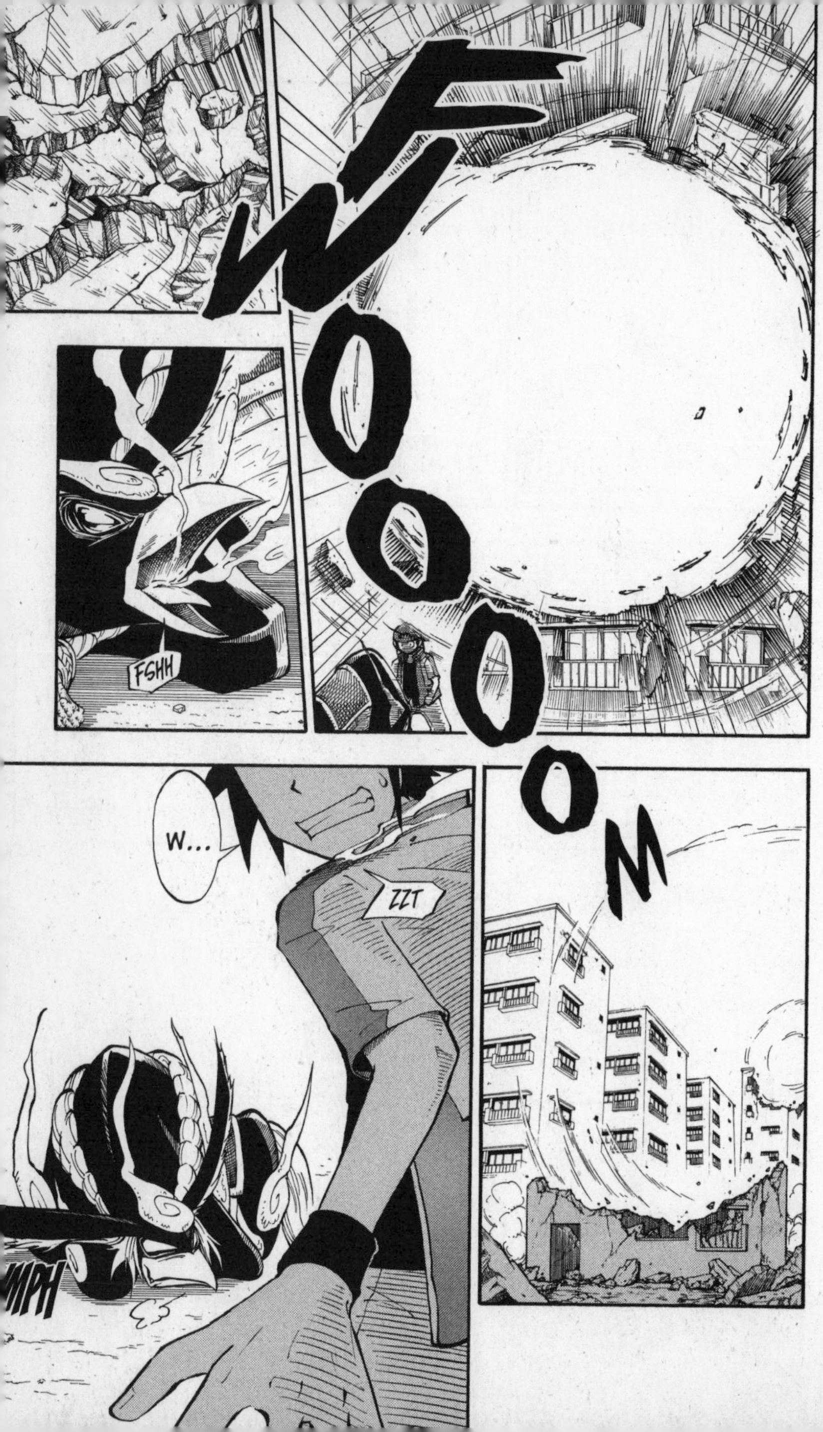
WOOOOOM
FSHH
W...
ZZT
MPH

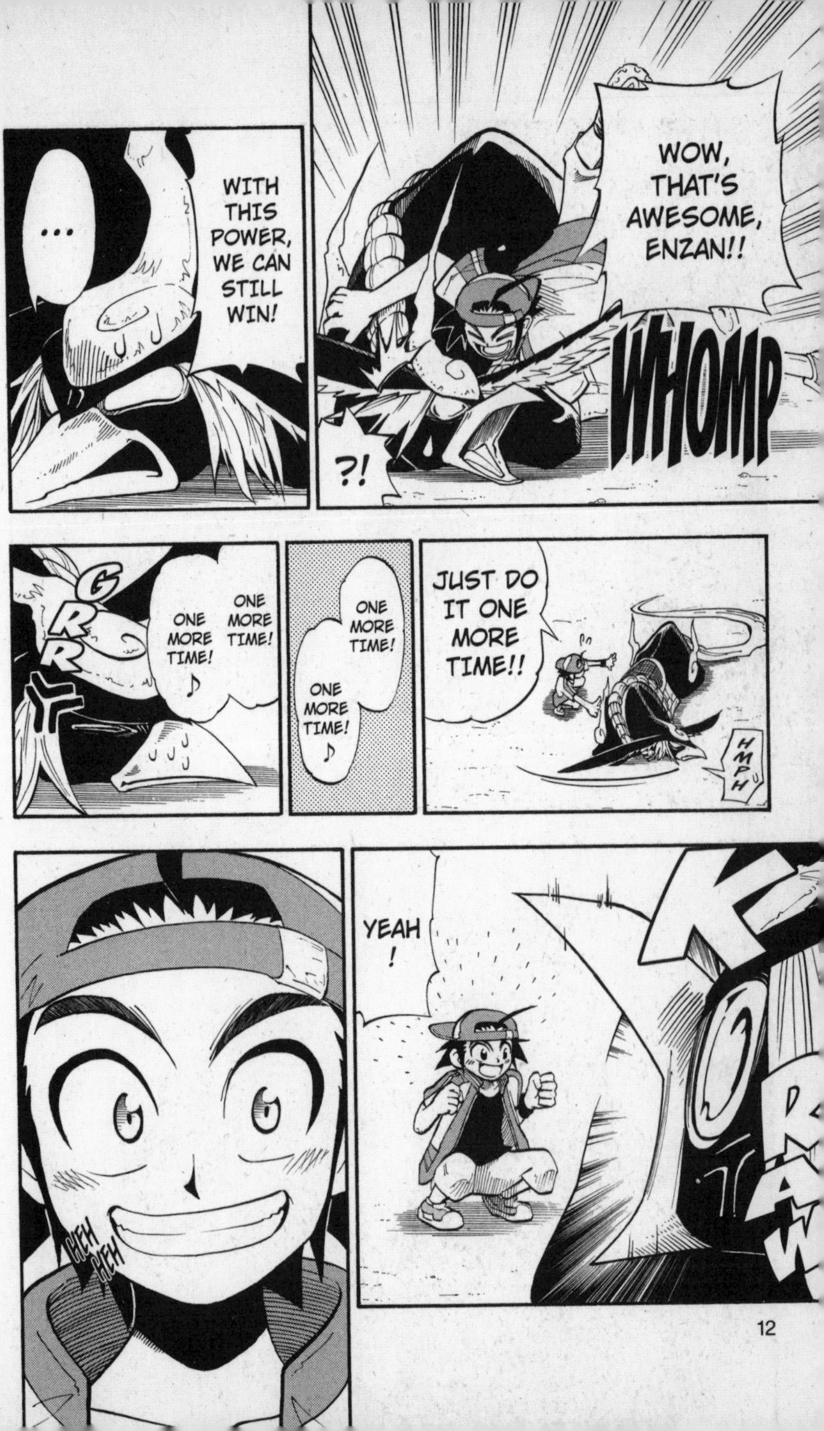

WOW, THAT'S AWESOME, ENZAN!!
WHOMP
?!
...
WITH THIS POWER, WE CAN STILL WIN!
JUST DO IT ONE MORE TIME!!
HMPH
ONE MORE TIME!
ONE MORE TIME! ♪
ONE MORE TIME!
ONE MORE TIME! ♪
GRR
YEAH!
HEH HEH

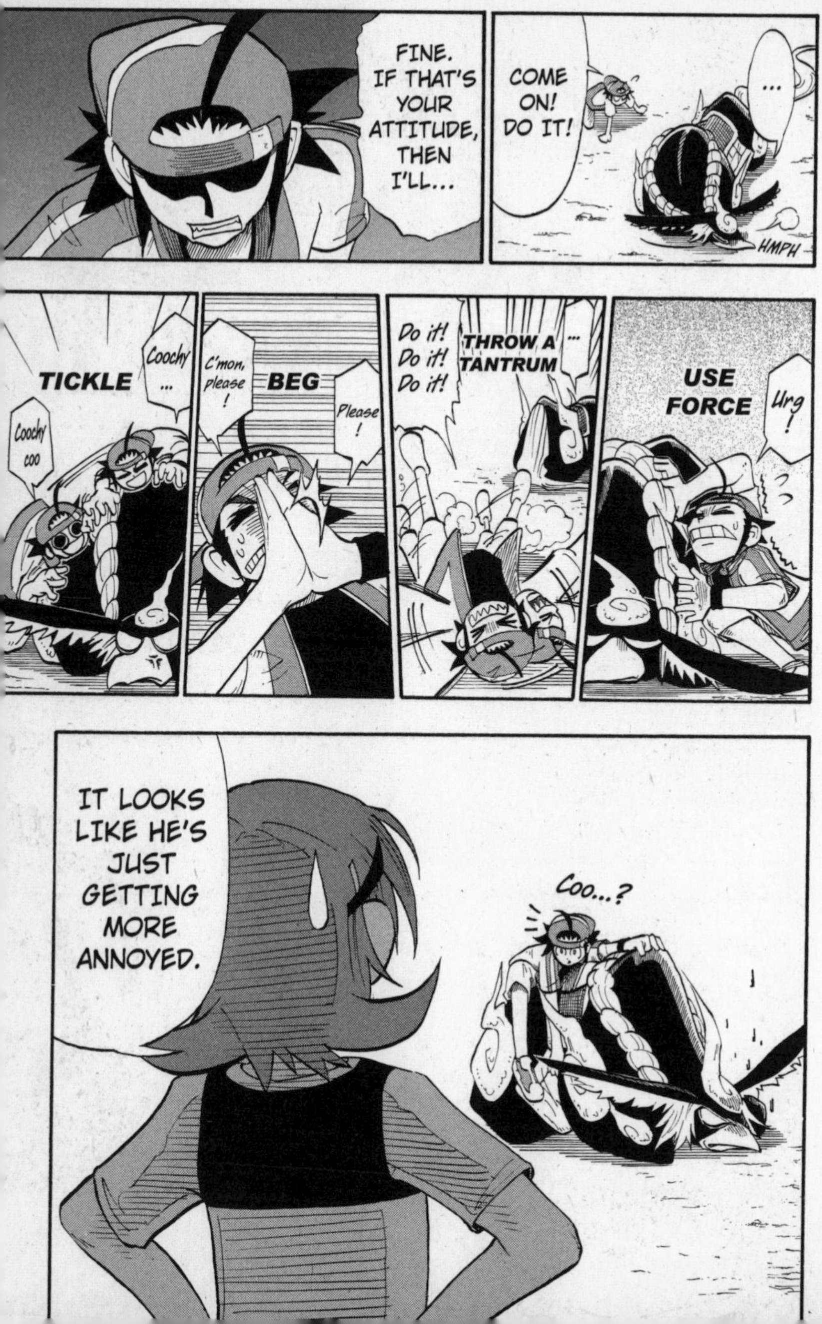
...
COME ON! DO IT!
HMPH
FINE. IF THAT'S YOUR ATTITUDE, THEN I'LL...
USE FORCE
Urg!
...
THROW A TANTRUM
Do it! Do it! Do it!
BEG
Please!
C'mon, please!
Coochy...
TICKLE
Coochy coo
Coo...?
IT LOOKS LIKE HE'S JUST GETTING MORE ANNOYED.

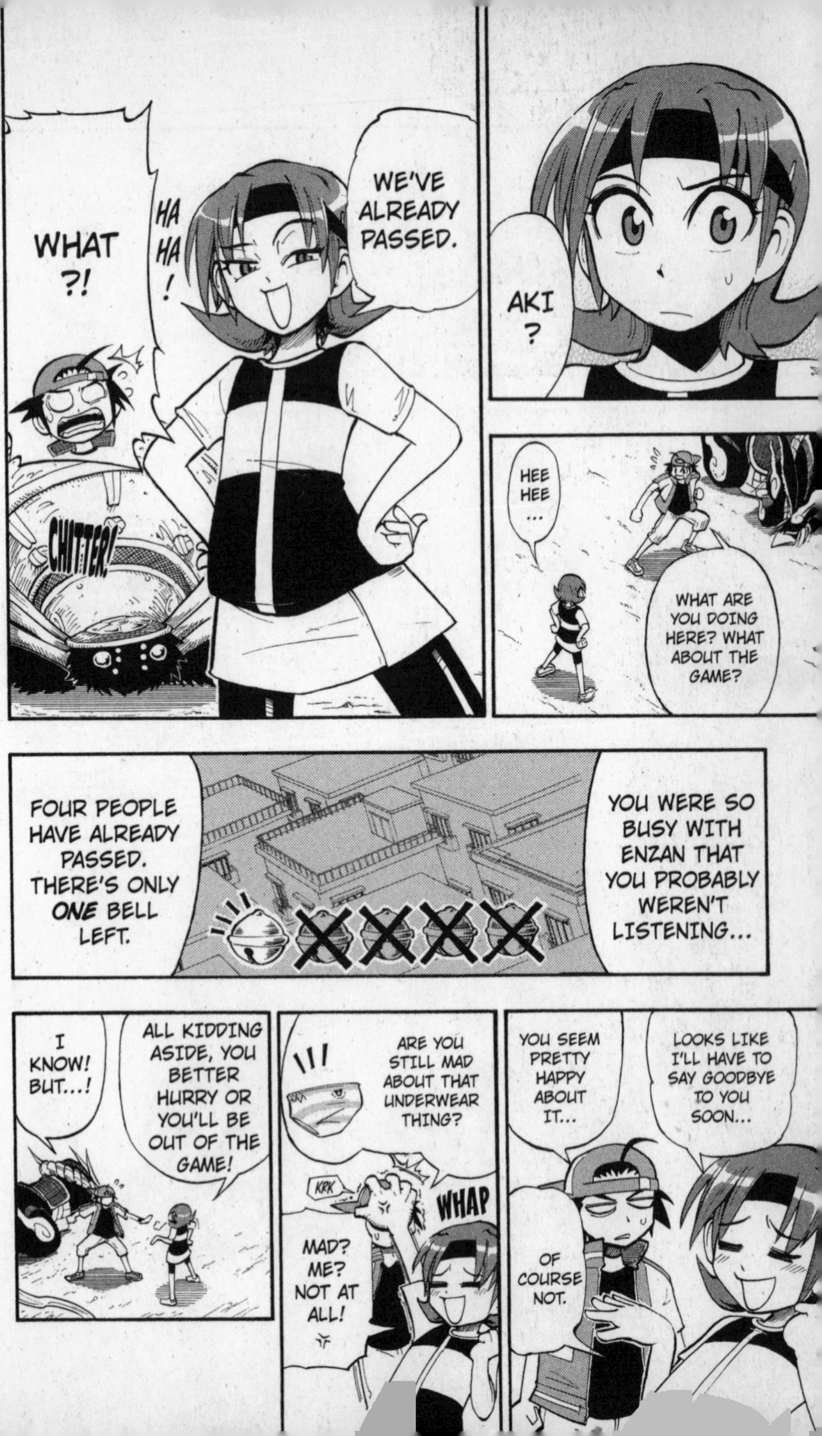
AKI?
HEE HEE...
WHAT ARE YOU DOING HERE? WHAT ABOUT THE GAME?
WE'VE ALREADY PASSED.
HA HA!
WHAT?!
CHITTER!
YOU WERE SO BUSY WITH ENZAN THAT YOU PROBABLY WEREN'T LISTENING...
FOUR PEOPLE HAVE ALREADY PASSED. THERE'S ONLY *ONE* BELL LEFT.
LOOKS LIKE I'LL HAVE TO SAY GOODBYE TO YOU SOON...
YOU SEEM PRETTY HAPPY ABOUT IT...
OF COURSE NOT.
ARE YOU STILL MAD ABOUT THAT UNDERWEAR THING?
KRK
WHAP
MAD? ME? NOT AT ALL!
ALL KIDDING ASIDE, YOU BETTER HURRY OR YOU'LL BE OUT OF THE GAME!
I KNOW! BUT...!

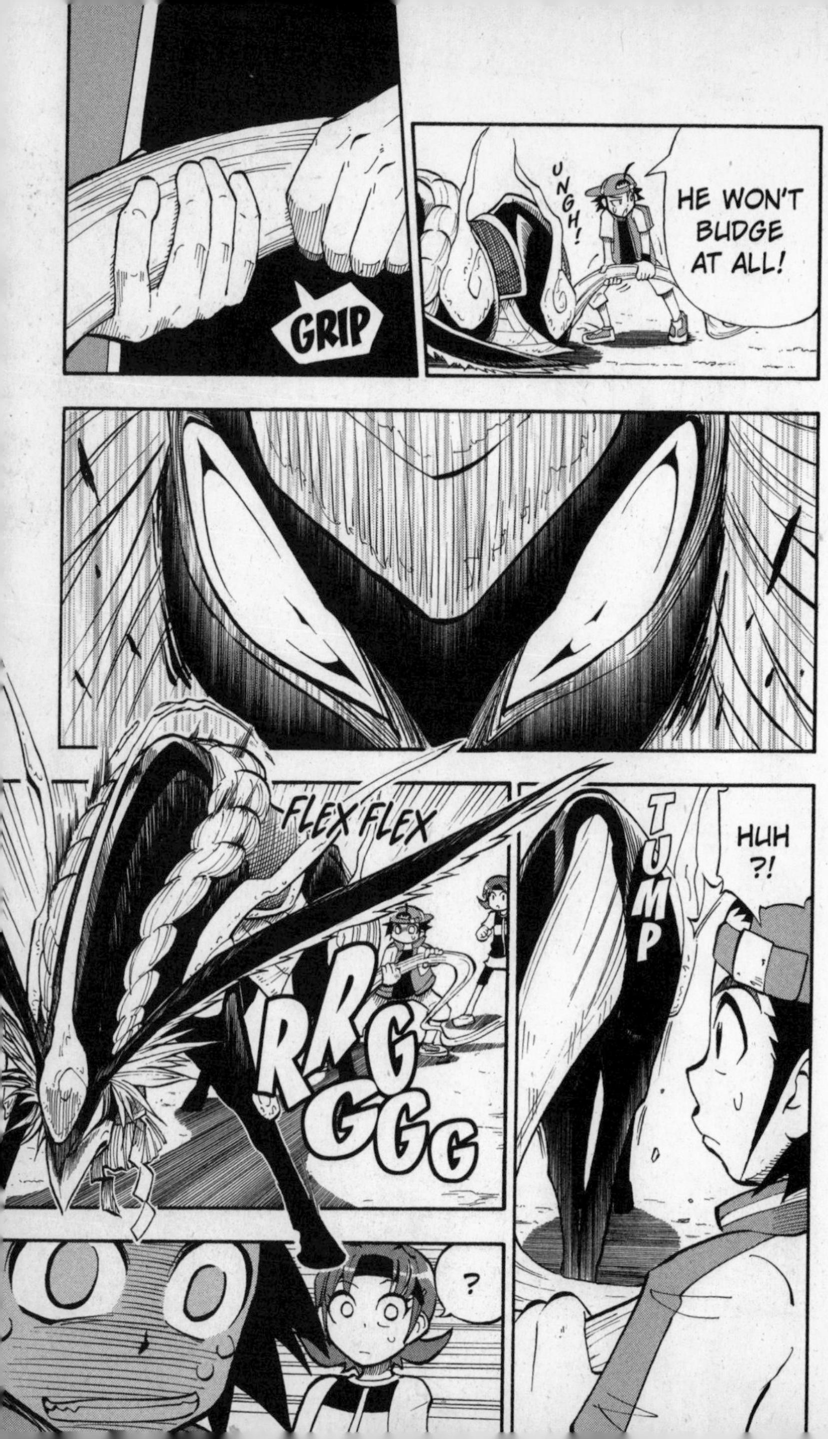
UNGH!
HE WON'T BUDGE AT ALL!
GRIP
TUMP
HUH ?!
FLEX FLEX
R-R-G GGGG
?

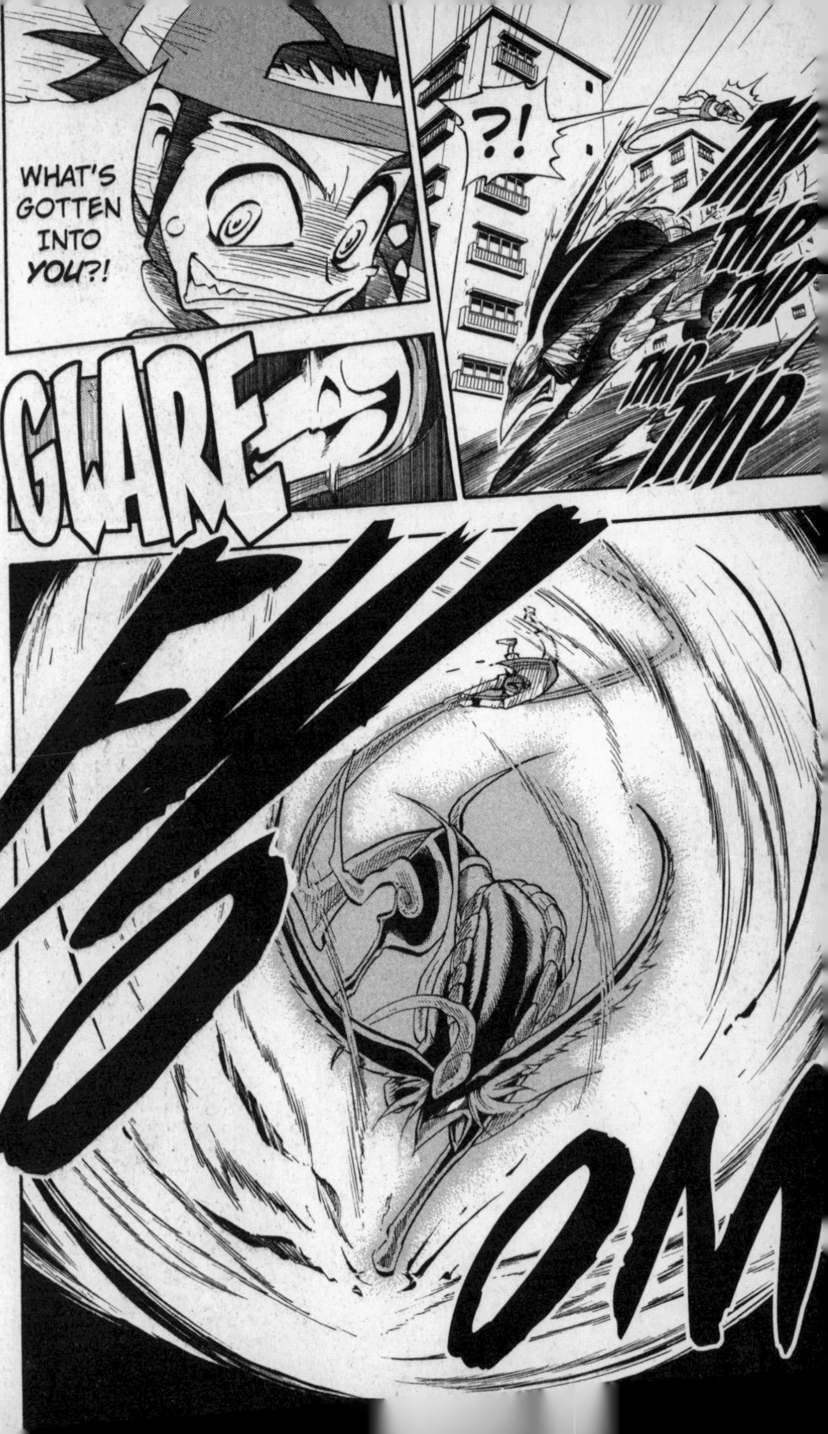
?!
TMP TMP TMP TMP
WHAT'S GOTTEN INTO *YOU*?!
GLARE

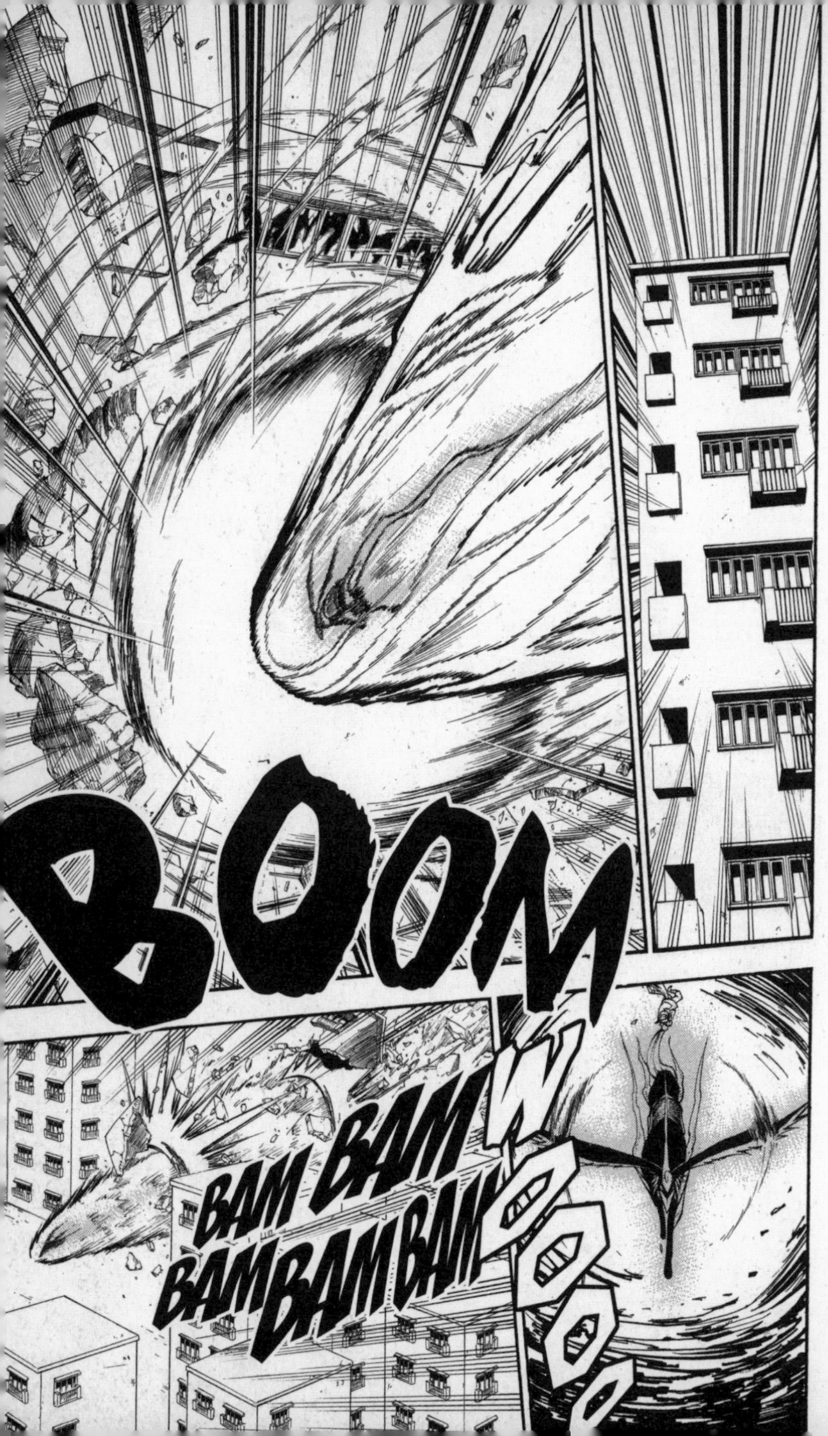
BOOM
BAM BAM BAM BAM BAM
WOOOO

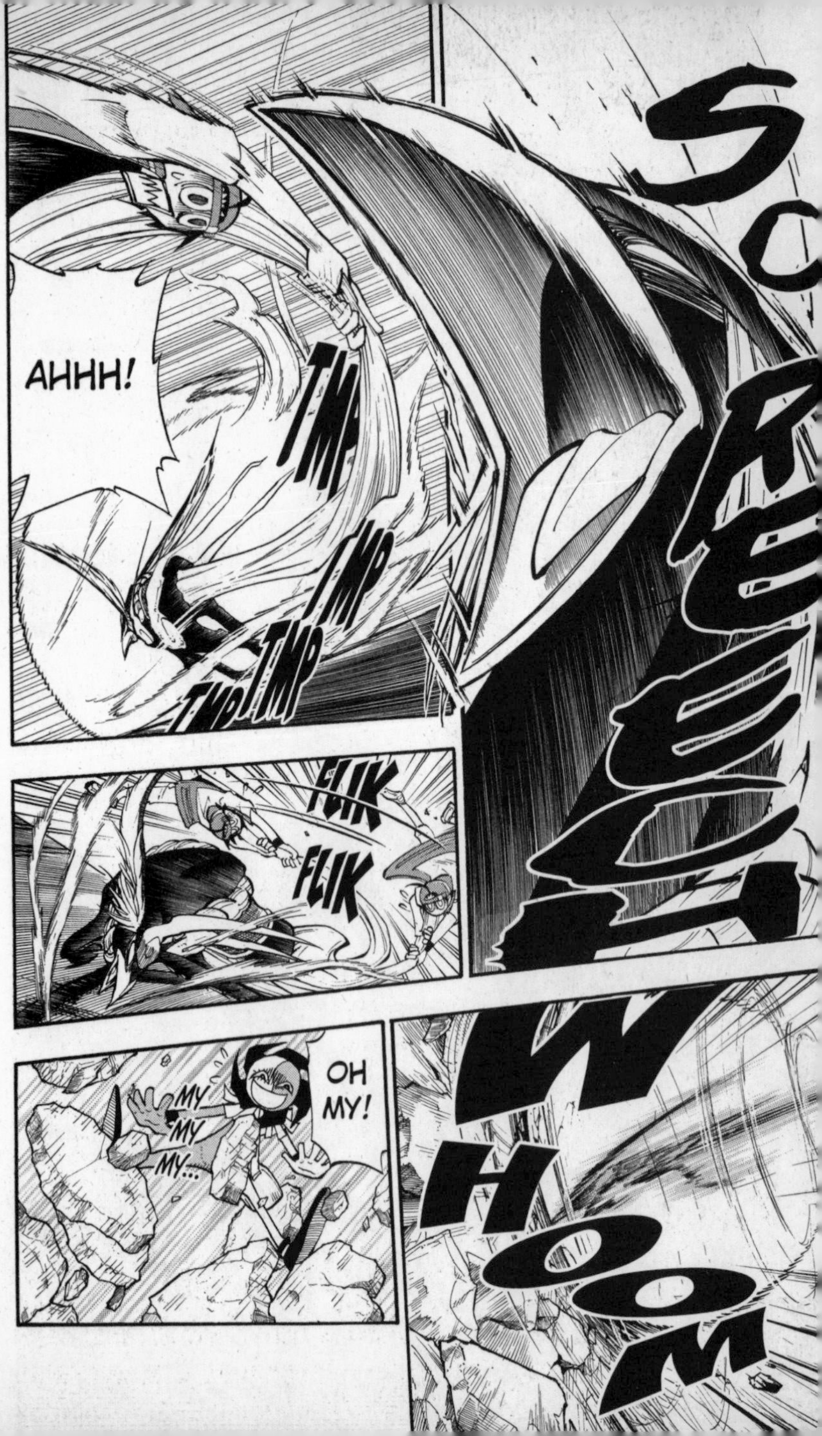
SCREECH
WHOOM
TMP
TMP
TMP
TMP
TMP
AHHH!
FLIK
FLIK
OH MY!
MY MY MY...

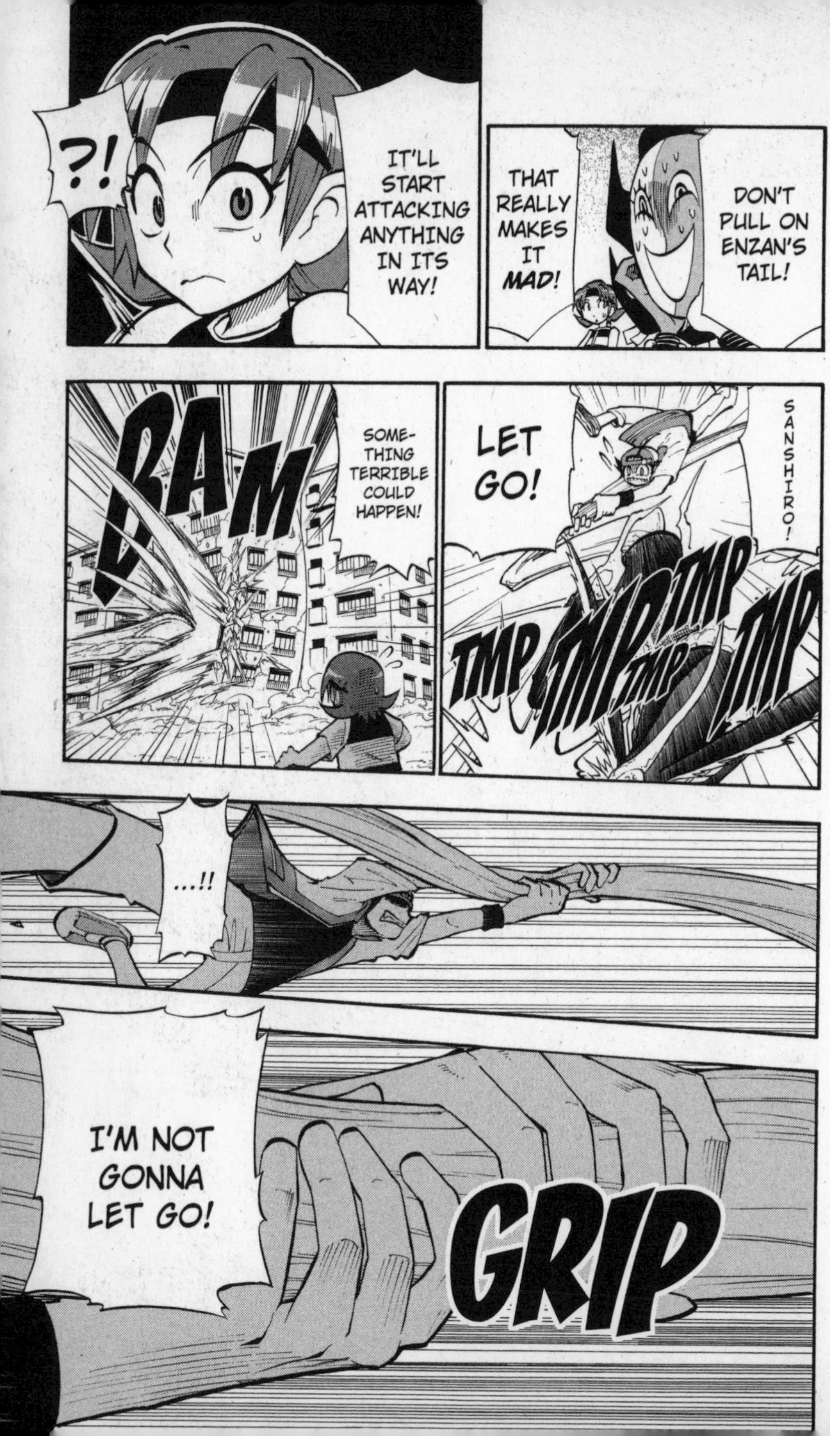
DON'T PULL ON ENZAN'S TAIL!
THAT REALLY MAKES IT *MAD*!
IT'LL START ATTACKING ANYTHING IN ITS WAY!
?!
SANSHIRO!
LET GO!
TMP TMP TMP TMP TMP
SOME-THING TERRIBLE COULD HAPPEN!
BAM
...!!
I'M NOT GONNA LET GO!
GRIP

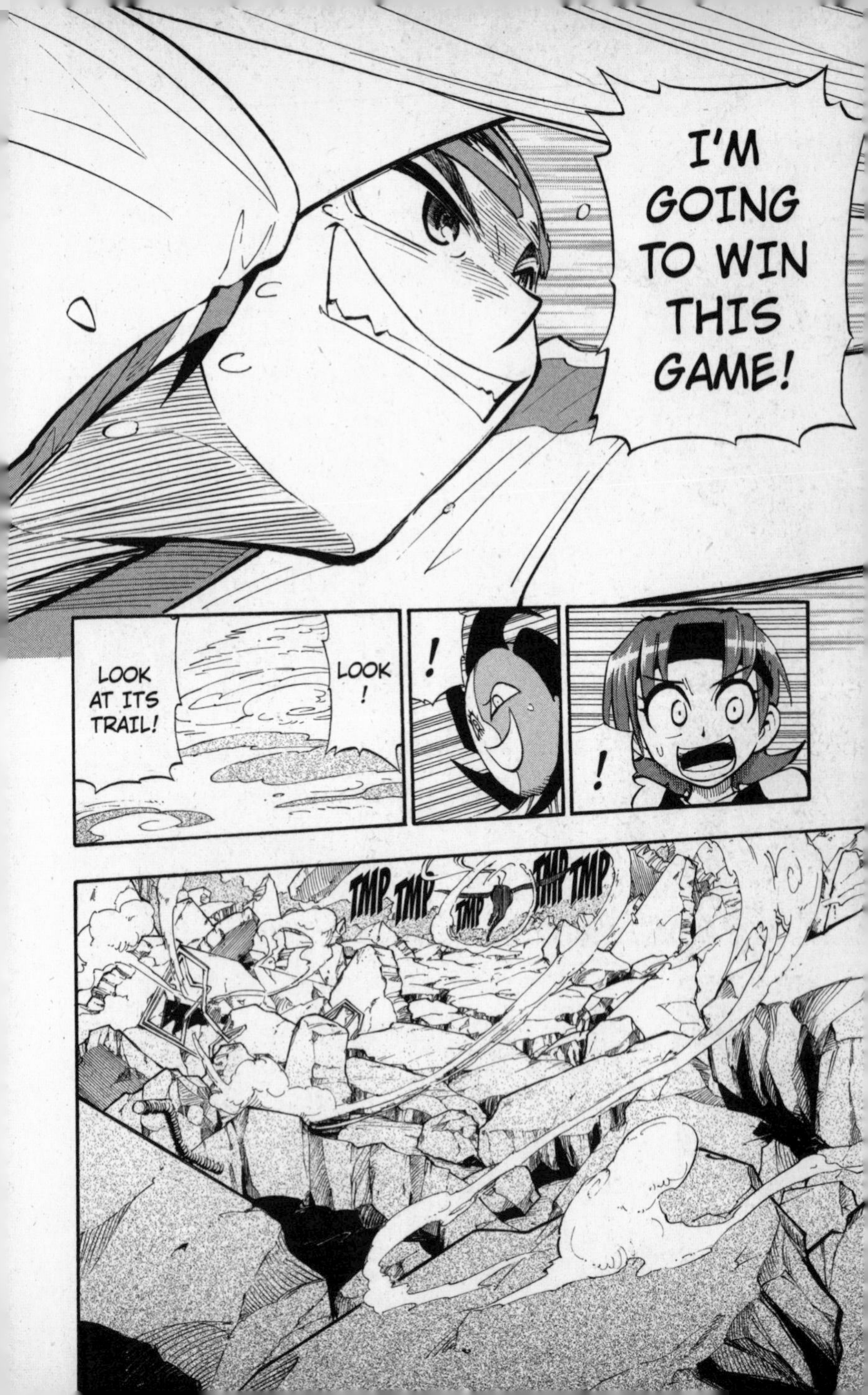
I'M GOING TO WIN THIS GAME!
!
!
LOOK!
LOOK AT ITS TRAIL!
TMP TMP TMP TMP TMP

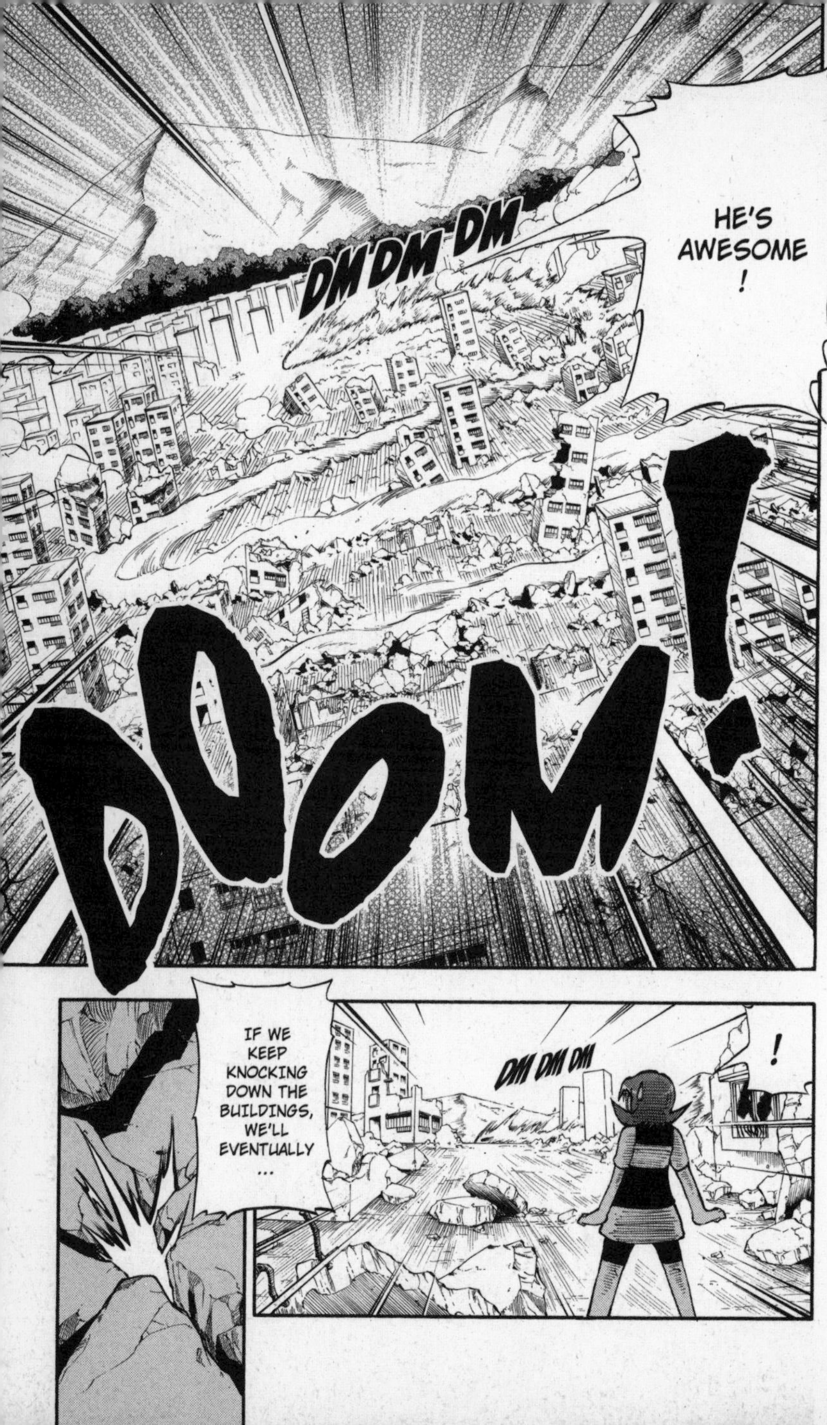
HE'S AWESOME!
DM DM DM
DOOM!
!
DM DM DM
IF WE KEEP KNOCKING DOWN THE BUILDINGS, WE'LL EVENTUALLY...

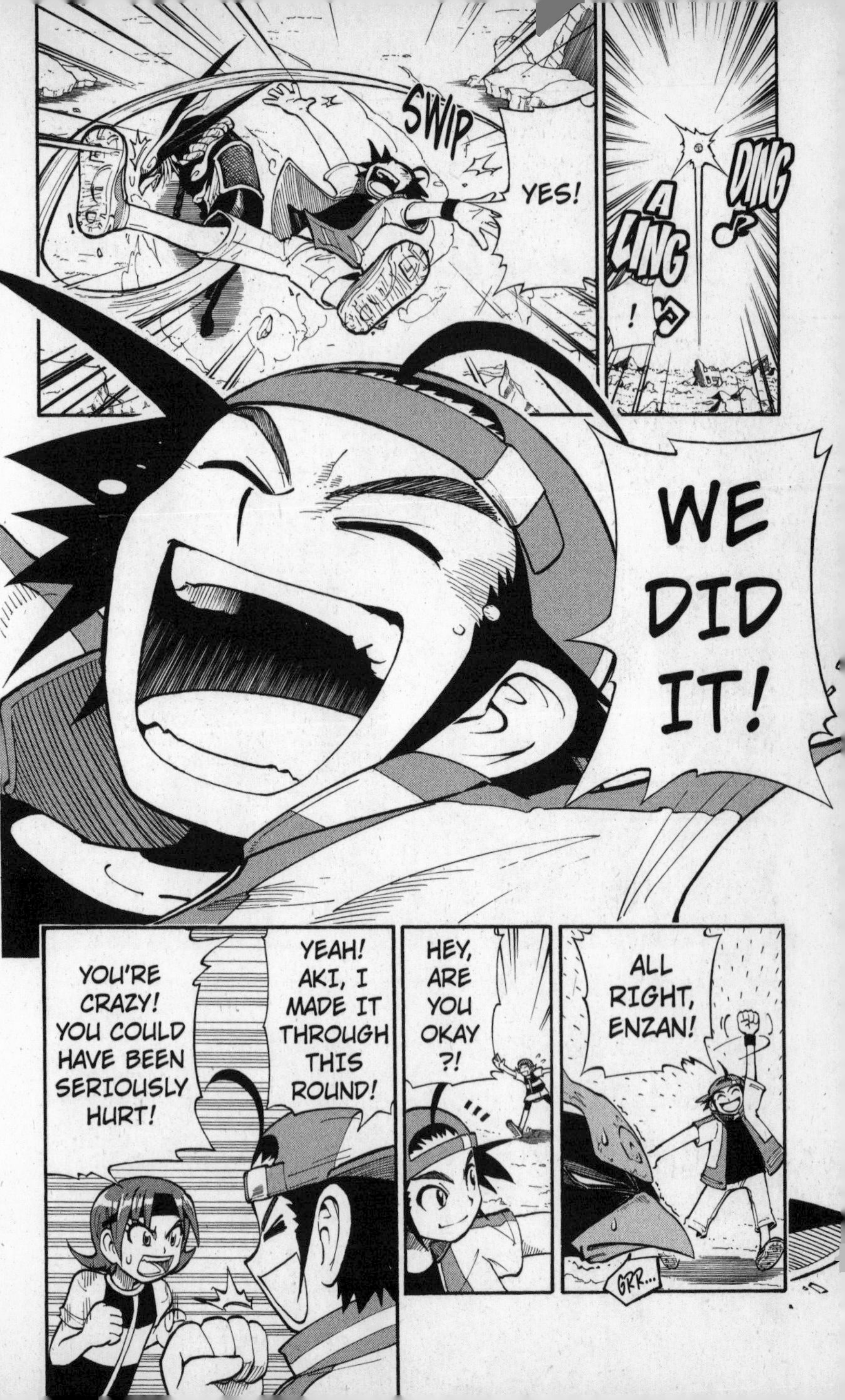
DING
A LING
!
SWIP
YES!
WE DID IT!
ALL RIGHT, ENZAN!
GRR...
HEY, ARE YOU OKAY ?!
YEAH! AKI, I MADE IT THROUGH THIS ROUND!
YOU'RE CRAZY! YOU COULD HAVE BEEN SERIOUSLY HURT!

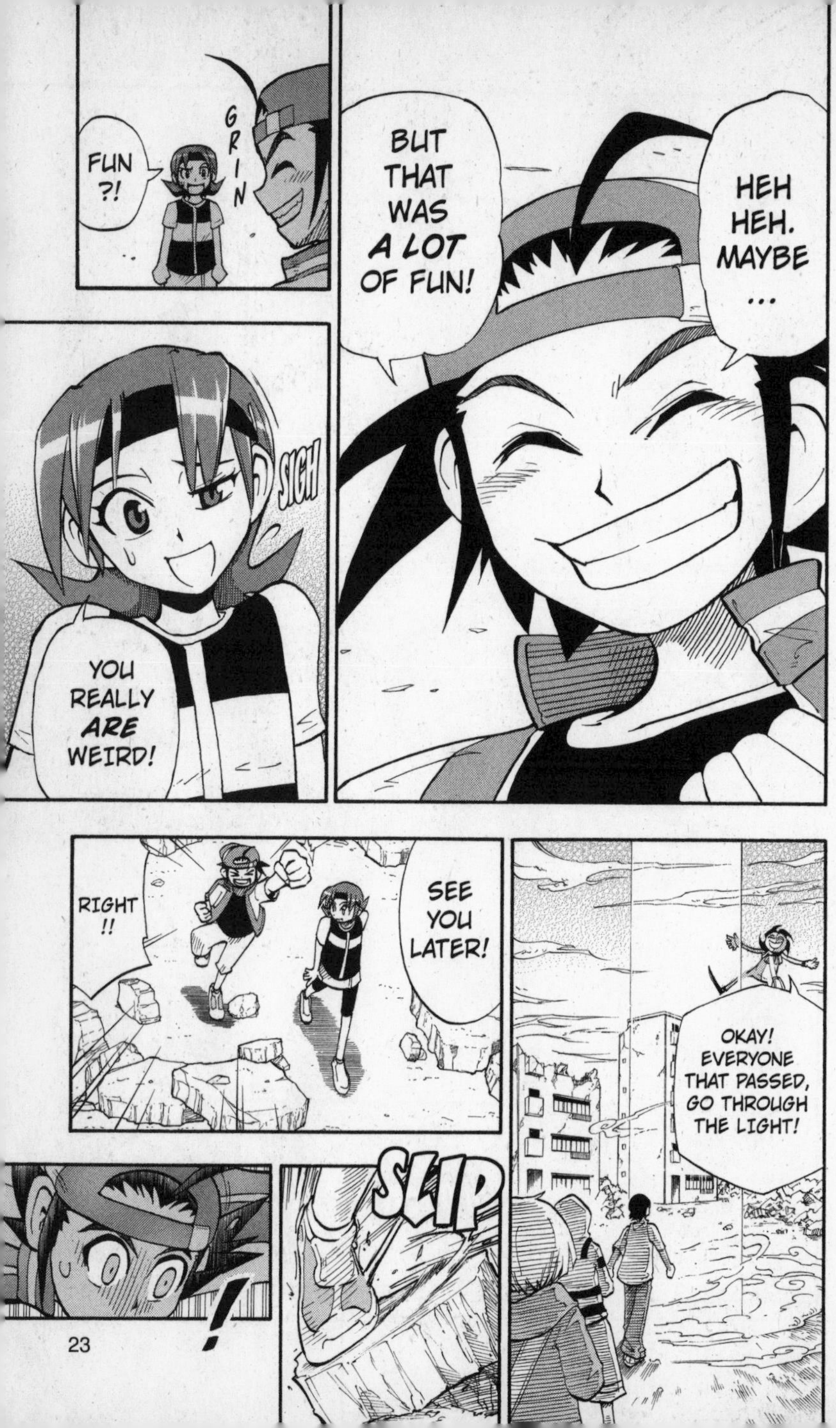
HEH HEH. MAYBE ...
BUT THAT WAS A LOT OF FUN!
GRIN
FUN ?!
SIGH
YOU REALLY ARE WEIRD!
OKAY! EVERYONE THAT PASSED, GO THROUGH THE LIGHT!
SEE YOU LATER!
RIGHT !!
SLIP
!

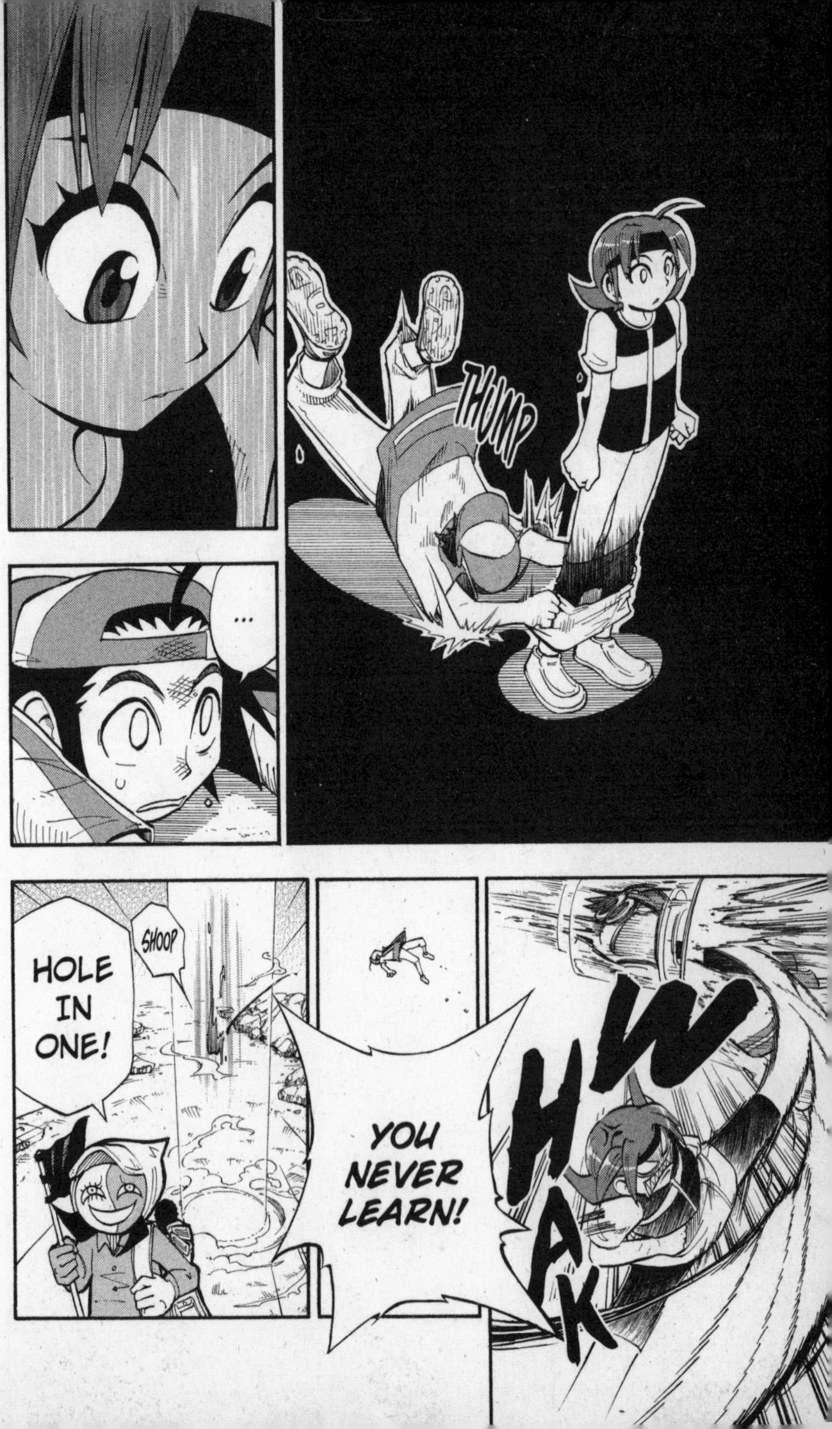
THUMP
...
WHAK
YOU NEVER LEARN!
SHOOP
HOLE IN ONE!

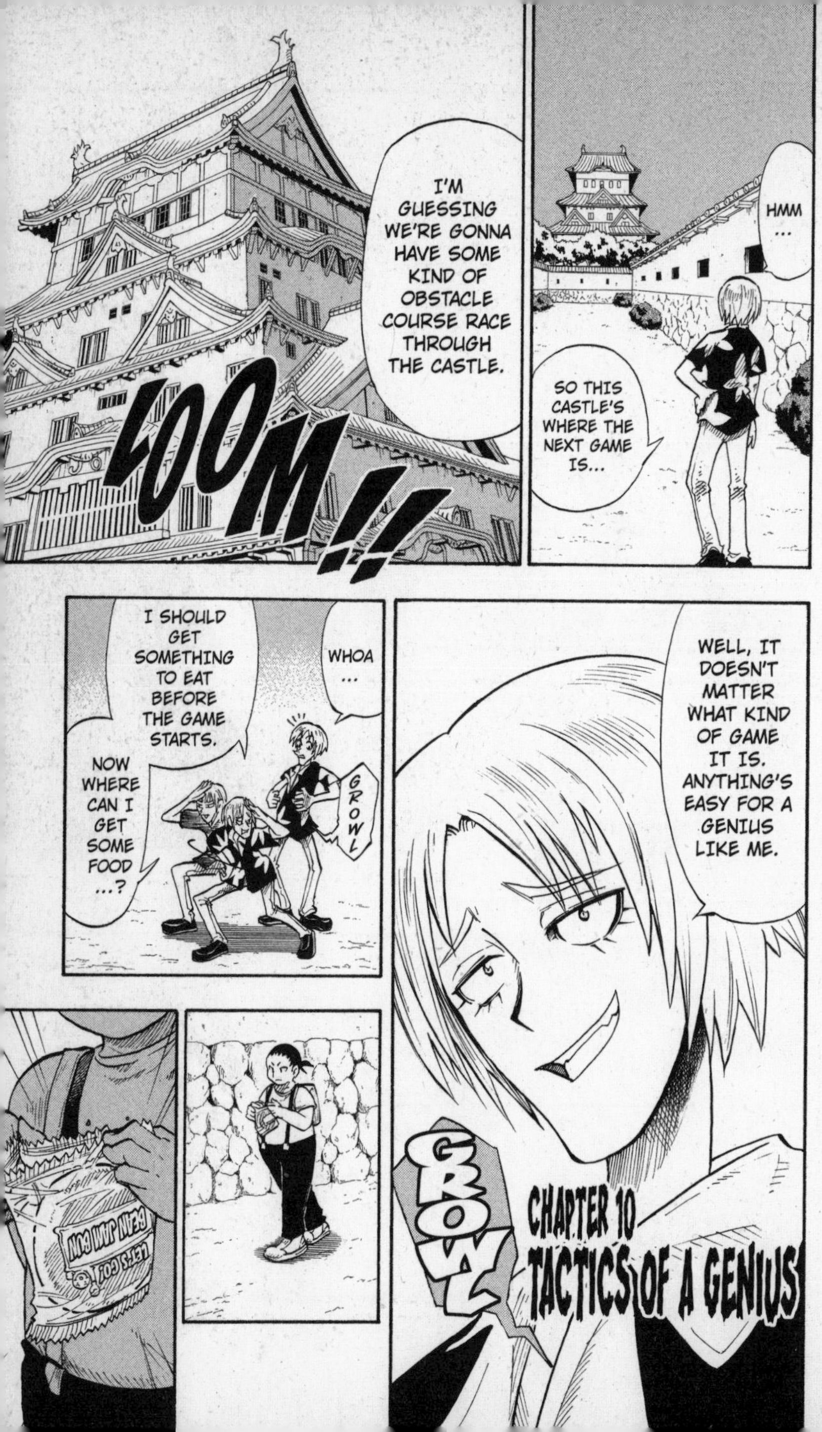
HMM ...
SO THIS CASTLE'S WHERE THE NEXT GAME IS...
I'M GUESSING WE'RE GONNA HAVE SOME KIND OF OBSTACLE COURSE RACE THROUGH THE CASTLE.
ZOOM!!
WELL, IT DOESN'T MATTER WHAT KIND OF GAME IT IS. ANYTHING'S EASY FOR A GENIUS LIKE ME.
GROWL
CHAPTER 10
TACTICS OF A GENIUS
WHOA ...
GROWL
I SHOULD GET SOMETHING TO EAT BEFORE THE GAME STARTS.
NOW WHERE CAN I GET SOME FOOD ...?
LET'S GO!!
BEAN JAM BUN

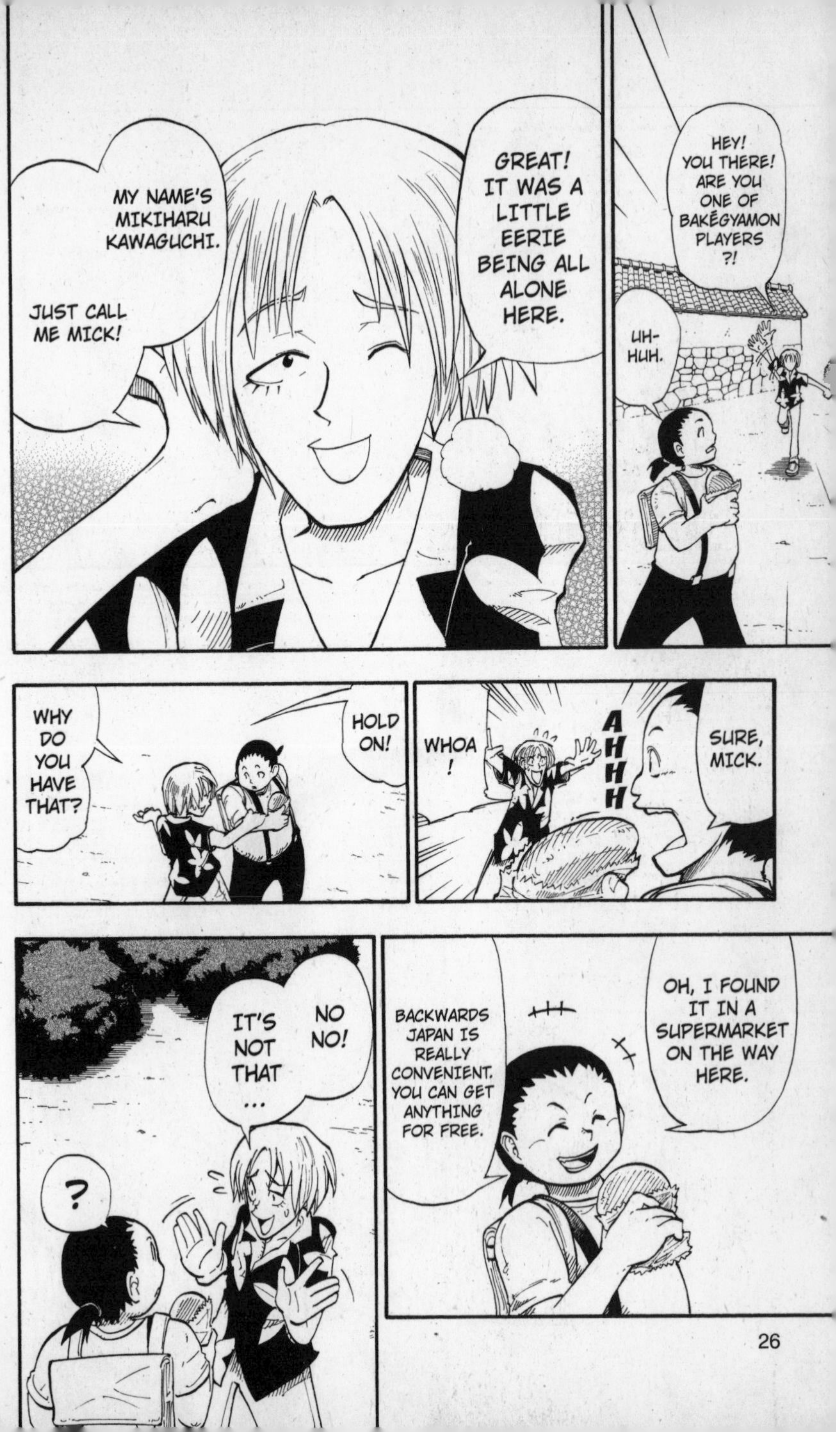
HEY! YOU THERE! ARE YOU ONE OF BAKĒGYAMON PLAYERS ?!
UH-HUH.
GREAT! IT WAS A LITTLE EERIE BEING ALL ALONE HERE.
MY NAME'S MIKIHARU KAWAGUCHI.
JUST CALL ME MICK!
SURE, MICK.
AHHH
WHOA !
HOLD ON!
WHY DO YOU HAVE THAT?
OH, I FOUND IT IN A SUPERMARKET ON THE WAY HERE.
BACKWARDS JAPAN IS REALLY CONVENIENT. YOU CAN GET ANYTHING FOR FREE.
NO NO!
IT'S NOT THAT ...
?

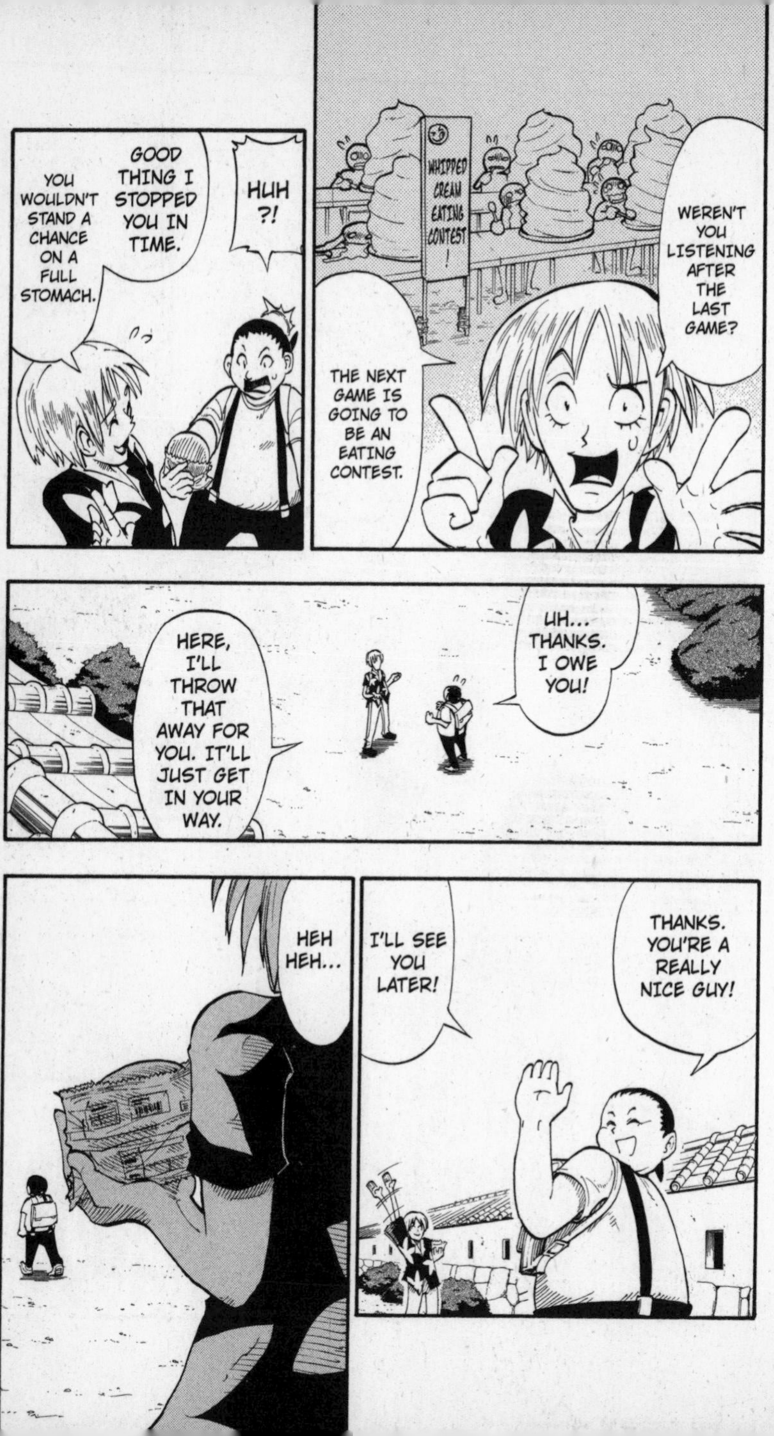
WEREN'T YOU LISTENING AFTER THE LAST GAME?
WHIPPED CREAM EATING CONTEST!
THE NEXT GAME IS GOING TO BE AN EATING CONTEST.
HUH ?!
GOOD THING I STOPPED YOU IN TIME.
YOU WOULDN'T STAND A CHANCE ON A FULL STOMACH.
UH... THANKS. I OWE YOU!
HERE, I'LL THROW THAT AWAY FOR YOU. IT'LL JUST GET IN YOUR WAY.
THANKS. YOU'RE A REALLY NICE GUY!
I'LL SEE YOU LATER!
HEH HEH...

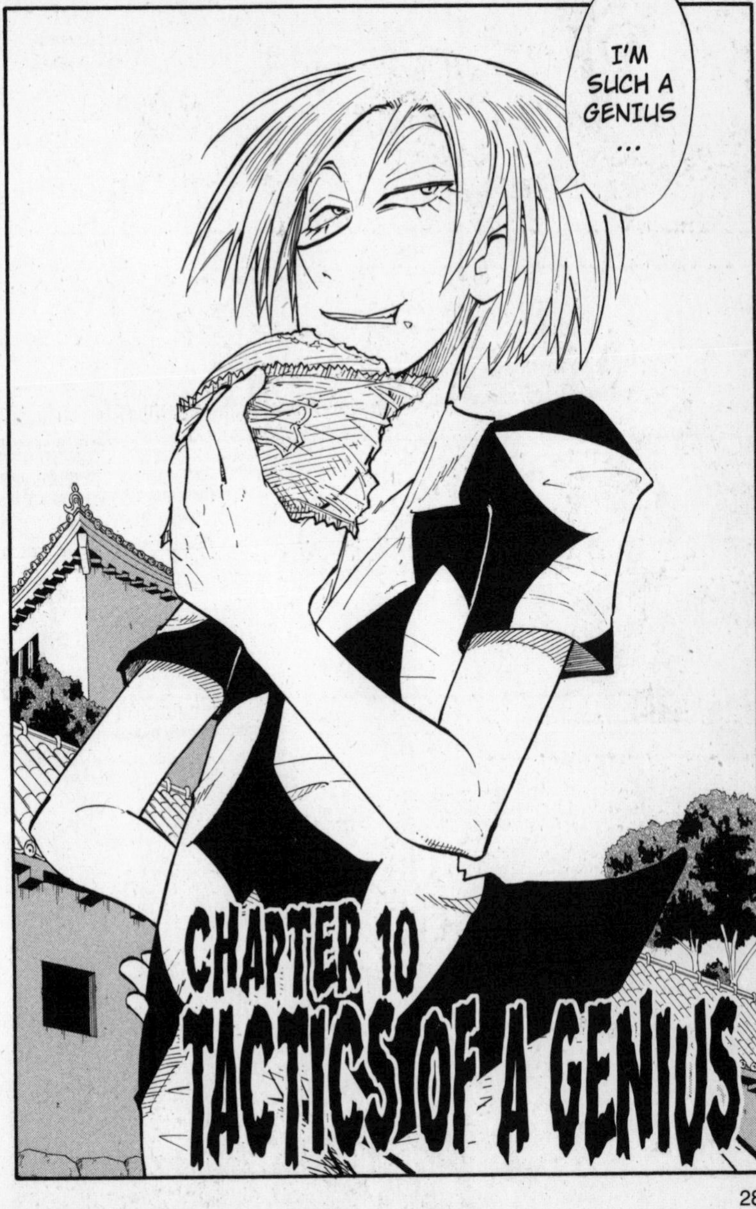
I'M SUCH A GENIUS ...
CHAPTER 10
TACTICS OF A GENIUS

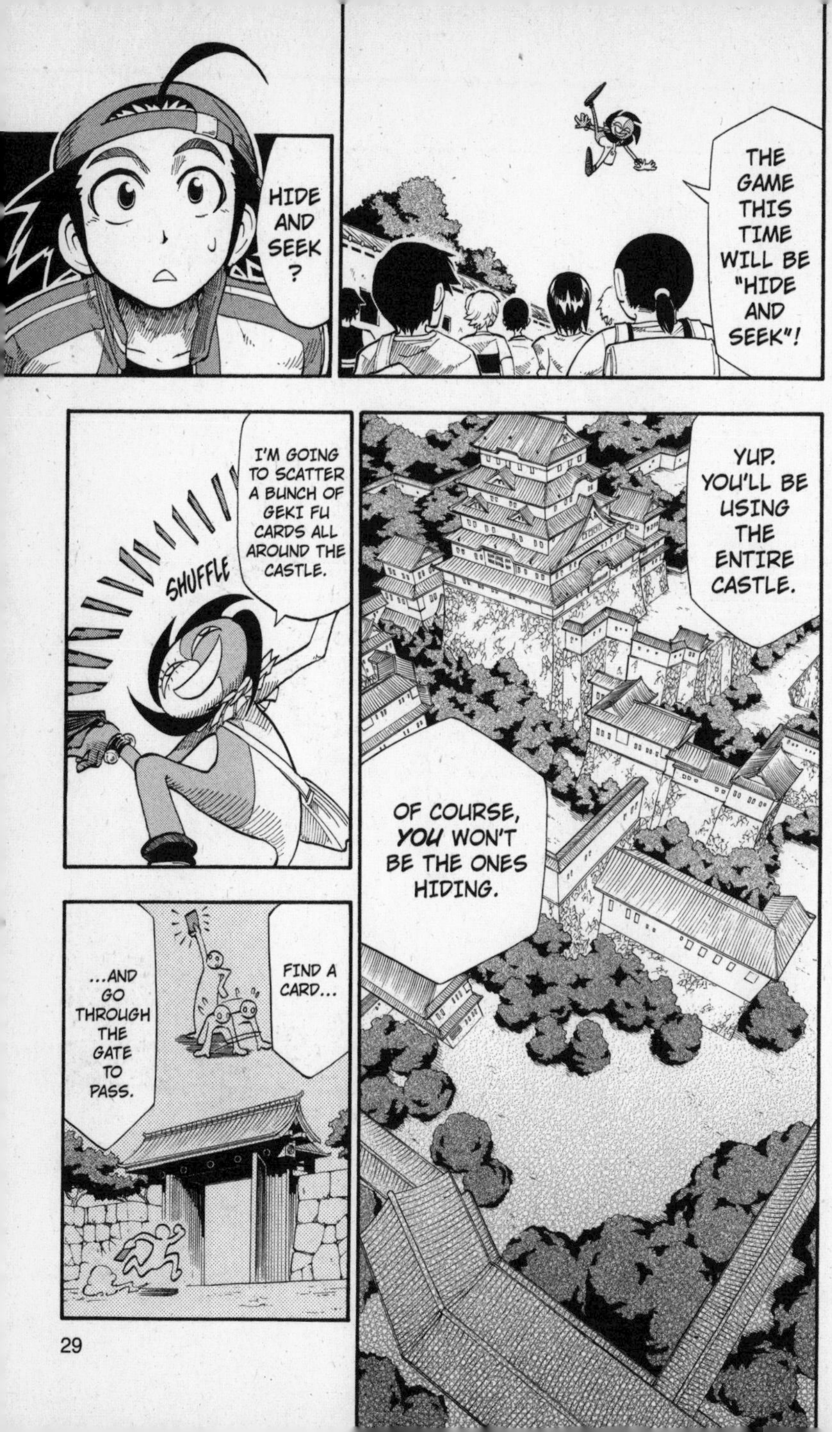
THE GAME THIS TIME WILL BE "HIDE AND SEEK"!
HIDE AND SEEK?
YUP. YOU'LL BE USING THE ENTIRE CASTLE.
OF COURSE, *YOU* WON'T BE THE ONES HIDING.
I'M GOING TO SCATTER A BUNCH OF GEKI FU CARDS ALL AROUND THE CASTLE.
SHUFFLE
FIND A CARD...
...AND GO THROUGH THE GATE TO PASS.

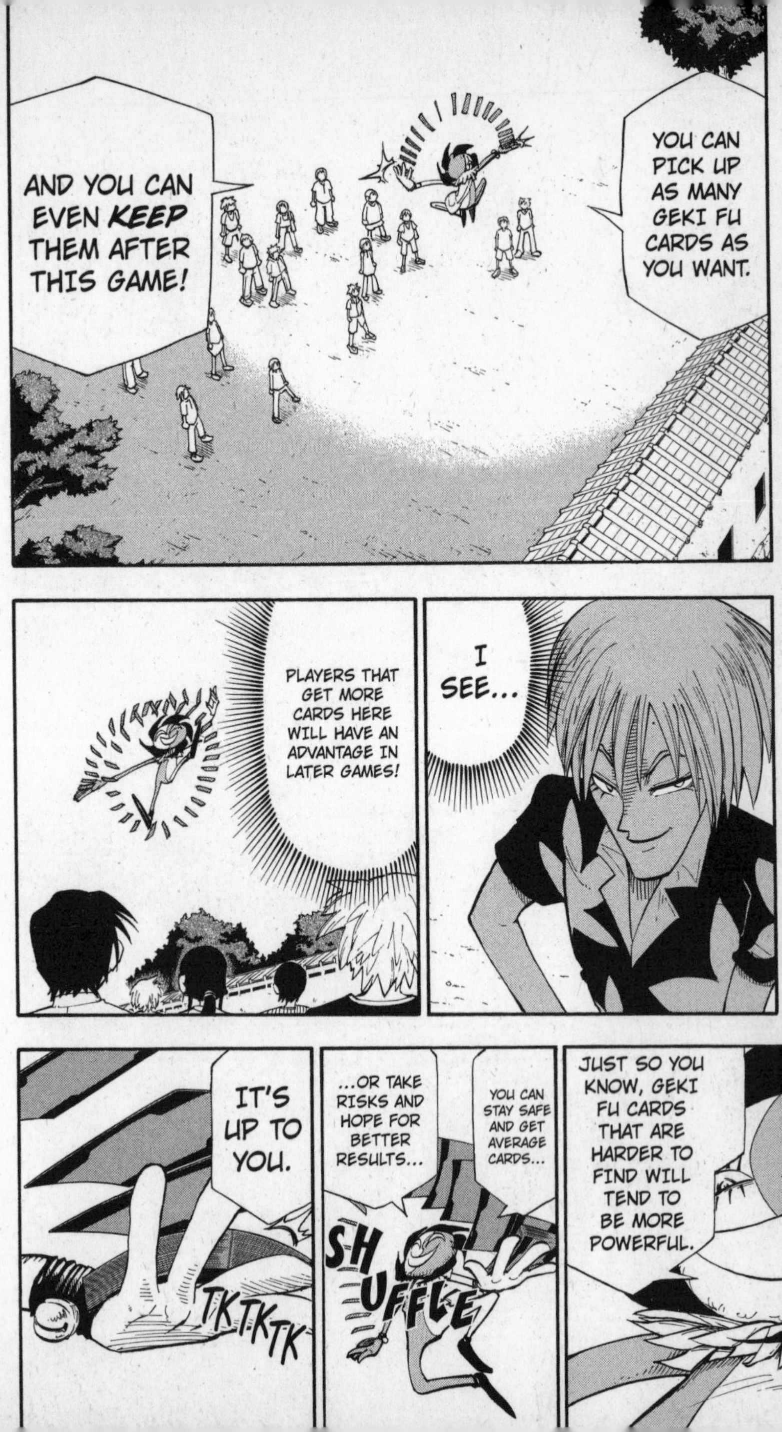
YOU CAN PICK UP AS MANY GEKI FU CARDS AS YOU WANT.
AND YOU CAN EVEN *KEEP* THEM AFTER THIS GAME!
I SEE...
PLAYERS THAT GET MORE CARDS HERE WILL HAVE AN ADVANTAGE IN LATER GAMES!
JUST SO YOU KNOW, GEKI FU CARDS THAT ARE HARDER TO FIND WILL TEND TO BE MORE POWERFUL.
YOU CAN STAY SAFE AND GET AVERAGE CARDS...
...OR TAKE RISKS AND HOPE FOR BETTER RESULTS...
SHUFFLE
IT'S UP TO YOU.
TKTKTK

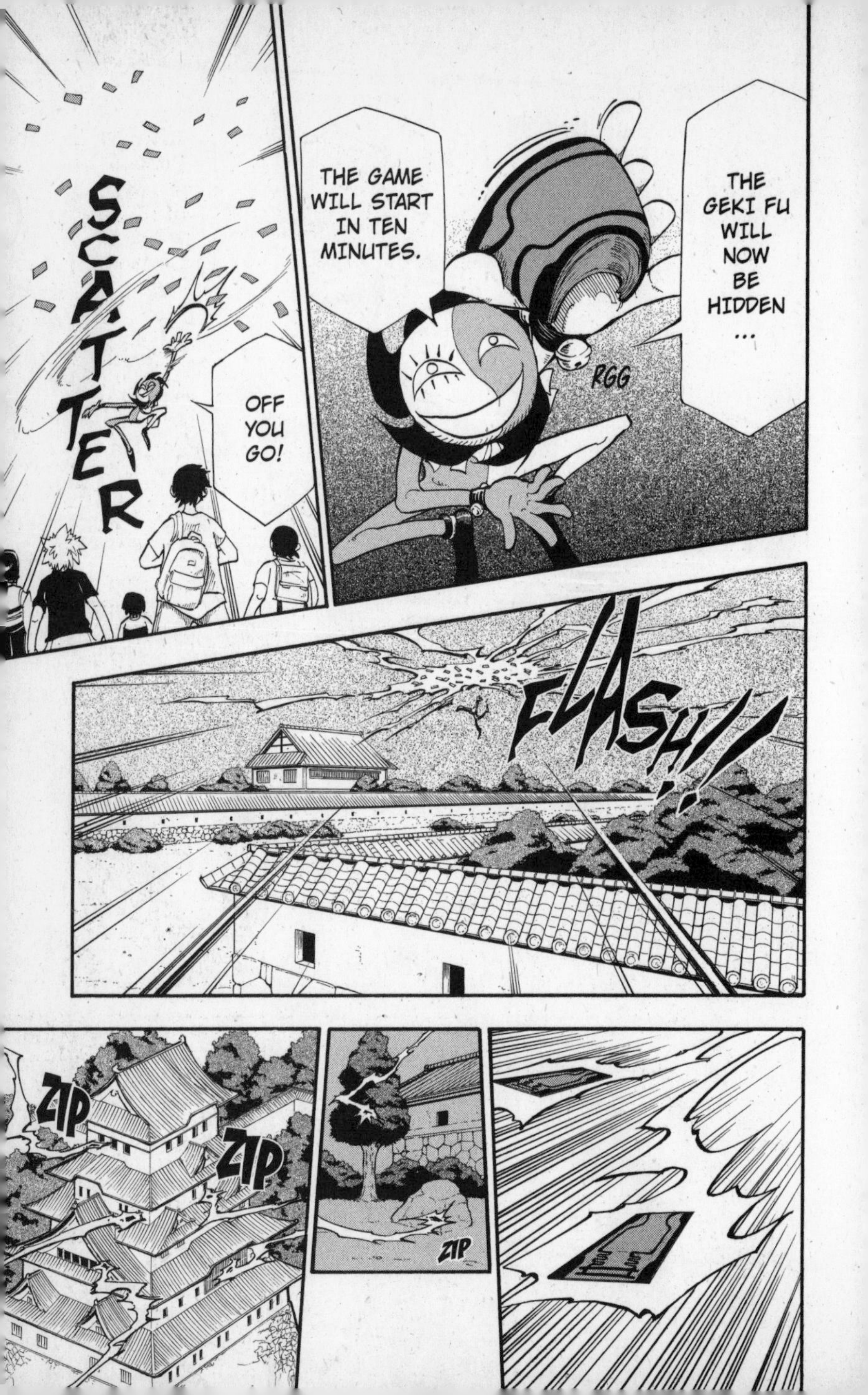
THE GEKI FU WILL NOW BE HIDDEN ...
THE GAME WILL START IN TEN MINUTES.
RGG
OFF YOU GO!
SCATTER
FLASH!!
ZIP
ZIP
ZIP

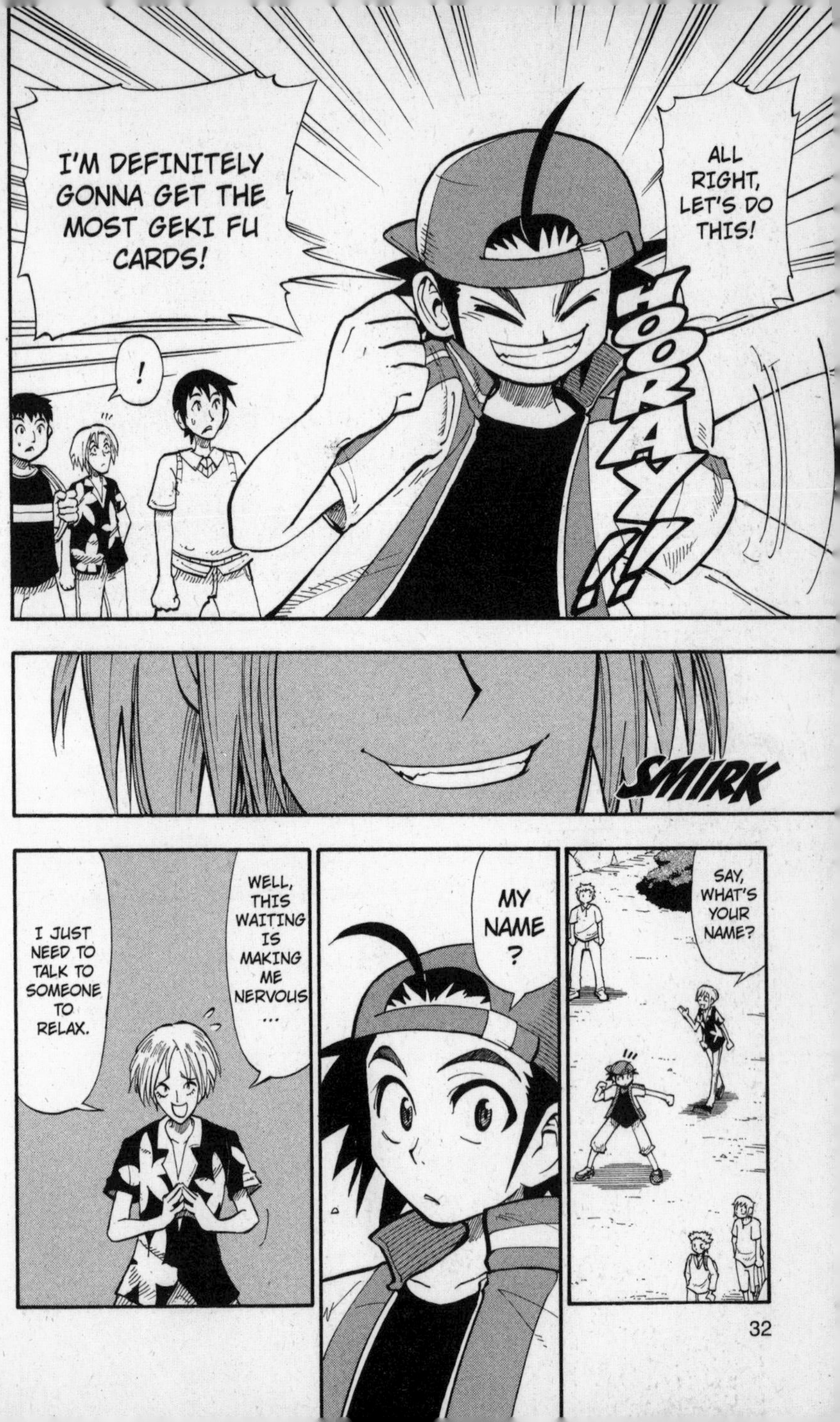
ALL RIGHT, LET'S DO THIS!
HOORAY!!
I'M DEFINITELY GONNA GET THE MOST GEKI FU CARDS!
!
SMIRK
SAY, WHAT'S YOUR NAME?
MY NAME?
WELL, THIS WAITING IS MAKING ME NERVOUS...
I JUST NEED TO TALK TO SOMEONE TO RELAX.

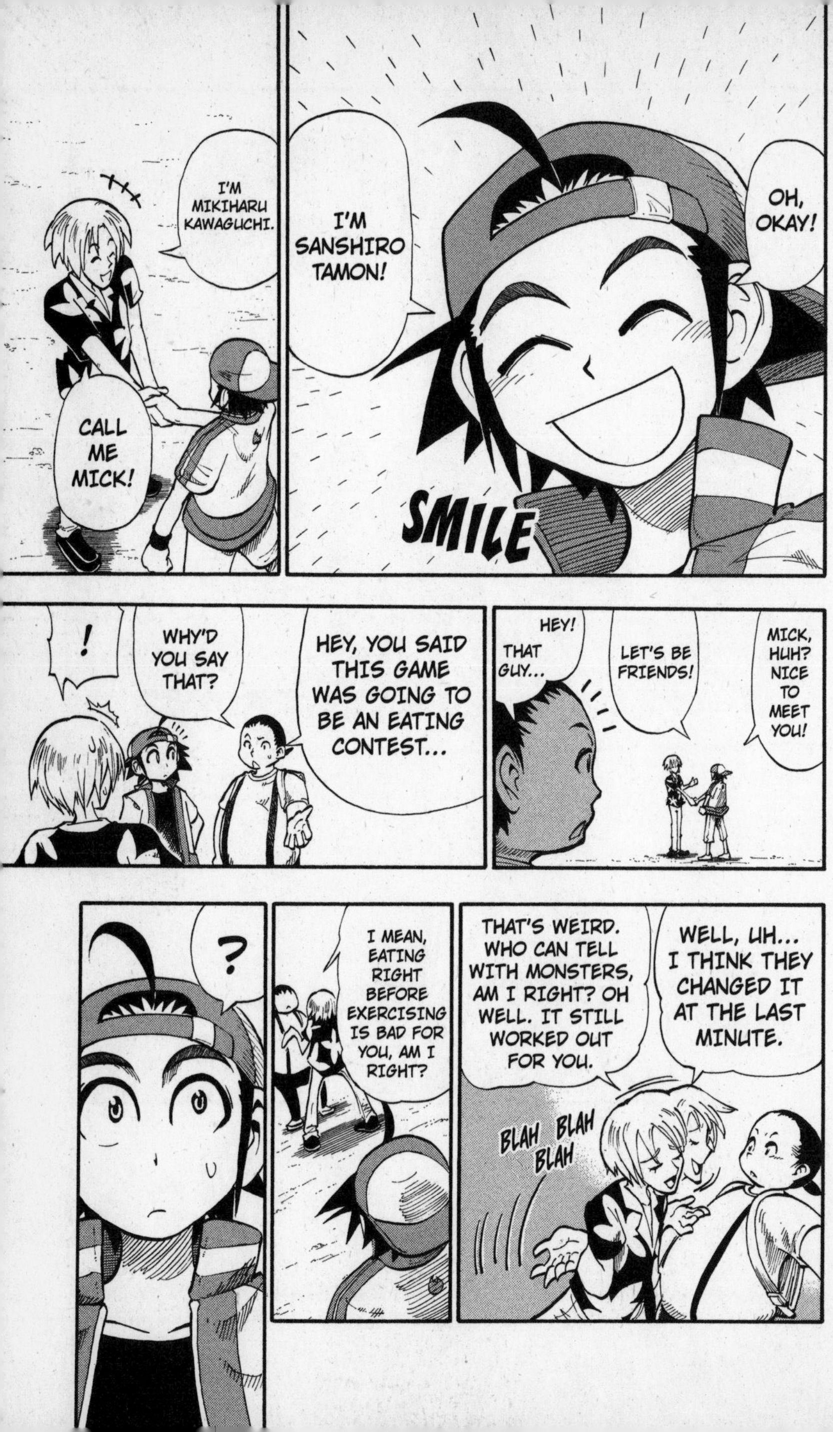
OH, OKAY!
I'M SANSHIRO TAMON!
SMILE
I'M MIKIHARU KAWAGUCHI.
CALL ME MICK!
MICK, HUH? NICE TO MEET YOU!
LET'S BE FRIENDS!
HEY! THAT GUY...
HEY, YOU SAID THIS GAME WAS GOING TO BE AN EATING CONTEST...
WHY'D YOU SAY THAT?
!
WELL, UH... I THINK THEY CHANGED IT AT THE LAST MINUTE.
THAT'S WEIRD. WHO CAN TELL WITH MONSTERS, AM I RIGHT? OH WELL. IT STILL WORKED OUT FOR YOU.
BLAH BLAH BLAH
I MEAN, EATING RIGHT BEFORE EXERCISING IS BAD FOR YOU, AM I RIGHT?
?

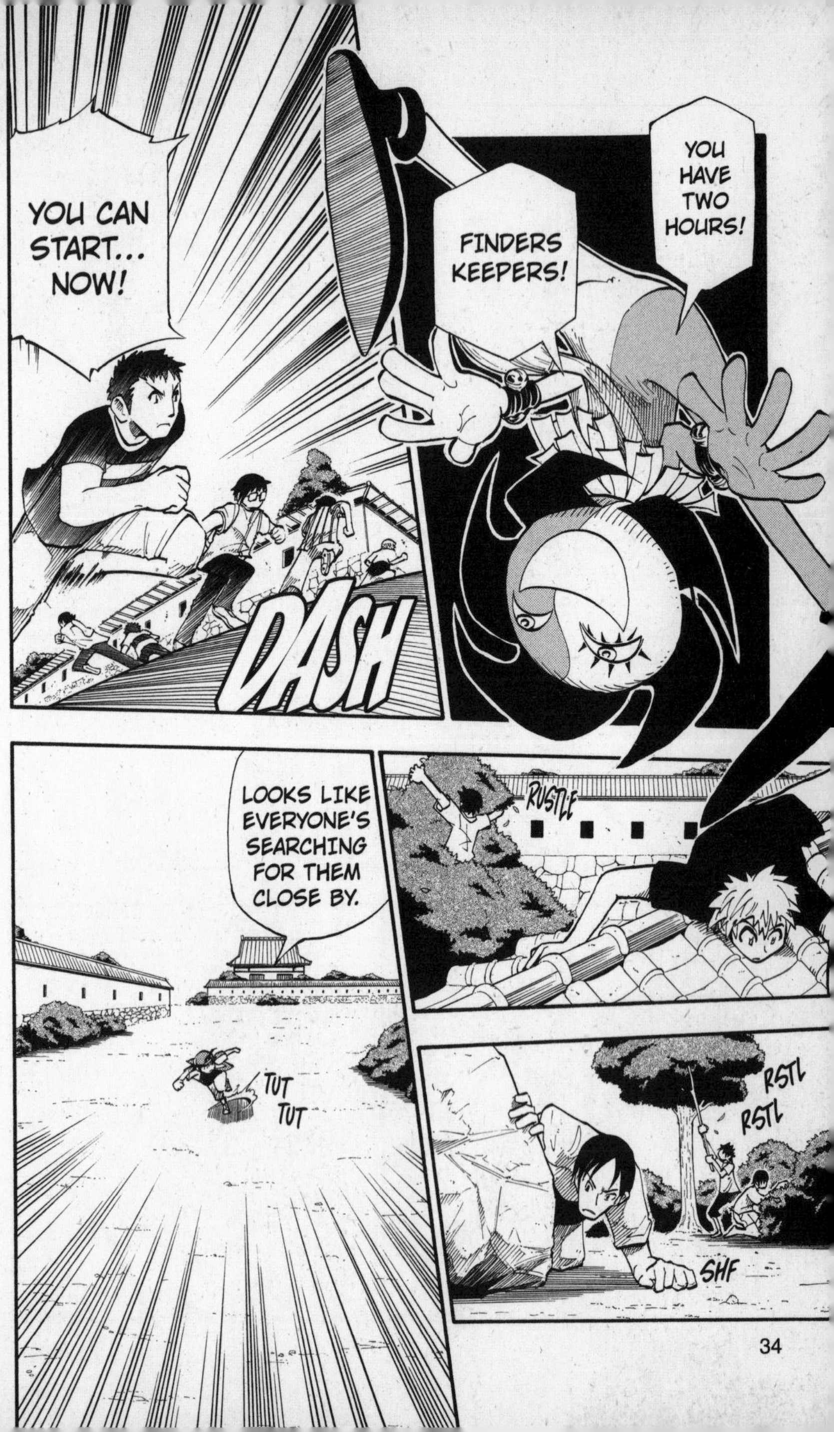
YOU HAVE TWO HOURS!
FINDERS KEEPERS!
YOU CAN START... NOW!
DASH
RUSTLE
RSTL RSTL
SHF
LOOKS LIKE EVERYONE'S SEARCHING FOR THEM CLOSE BY.
TUT TUT

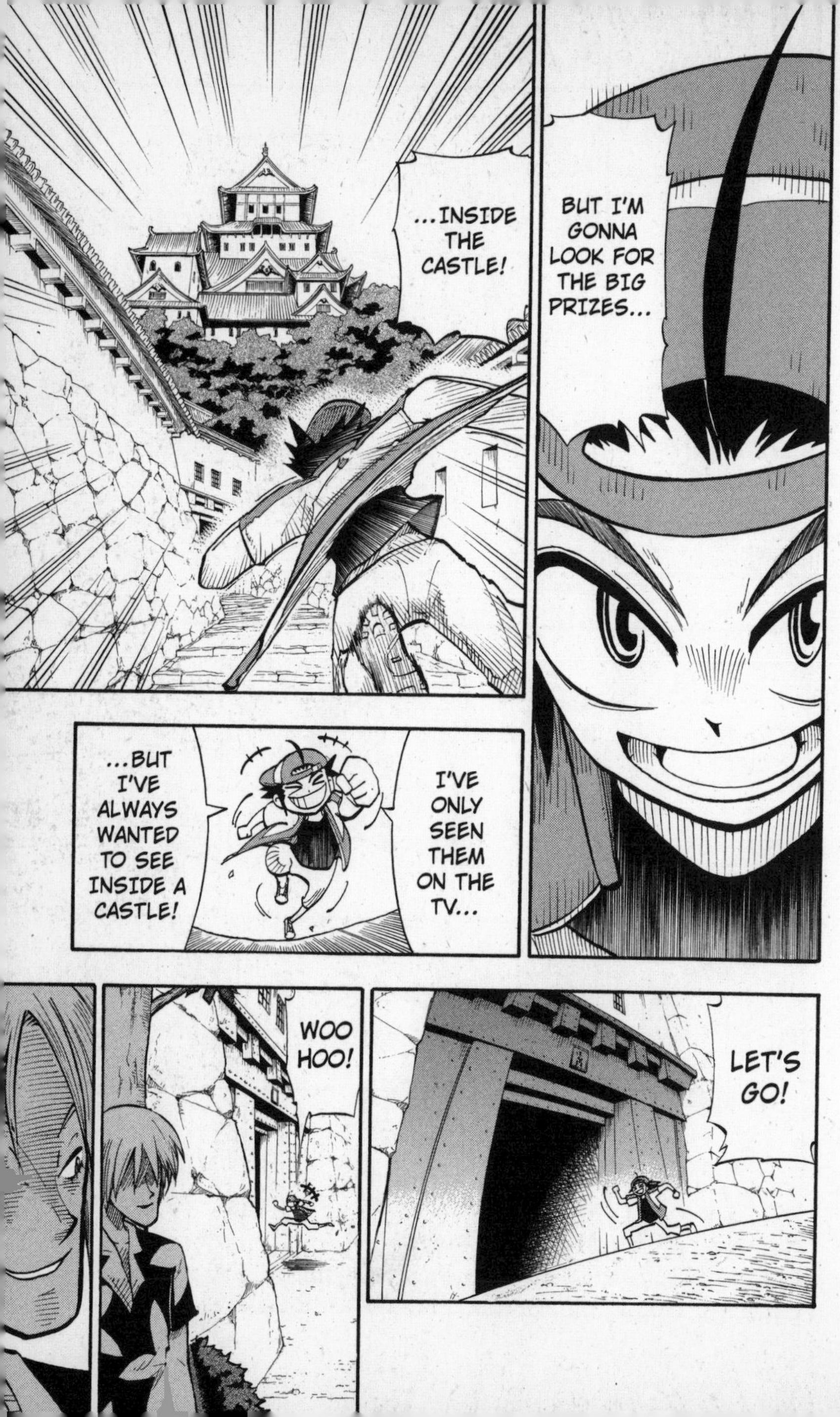
BUT I'M GONNA LOOK FOR THE BIG PRIZES...
...INSIDE THE CASTLE!
I'VE ONLY SEEN THEM ON THE TV...
...BUT I'VE ALWAYS WANTED TO SEE INSIDE A CASTLE!
LET'S GO!
WOO HOO!

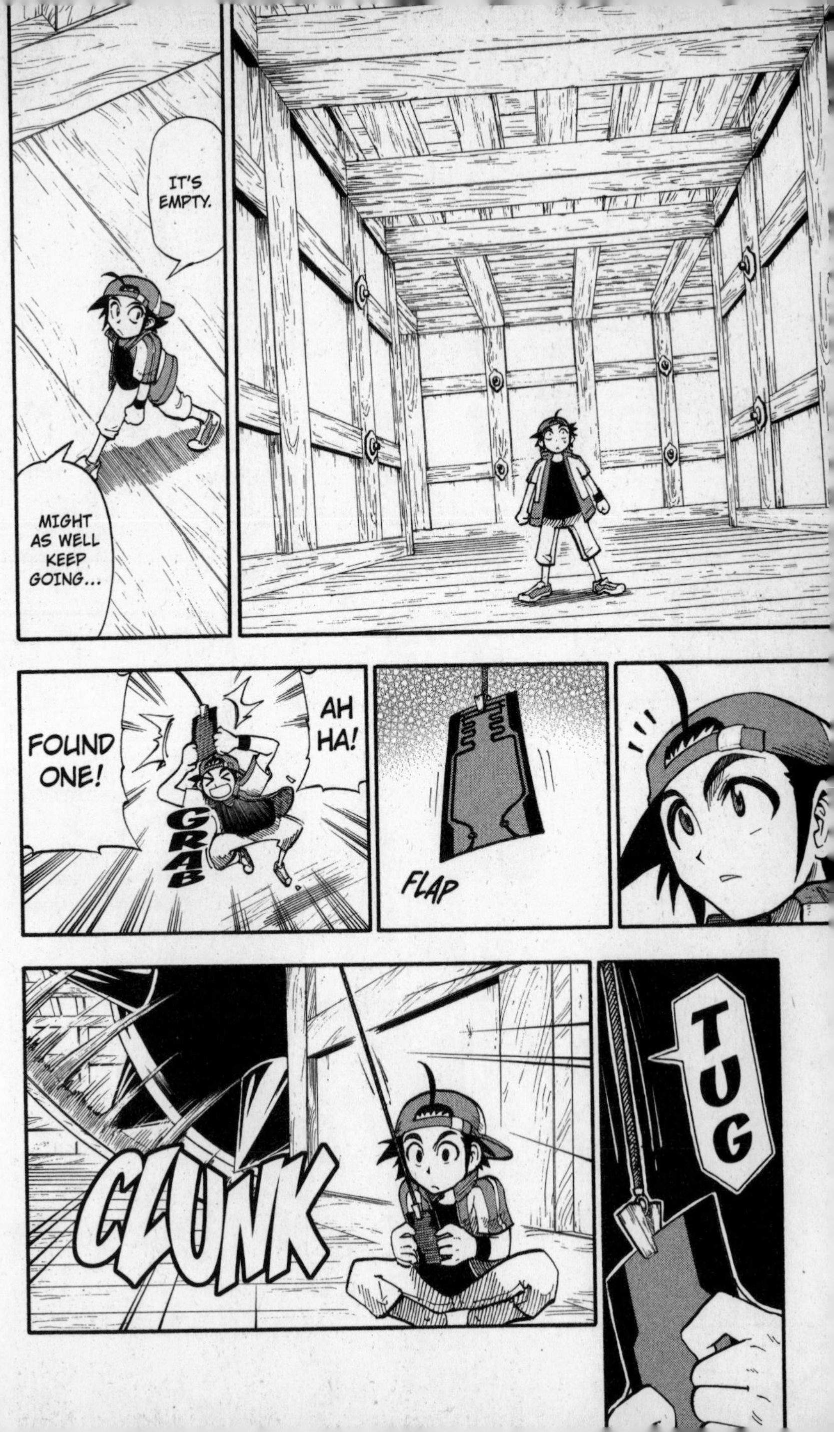
IT'S EMPTY.
MIGHT AS WELL KEEP GOING...
FLAP
AH HA!
FOUND ONE!
GRAB
TUG
CLUNK

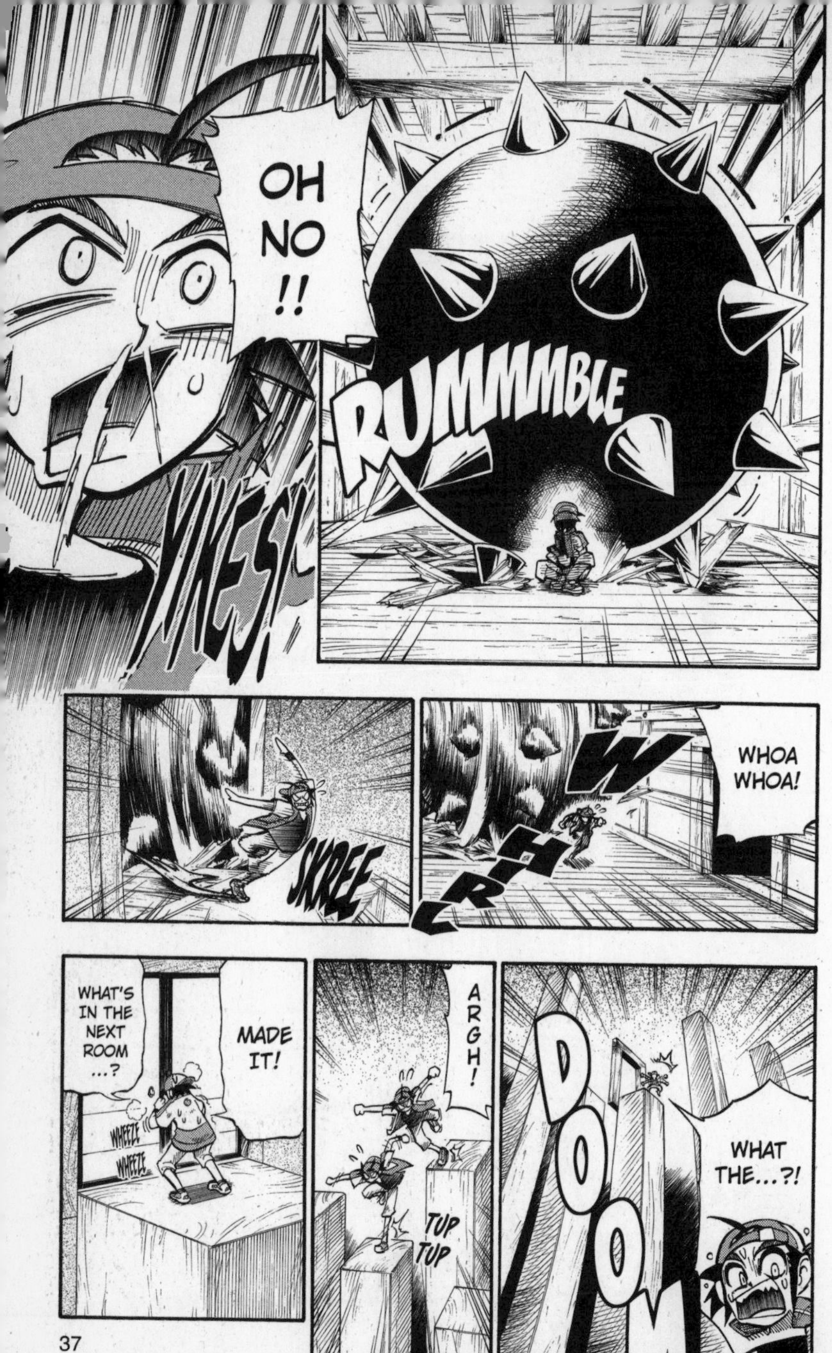
RUMMMBLE
OH NO!!
YIKES!
WHOA WHOA!
WHIRL
SKREE
WHAT THE...?!
DOOM
ARGH!
TUP TUP
MADE IT!
WHAT'S IN THE NEXT ROOM ...?
WHEEZE WHEEZE

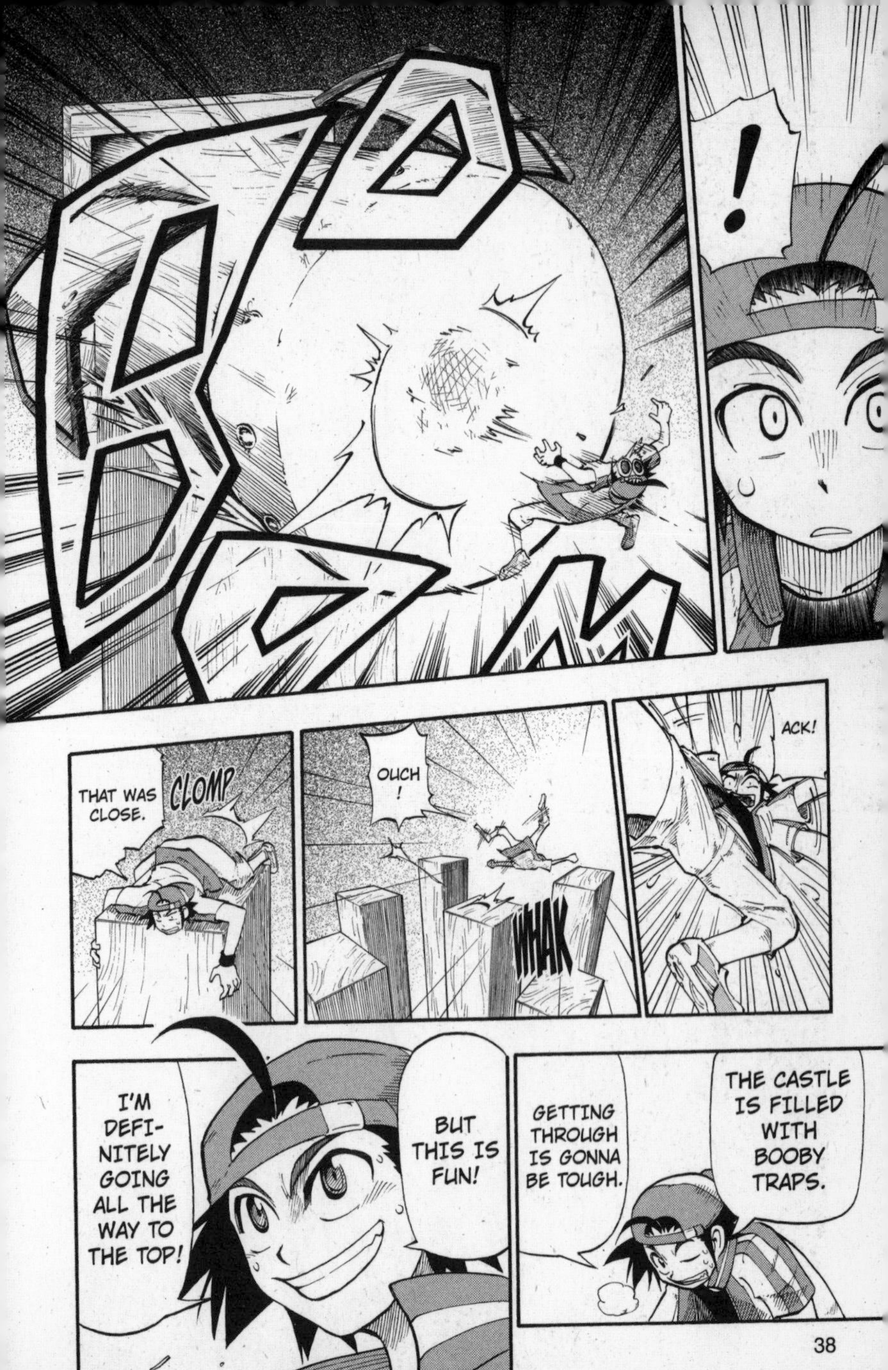
!
ACK!
OUCH!
WHAK
CLOMP
THAT WAS CLOSE.
THE CASTLE IS FILLED WITH BOOBY TRAPS.
GETTING THROUGH IS GONNA BE TOUGH.
BUT THIS IS FUN!
I'M DEFI-NITELY GOING ALL THE WAY TO THE TOP!

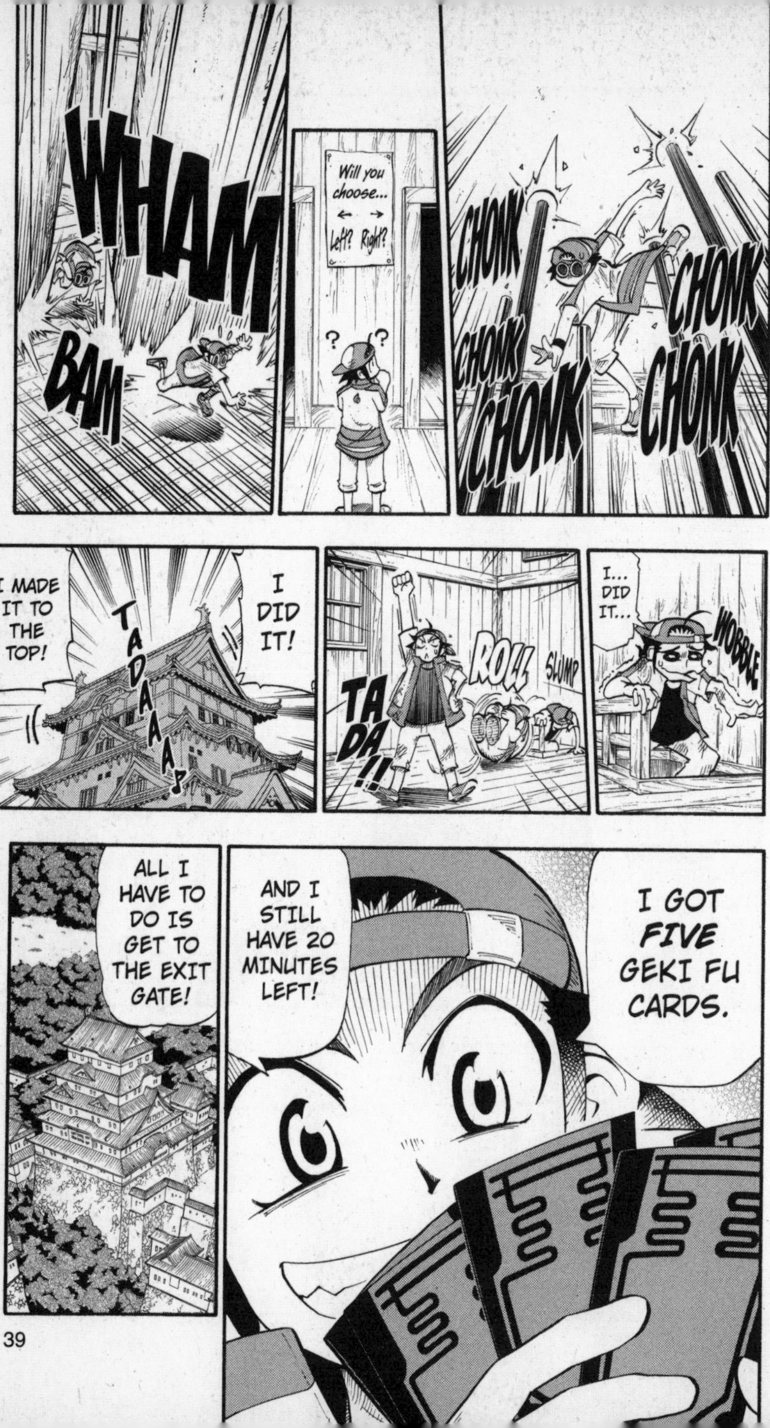
CHONK
CHONK
CHONK
CHONK
CHONK
Will you choose... ← → Left? Right?
??
WHAM
BAM
I... DID IT...
WOBBLE
ROLL
SLUMP
TADA!!
I DID IT!
I MADE IT TO THE TOP!
TADAAAA♪
I GOT *FIVE* GEKI FU CARDS.
AND I STILL HAVE 20 MINUTES LEFT!
ALL I HAVE TO DO IS GET TO THE EXIT GATE!

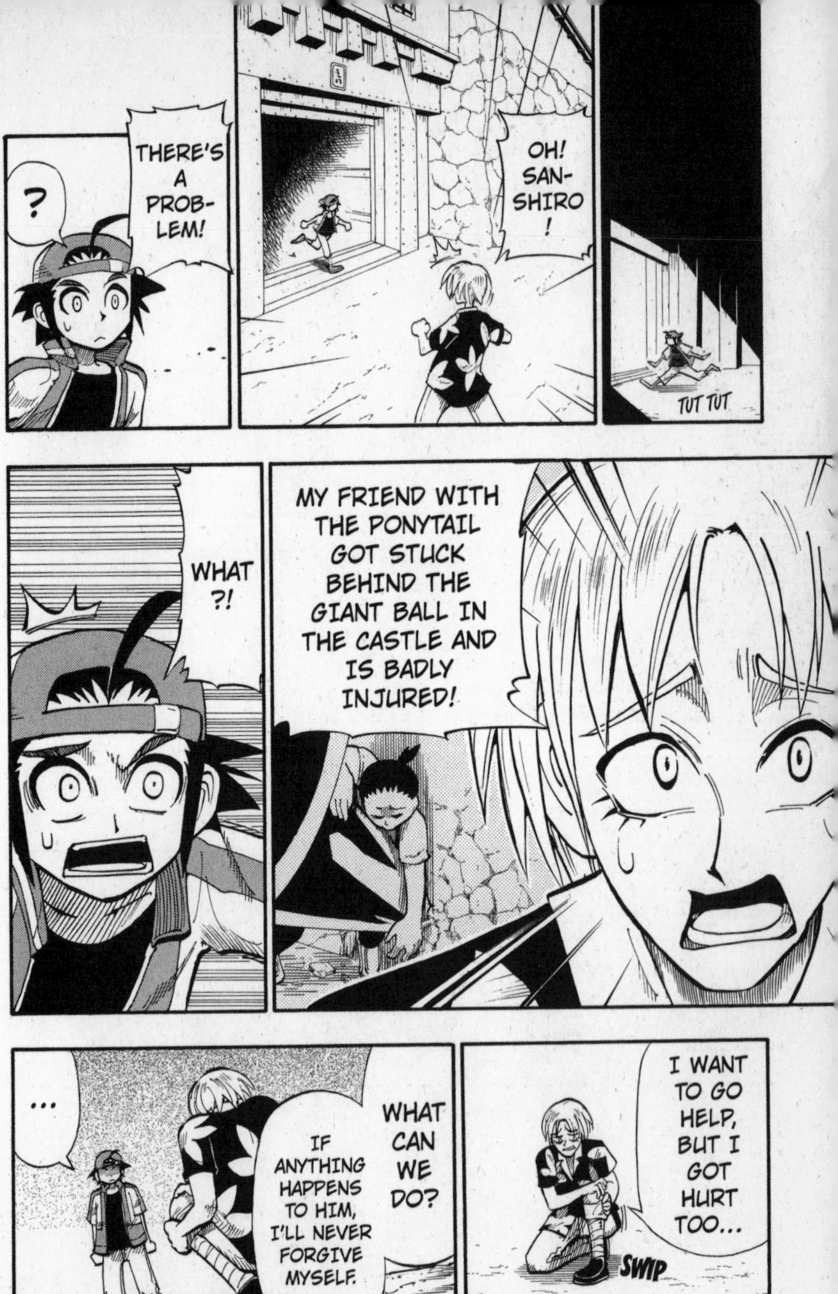
TUT TUT
OH! SAN-SHIRO!
THERE'S A PROB-LEM!
?
MY FRIEND WITH THE PONYTAIL GOT STUCK BEHIND THE GIANT BALL IN THE CASTLE AND IS BADLY INJURED!
WHAT?!
I WANT TO GO HELP, BUT I GOT HURT TOO...
SWIP
WHAT CAN WE DO?
IF ANYTHING HAPPENS TO HIM, I'LL NEVER FORGIVE MYSELF.
...

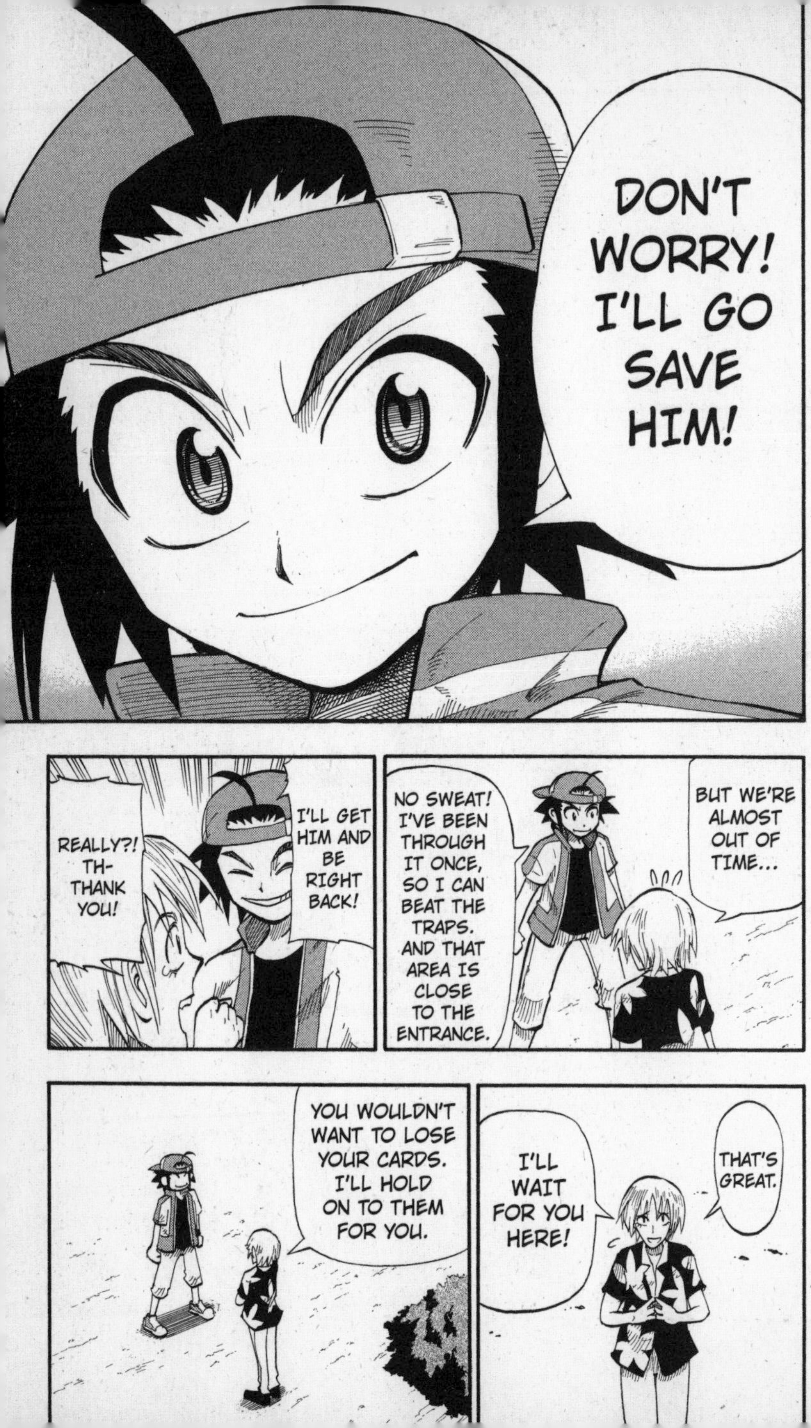
DON'T WORRY! I'LL GO SAVE HIM!
BUT WE'RE ALMOST OUT OF TIME...
NO SWEAT! I'VE BEEN THROUGH IT ONCE, SO I CAN BEAT THE TRAPS. AND THAT AREA IS CLOSE TO THE ENTRANCE.
I'LL GET HIM AND BE RIGHT BACK!
REALLY?! TH-THANK YOU!
THAT'S GREAT.
I'LL WAIT FOR YOU HERE!
YOU WOULDN'T WANT TO LOSE YOUR CARDS. I'LL HOLD ON TO THEM FOR YOU.

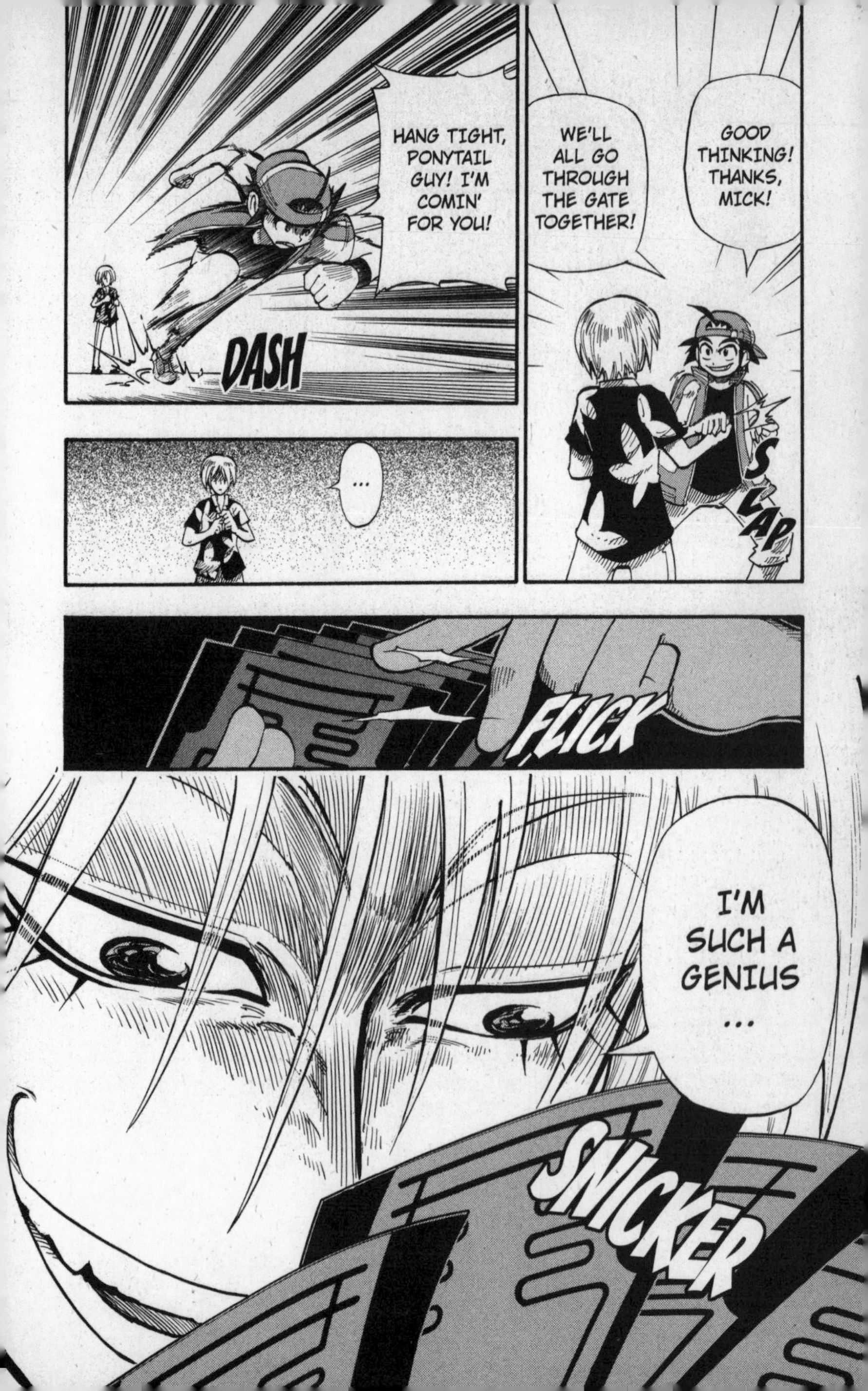
GOOD THINKING! THANKS, MICK!
WE'LL ALL GO THROUGH THE GATE TOGETHER!
SLAP
HANG TIGHT, PONYTAIL GUY! I'M COMIN' FOR YOU!
DASH
...
FLICK
I'M SUCH A GENIUS ...
SNICKER

CHAPTER 11 WILL OF THE GEKI FU

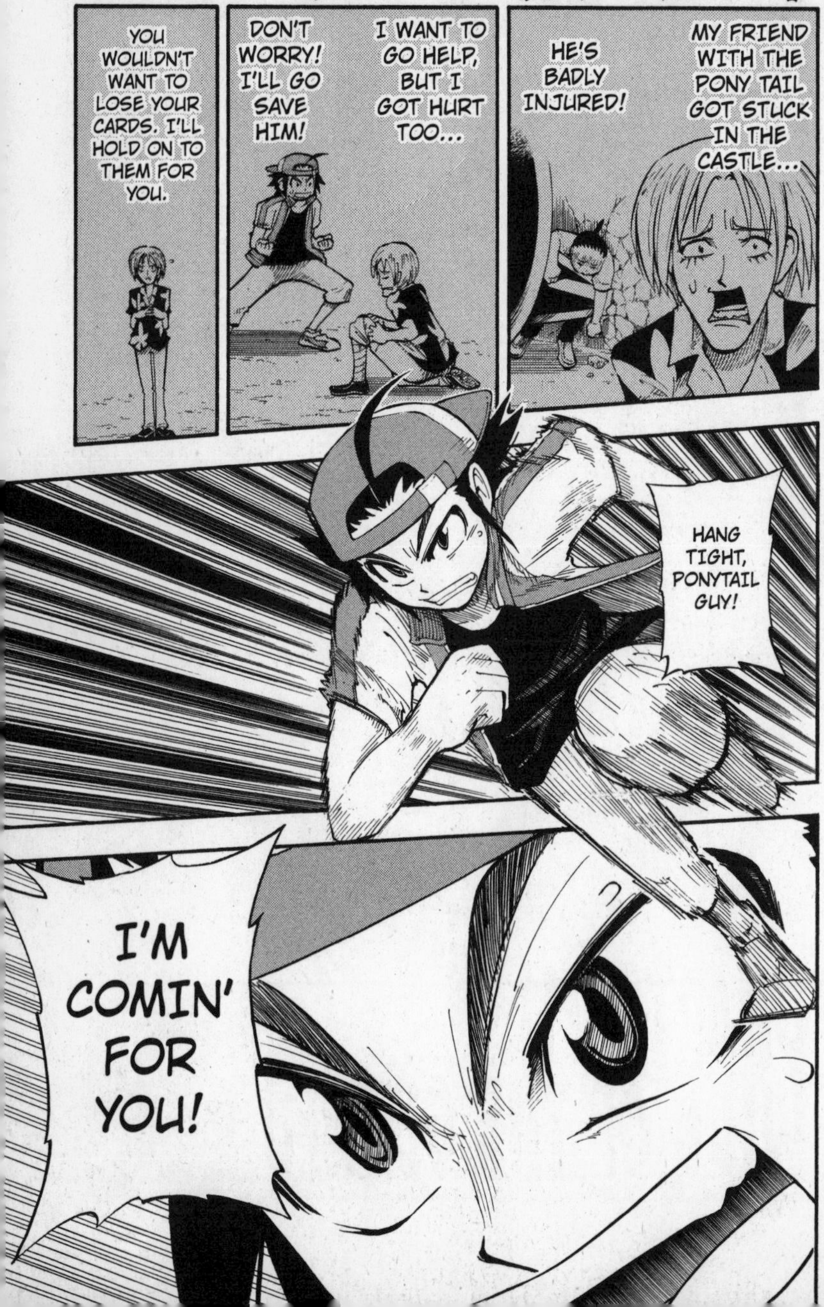
MY FRIEND WITH THE PONY TAIL GOT STUCK IN THE CASTLE...
HE'S BADLY INJURED!
I WANT TO GO HELP, BUT I GOT HURT TOO...
DON'T WORRY! I'LL GO SAVE HIM!
YOU WOULDN'T WANT TO LOSE YOUR CARDS. I'LL HOLD ON TO THEM FOR YOU.
HANG TIGHT, PONYTAIL GUY!
I'M COMIN' FOR YOU!

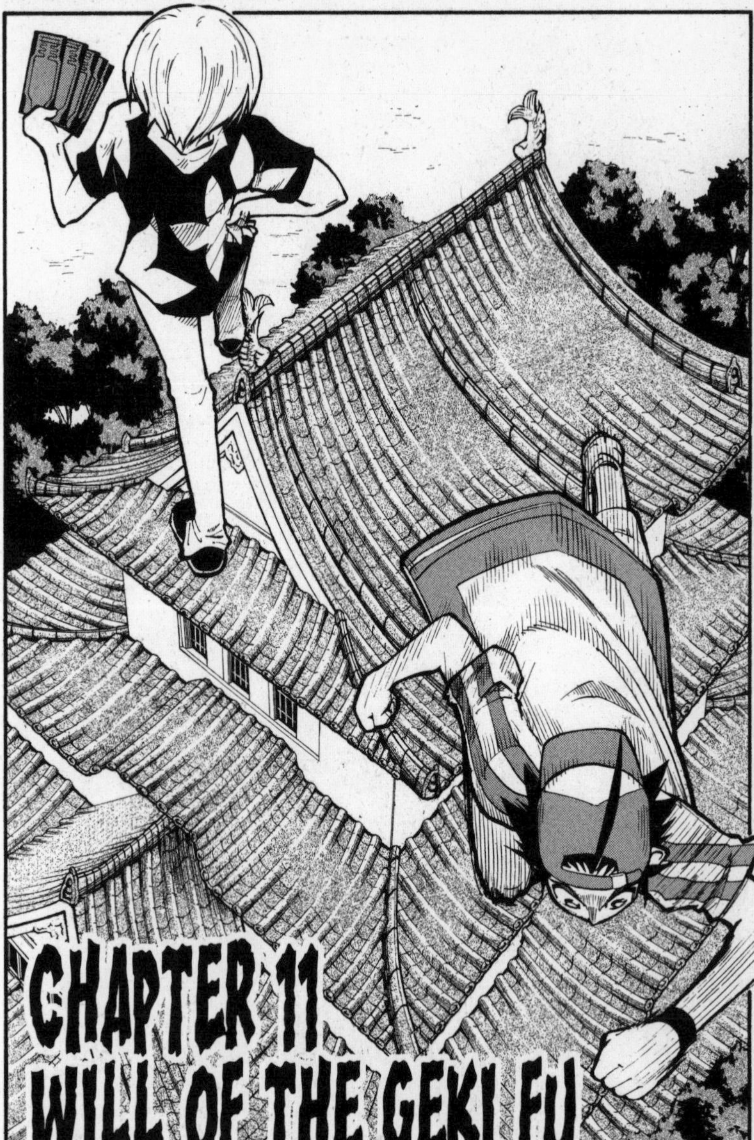
CHAPTER 11
WILL OF THE GEKI FU

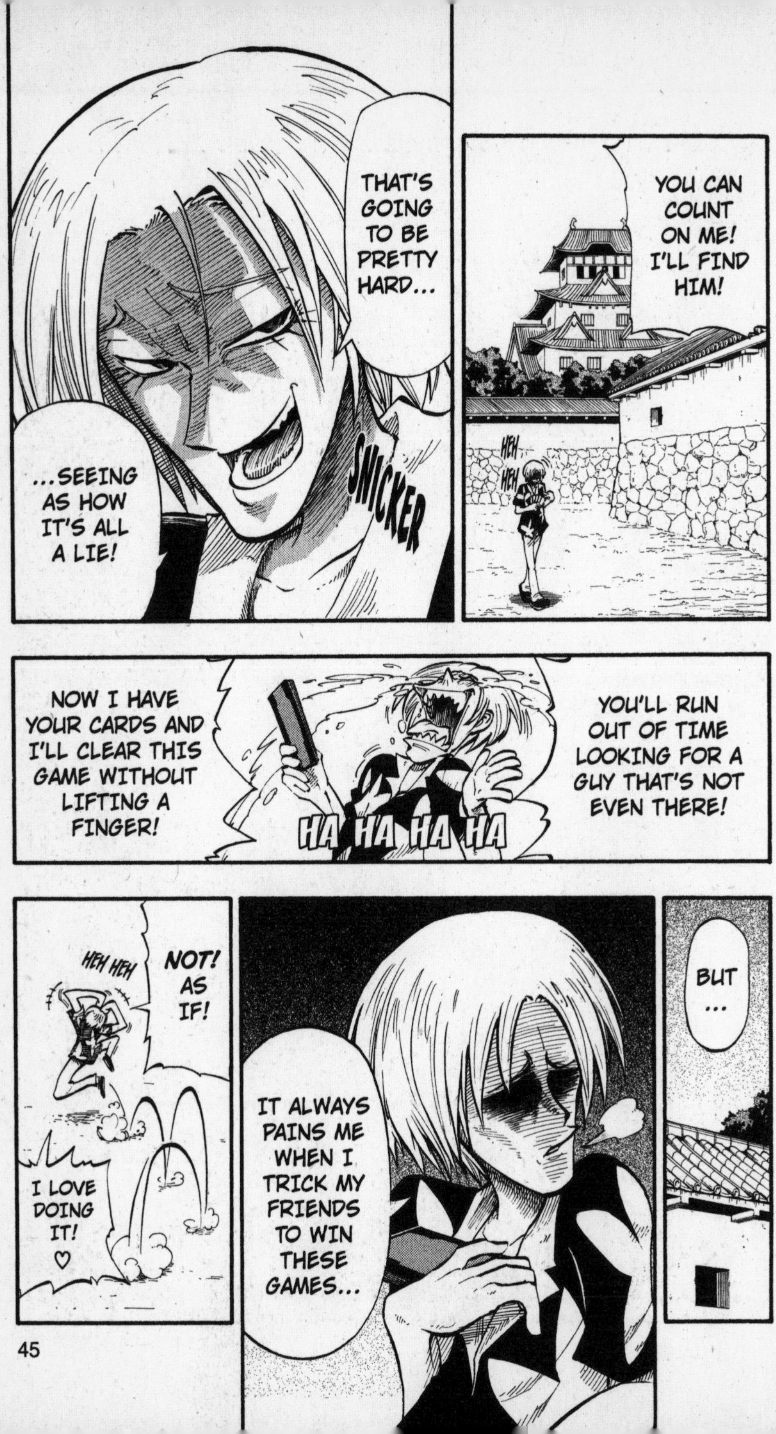
YOU CAN COUNT ON ME! I'LL FIND HIM!
HEH HEH
THAT'S GOING TO BE PRETTY HARD...
SNICKER
...SEEING AS HOW IT'S ALL A LIE!
YOU'LL RUN OUT OF TIME LOOKING FOR A GUY THAT'S NOT EVEN THERE!
NOW I HAVE YOUR CARDS AND I'LL CLEAR THIS GAME WITHOUT LIFTING A FINGER!
HA HA HA HA
BUT...
IT ALWAYS PAINS ME WHEN I TRICK MY FRIENDS TO WIN THESE GAMES...
NOT! AS IF!
HEH HEH
I LOVE DOING IT! ♡

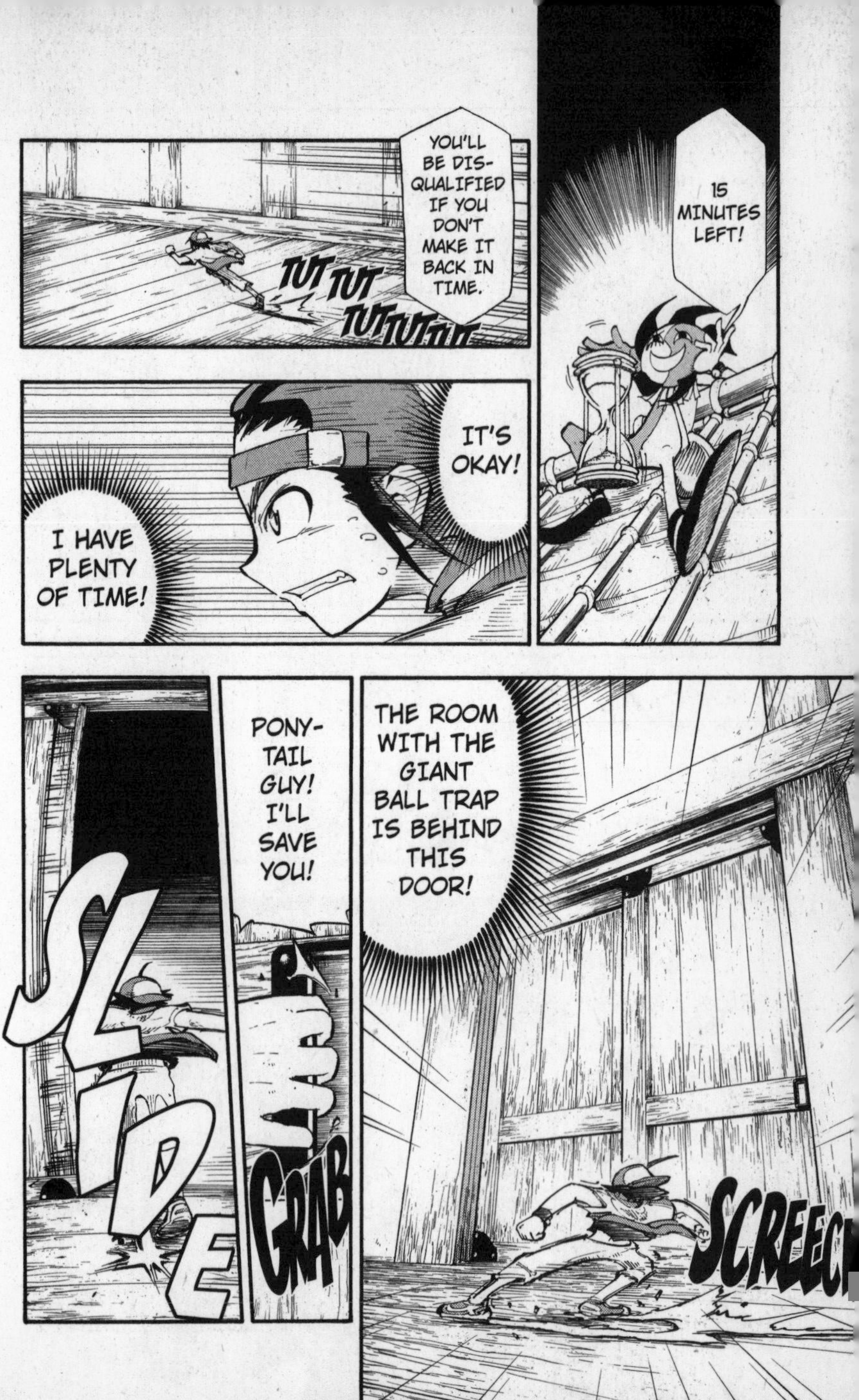
15 MINUTES LEFT!
YOU'LL BE DIS-QUALIFIED IF YOU DON'T MAKE IT BACK IN TIME.
TUT TUT
TUT
IT'S OKAY!
I HAVE PLENTY OF TIME!
THE ROOM WITH THE GIANT BALL TRAP IS BEHIND THIS DOOR!
SCREEC
PONY-TAIL GUY! I'LL SAVE YOU!
GRAB
SLIDE

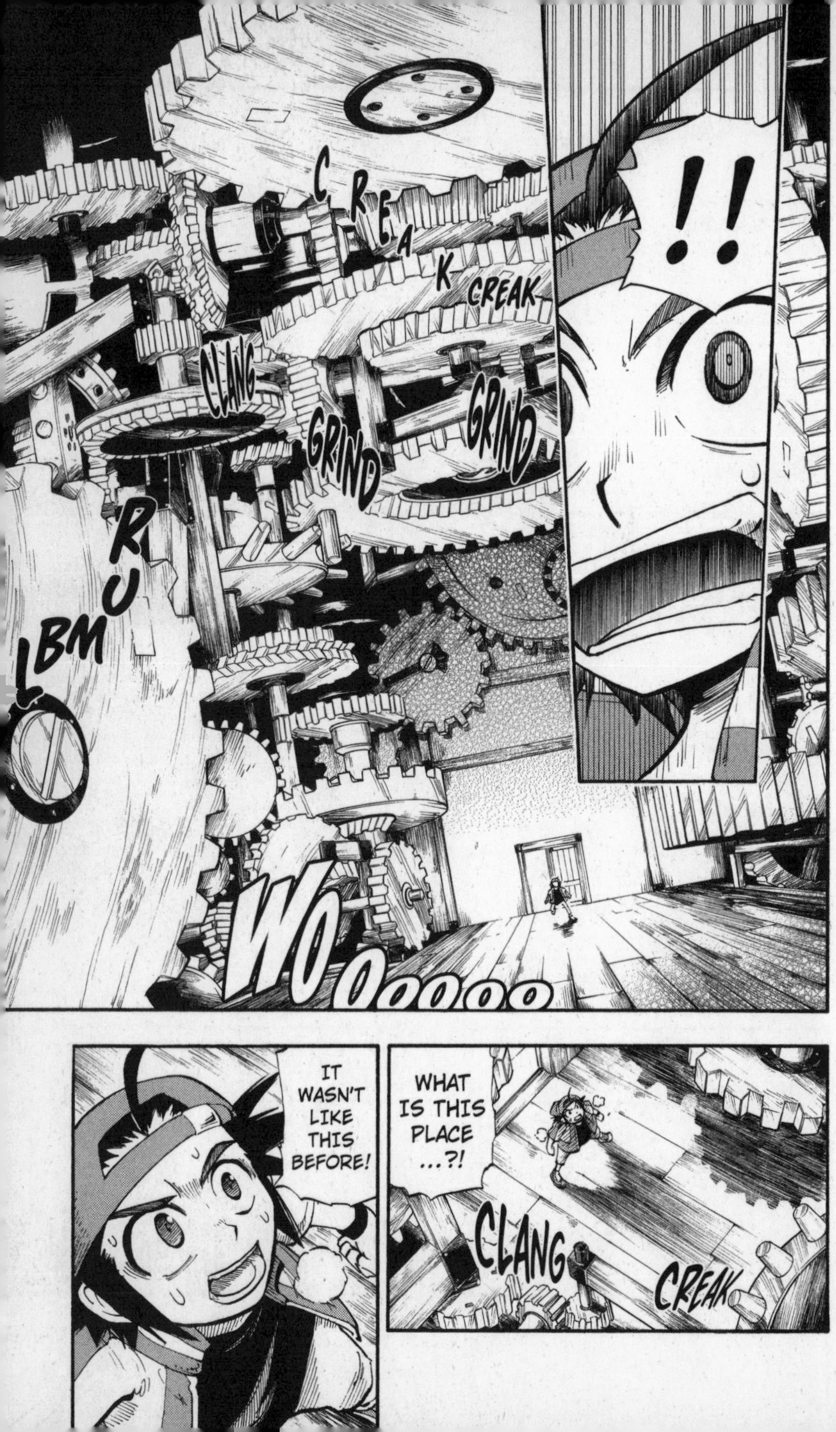
!!
CREAK
CREAK
CLANG
GRIND
GRIND
RUMBL
WOOOOOO
WHAT IS THIS PLACE ...?!
CLANG
CREAK
IT WASN'T LIKE THIS BEFORE!

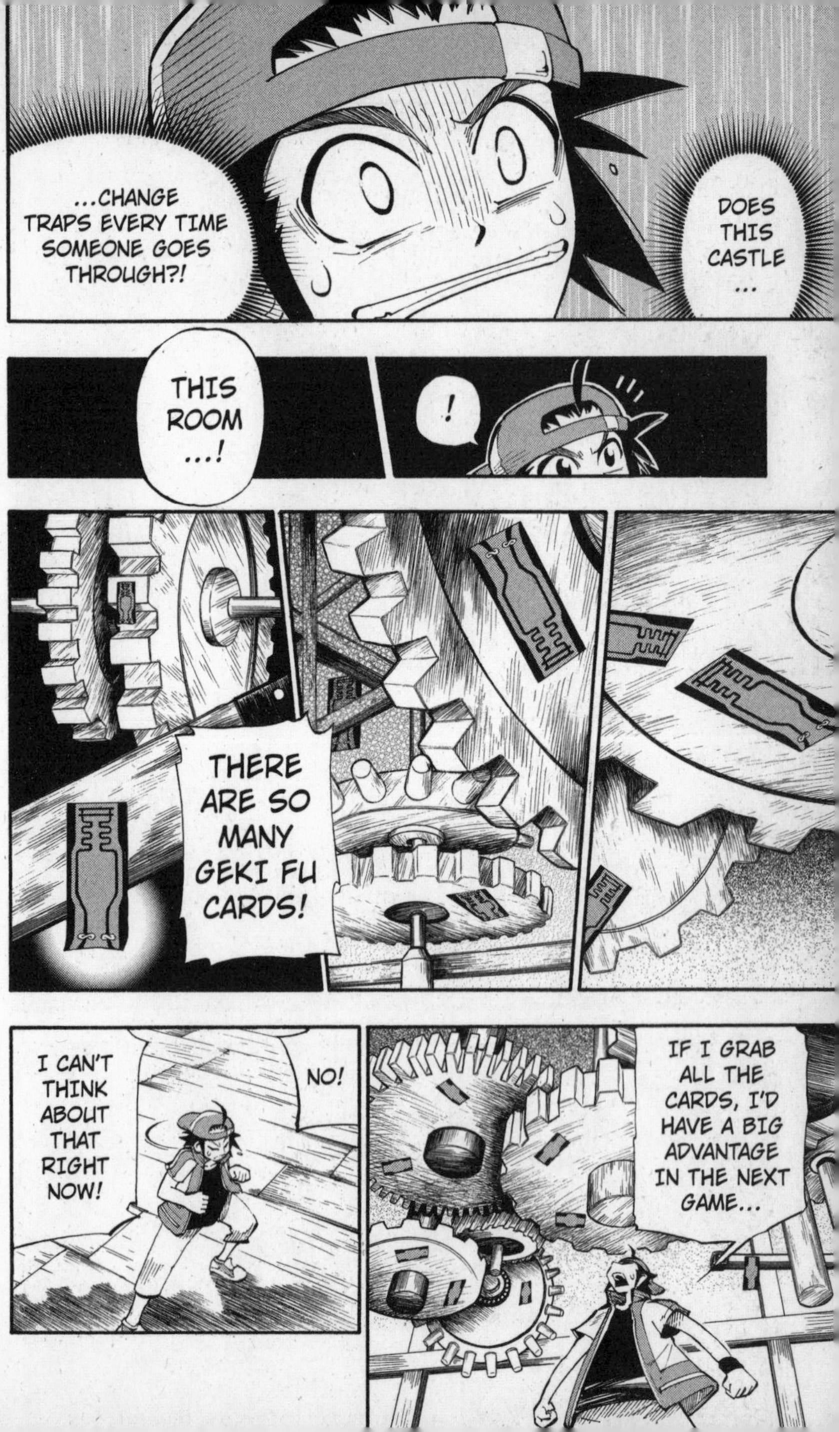
DOES THIS CASTLE ...
...CHANGE TRAPS EVERY TIME SOMEONE GOES THROUGH?!
!
THIS ROOM ...!
THERE ARE SO MANY GEKI FU CARDS!
IF I GRAB ALL THE CARDS, I'D HAVE A BIG ADVANTAGE IN THE NEXT GAME...
NO!
I CAN'T THINK ABOUT THAT RIGHT NOW!

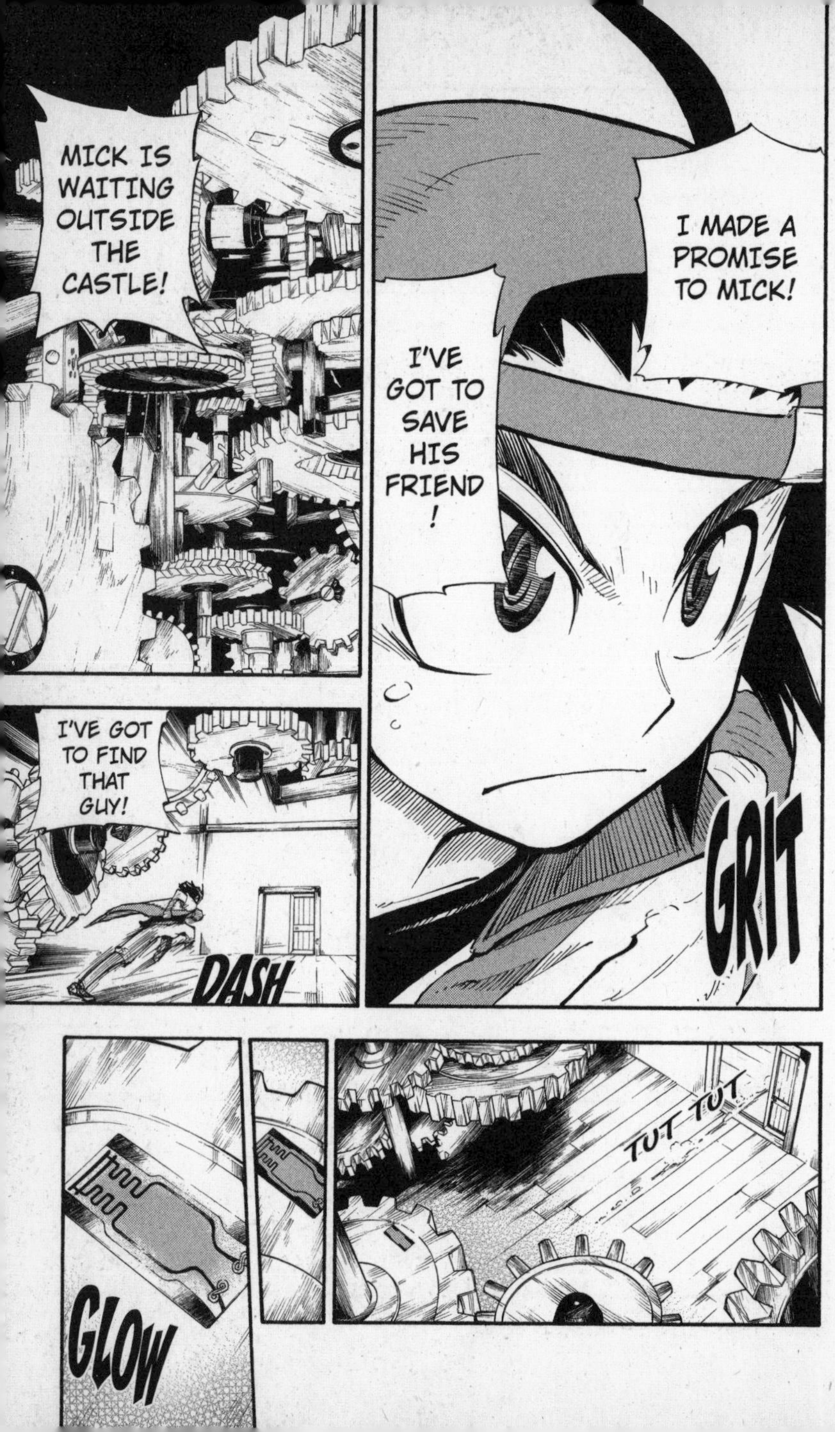
I MADE A PROMISE TO MICK!
I'VE GOT TO SAVE HIS FRIEND!
GRIT
MICK IS WAITING OUTSIDE THE CASTLE!
I'VE GOT TO FIND THAT GUY!
DASH
TUT TUT
GLOW

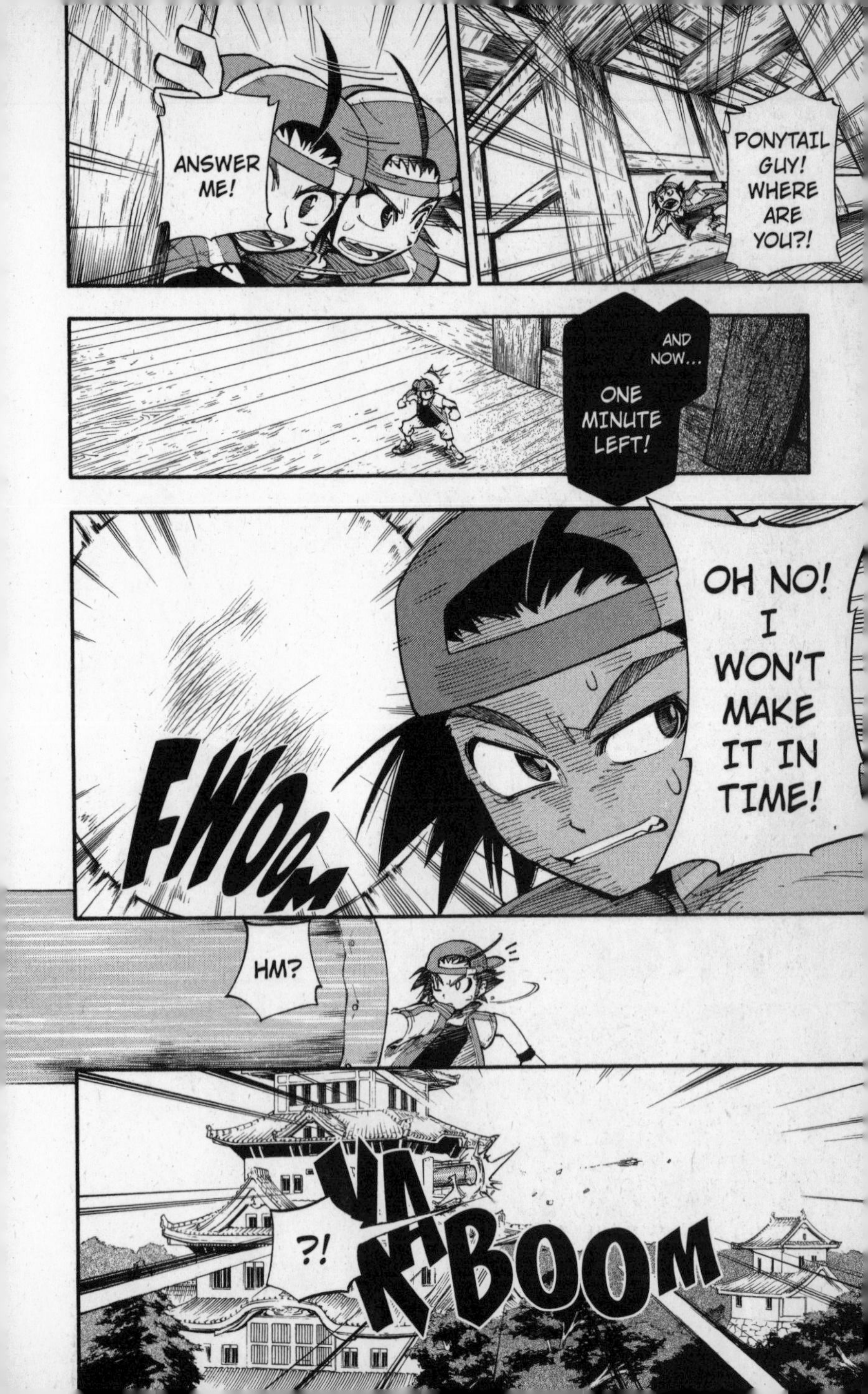
PONYTAIL GUY! WHERE ARE YOU?!
ANSWER ME!
AND NOW...
ONE MINUTE LEFT!
OH NO! I WON'T MAKE IT IN TIME!
FWOOM
HM?
KABOOM
?!

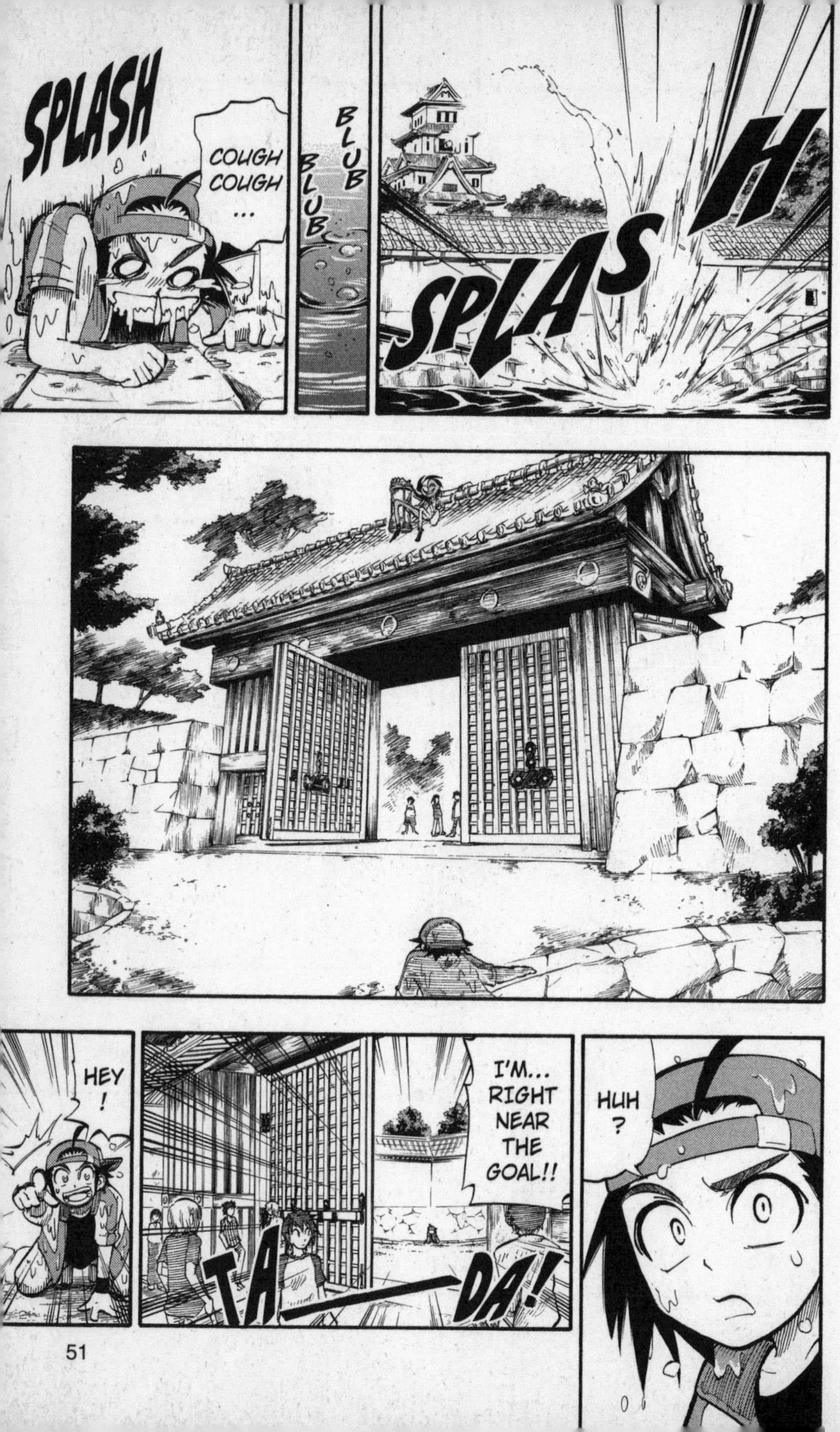
SPLASH
BLUB BLUB
SPLASH
COUGH COUGH ...
HUH ?
I'M... RIGHT NEAR THE GOAL!!
TA—DA!
HEY !

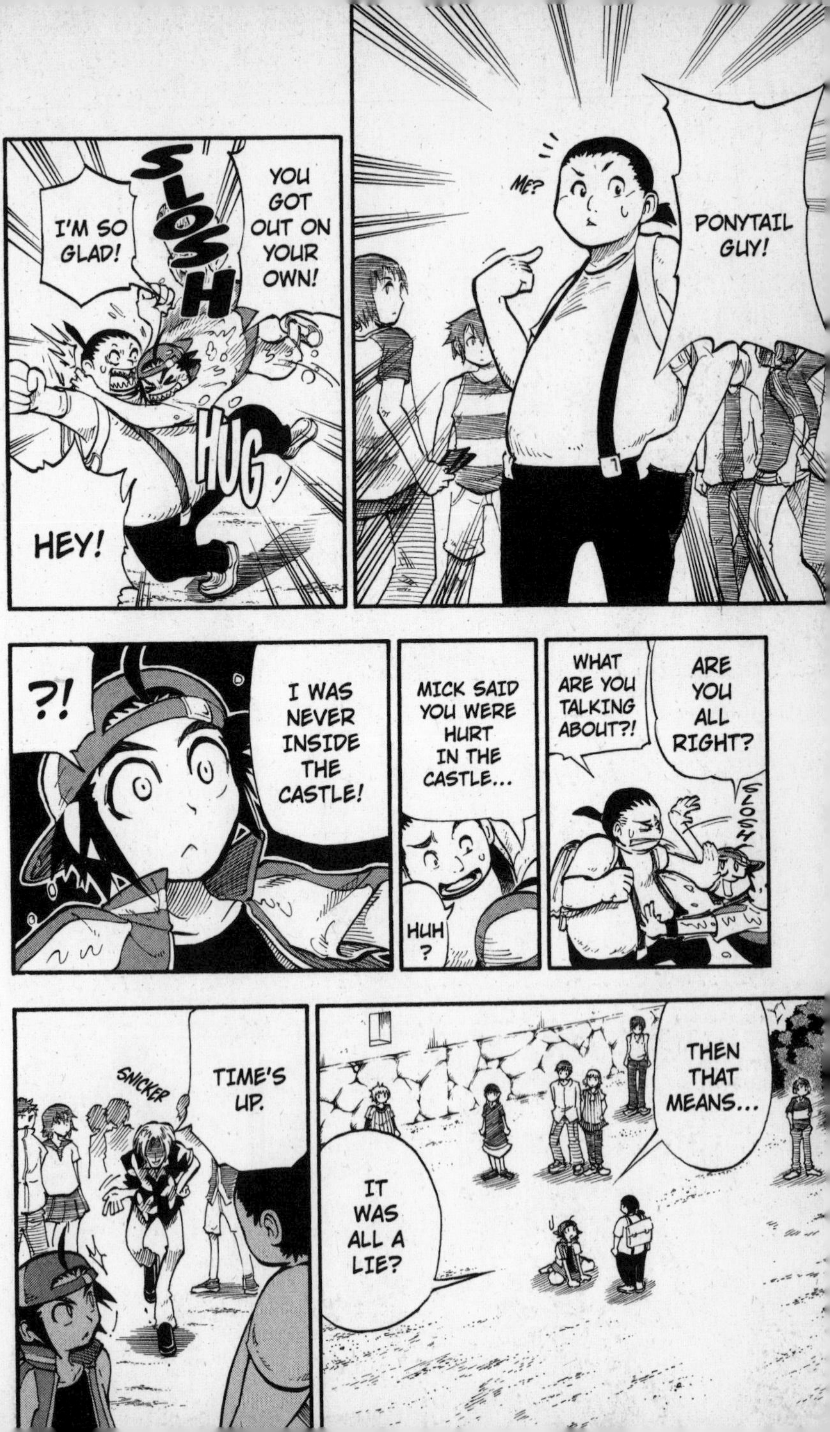
PONYTAIL GUY!
ME?
YOU GOT OUT ON YOUR OWN!
SLOSH
I'M SO GLAD!
HUG
HEY!
ARE YOU ALL RIGHT?
WHAT ARE YOU TALKING ABOUT?!
SLOSH
MICK SAID YOU WERE HURT IN THE CASTLE...
HUH?
I WAS NEVER INSIDE THE CASTLE!
?!
THEN THAT MEANS...
IT WAS ALL A LIE?
TIME'S UP.
SNICKER

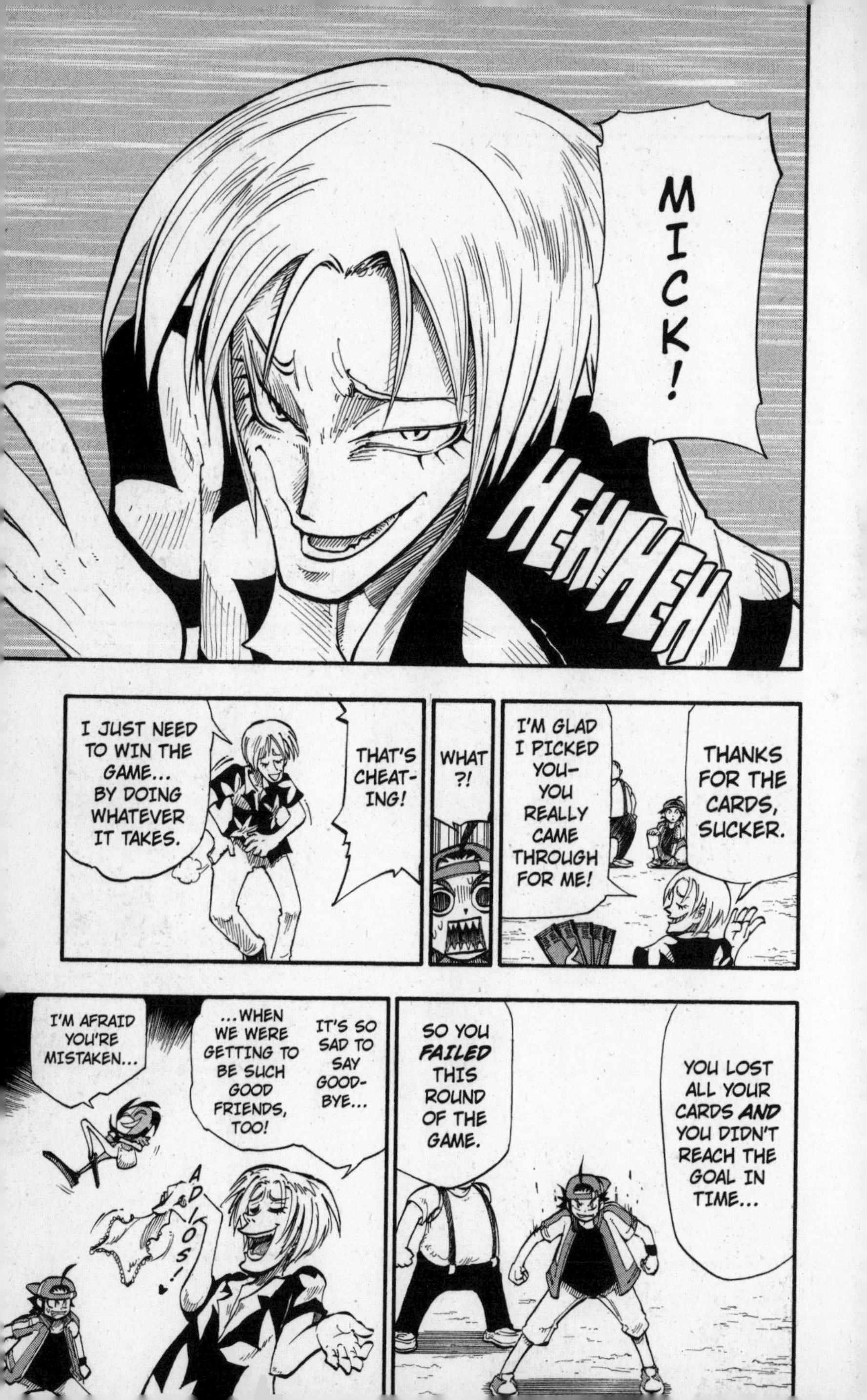
MICK!
HEH HEH
THANKS FOR THE CARDS, SUCKER.
I'M GLAD I PICKED YOU— YOU REALLY CAME THROUGH FOR ME!
WHAT?!
THAT'S CHEAT-ING!
I JUST NEED TO WIN THE GAME... BY DOING WHATEVER IT TAKES.
YOU LOST ALL YOUR CARDS *AND* YOU DIDN'T REACH THE GOAL IN TIME...
SO YOU *FAILED* THIS ROUND OF THE GAME.
IT'S SO SAD TO SAY GOOD-BYE...
...WHEN WE WERE GETTING TO BE SUCH GOOD FRIENDS, TOO!
I'M AFRAID YOU'RE MISTAKEN...
ADIOS!

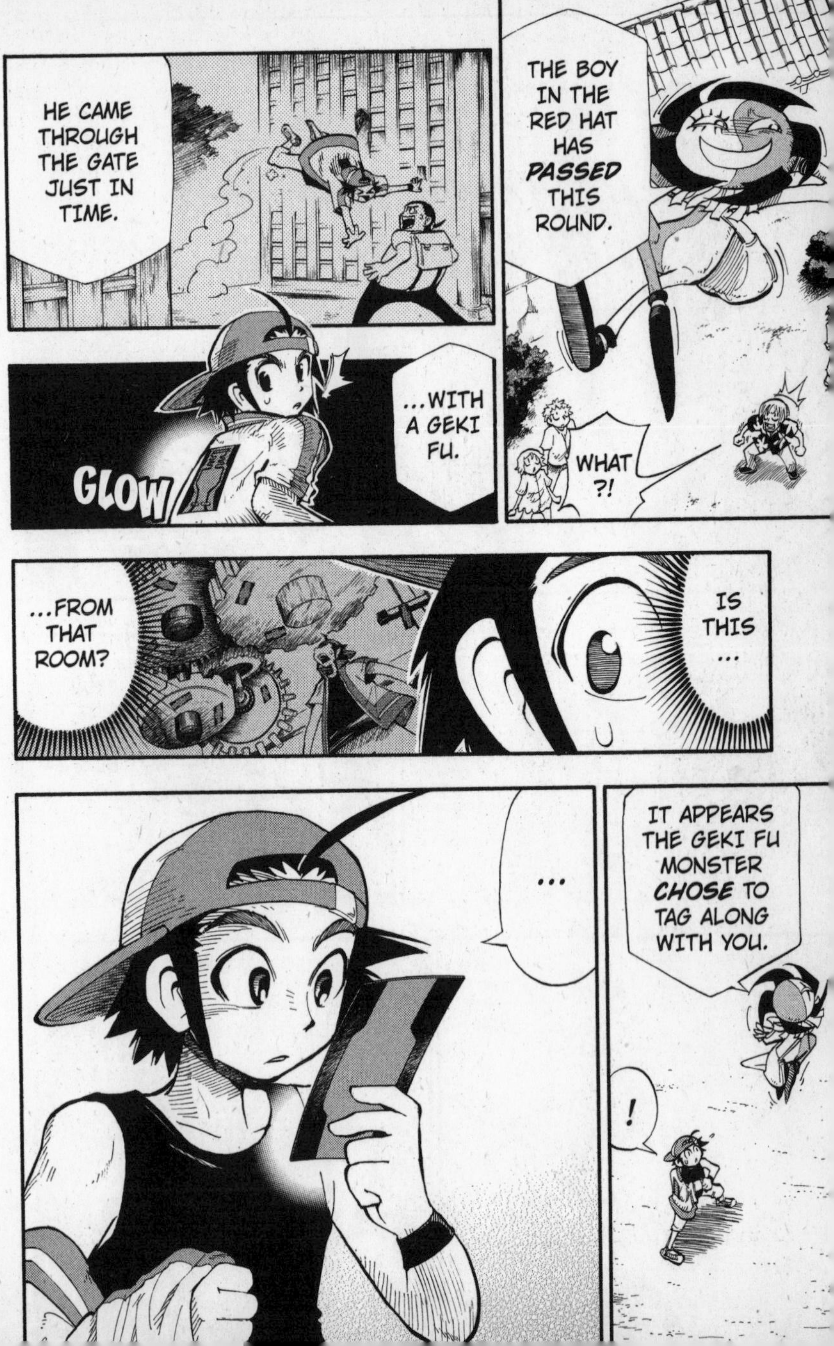
THE BOY IN THE RED HAT HAS PASSED THIS ROUND.
WHAT?!
HE CAME THROUGH THE GATE JUST IN TIME.
...WITH A GEKI FU.
GLOW
IS THIS ...
...FROM THAT ROOM?
IT APPEARS THE GEKI FU MONSTER CHOSE TO TAG ALONG WITH YOU.
!
...

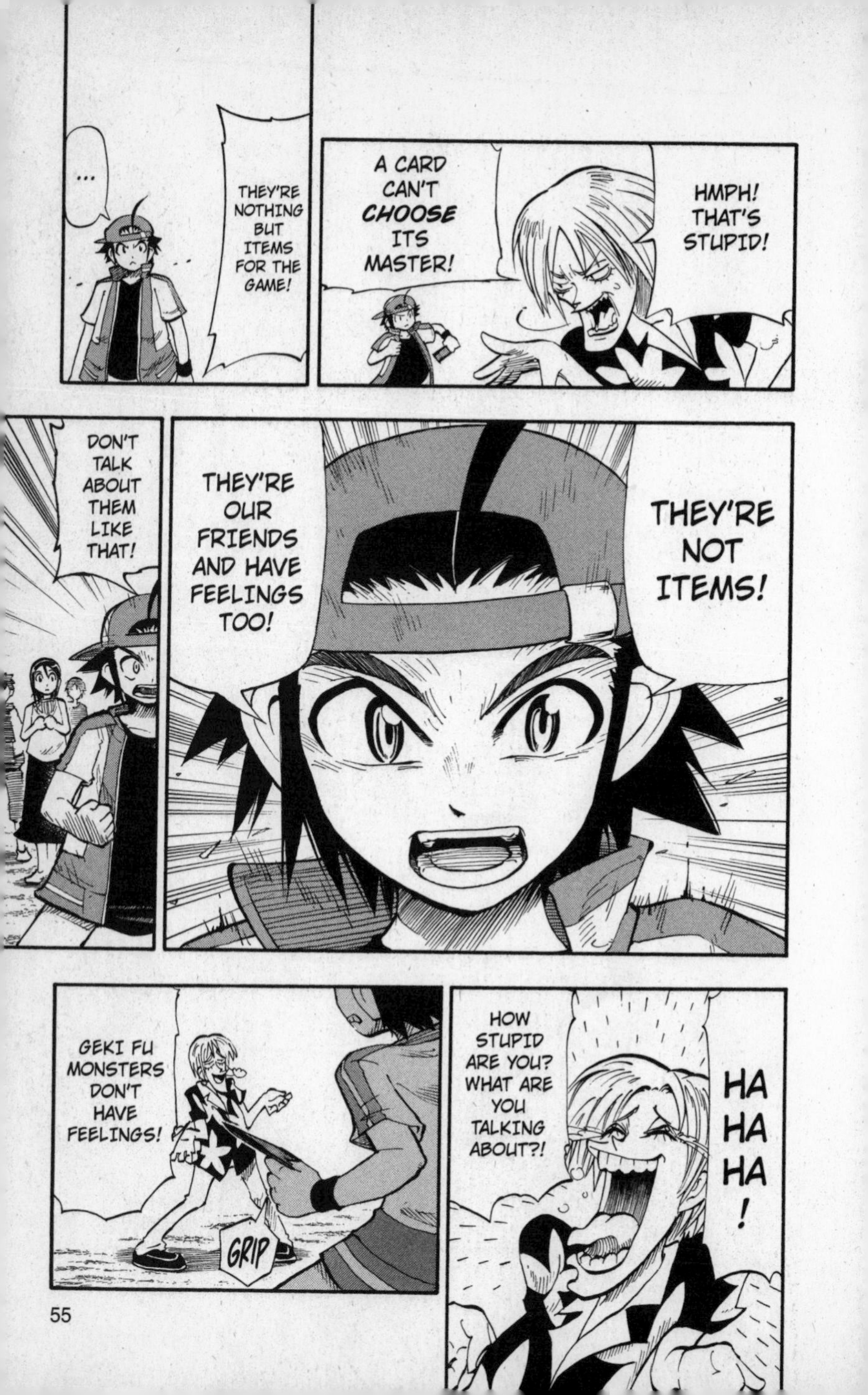
HMPH! THAT'S STUPID!
A CARD CAN'T CHOOSE ITS MASTER!
THEY'RE NOTHING BUT ITEMS FOR THE GAME!
...
THEY'RE NOT ITEMS!
THEY'RE OUR FRIENDS AND HAVE FEELINGS TOO!
DON'T TALK ABOUT THEM LIKE THAT!
HA HA HA!
HOW STUPID ARE YOU? WHAT ARE YOU TALKING ABOUT?!
GEKI FU MONSTERS DON'T HAVE FEELINGS!
GRIP

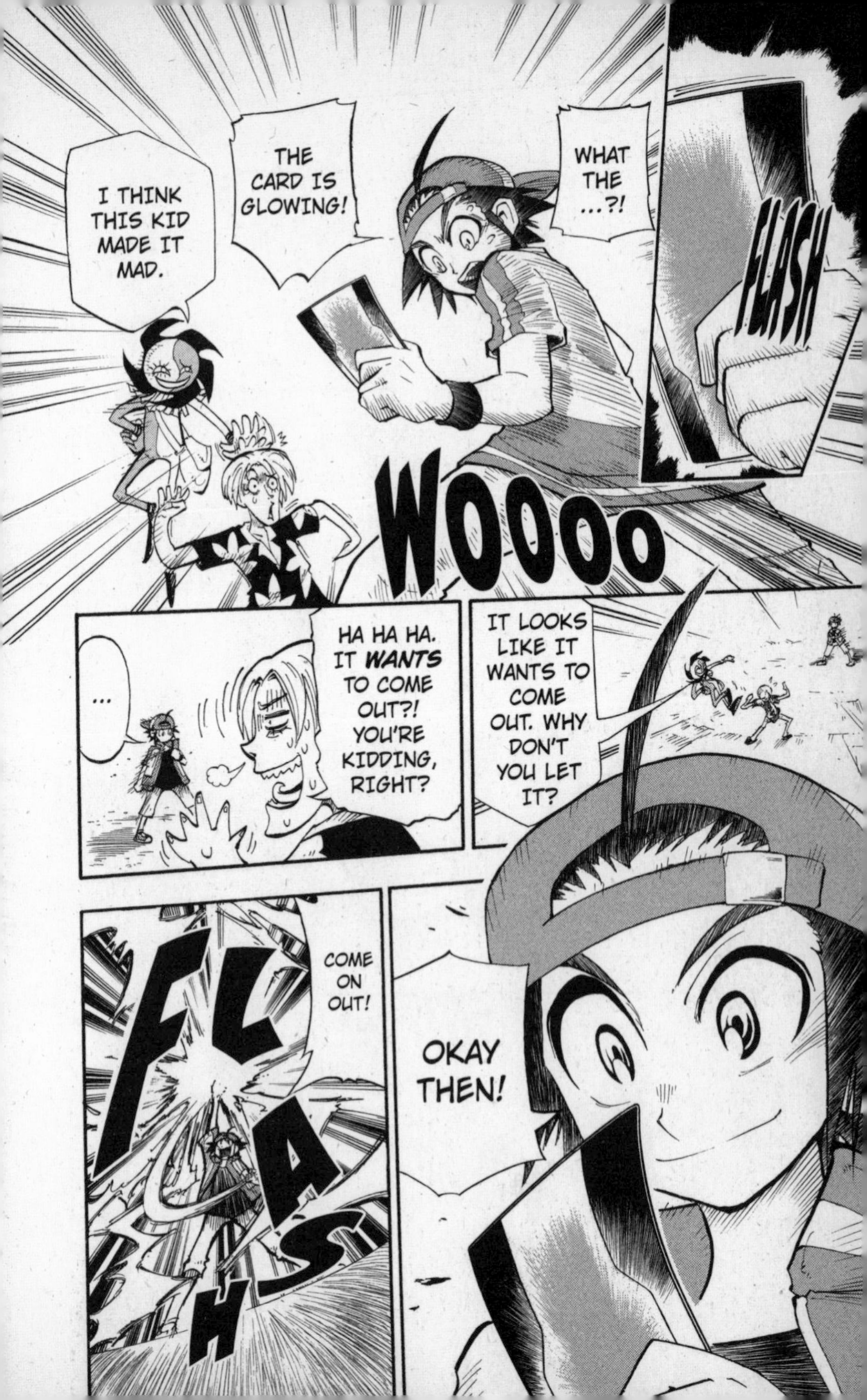
FLASH
WHAT THE ...?!
THE CARD IS GLOWING!
I THINK THIS KID MADE IT MAD.
WOOOO
IT LOOKS LIKE IT WANTS TO COME OUT. WHY DON'T YOU LET IT?
HA HA HA. IT ***WANTS*** TO COME OUT?! YOU'RE KIDDING, RIGHT?
...
OKAY THEN!
COME ON OUT!
FLASH

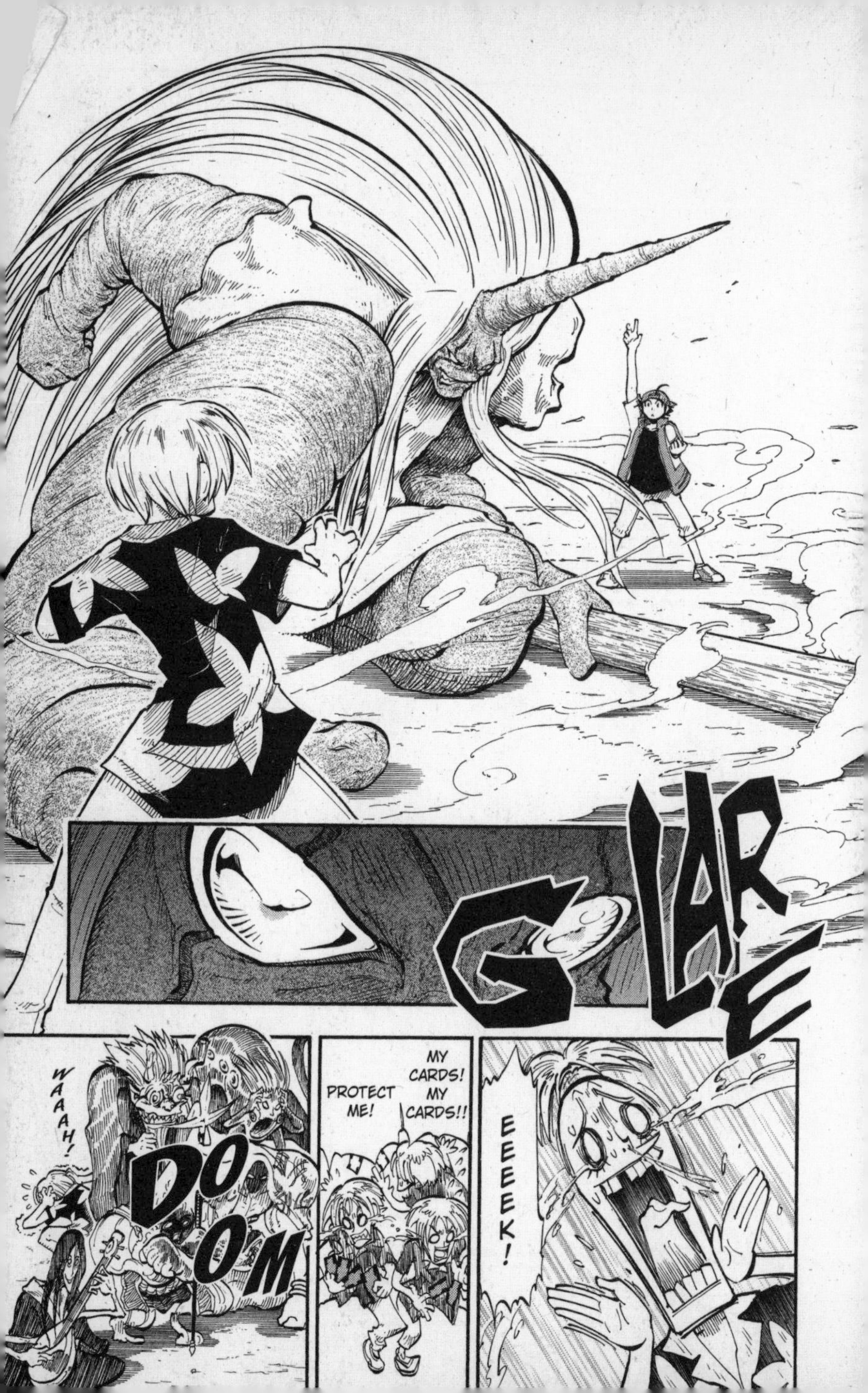
GLARE
EEEEK!
MY CARDS! MY CARDS!!
PROTECT ME!
WAAAH!
DOOM

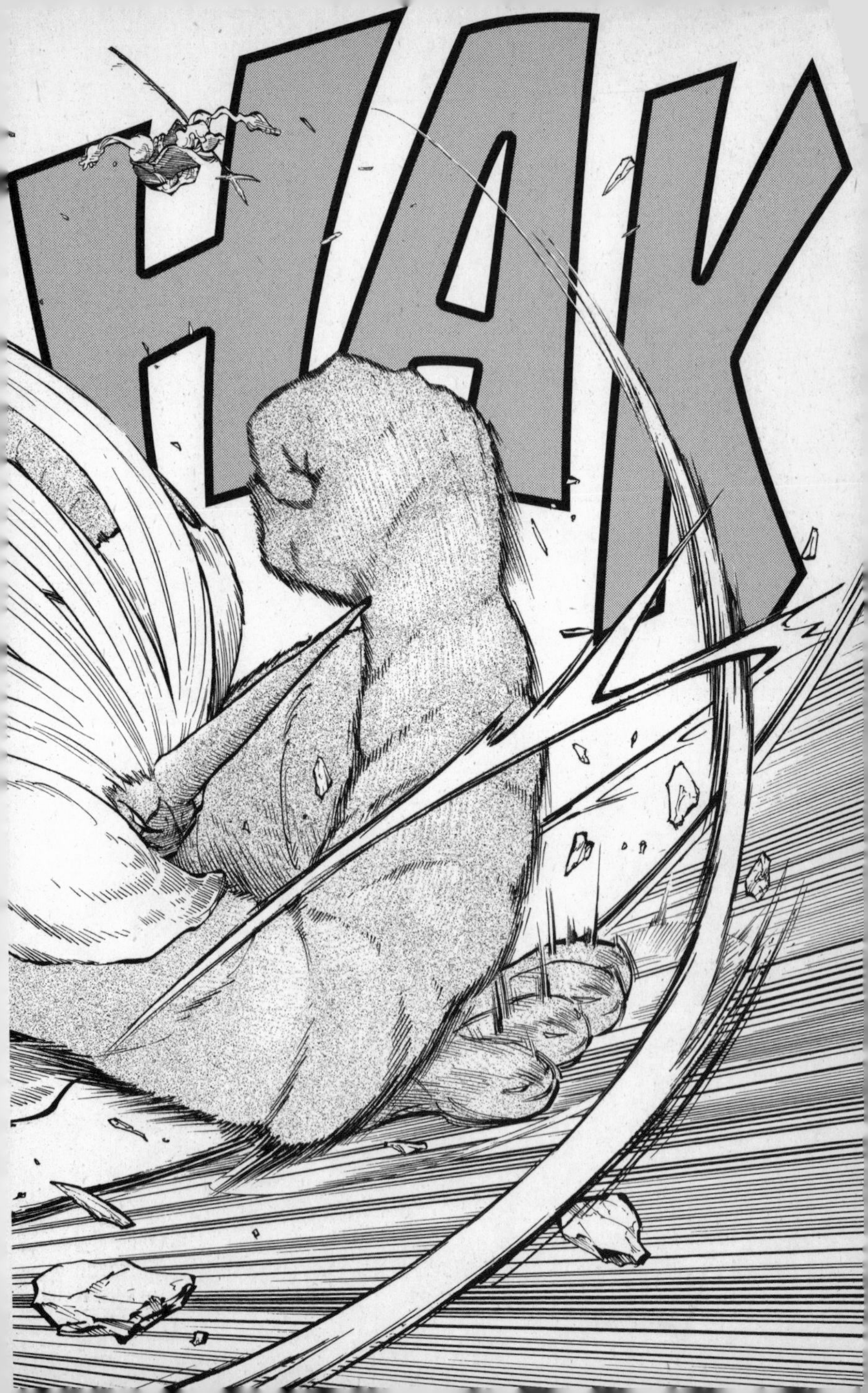
HAK

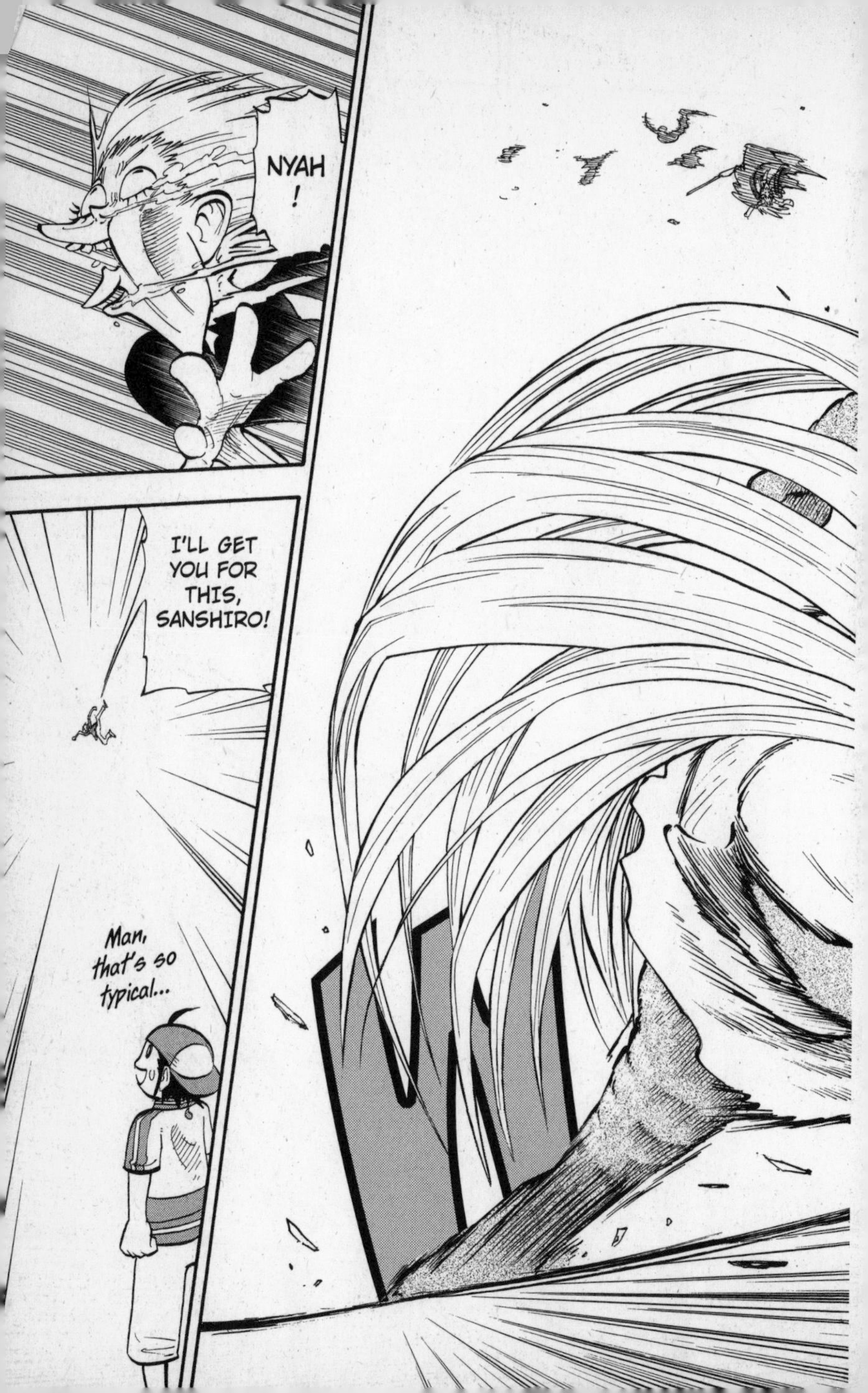
NYAH!
I'LL GET YOU FOR THIS, SANSHIRO!
Man, that's so typical...

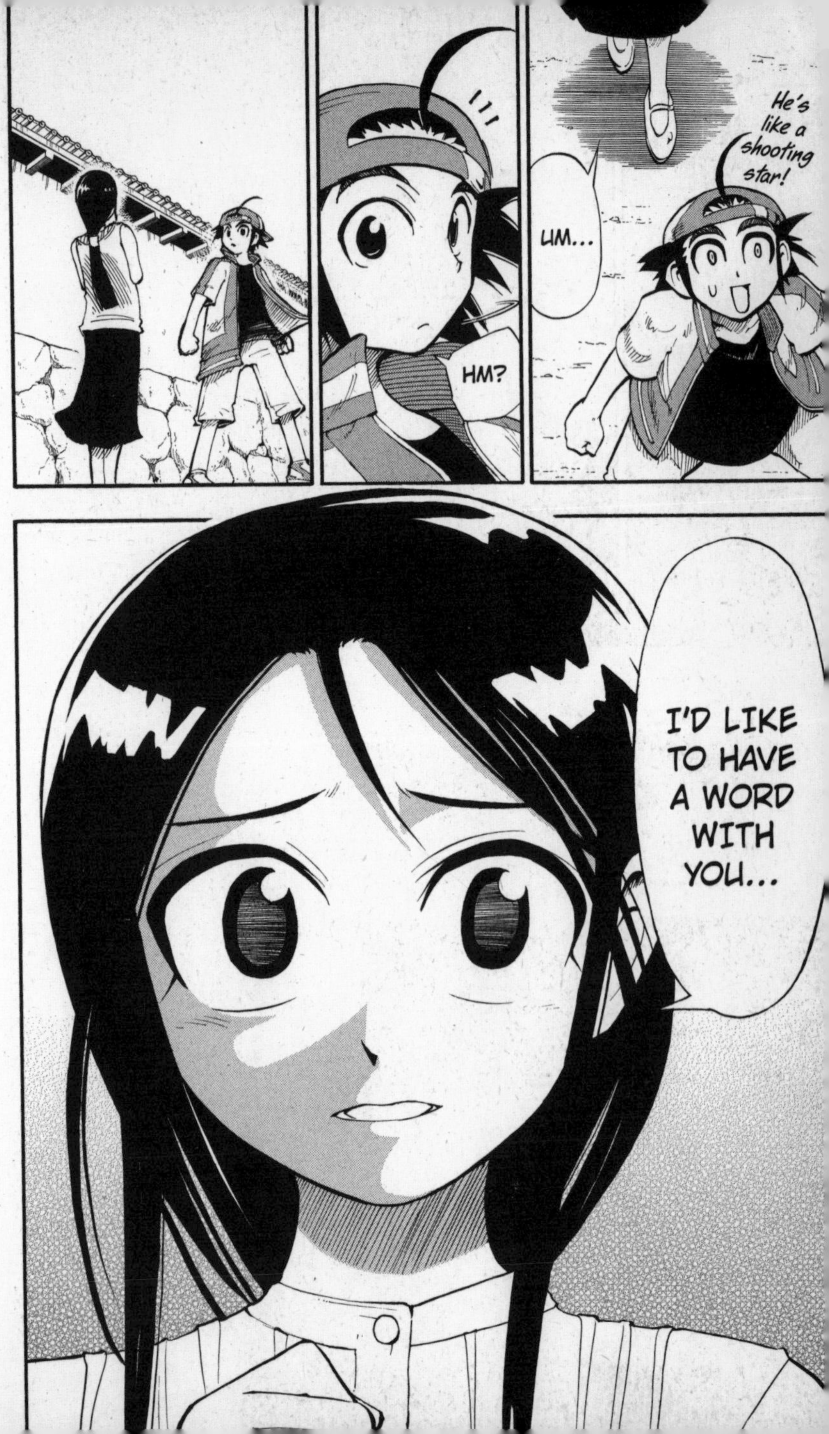
UM...
He's like a shooting star!
HM?
I'D LIKE TO HAVE A WORD WITH YOU...

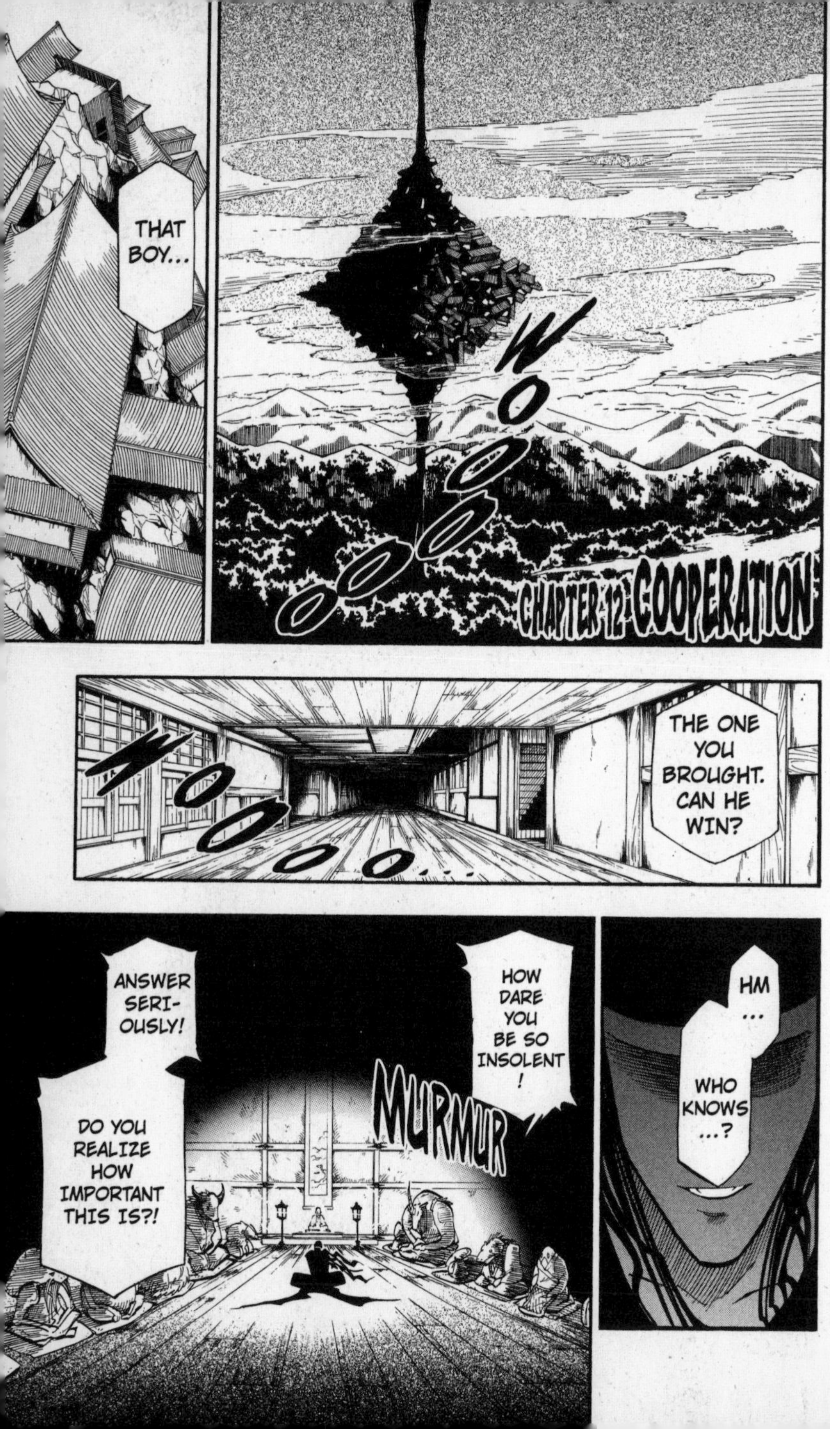
WOOOOOOO
CHAPTER 12 COOPERATION
THAT BOY...
THE ONE YOU BROUGHT. CAN HE WIN?
WOOOOO...
HM... WHO KNOWS...?
HOW DARE YOU BE SO INSOLENT!
MURMUR
ANSWER SERIOUSLY!
DO YOU REALIZE HOW IMPORTANT THIS IS?!

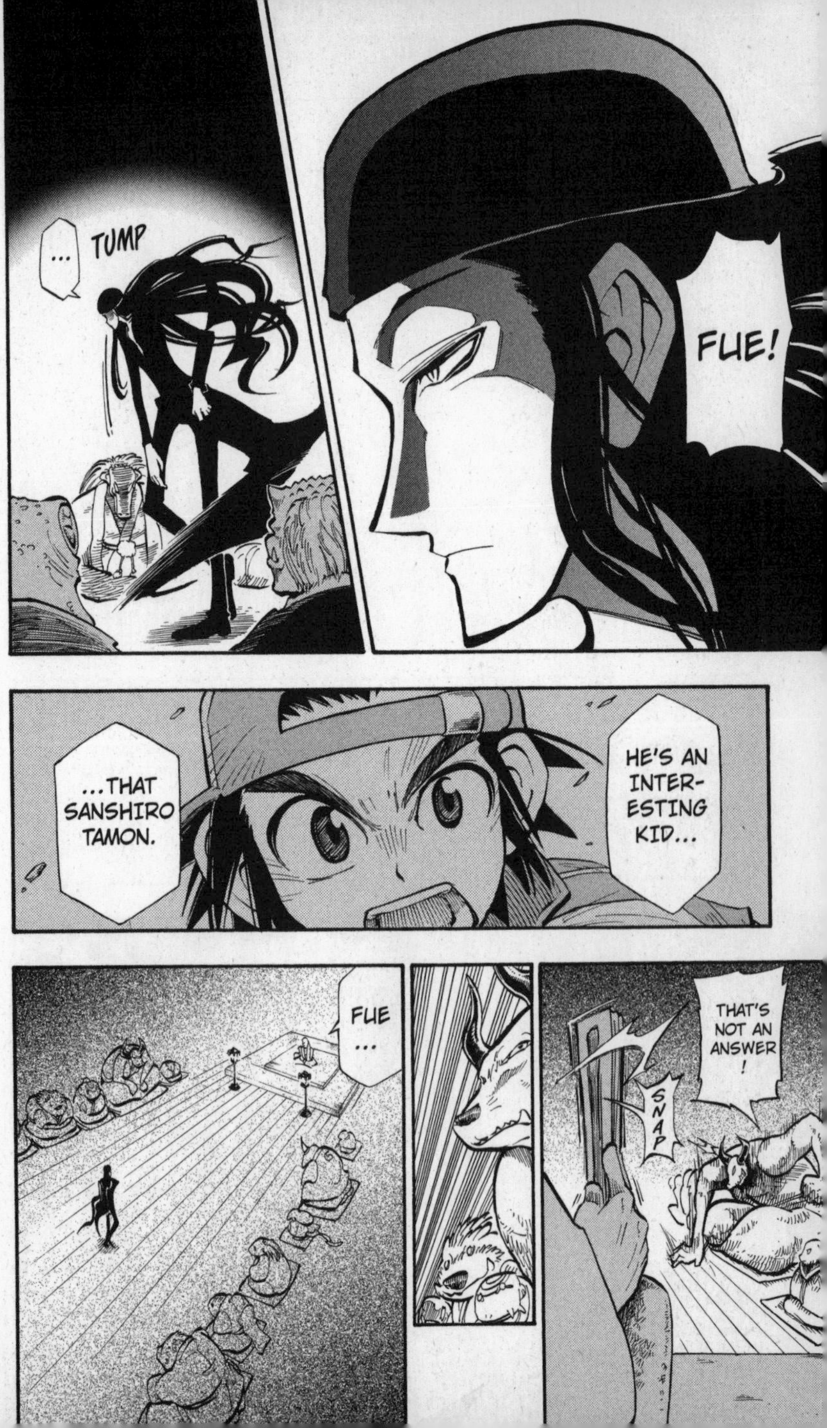
FUE!
...
TUMP
HE'S AN INTER-ESTING KID...
...THAT SANSHIRO TAMON.
THAT'S NOT AN ANSWER!
SNAP
FUE ...

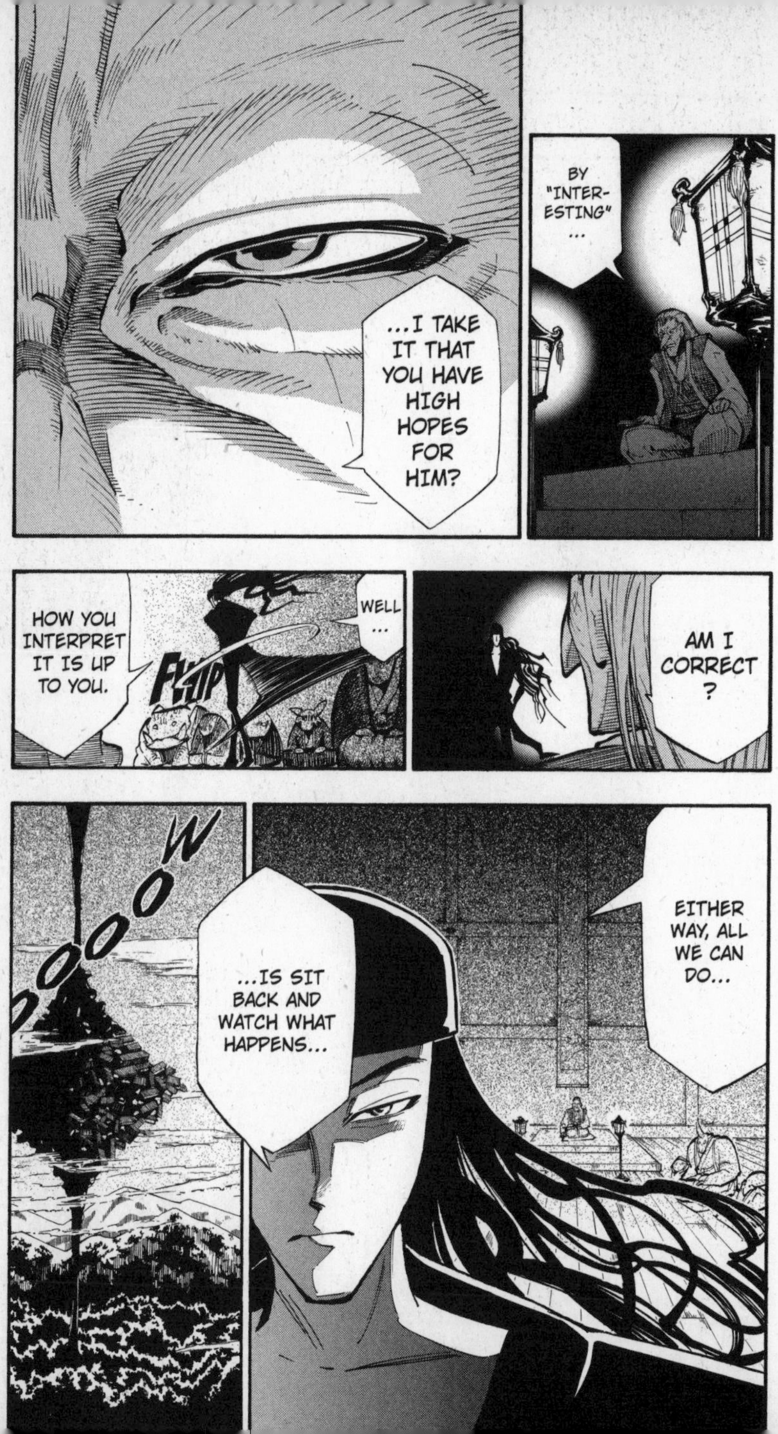
BY "INTER-ESTING"...
...I TAKE IT THAT YOU HAVE HIGH HOPES FOR HIM?
AM I CORRECT?
WELL...
FWIP
HOW YOU INTERPRET IT IS UP TO YOU.
EITHER WAY, ALL WE CAN DO...
...IS SIT BACK AND WATCH WHAT HAPPENS...
WOOOOOO

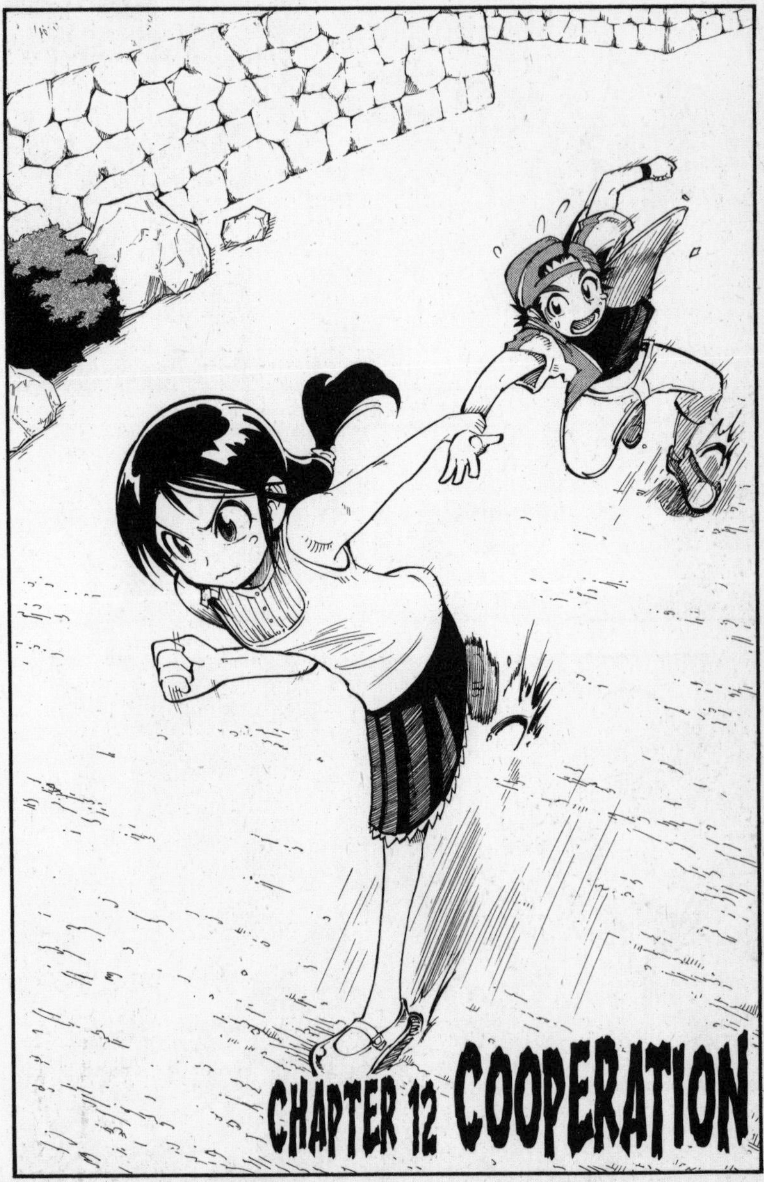
CHAPTER 12 COOPERATION

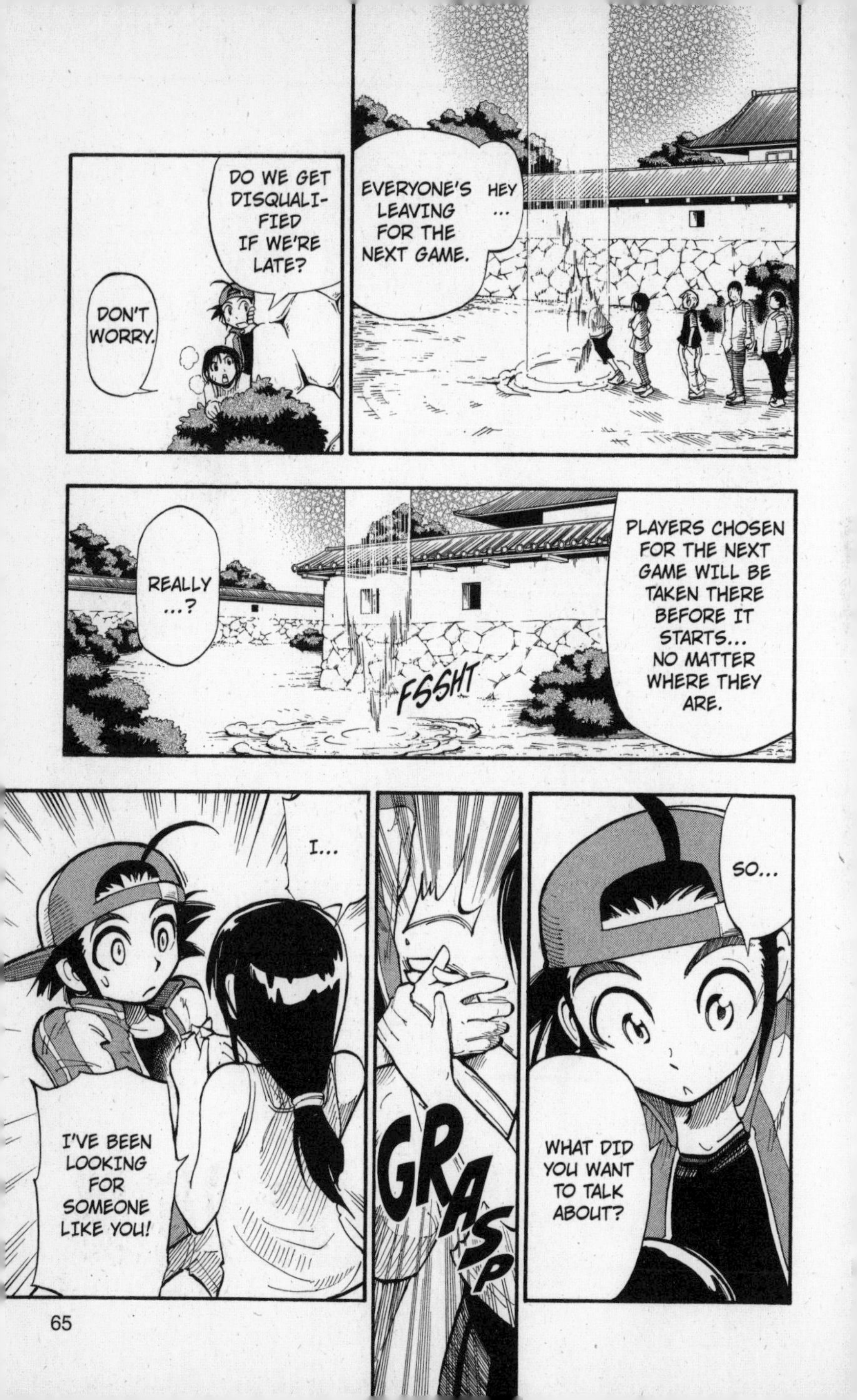
HEY ...
EVERYONE'S LEAVING FOR THE NEXT GAME.
DO WE GET DISQUALI-FIED IF WE'RE LATE?
DON'T WORRY.
PLAYERS CHOSEN FOR THE NEXT GAME WILL BE TAKEN THERE BEFORE IT STARTS... NO MATTER WHERE THEY ARE.
FSSHT
REALLY ...?
SO...
WHAT DID YOU WANT TO TALK ABOUT?
GRASP
I...
I'VE BEEN LOOKING FOR SOMEONE LIKE YOU!

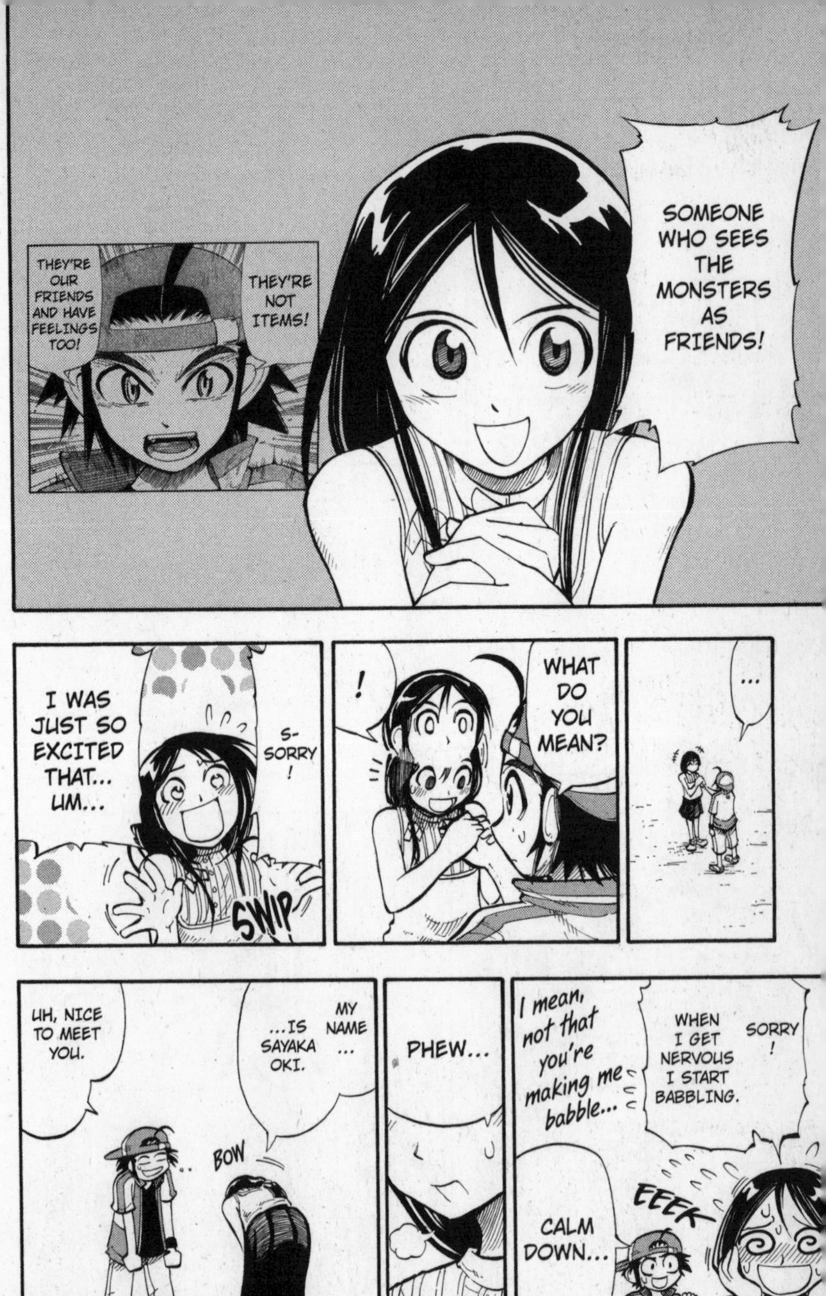
SOMEONE WHO SEES THE MONSTERS AS FRIENDS!
THEY'RE NOT ITEMS!
THEY'RE OUR FRIENDS AND HAVE FEELINGS TOO!
...
WHAT DO YOU MEAN?
!
S-SORRY!
I WAS JUST SO EXCITED THAT... UM...
SWIP
SORRY!
WHEN I GET NERVOUS I START BABBLING.
I mean, not that you're making me babble...
EEEK
CALM DOWN...
PHEW...
MY NAME...
...IS SAYAKA OKI.
BOW
UH, NICE TO MEET YOU.

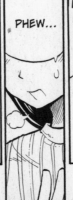

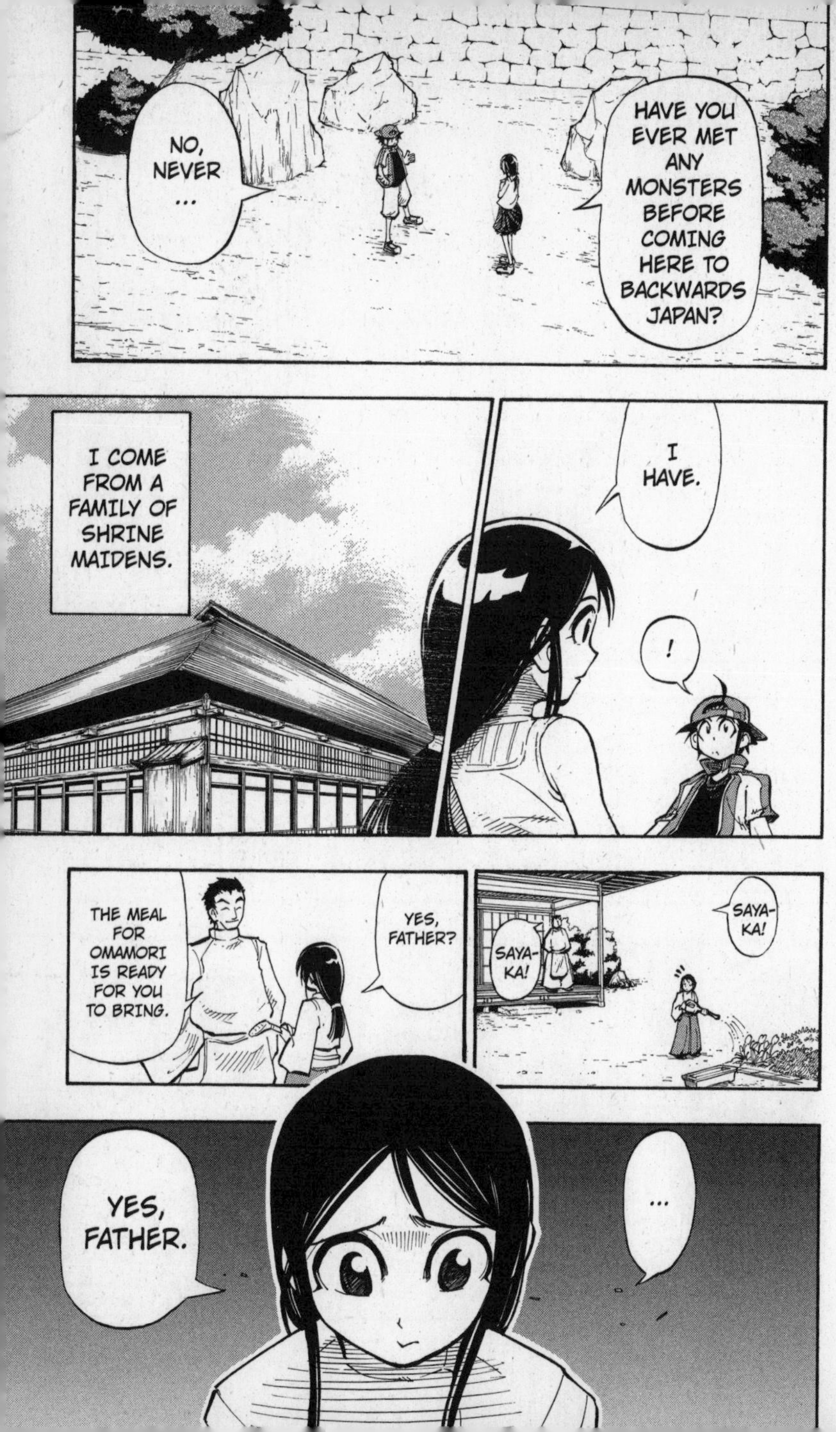
HAVE YOU EVER MET ANY MONSTERS BEFORE COMING HERE TO BACKWARDS JAPAN?
NO, NEVER ...
I HAVE.
!
I COME FROM A FAMILY OF SHRINE MAIDENS.
SAYA-KA!
SAYA-KA!
YES, FATHER?
THE MEAL FOR OMAMORI IS READY FOR YOU TO BRING.
...
YES, FATHER.

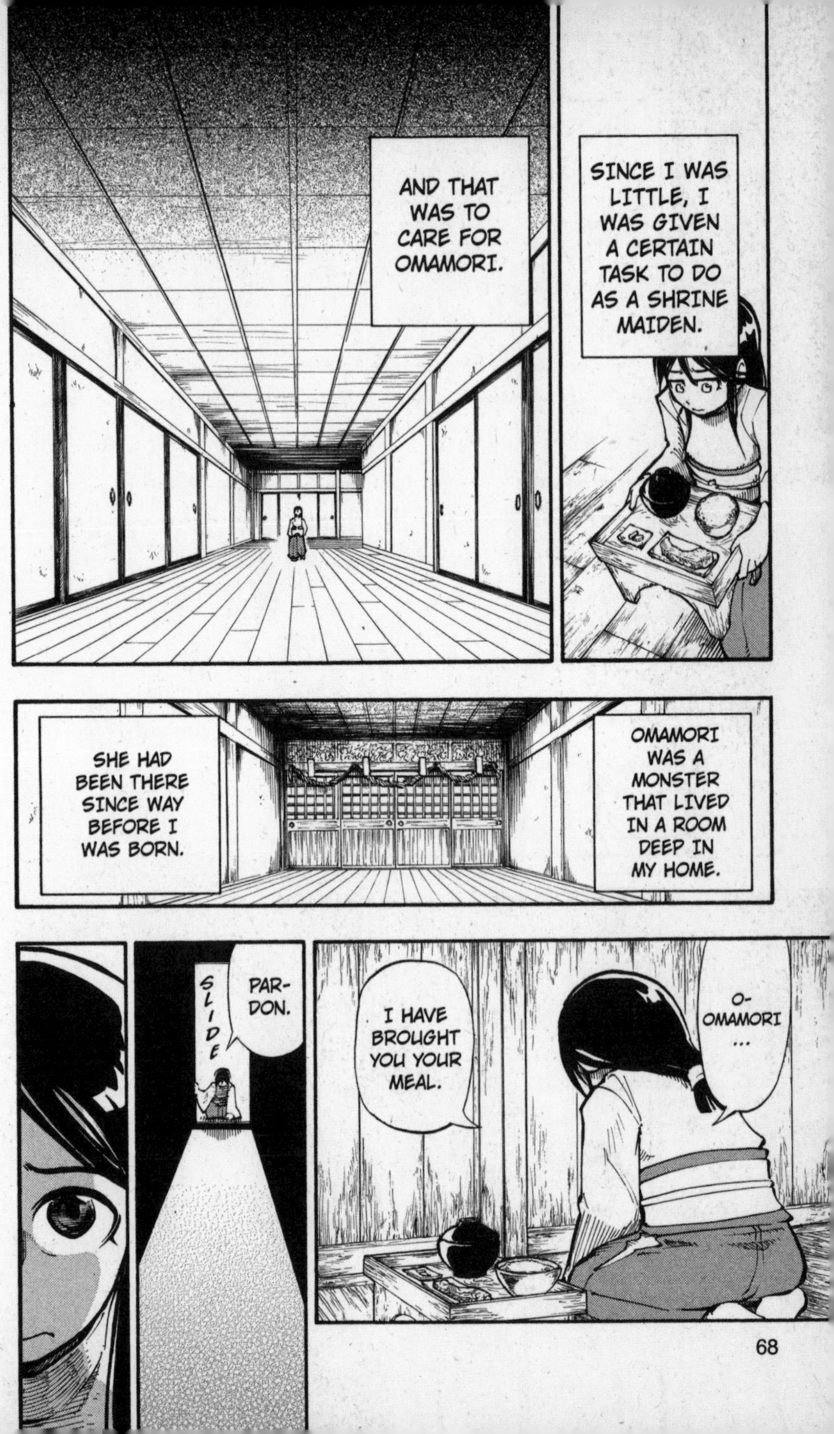
SINCE I WAS LITTLE, I WAS GIVEN A CERTAIN TASK TO DO AS A SHRINE MAIDEN.
AND THAT WAS TO CARE FOR OMAMORI.
OMAMORI WAS A MONSTER THAT LIVED IN A ROOM DEEP IN MY HOME.
SHE HAD BEEN THERE SINCE WAY BEFORE I WAS BORN.
O-OMAMORI...
I HAVE BROUGHT YOU YOUR MEAL.
PAR-DON.
SLIDE

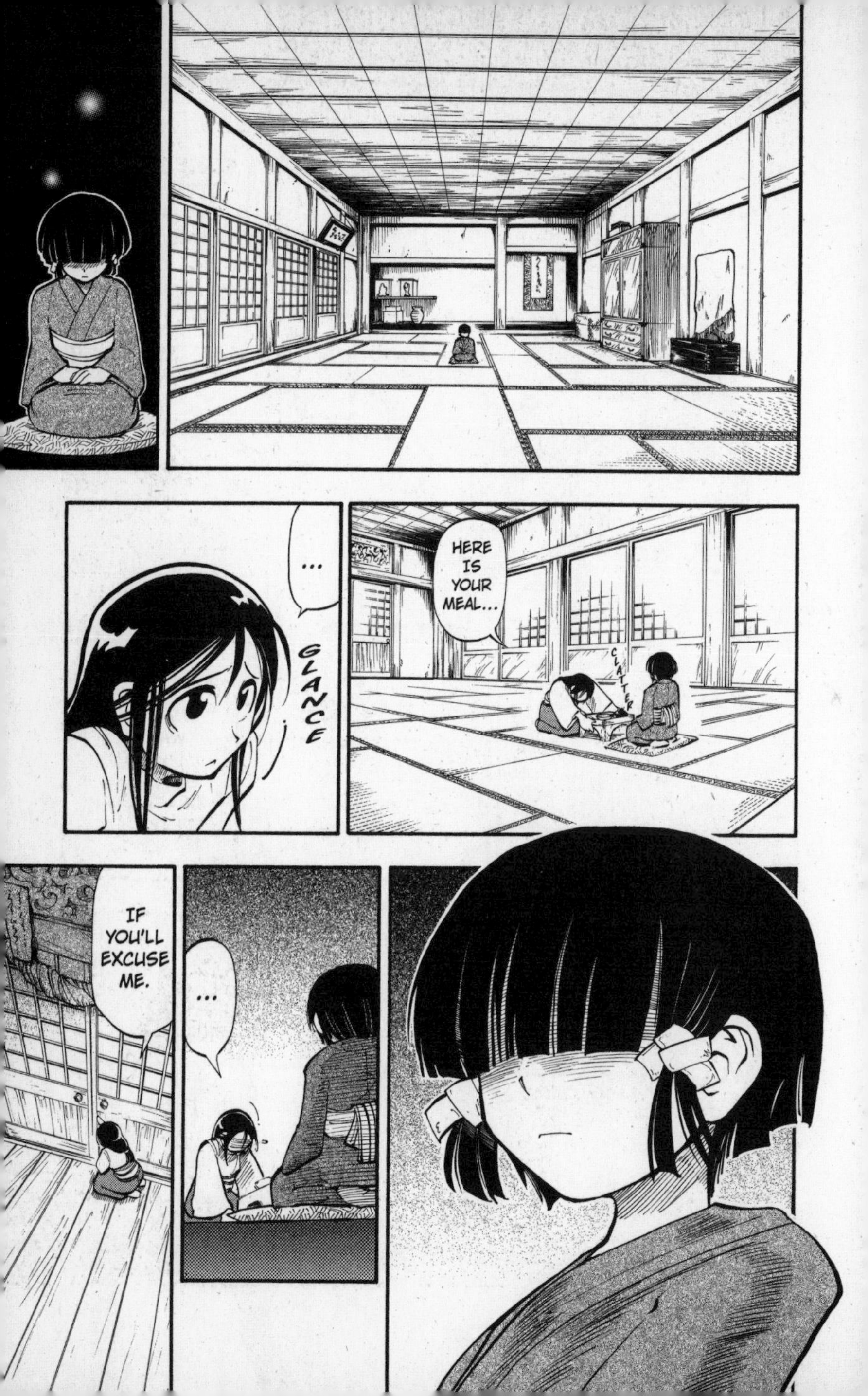
HERE IS YOUR MEAL...
CLATTER
...
GLANCE
...
IF YOU'LL EXCUSE ME.

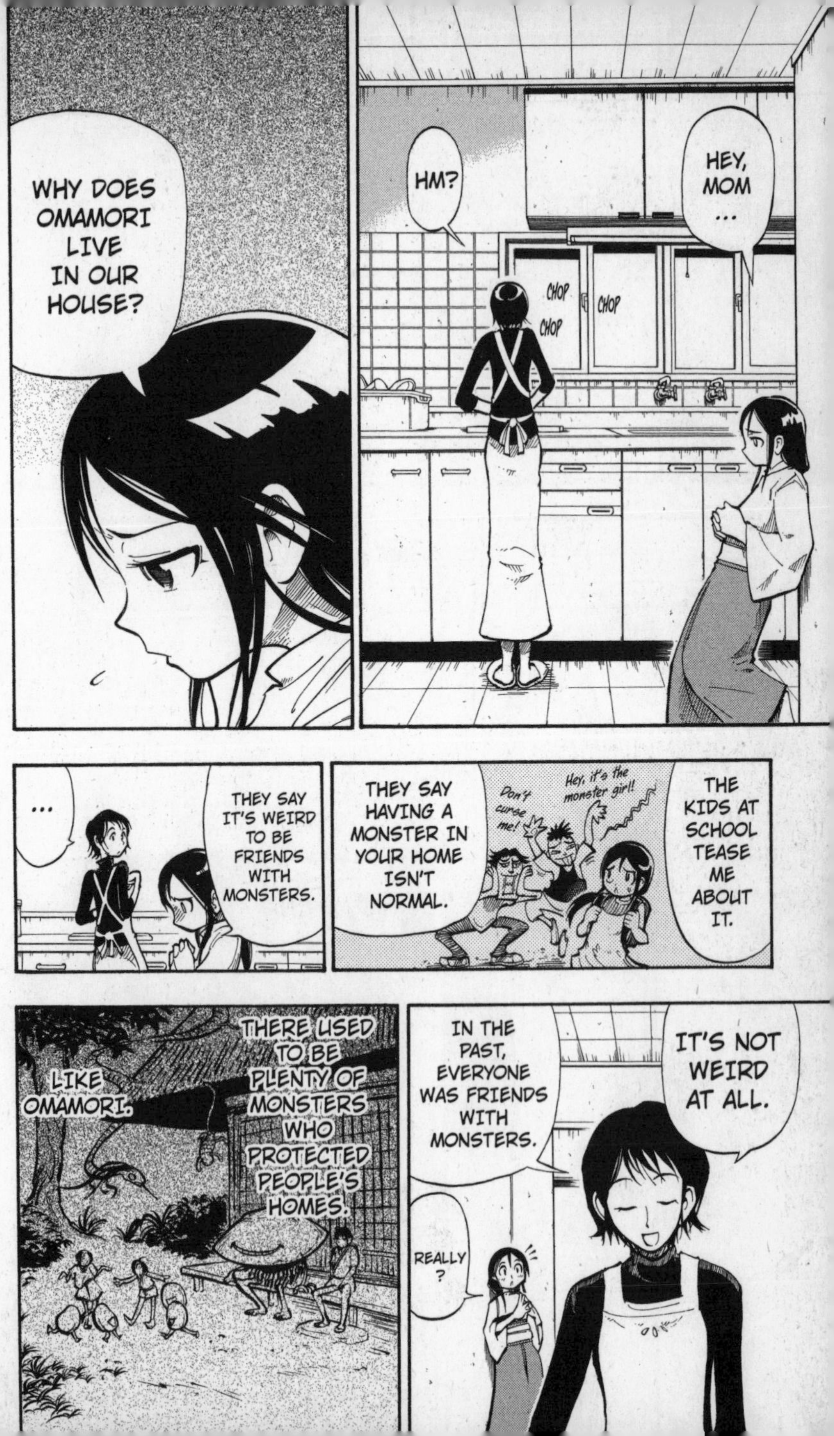
HEY, MOM ...
HM?
CHOP
CHOP
CHOP
WHY DOES OMAMORI LIVE IN OUR HOUSE?
THE KIDS AT SCHOOL TEASE ME ABOUT IT.
Hey, it's the monster girl!
Don't curse me!
THEY SAY HAVING A MONSTER IN YOUR HOME ISN'T NORMAL.
THEY SAY IT'S WEIRD TO BE FRIENDS WITH MONSTERS.
...
IT'S NOT WEIRD AT ALL.
IN THE PAST, EVERYONE WAS FRIENDS WITH MONSTERS.
REALLY?
THERE USED TO BE PLENTY OF MONSTERS WHO PROTECTED PEOPLE'S HOMES.
LIKE OMAMORI.

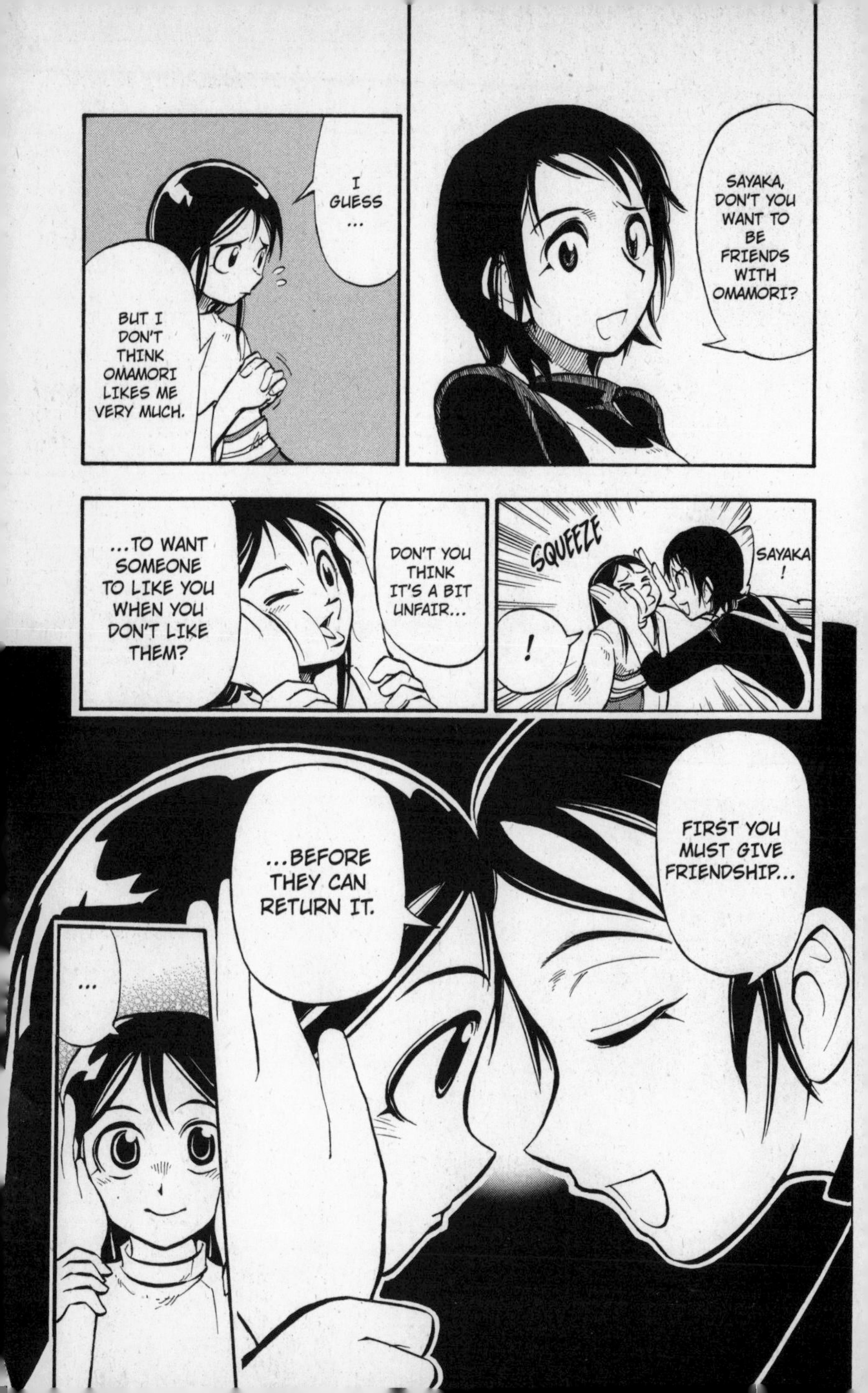
SAYAKA, DON'T YOU WANT TO BE FRIENDS WITH OMAMORI?
I GUESS...
BUT I DON'T THINK OMAMORI LIKES ME VERY MUCH.
SAYAKA!
SQUEEZE
!
DON'T YOU THINK IT'S A BIT UNFAIR...
...TO WANT SOMEONE TO LIKE YOU WHEN YOU DON'T LIKE THEM?
FIRST YOU MUST GIVE FRIENDSHIP...
...BEFORE THEY CAN RETURN IT.
...

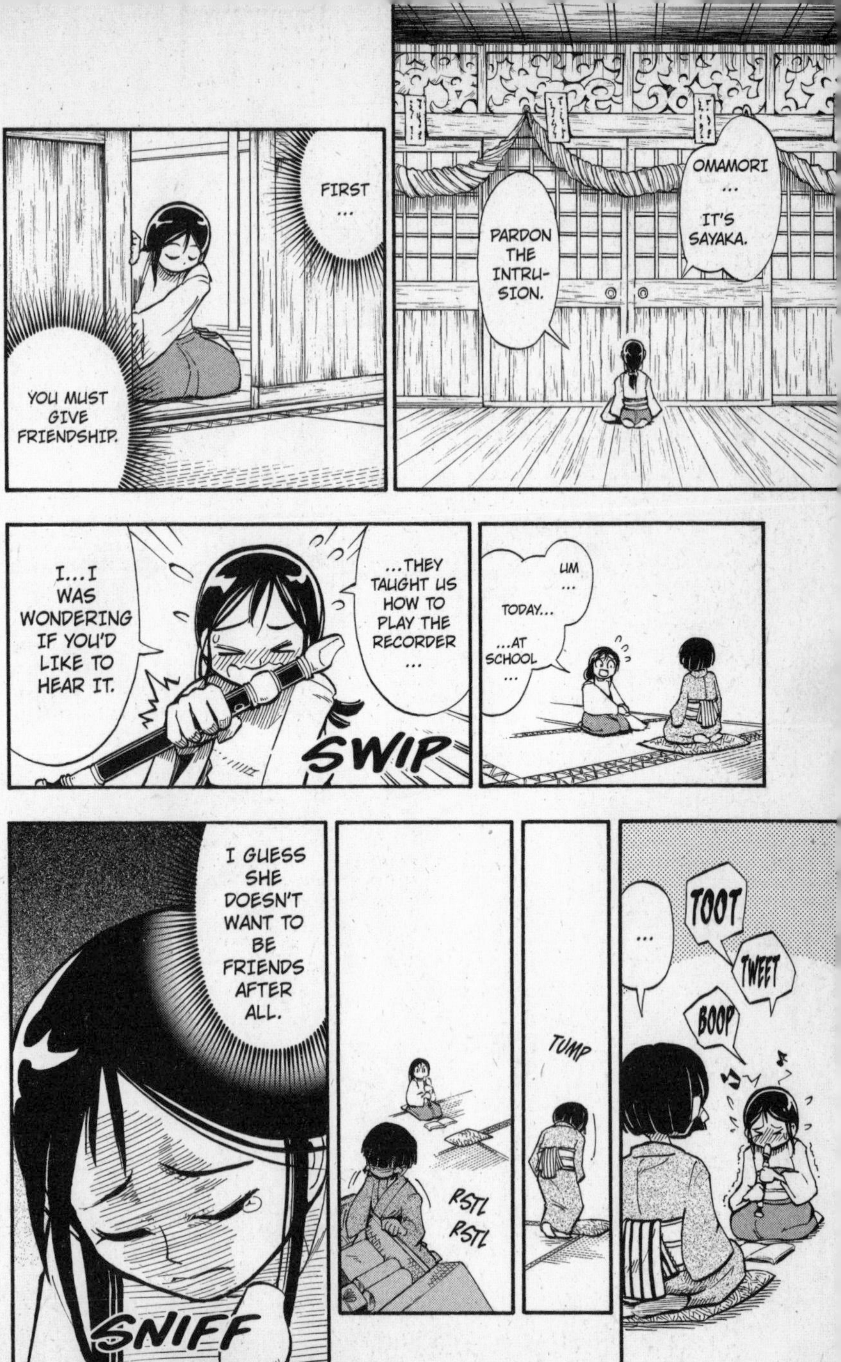
OMAMORI ... IT'S SAYAKA.
PARDON THE INTRUSION.
FIRST ...
YOU MUST GIVE FRIENDSHIP.
UM ...
TODAY...
...AT SCHOOL ...
...THEY TAUGHT US HOW TO PLAY THE RECORDER ...
I...I WAS WONDERING IF YOU'D LIKE TO HEAR IT.
SWIP
...
TOOT
TWEET
BOOP
TUMP
RSTL RSTL
I GUESS SHE DOESN'T WANT TO BE FRIENDS AFTER ALL.
SNIFF

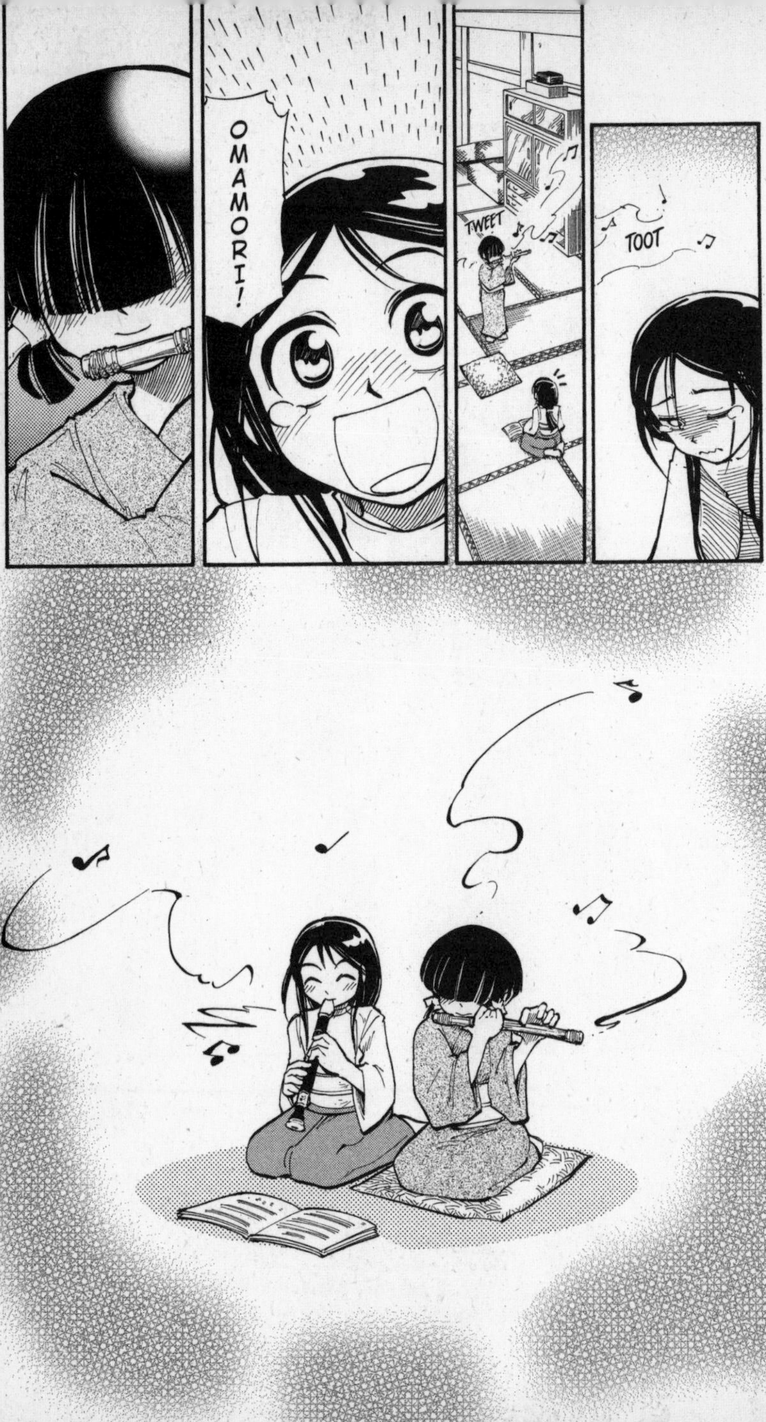
TOOT
TWEET
OMAMORI!

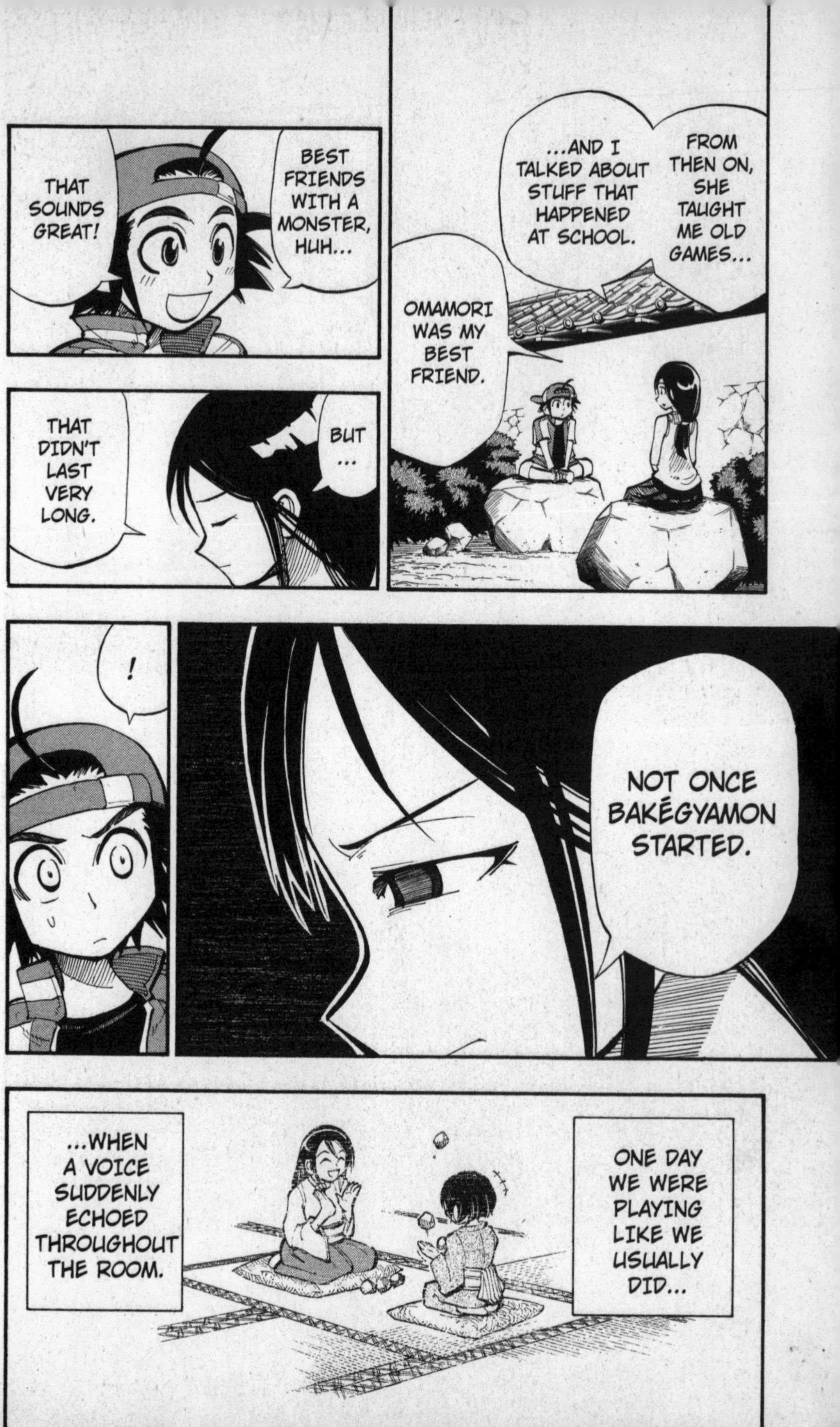
FROM THEN ON, SHE TAUGHT ME OLD GAMES...
...AND I TALKED ABOUT STUFF THAT HAPPENED AT SCHOOL.
OMAMORI WAS MY BEST FRIEND.
BEST FRIENDS WITH A MONSTER, HUH...
THAT SOUNDS GREAT!
BUT...
THAT DIDN'T LAST VERY LONG.
NOT ONCE BAKÉGYAMON STARTED.
!
ONE DAY WE WERE PLAYING LIKE WE USUALLY DID...
...WHEN A VOICE SUDDENLY ECHOED THROUGHOUT THE ROOM.

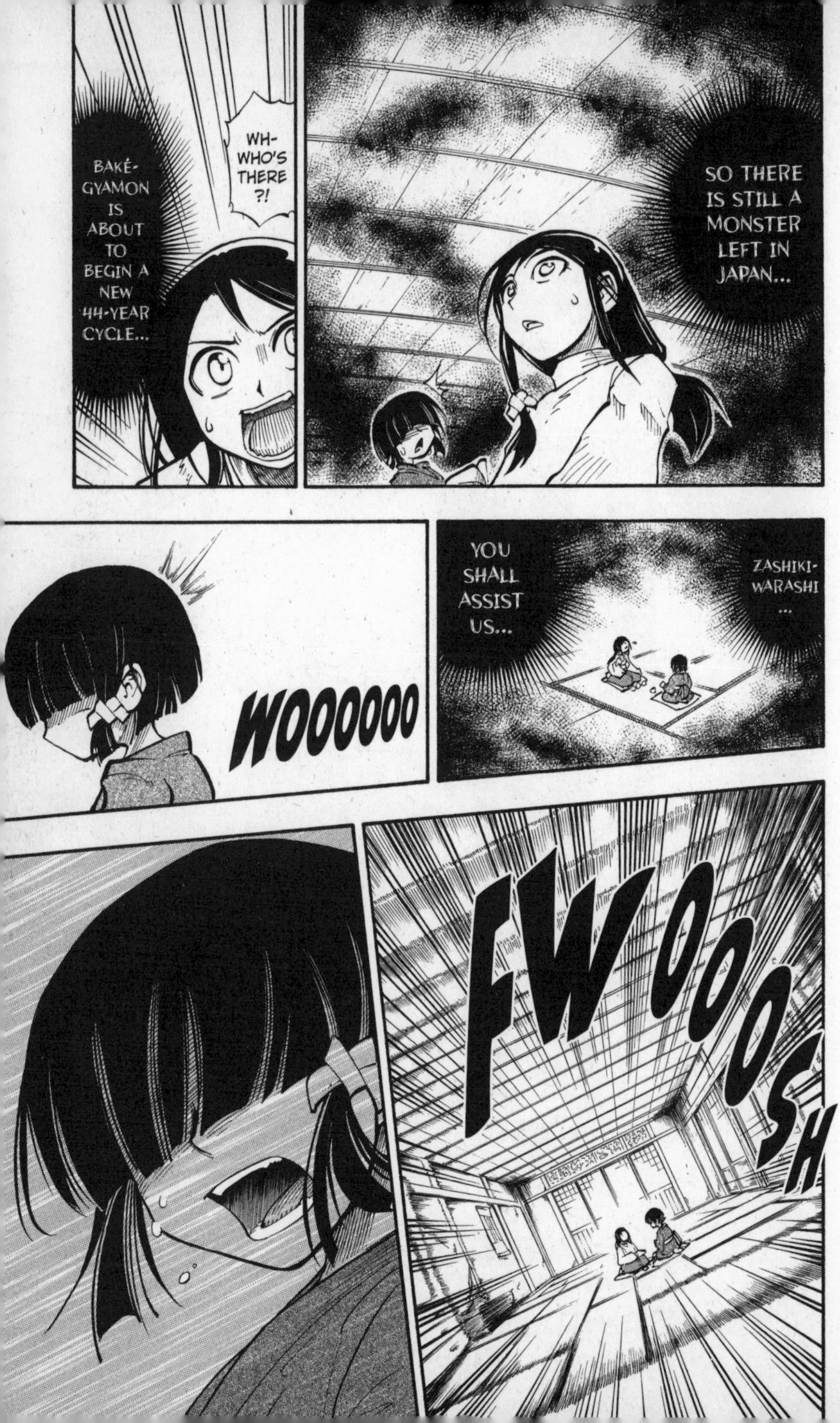
SO THERE IS STILL A MONSTER LEFT IN JAPAN...
WH- WHO'S THERE ?!
BAKÉ-GYAMON IS ABOUT TO BEGIN A NEW 44-YEAR CYCLE...
ZASHIKI-WARASHI ...
YOU SHALL ASSIST US...
WOOOOOO
FWOOOSH

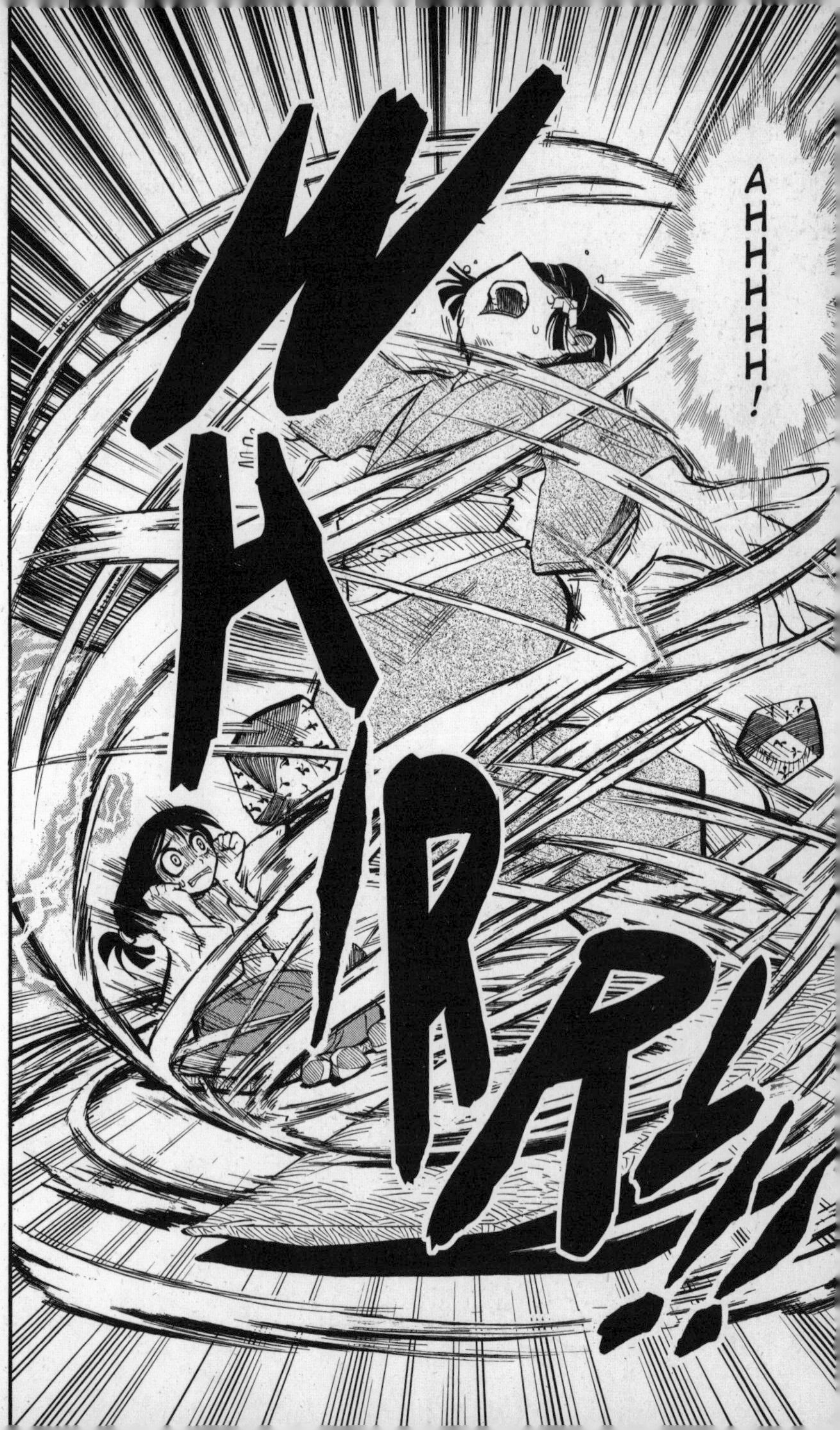
AHHHHH!
WHIRRL!!

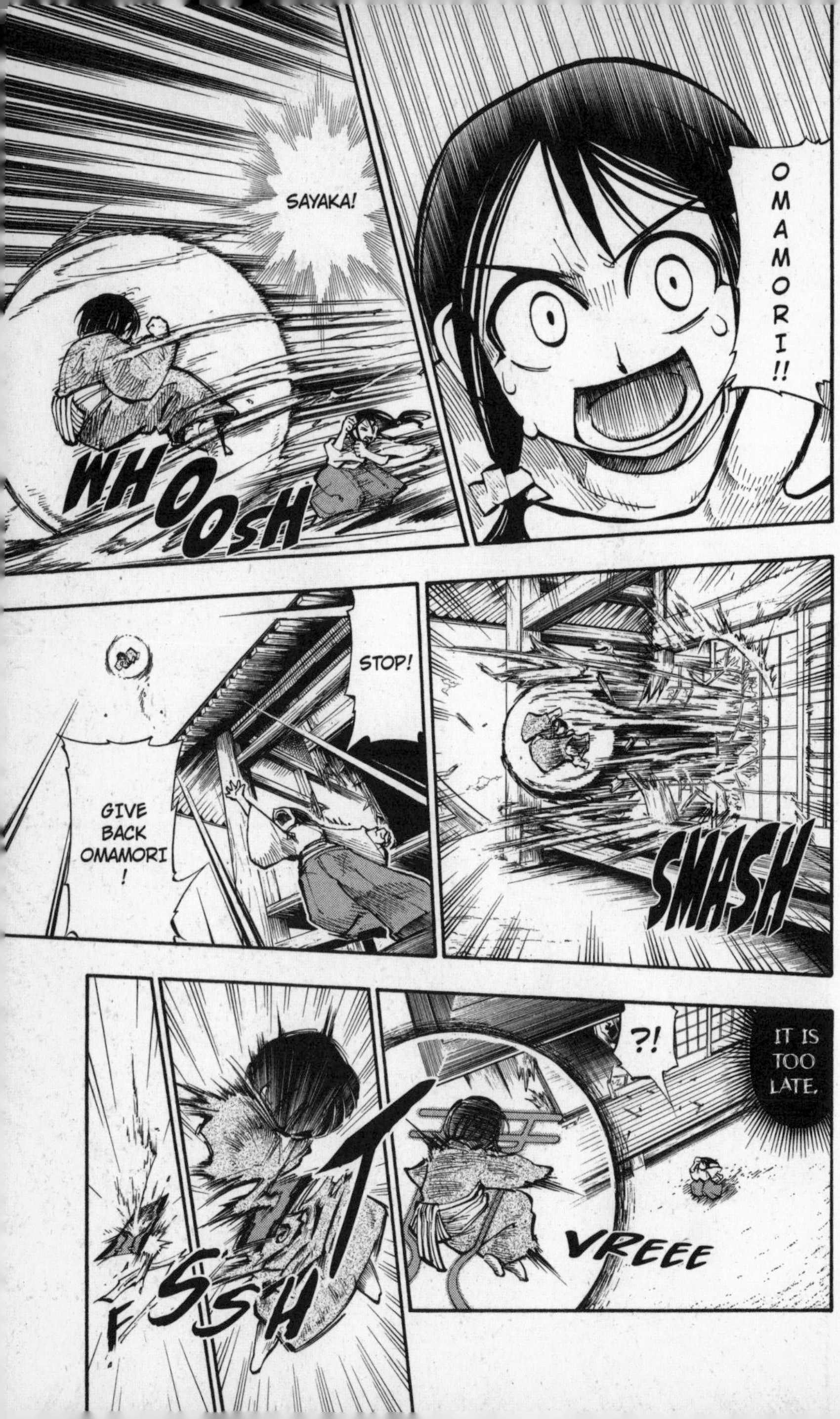
OMAMORI!!
SAYAKA!
WHOOSH
SMASH
STOP!
GIVE BACK OMAMORI!
IT IS TOO LATE.
?!
VREEE
FSSH

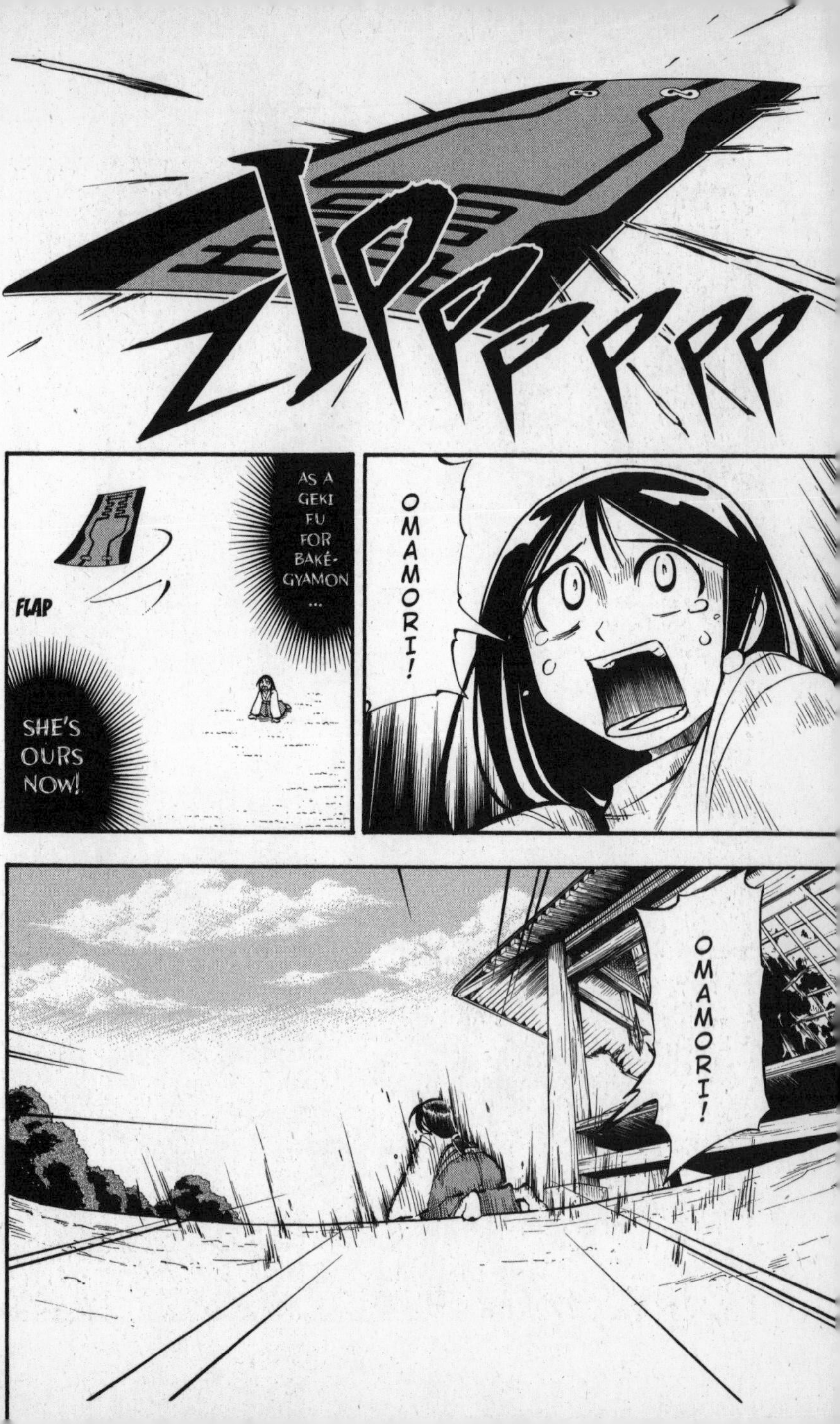
ZIPPPPPP
OMAMORI!
AS A GEKI FU FOR BAKÉ-GYAMON...
FLAP
SHE'S OURS NOW!
OMAMORI!

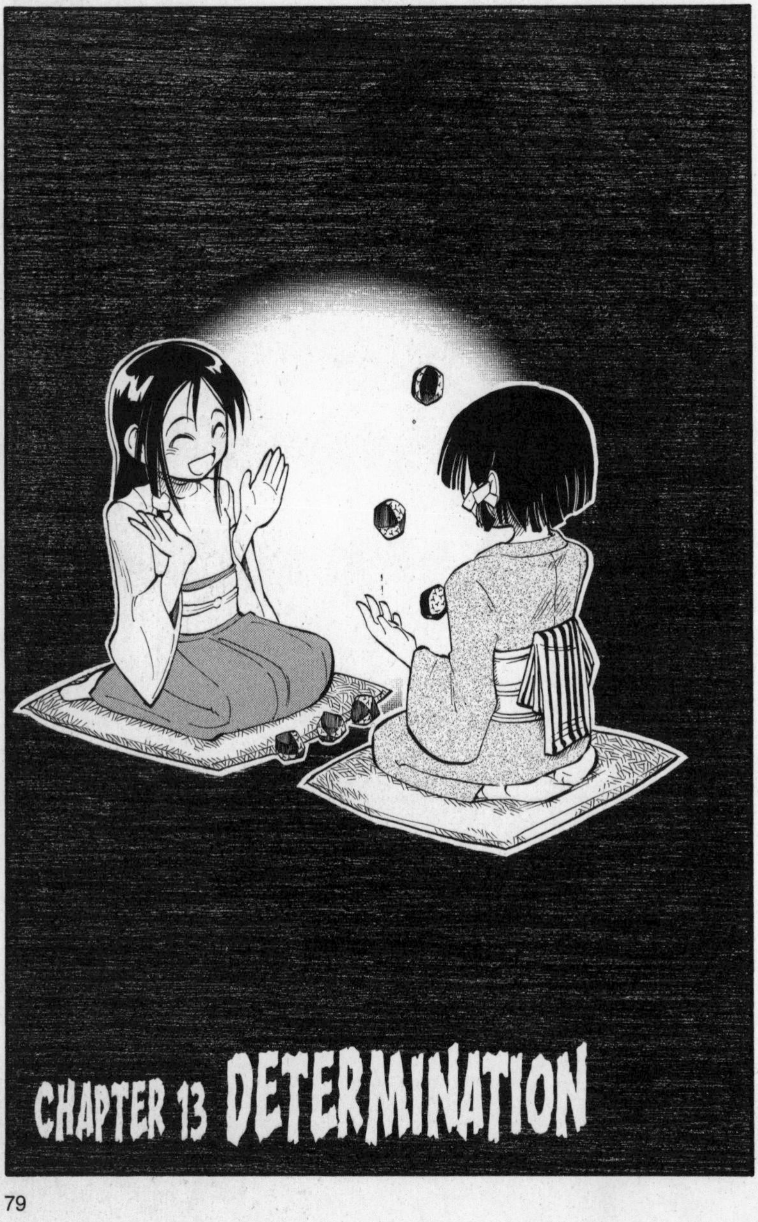
CHAPTER 13 DETERMINATION

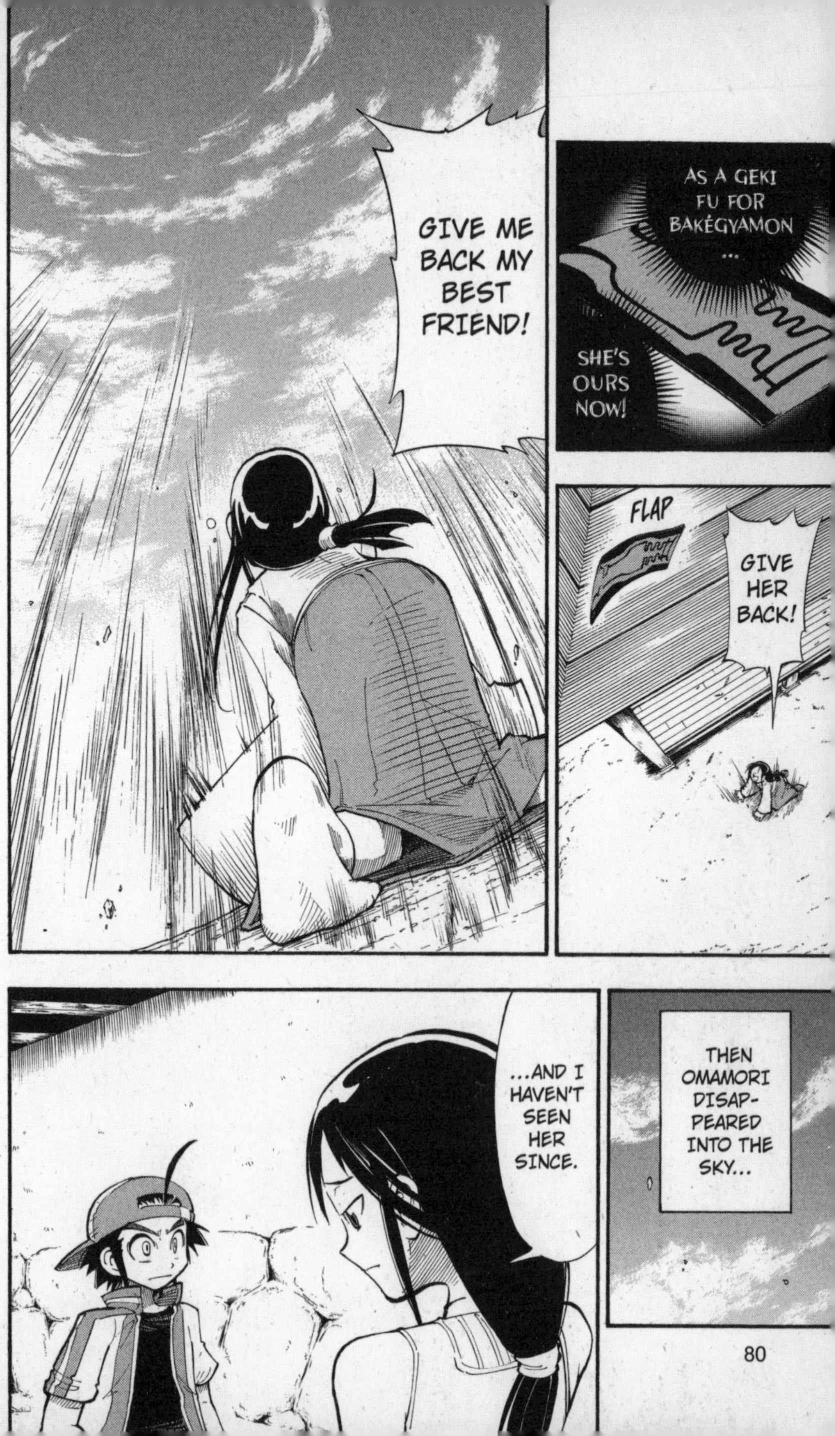
AS A GEKI FU FOR BAKÉGYAMON ...
SHE'S OURS NOW!
FLAP
GIVE HER BACK!
GIVE ME BACK MY BEST FRIEND!
THEN OMAMORI DISAPPEARED INTO THE SKY...
...AND I HAVEN'T SEEN HER SINCE.

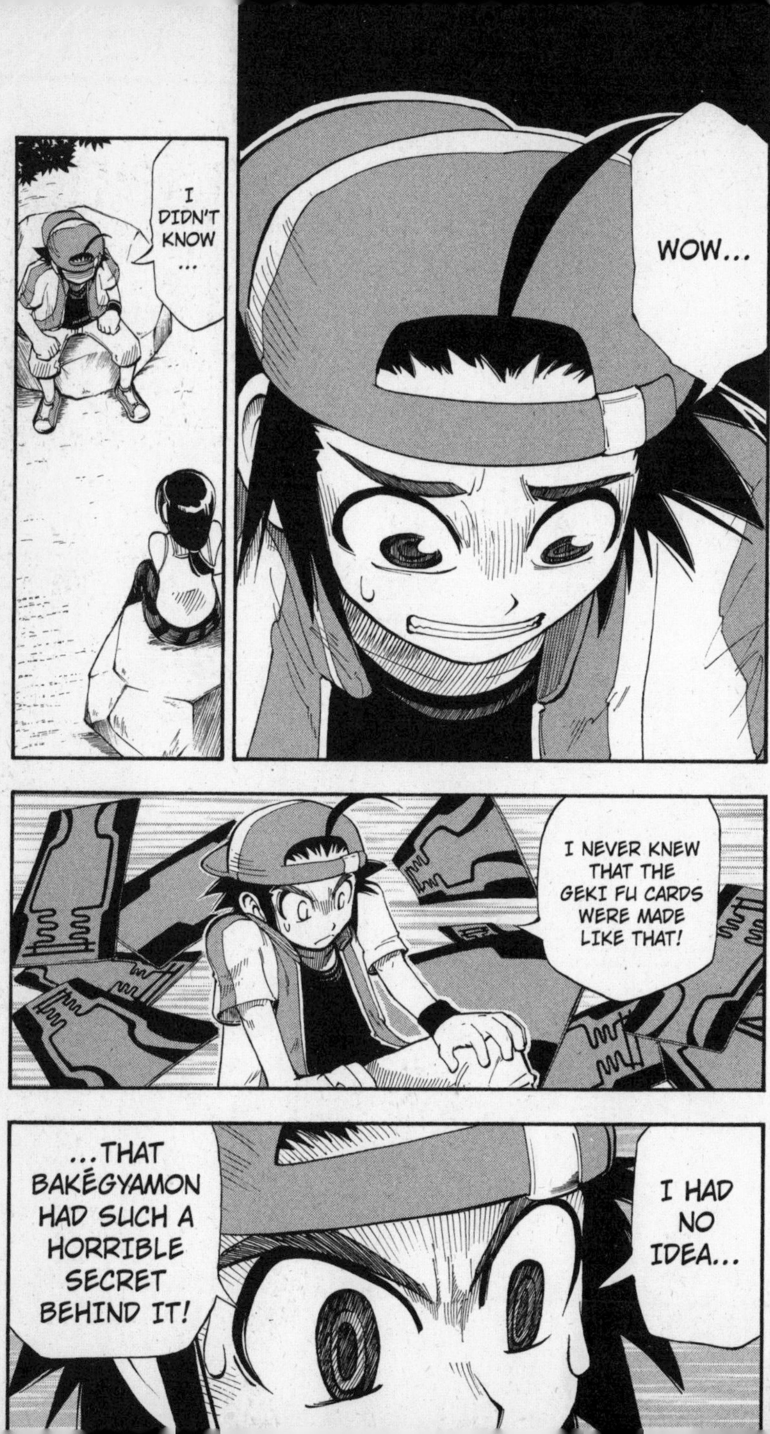
WOW...
I DIDN'T KNOW ...
I NEVER KNEW THAT THE GEKI FU CARDS WERE MADE LIKE THAT!
I HAD NO IDEA...
...THAT BAKÉGYAMON HAD SUCH A HORRIBLE SECRET BEHIND IT!

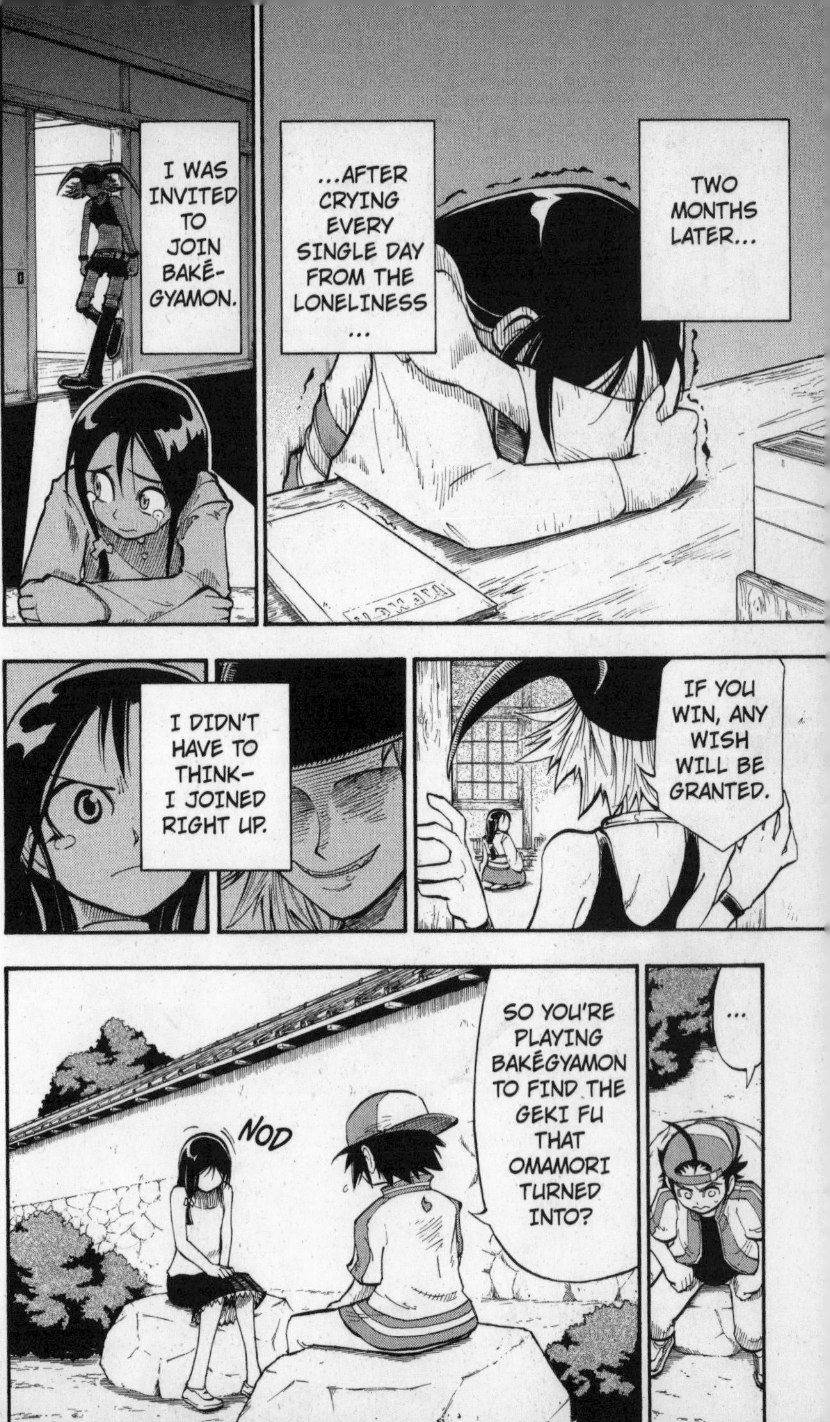
TWO MONTHS LATER...
...AFTER CRYING EVERY SINGLE DAY FROM THE LONELINESS ...
I WAS INVITED TO JOIN BAKÉ-GYAMON.
IF YOU WIN, ANY WISH WILL BE GRANTED.
I DIDN'T HAVE TO THINK- I JOINED RIGHT UP.
...
SO YOU'RE PLAYING BAKÉGYAMON TO FIND THE GEKI FU THAT OMAMORI TURNED INTO?
NOD

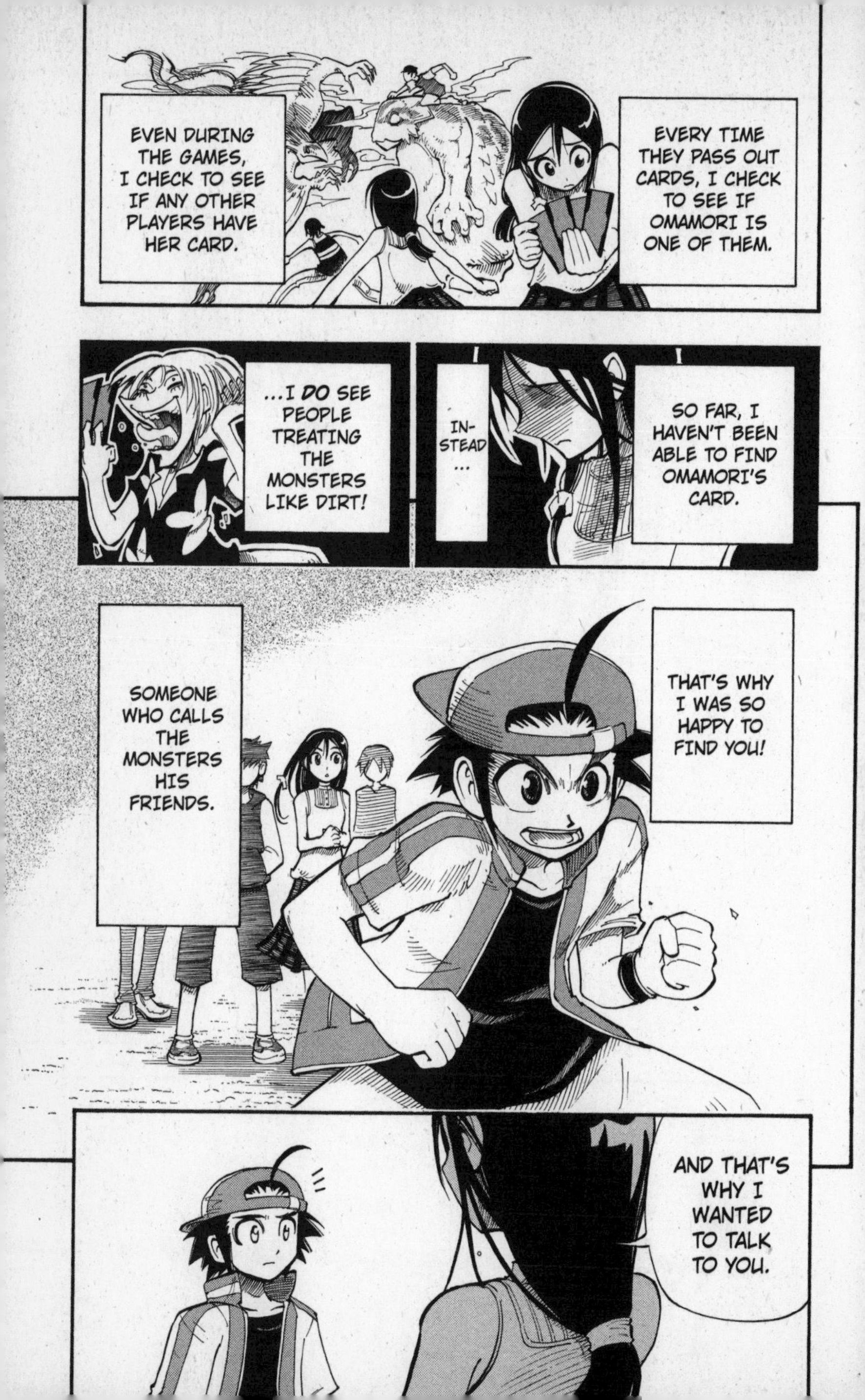
EVERY TIME THEY PASS OUT CARDS, I CHECK TO SEE IF OMAMORI IS ONE OF THEM.
EVEN DURING THE GAMES, I CHECK TO SEE IF ANY OTHER PLAYERS HAVE HER CARD.
SO FAR, I HAVEN'T BEEN ABLE TO FIND OMAMORI'S CARD.
IN-STEAD...
...I *DO* SEE PEOPLE TREATING THE MONSTERS LIKE DIRT!
THAT'S WHY I WAS SO HAPPY TO FIND YOU!
SOMEONE WHO CALLS THE MONSTERS HIS FRIENDS.
AND THAT'S WHY I WANTED TO TALK TO YOU.

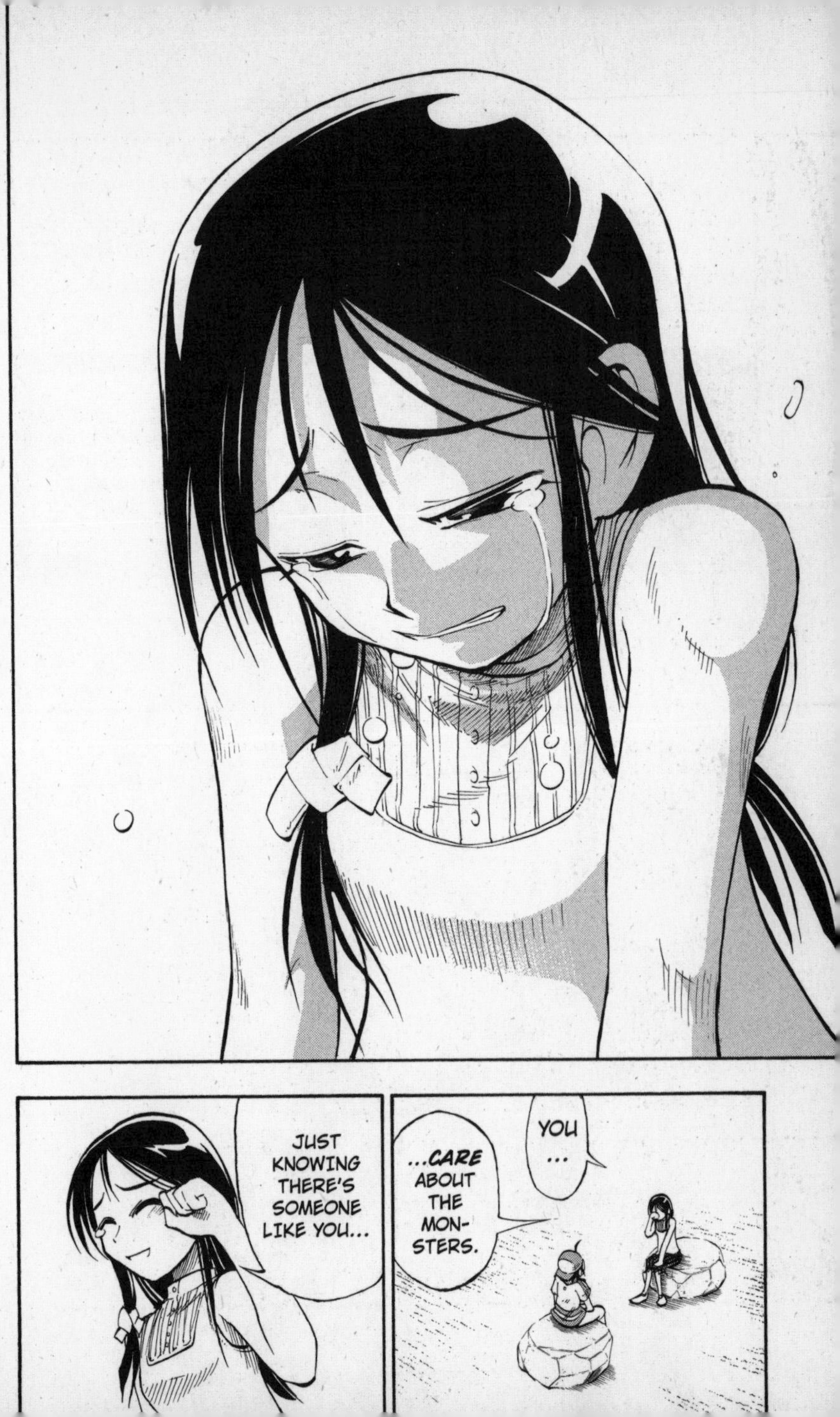
YOU...
...CARE ABOUT THE MON-STERS.
JUST KNOWING THERE'S SOMEONE LIKE YOU...

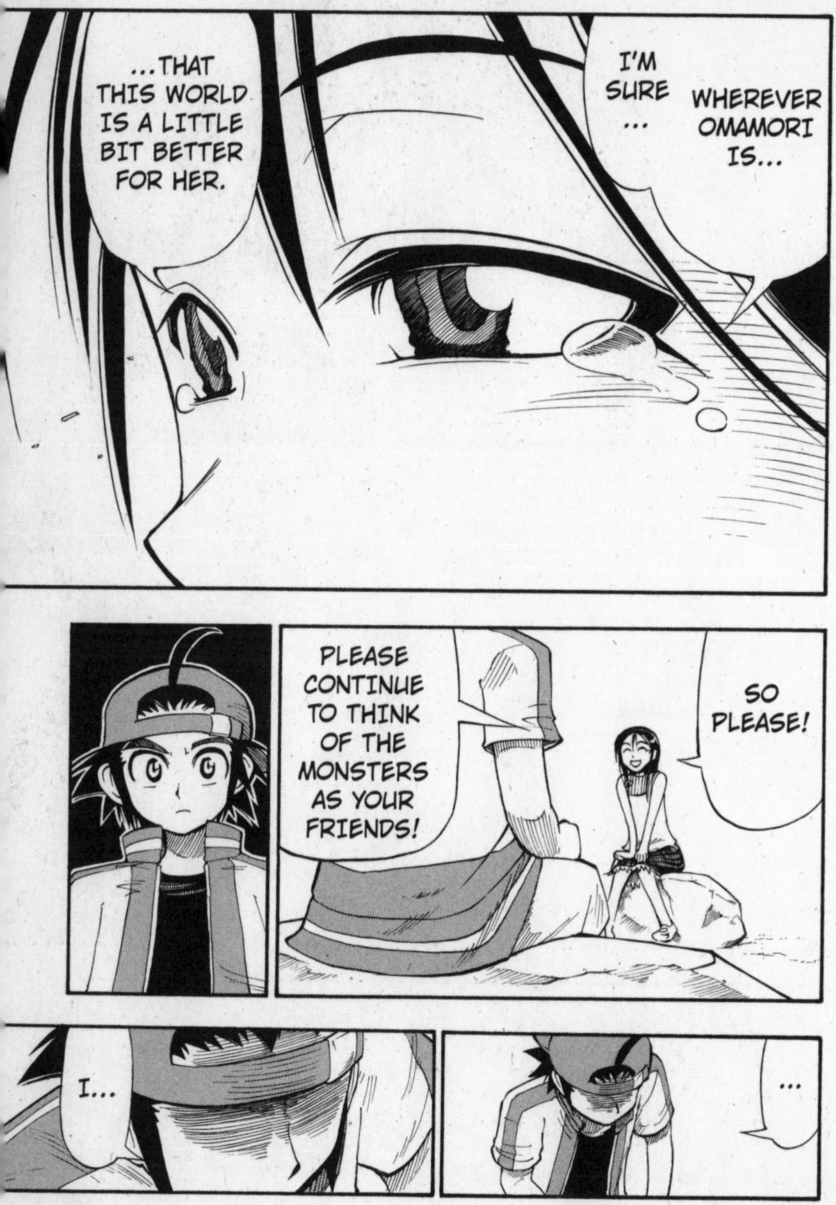
WHEREVER OMAMORI IS...
I'M SURE ...
...THAT THIS WORLD IS A LITTLE BIT BETTER FOR HER.
SO PLEASE!
PLEASE CONTINUE TO THINK OF THE MONSTERS AS YOUR FRIENDS!
...
I...

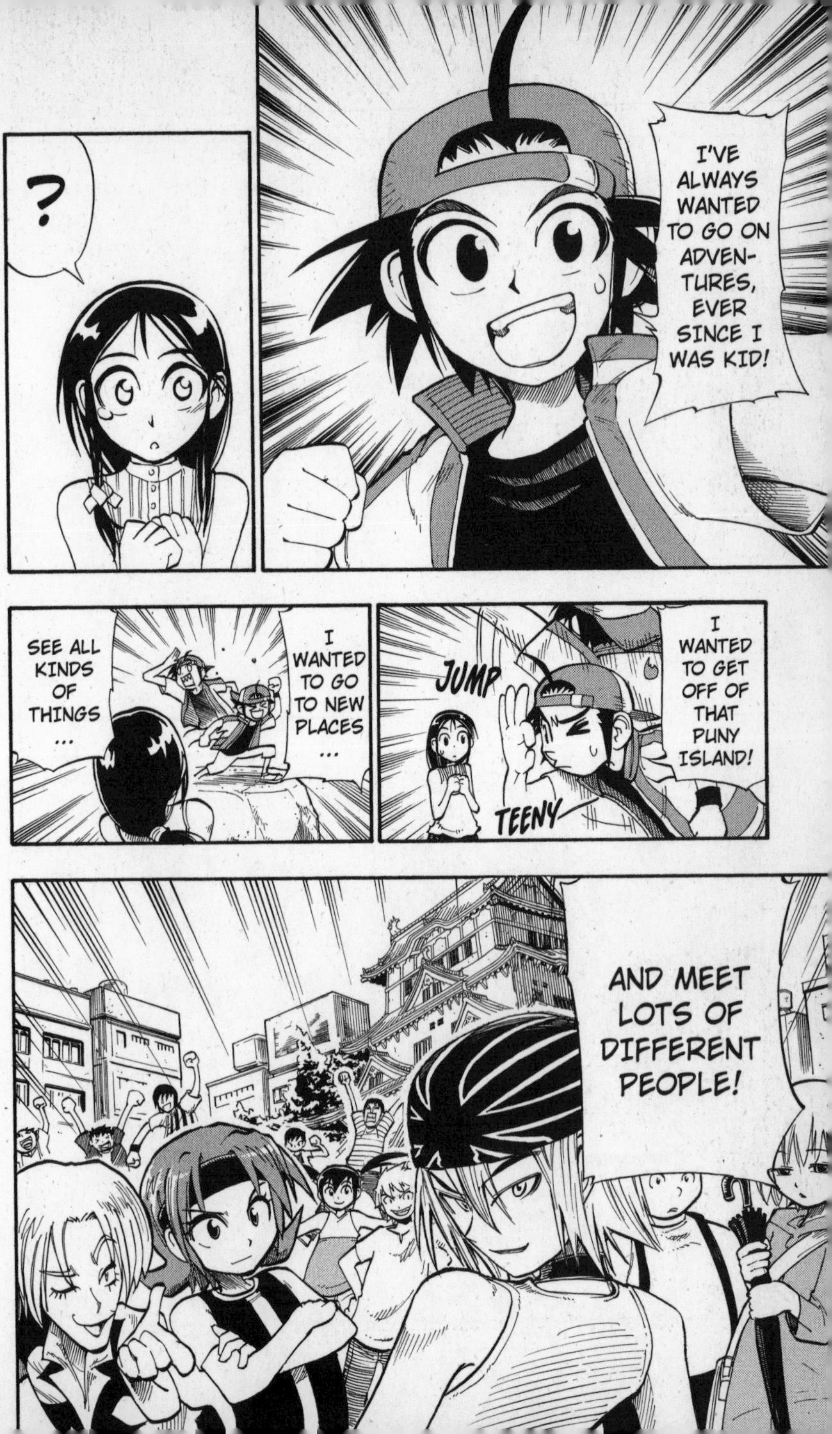
I'VE ALWAYS WANTED TO GO ON ADVEN-TURES, EVER SINCE I WAS KID!
?
I WANTED TO GET OFF OF THAT PUNY ISLAND!
JUMP
TEENY
I WANTED TO GO TO NEW PLACES ...
SEE ALL KINDS OF THINGS ...
AND MEET LOTS OF DIFFERENT PEOPLE!

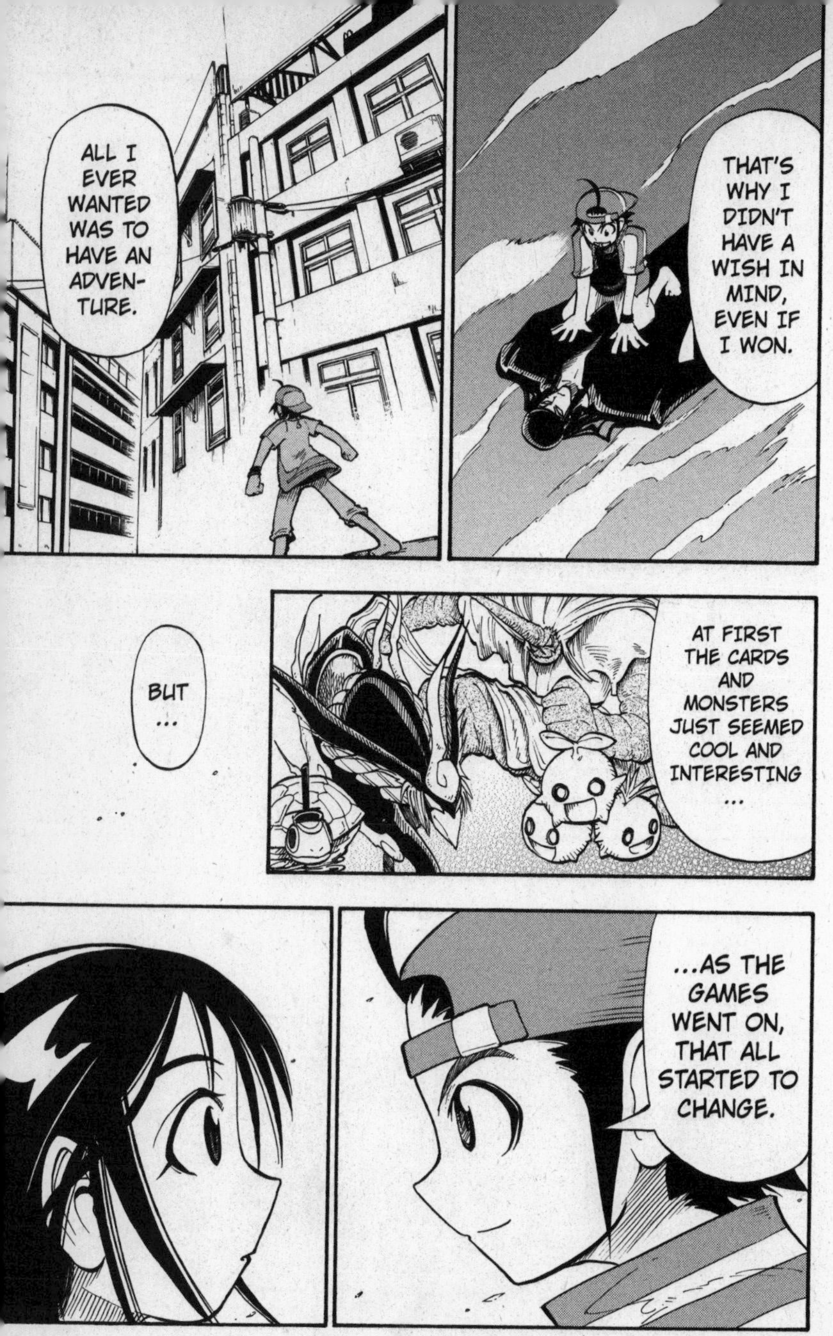
THAT'S WHY I DIDN'T HAVE A WISH IN MIND, EVEN IF I WON.
ALL I EVER WANTED WAS TO HAVE AN ADVENTURE.
AT FIRST THE CARDS AND MONSTERS JUST SEEMED COOL AND INTERESTING...
BUT...
...AS THE GAMES WENT ON, THAT ALL STARTED TO CHANGE.

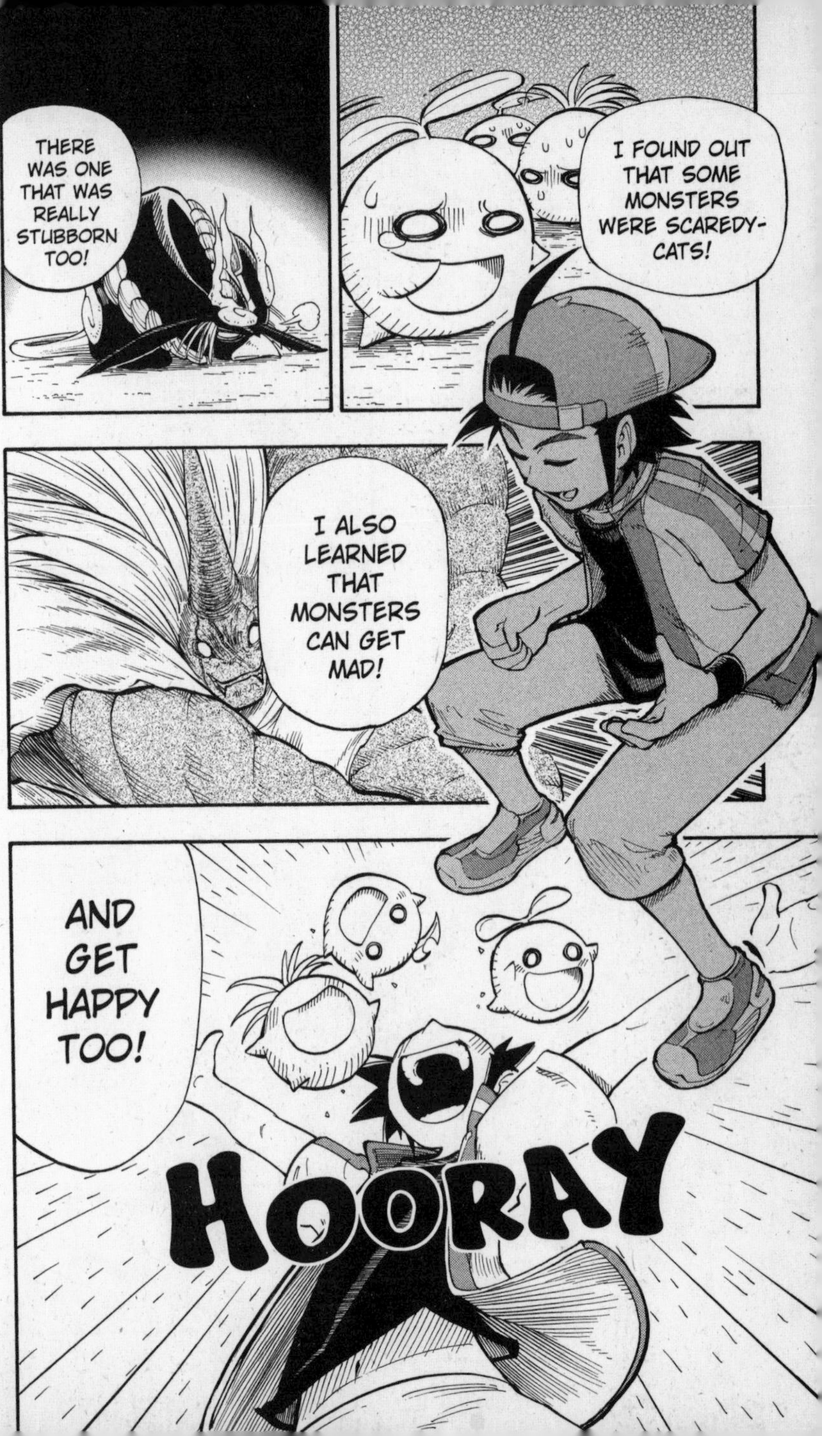
I FOUND OUT THAT SOME MONSTERS WERE SCAREDY-CATS!
THERE WAS ONE THAT WAS REALLY STUBBORN TOO!
I ALSO LEARNED THAT MONSTERS CAN GET MAD!
AND GET HAPPY TOO!
HOORAY

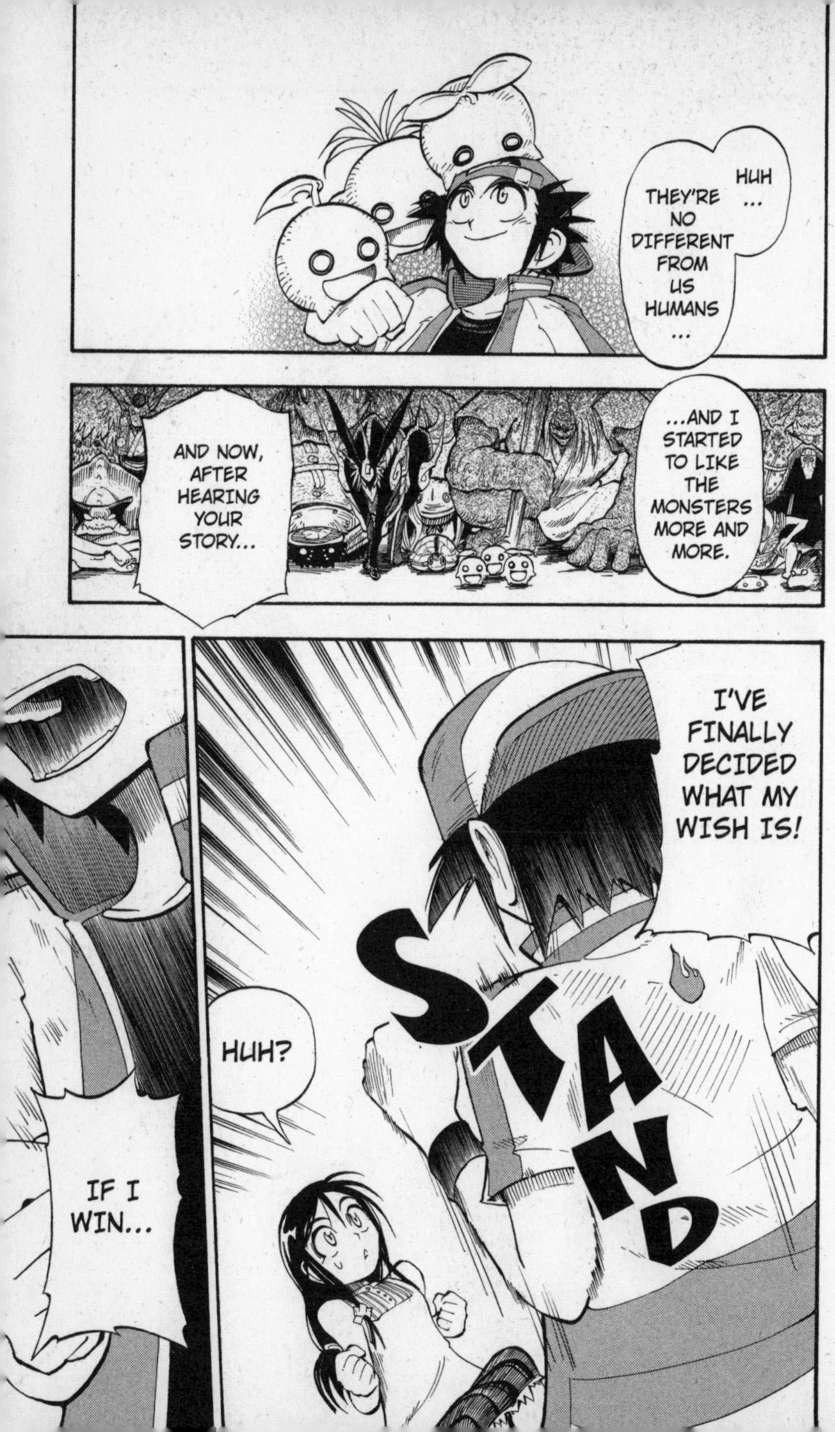
HUH ... THEY'RE NO DIFFERENT FROM US HUMANS ...
...AND I STARTED TO LIKE THE MONSTERS MORE AND MORE.
AND NOW, AFTER HEARING YOUR STORY...
I'VE FINALLY DECIDED WHAT MY WISH IS!
STAND
HUH?
IF I WIN...

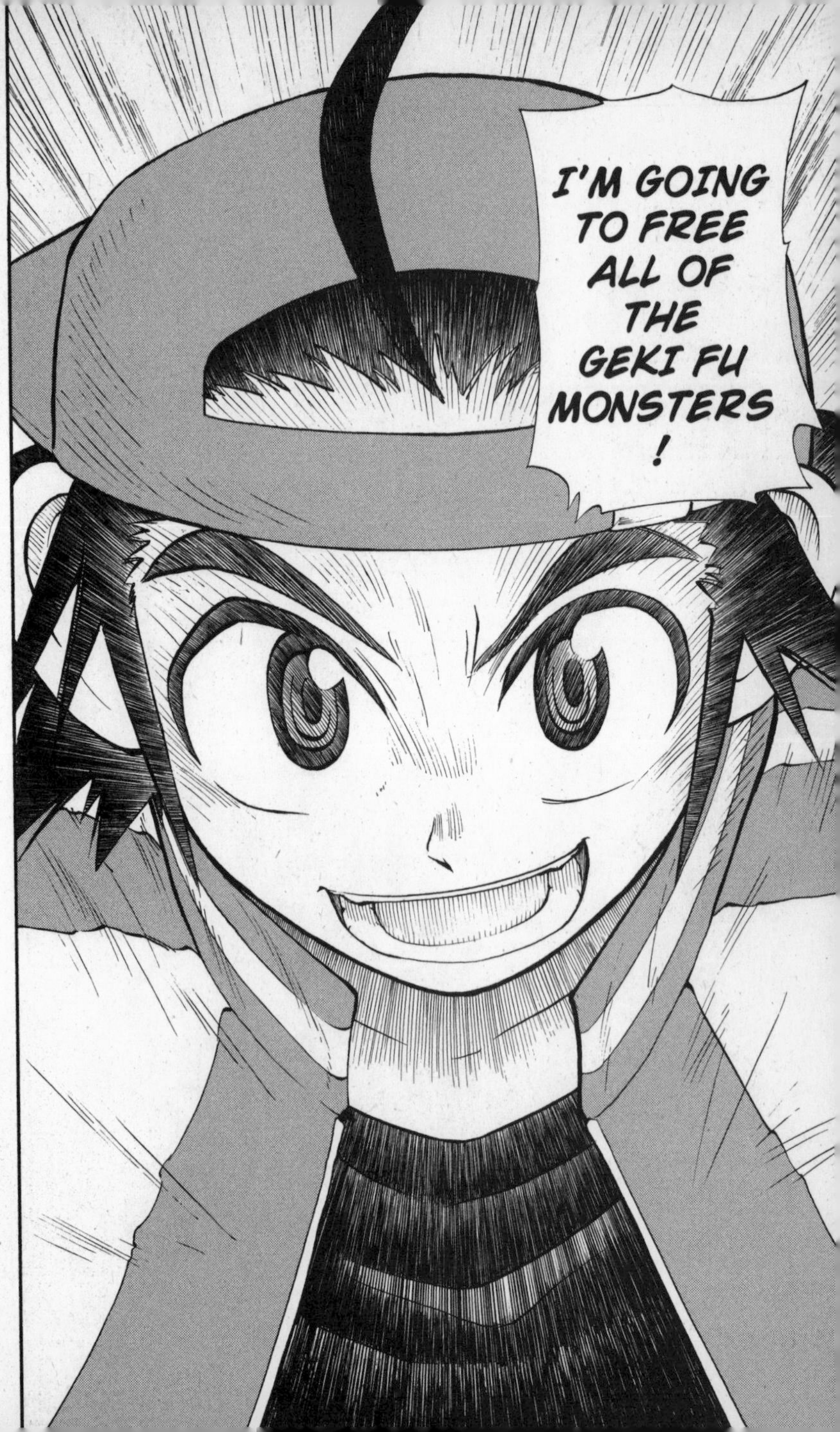
I'M GOING TO FREE ALL OF THE GEKI FU MONSTERS!

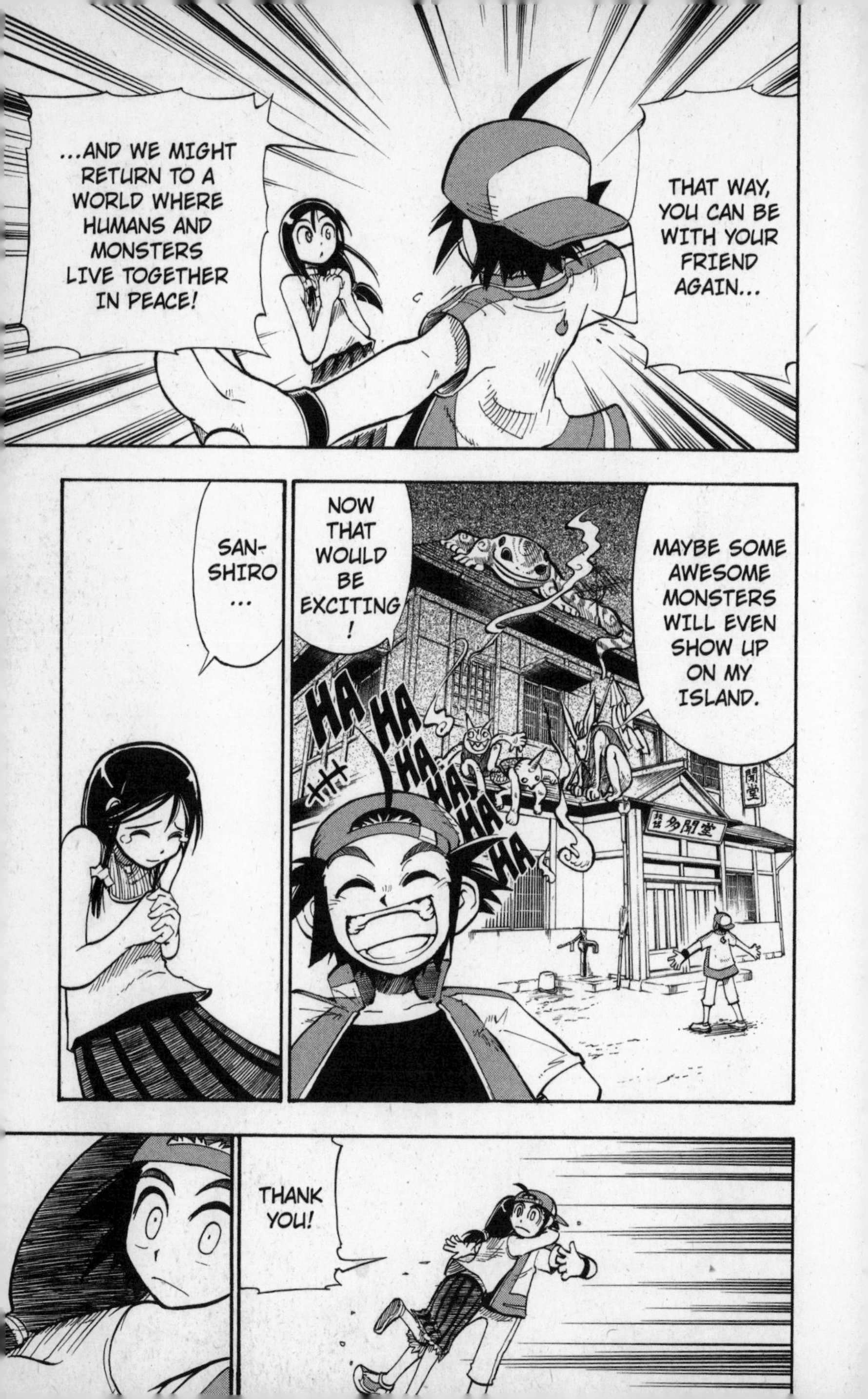
THAT WAY, YOU CAN BE WITH YOUR FRIEND AGAIN...
...AND WE MIGHT RETURN TO A WORLD WHERE HUMANS AND MONSTERS LIVE TOGETHER IN PEACE!
MAYBE SOME AWESOME MONSTERS WILL EVEN SHOW UP ON MY ISLAND.
NOW THAT WOULD BE EXCITING!
HA HA HA HA HA HA HA HA
SAN-SHIRO...
THANK YOU!

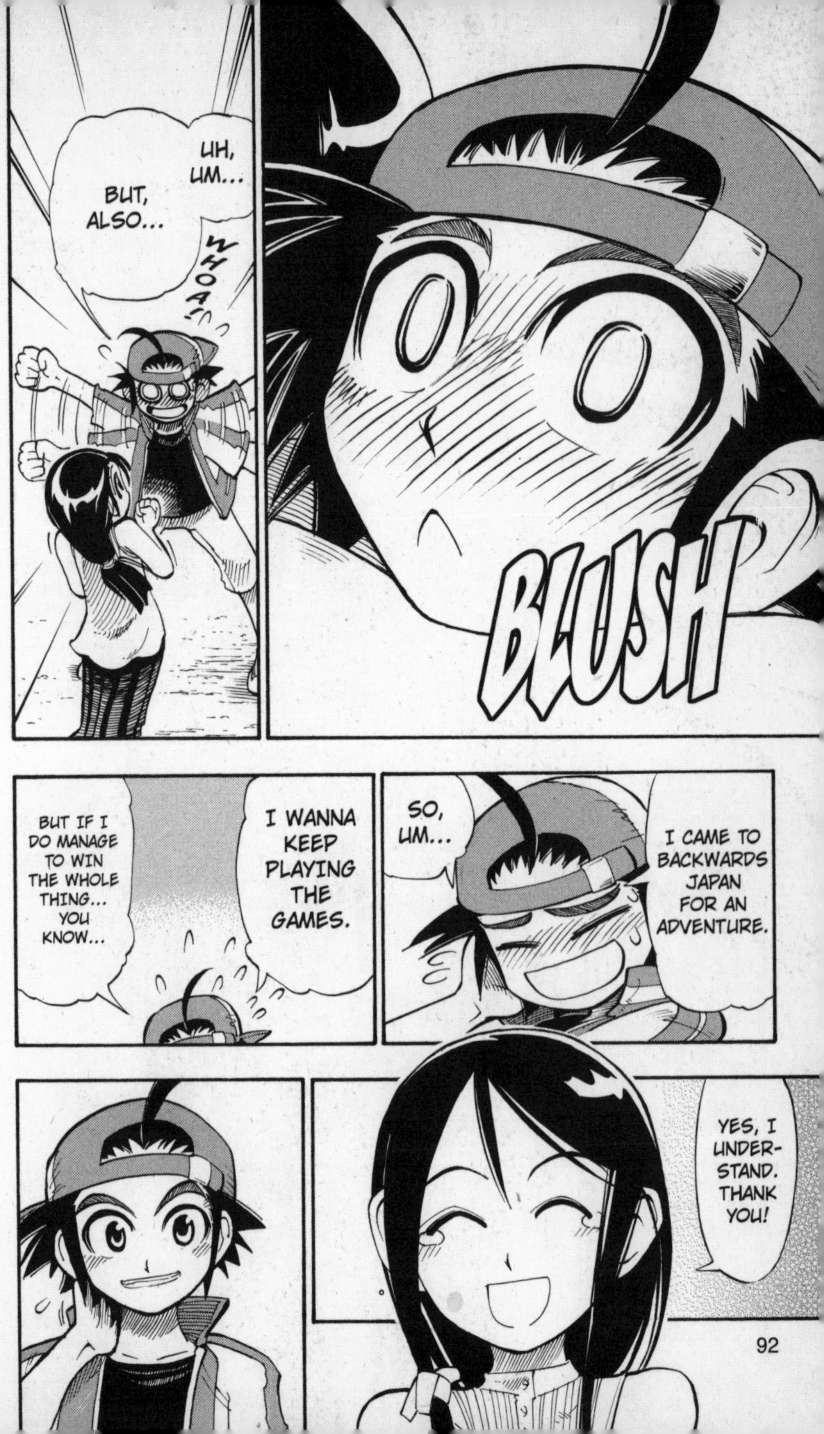
BLUSH
UH, UM...
BUT, ALSO...
WHOA!
I CAME TO BACKWARDS JAPAN FOR AN ADVENTURE.
SO, UM...
I WANNA KEEP PLAYING THE GAMES.
BUT IF I DO MANAGE TO WIN THE WHOLE THING... YOU KNOW...
YES, I UNDER-STAND. THANK YOU!

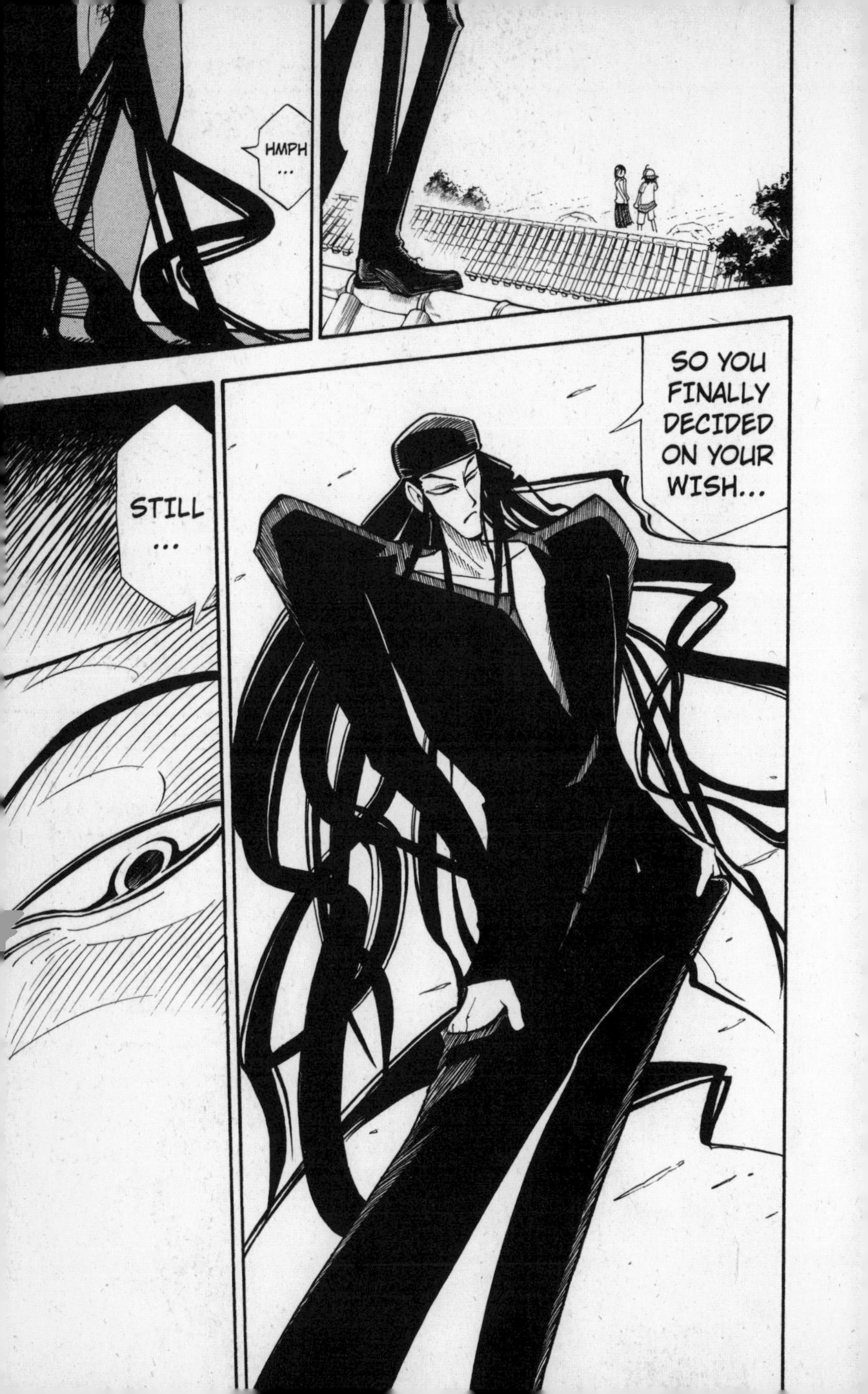
HMPH ...
SO YOU FINALLY DECIDED ON YOUR WISH...
STILL ...

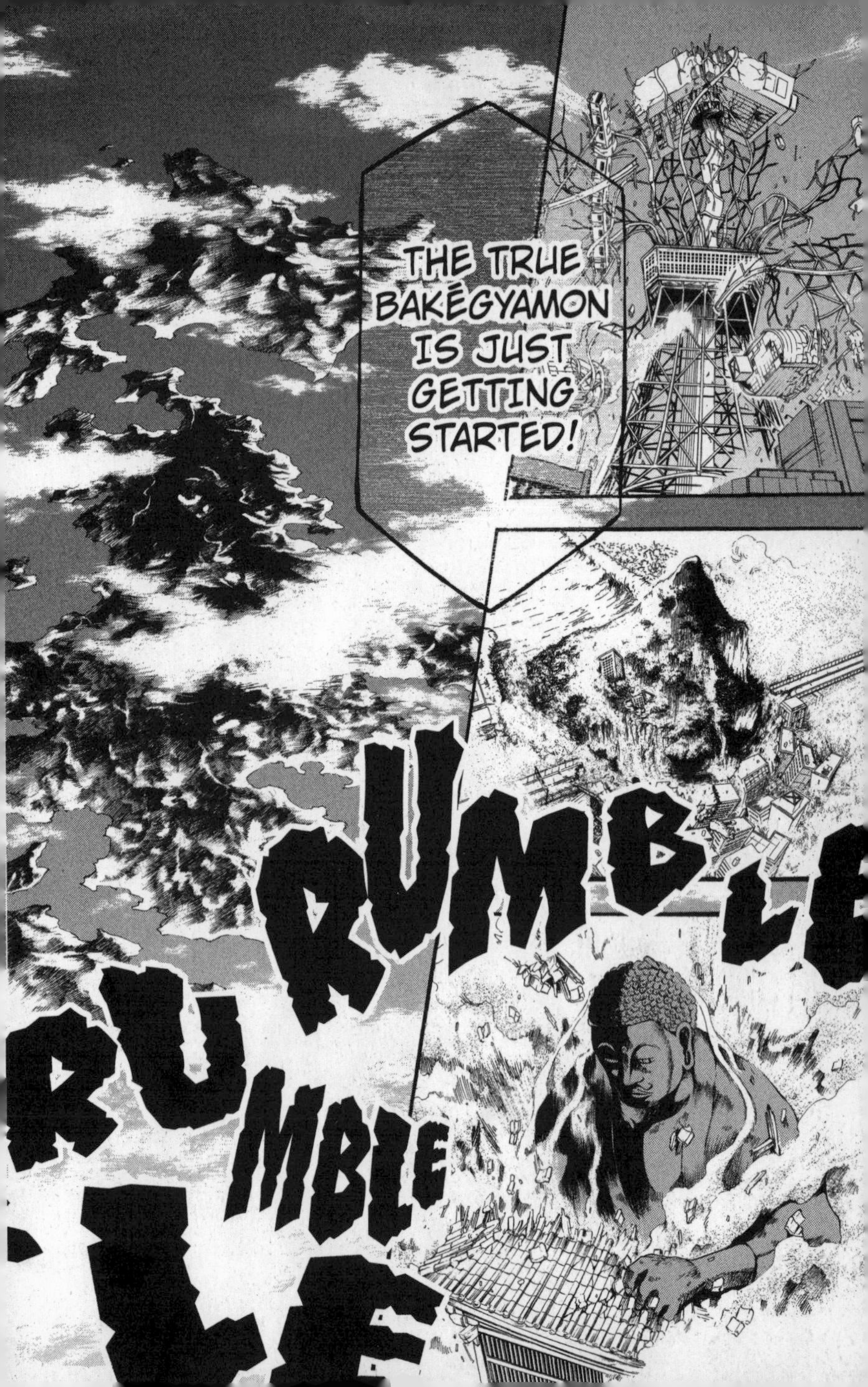
THE TRUE BAKÉGYAMON IS JUST GETTING STARTED!
RUMBLE
RUMBLE

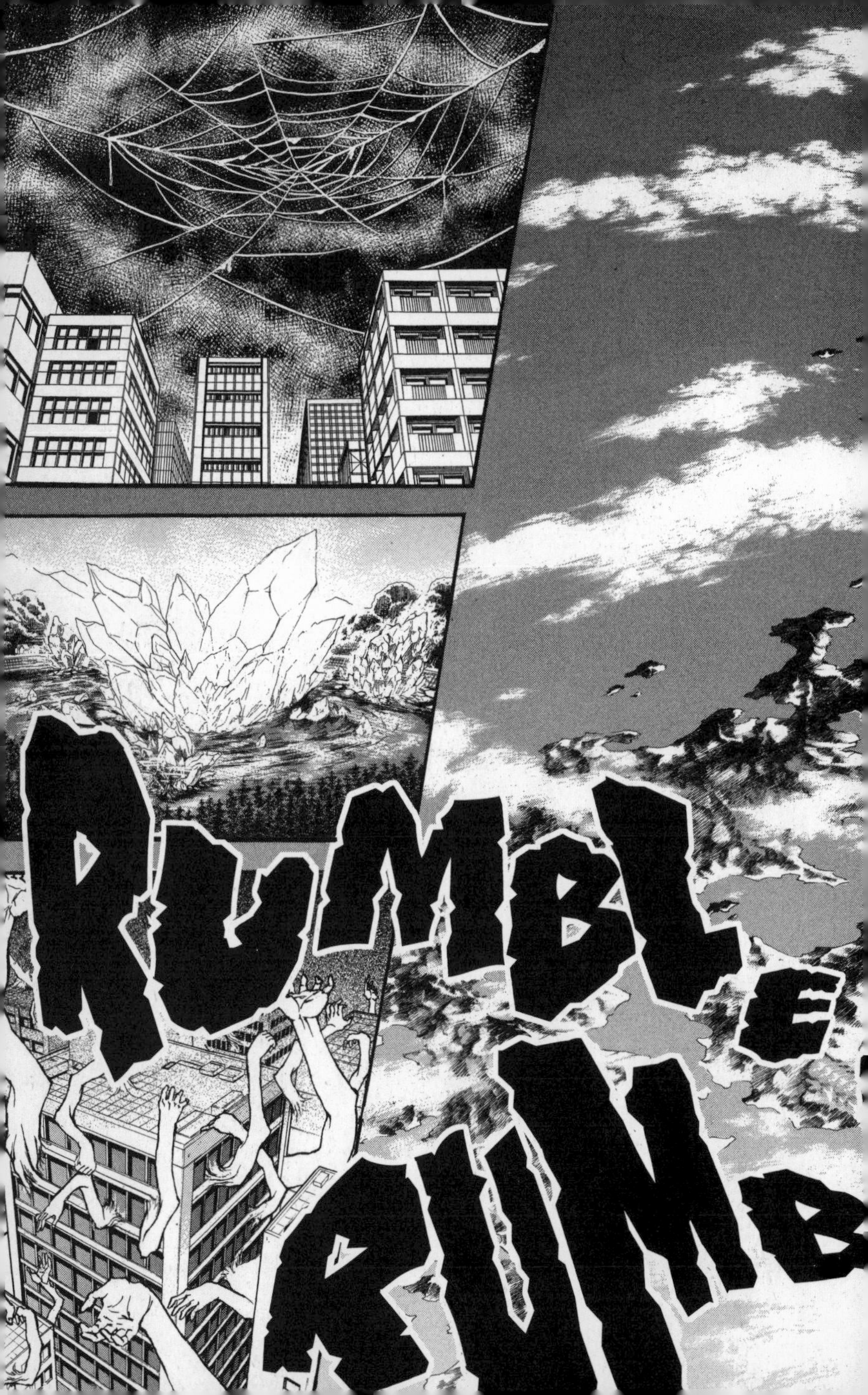
RUMBLE
RUMB

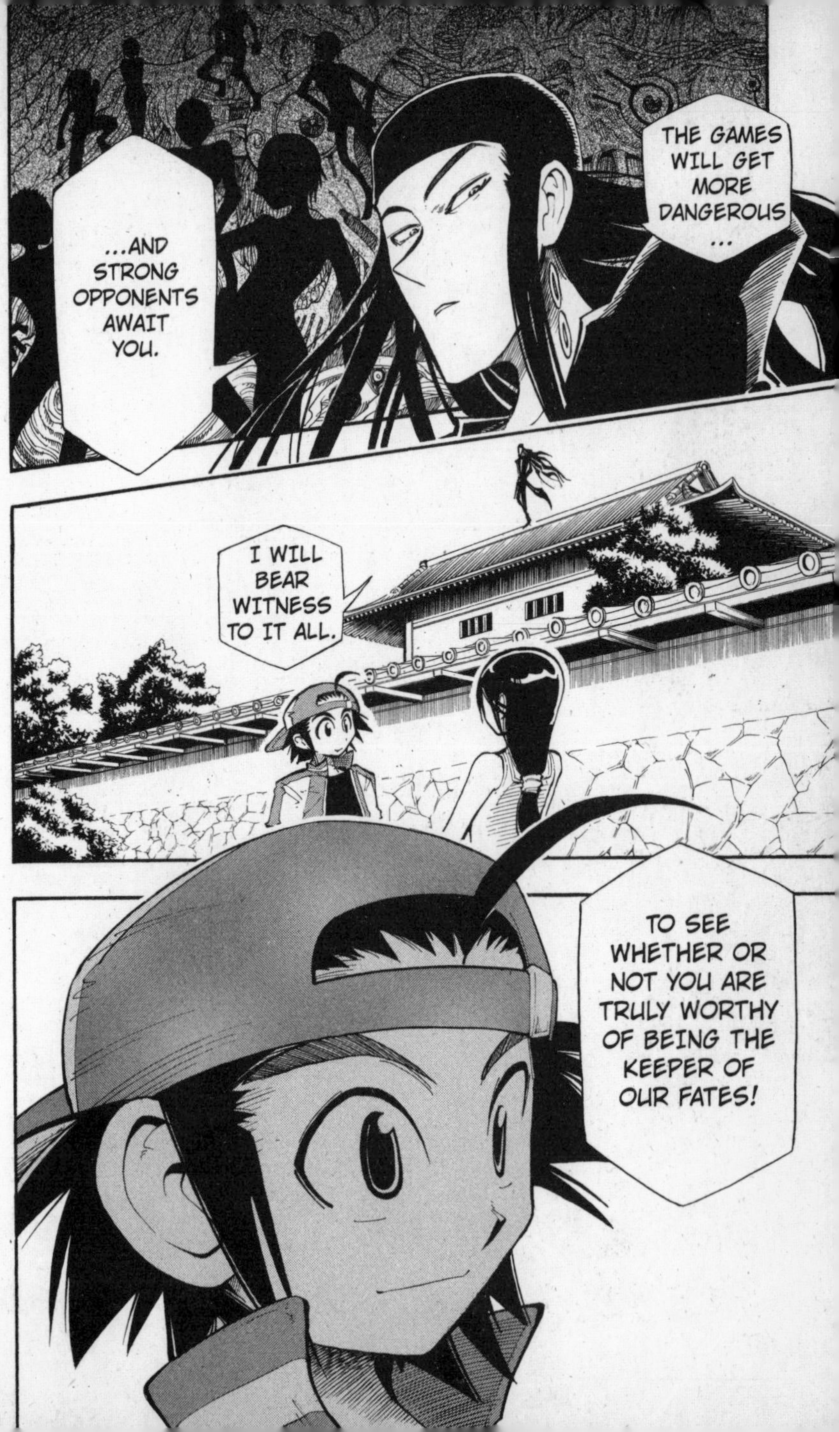
THE GAMES WILL GET MORE DANGEROUS ...
...AND STRONG OPPONENTS AWAIT YOU.
I WILL BEAR WITNESS TO IT ALL.
TO SEE WHETHER OR NOT YOU ARE TRULY WORTHY OF BEING THE KEEPER OF OUR FATES!

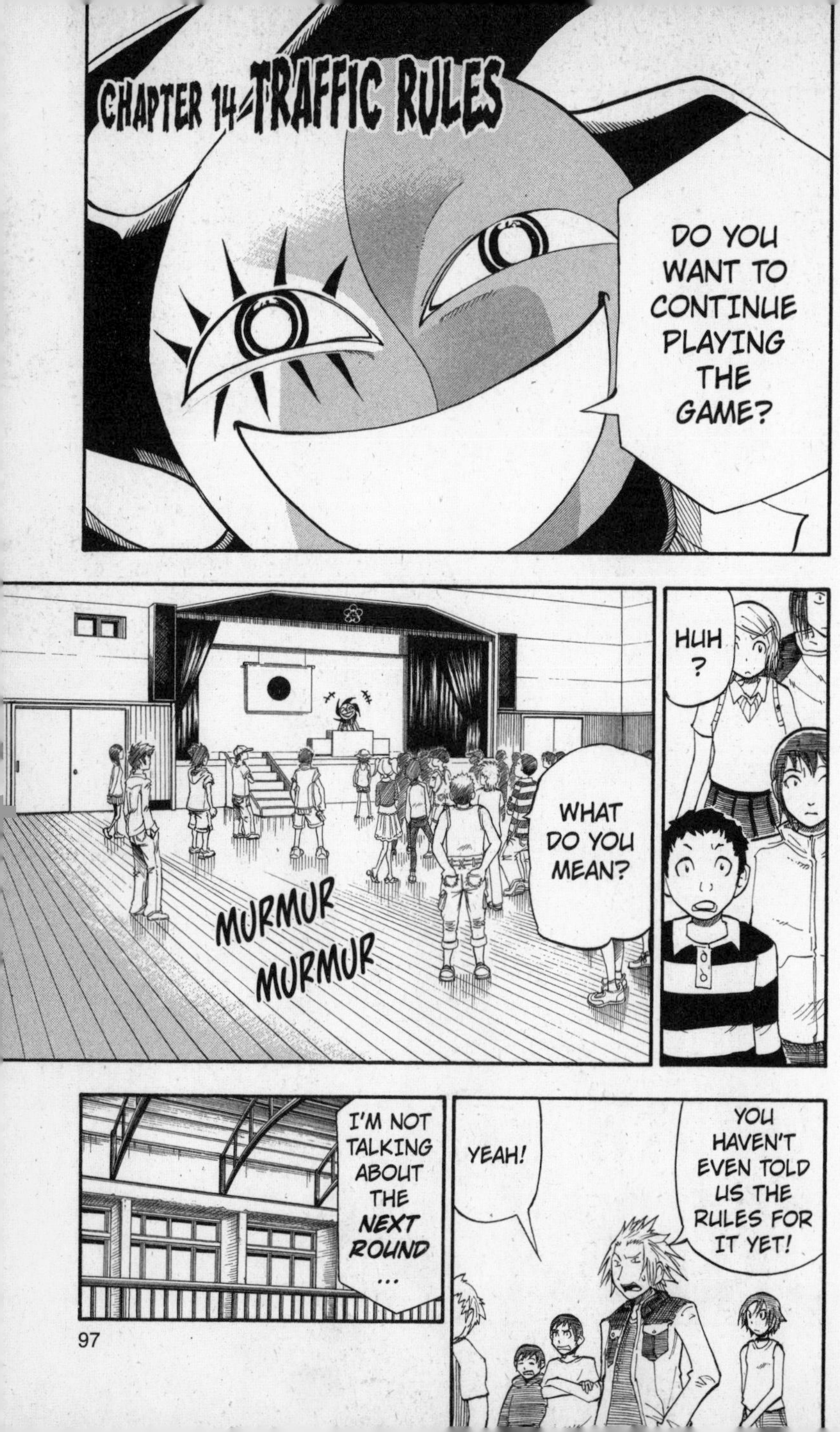
CHAPTER 14: TRAFFIC RULES
DO YOU WANT TO CONTINUE PLAYING THE GAME?
HUH?
WHAT DO YOU MEAN?
MURMUR MURMUR
YOU HAVEN'T EVEN TOLD US THE RULES FOR IT YET!
YEAH!
I'M NOT TALKING ABOUT THE *NEXT ROUND*...

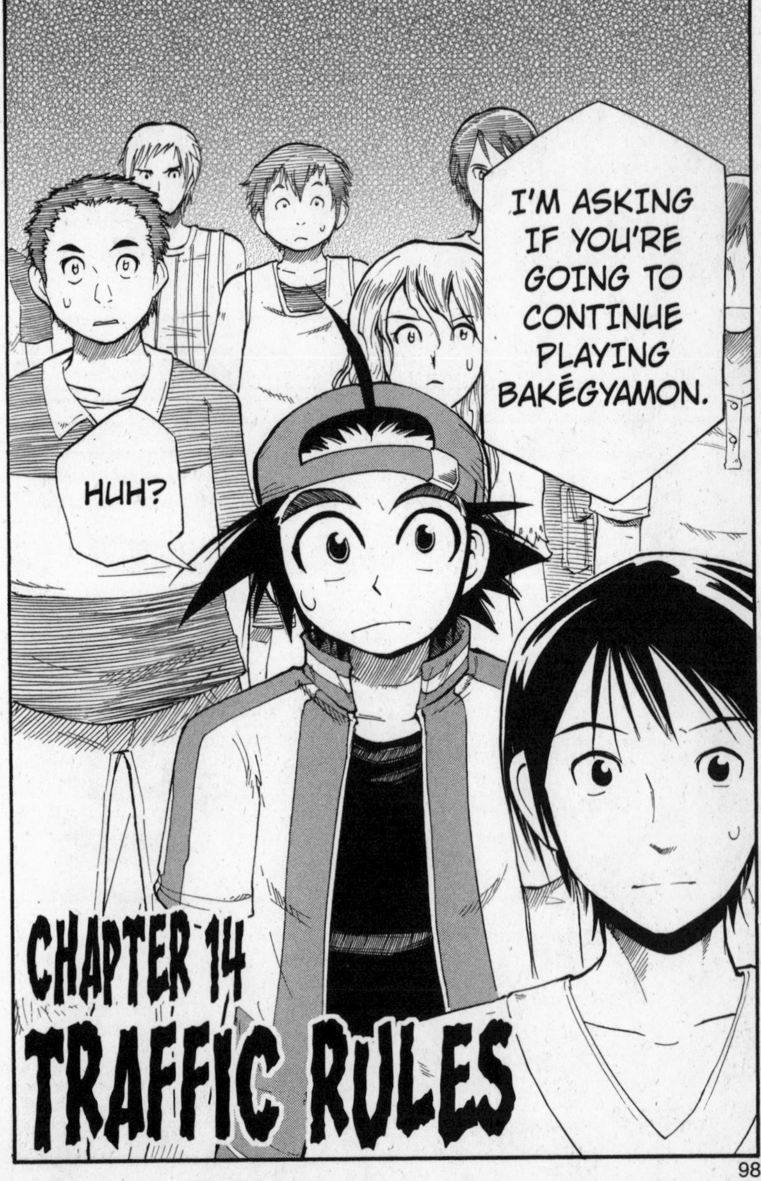
I'M ASKING IF YOU'RE GOING TO CONTINUE PLAYING BAKÉGYAMON.
HUH?
CHAPTER 14
TRAFFIC RULES

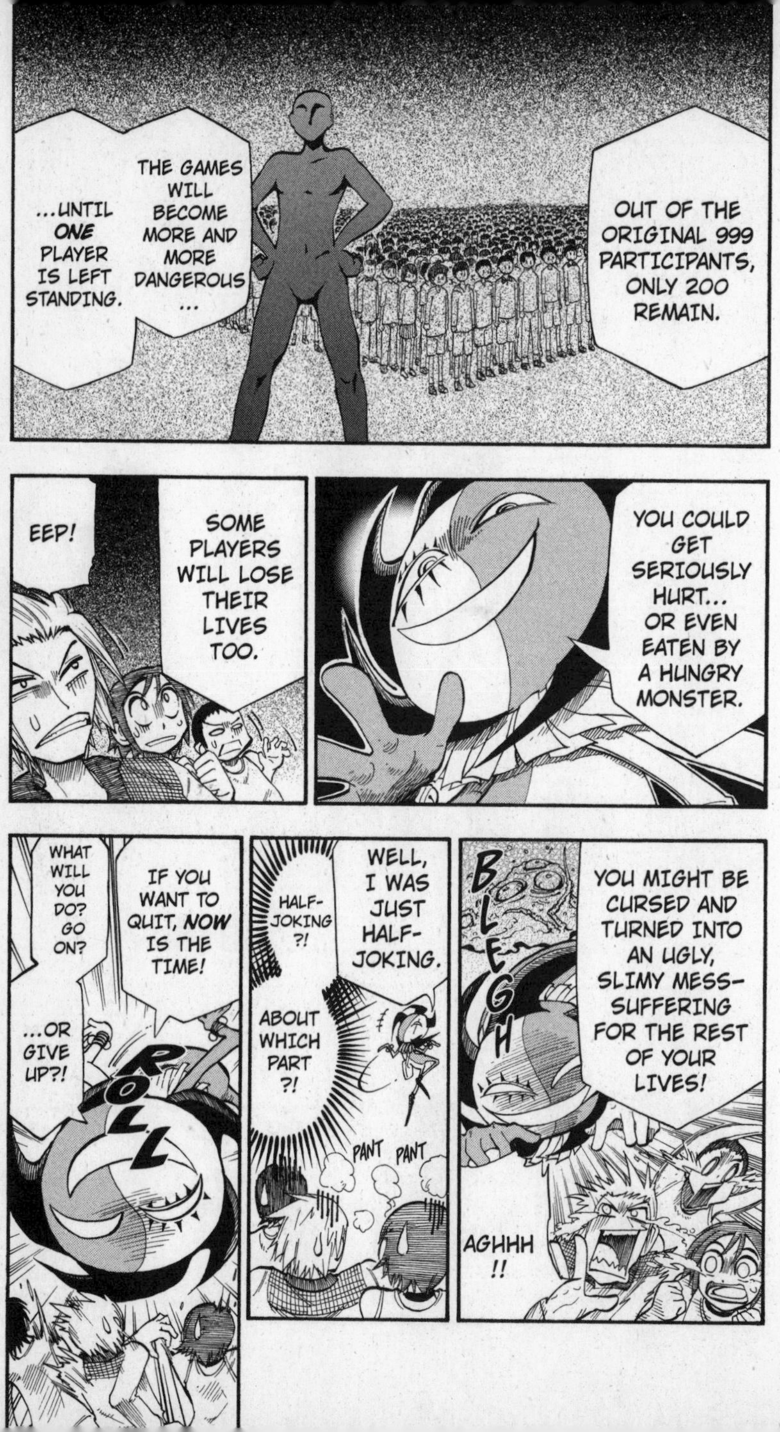
OUT OF THE ORIGINAL 999 PARTICIPANTS, ONLY 200 REMAIN.
THE GAMES WILL BECOME MORE AND MORE DANGEROUS...
...UNTIL ONE PLAYER IS LEFT STANDING.
YOU COULD GET SERIOUSLY HURT... OR EVEN EATEN BY A HUNGRY MONSTER.
SOME PLAYERS WILL LOSE THEIR LIVES TOO.
EEP!
YOU MIGHT BE CURSED AND TURNED INTO AN UGLY, SLIMY MESS-SUFFERING FOR THE REST OF YOUR LIVES!
BLEGH
AGHHH!!
WELL, I WAS JUST HALF-JOKING.
HALF-JOKING?!
ABOUT WHICH PART?!
PANT PANT
IF YOU WANT TO QUIT, NOW IS THE TIME!
WHAT WILL YOU DO? GO ON?
...OR GIVE UP?!
ROLL

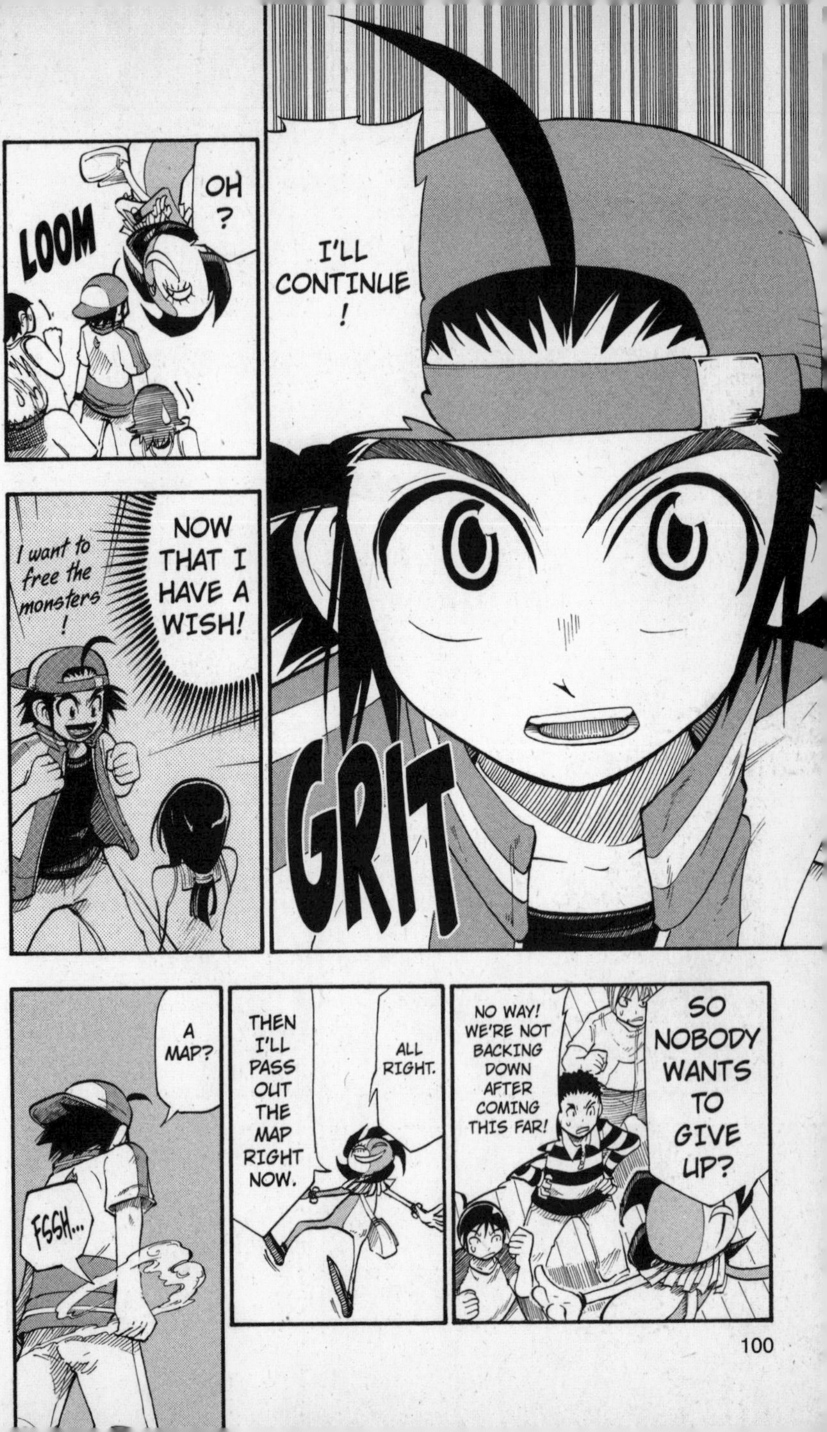
I'LL CONTINUE!
GRIT
OH?
LOOM
NOW THAT I HAVE A WISH!
I want to free the monsters!
SO NOBODY WANTS TO GIVE UP?
NO WAY! WE'RE NOT BACKING DOWN AFTER COMING THIS FAR!
ALL RIGHT.
THEN I'LL PASS OUT THE MAP RIGHT NOW.
A MAP?
FSSH...

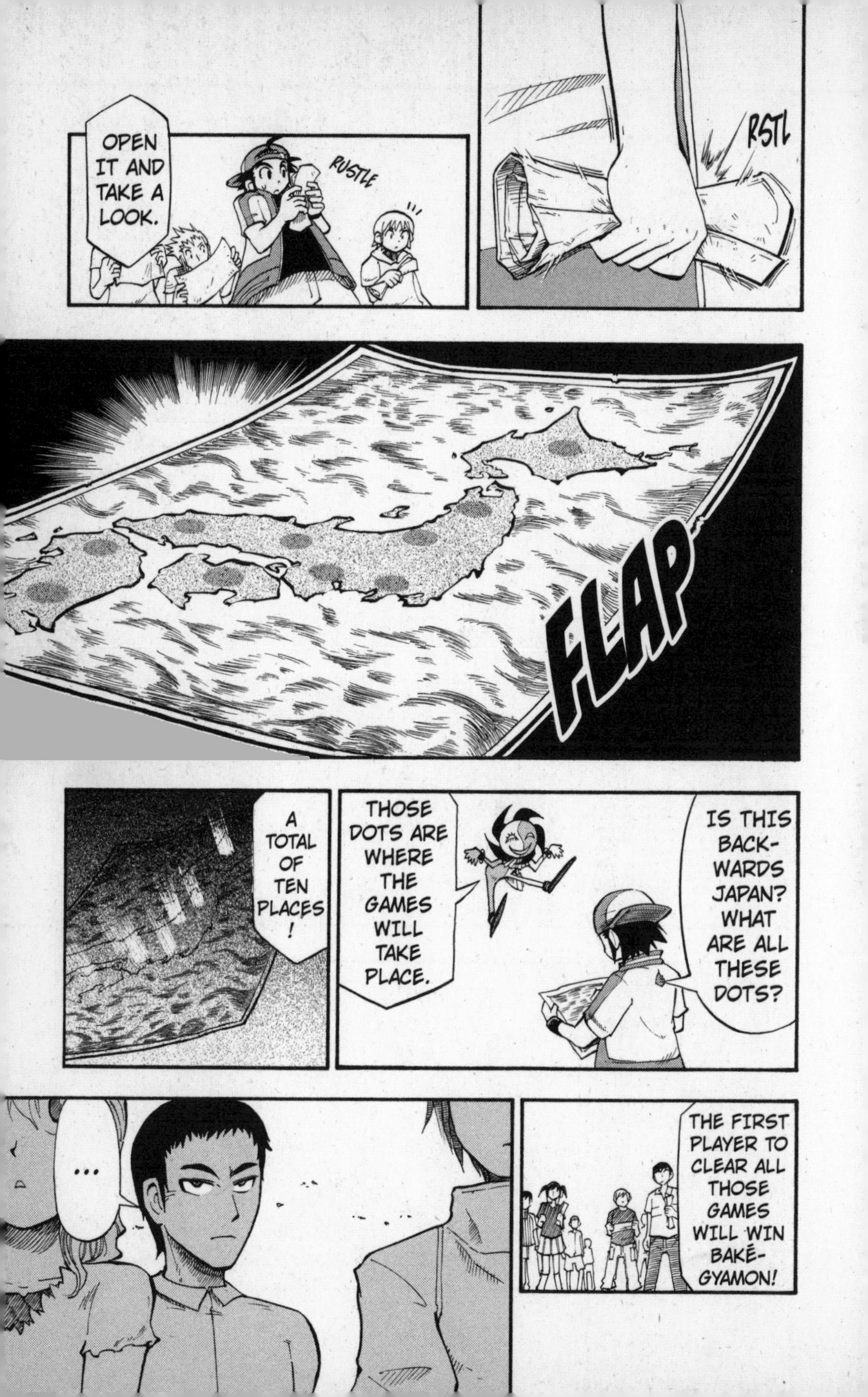
RSTL
OPEN IT AND TAKE A LOOK.
RUSTLE
FLAP
IS THIS BACKWARDS JAPAN? WHAT ARE ALL THESE DOTS?
THOSE DOTS ARE WHERE THE GAMES WILL TAKE PLACE.
A TOTAL OF TEN PLACES!
THE FIRST PLAYER TO CLEAR ALL THOSE GAMES WILL WIN BAKÉ-GYAMON!
...

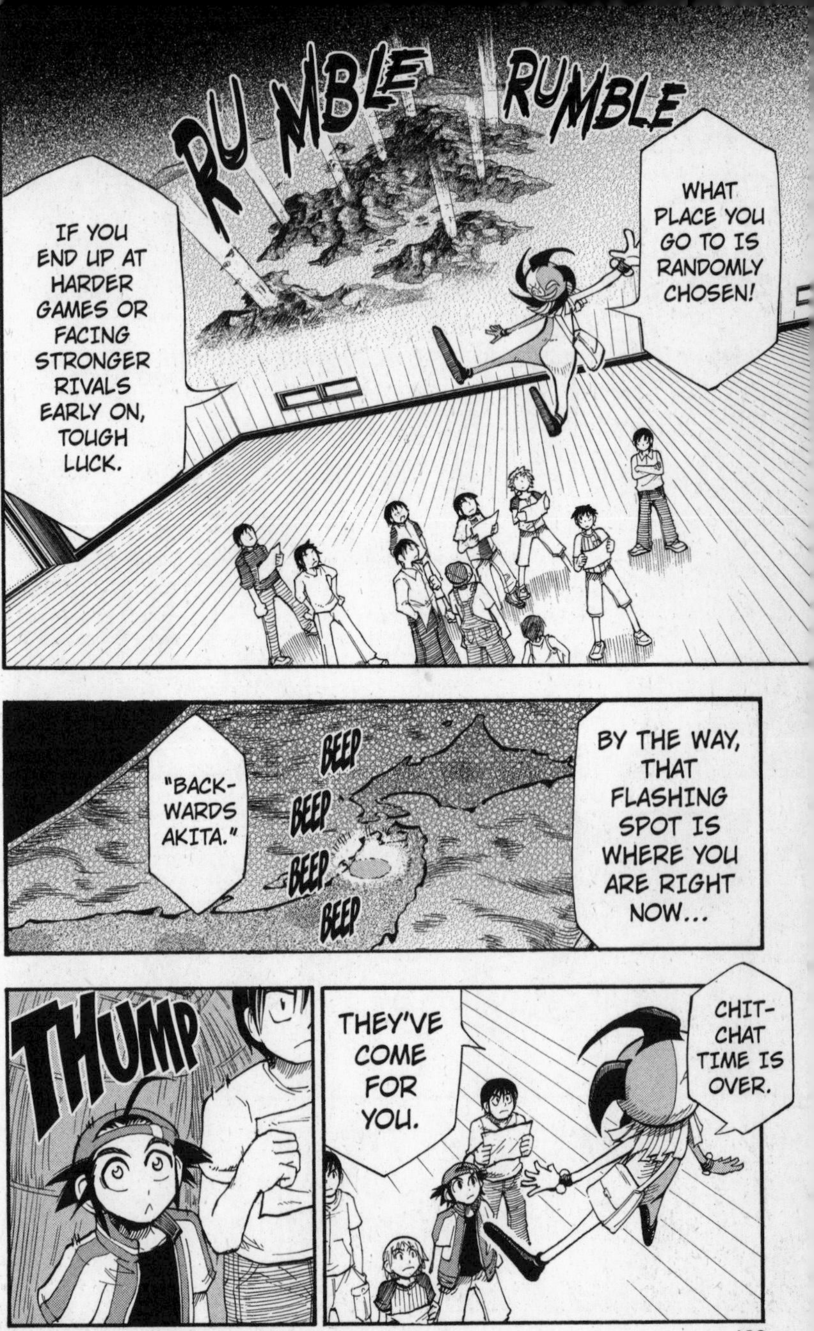
RUMBLE RUMBLE
WHAT PLACE YOU GO TO IS RANDOMLY CHOSEN!
IF YOU END UP AT HARDER GAMES OR FACING STRONGER RIVALS EARLY ON, TOUGH LUCK.
BY THE WAY, THAT FLASHING SPOT IS WHERE YOU ARE RIGHT NOW...
BEEP BEEP BEEP BEEP
"BACK-WARDS AKITA."
CHIT-CHAT TIME IS OVER.
THEY'VE COME FOR YOU.
THUMP

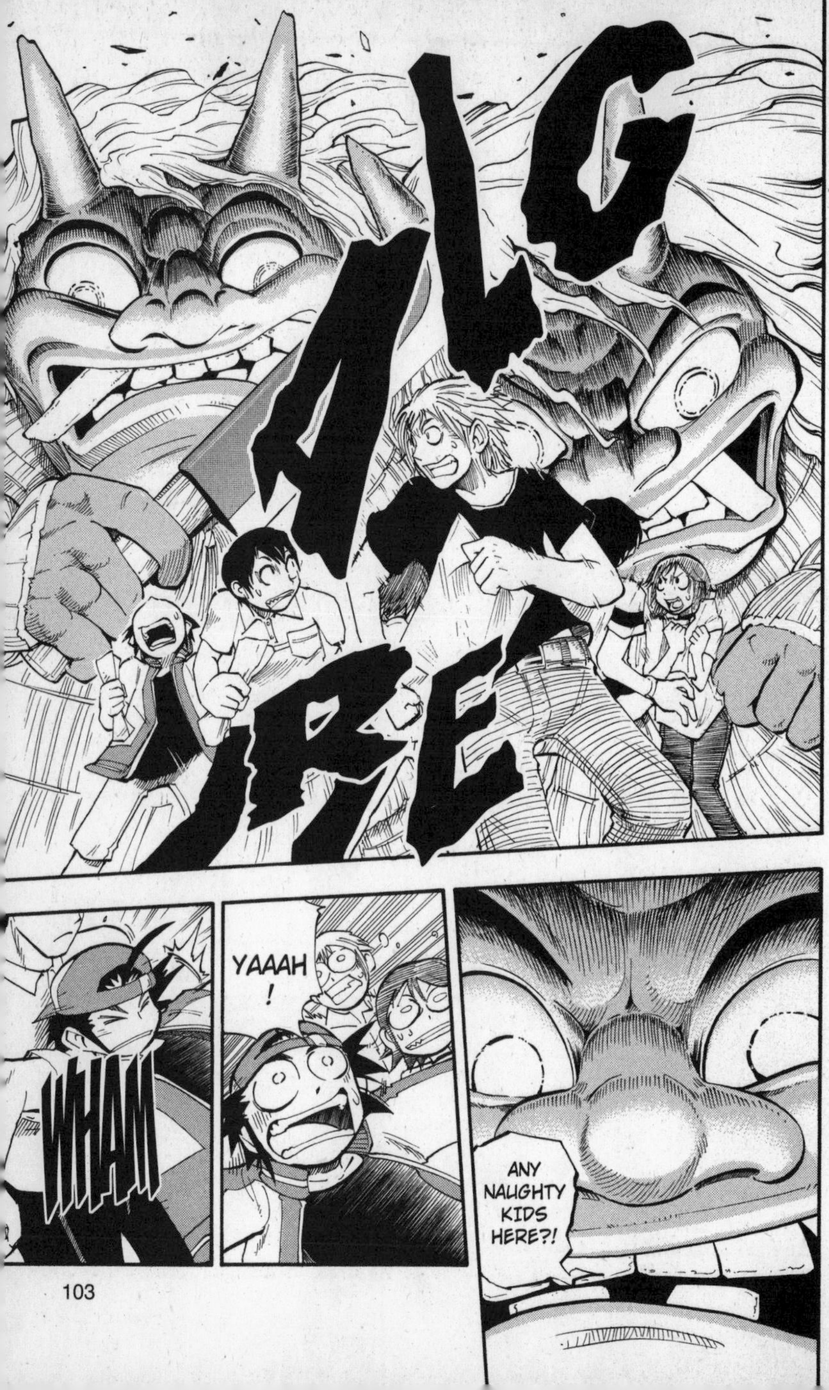
ANY NAUGHTY KIDS HERE?!
YAAAH!
WHAM

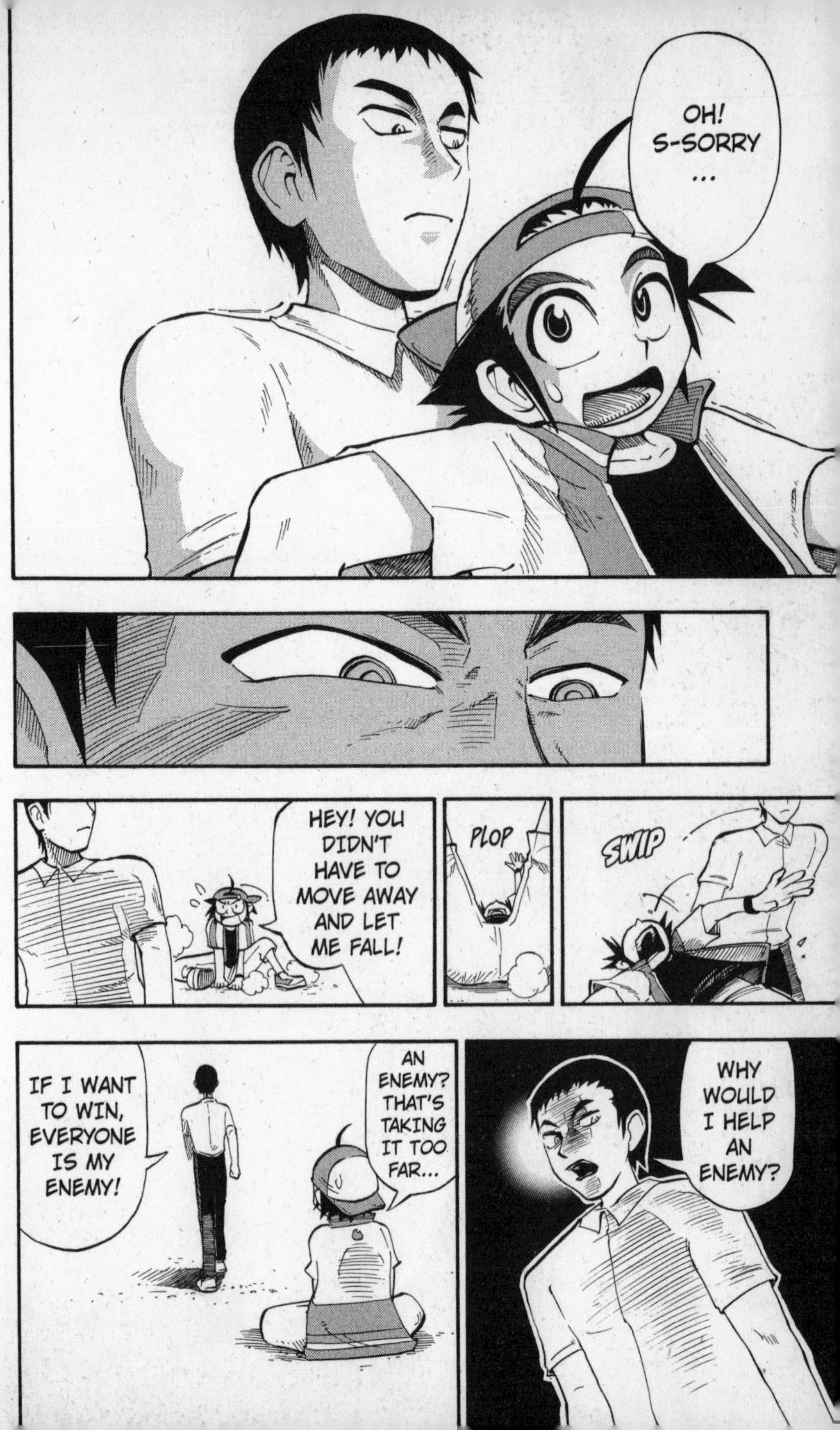
OH! S-SORRY ...
SWIP
PLOP
HEY! YOU DIDN'T HAVE TO MOVE AWAY AND LET ME FALL!
WHY WOULD I HELP AN ENEMY?
AN ENEMY? THAT'S TAKING IT TOO FAR...
IF I WANT TO WIN, EVERYONE IS MY ENEMY!

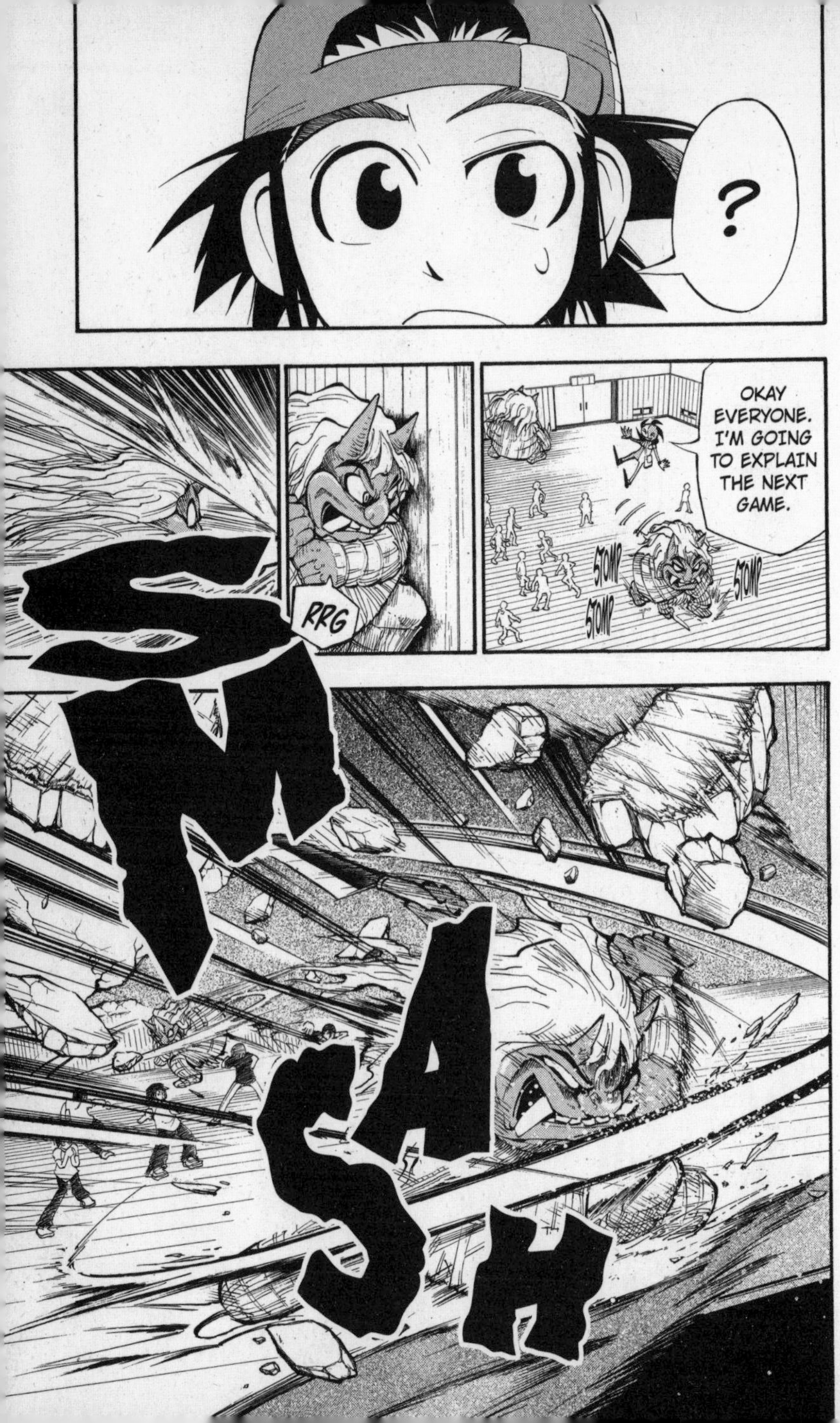
?
OKAY EVERYONE. I'M GOING TO EXPLAIN THE NEXT GAME.
STOMP
STOMP
STOMP
STOMP
RRG
SMASH

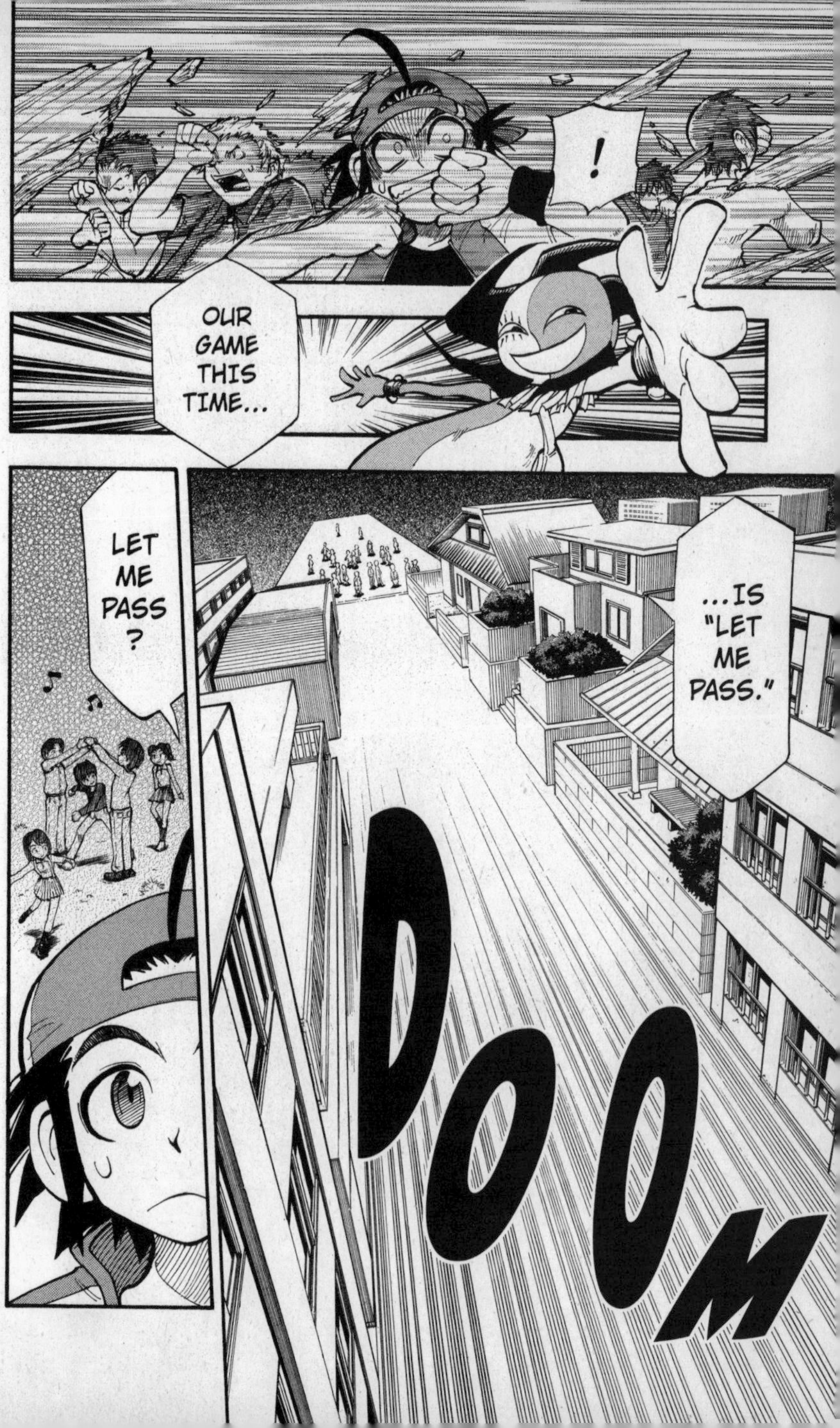
!
OUR GAME THIS TIME...
...IS "LET ME PASS."
DOOM
LET ME PASS?

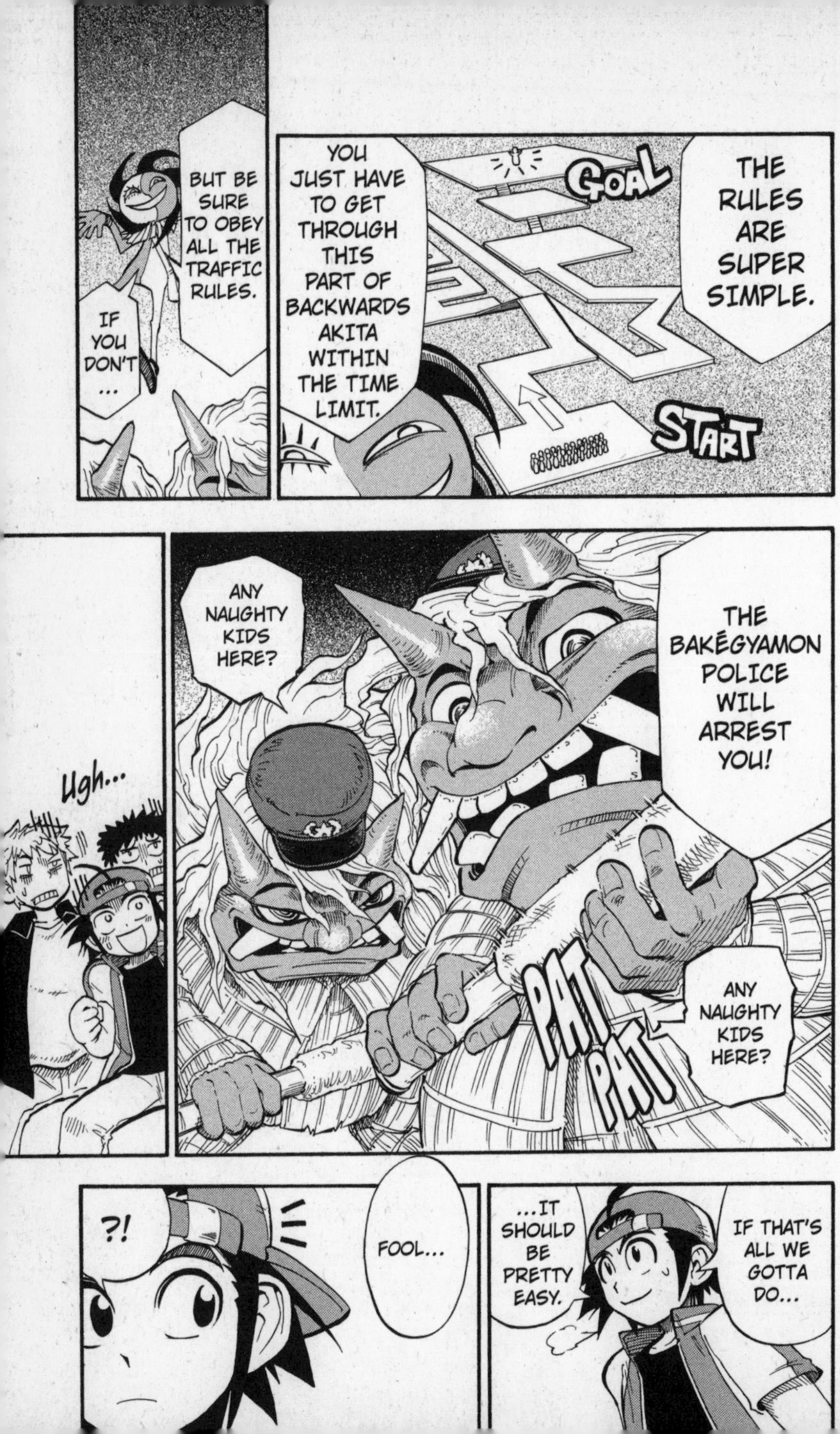
THE RULES ARE SUPER SIMPLE.
GOAL
YOU JUST HAVE TO GET THROUGH THIS PART OF BACKWARDS AKITA WITHIN THE TIME LIMIT.
START
BUT BE SURE TO OBEY ALL THE TRAFFIC RULES.
IF YOU DON'T ...
THE BAKÉGYAMON POLICE WILL ARREST YOU!
ANY NAUGHTY KIDS HERE?
PAT PAT
ANY NAUGHTY KIDS HERE?
Ugh...
IF THAT'S ALL WE GOTTA DO...
...IT SHOULD BE PRETTY EASY.
FOOL...
?!

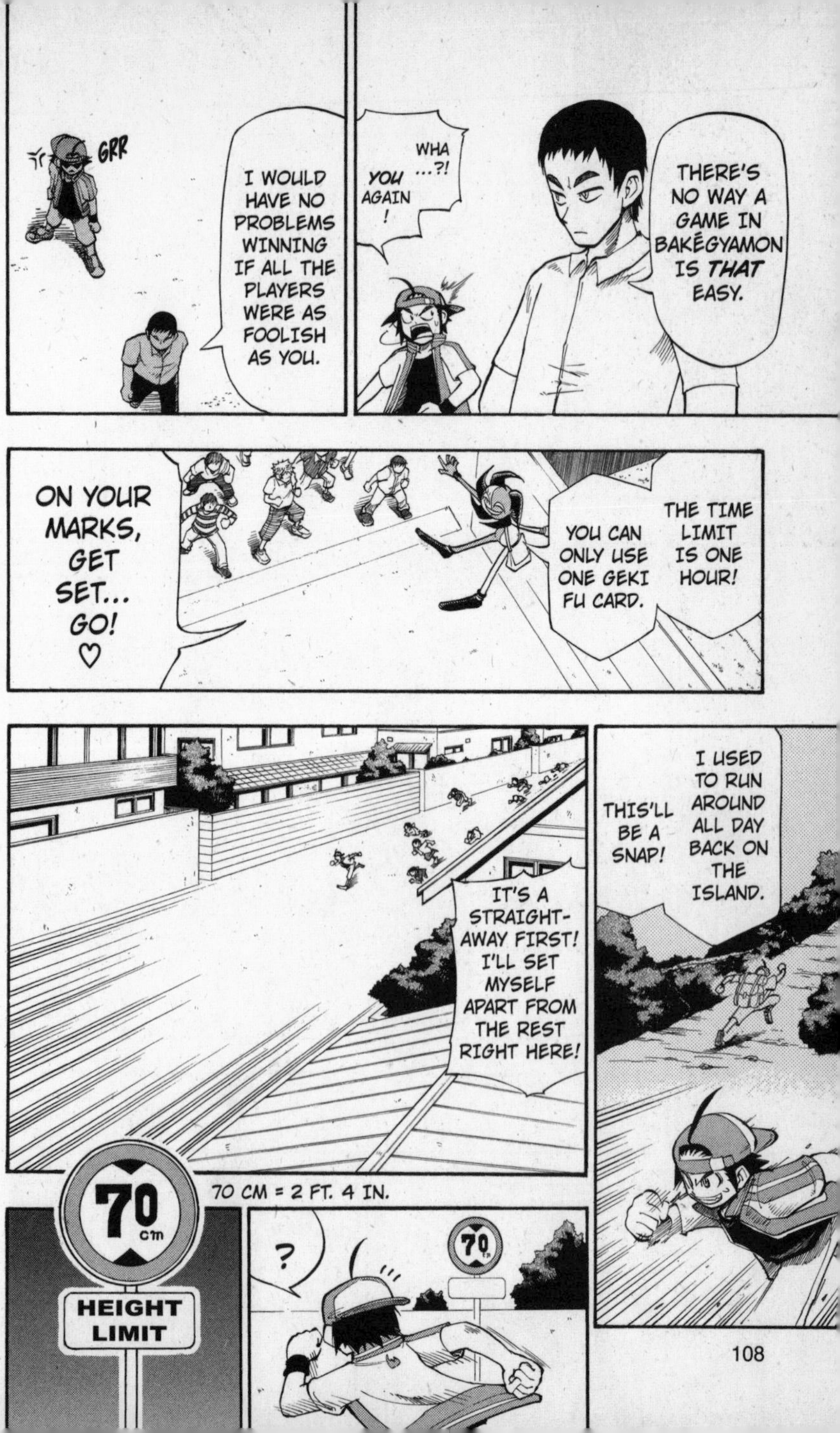
THERE'S NO WAY A GAME IN BAKĒGYAMON IS *THAT* EASY.
WHA ...?!
YOU AGAIN!
I WOULD HAVE NO PROBLEMS WINNING IF ALL THE PLAYERS WERE AS FOOLISH AS YOU.
GRR
THE TIME LIMIT IS ONE HOUR!
YOU CAN ONLY USE ONE GEKI FU CARD.
ON YOUR MARKS, GET SET... GO! ♡
I USED TO RUN AROUND ALL DAY BACK ON THE ISLAND.
THIS'LL BE A SNAP!
IT'S A STRAIGHT-AWAY FIRST! I'LL SET MYSELF APART FROM THE REST RIGHT HERE!
?
70
70 CM = 2 FT. 4 IN.
70 cm
HEIGHT LIMIT

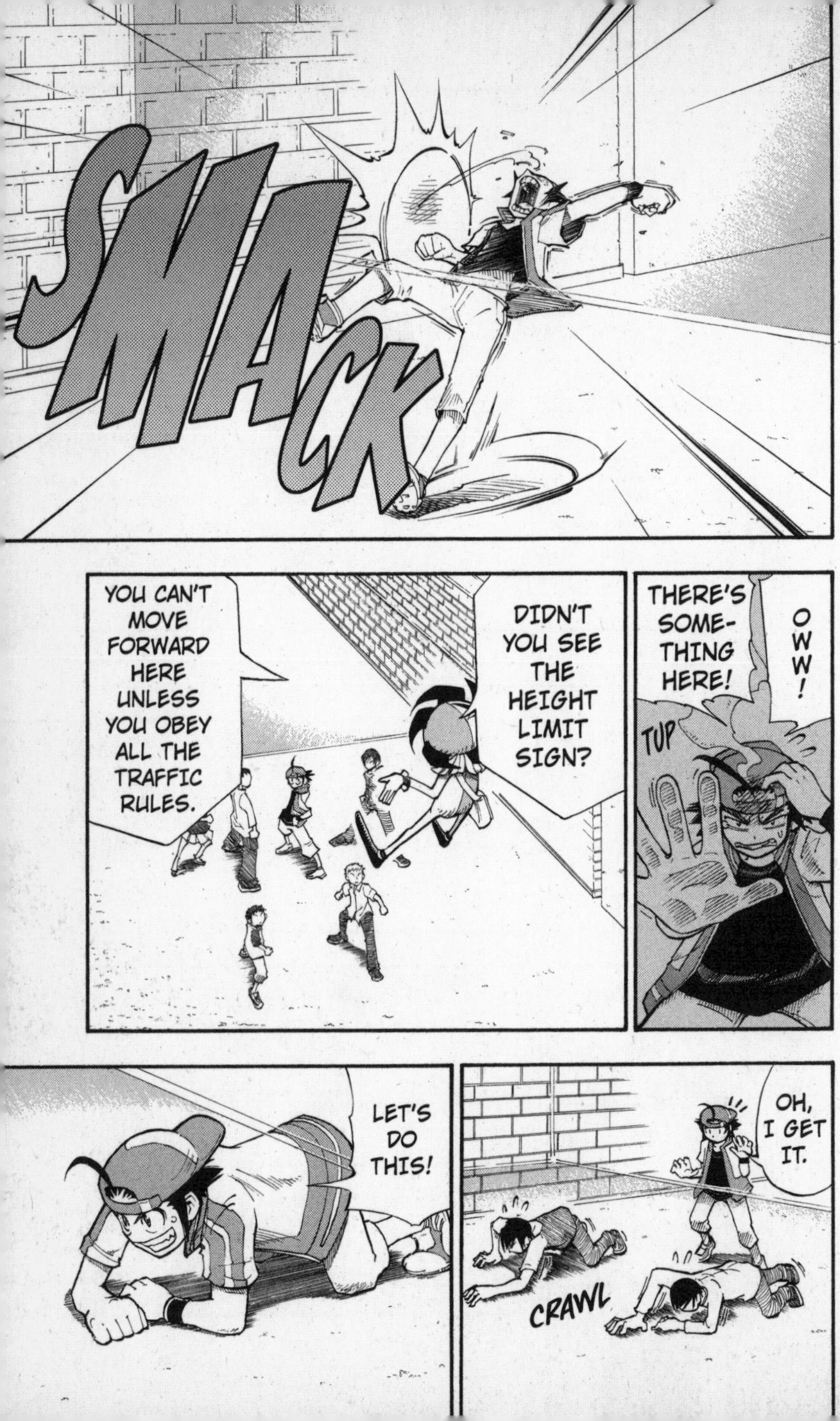
SMACK
OWW!
THERE'S SOMETHING HERE!
TUP
DIDN'T YOU SEE THE HEIGHT LIMIT SIGN?
YOU CAN'T MOVE FORWARD HERE UNLESS YOU OBEY ALL THE TRAFFIC RULES.
OH, I GET IT.
CRAWL
LET'S DO THIS!

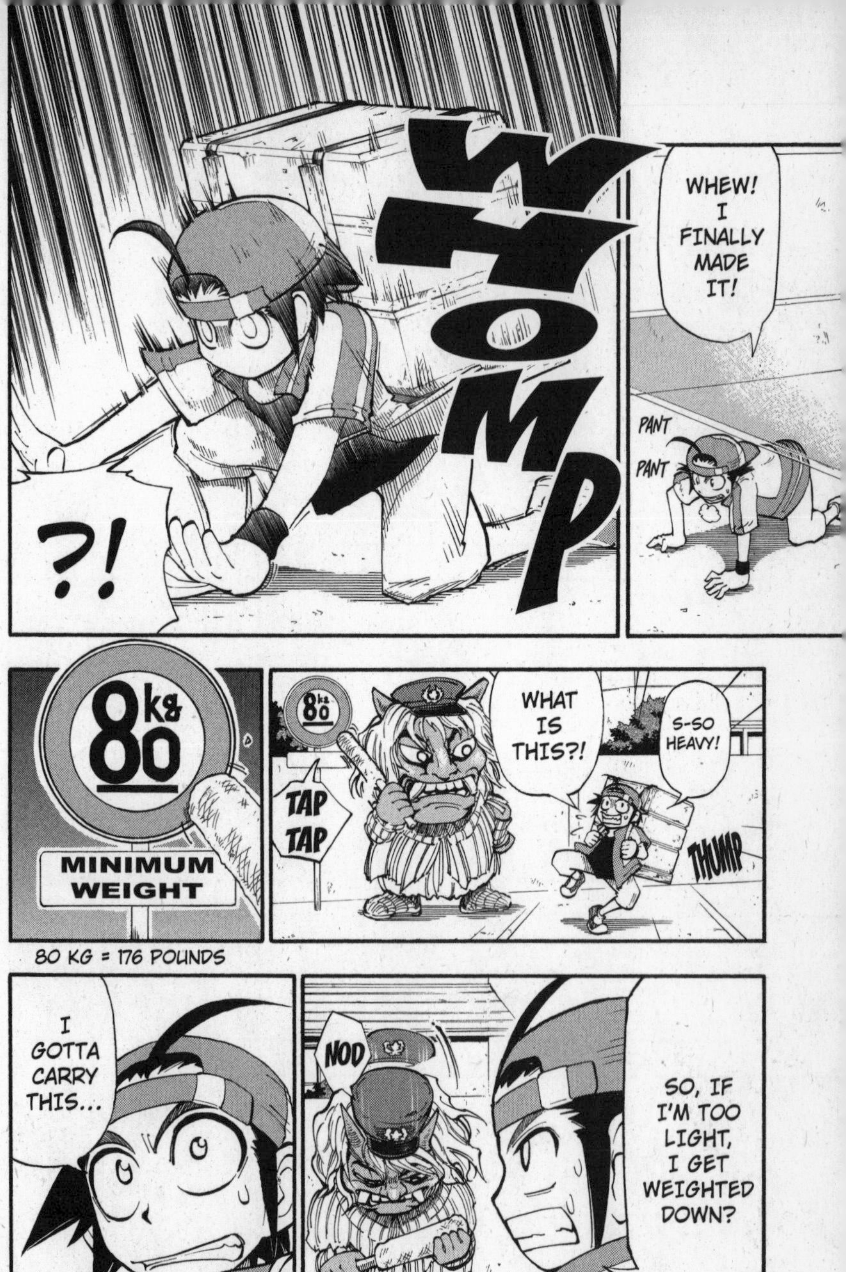
WHEW! I FINALLY MADE IT!
PANT
PANT
WHOMP
?!
S-SO HEAVY!
THUMP
WHAT IS THIS?!
TAP TAP
80 kg
MINIMUM WEIGHT
SO, IF I'M TOO LIGHT, I GET WEIGHTED DOWN?
NOD
I GOTTA CARRY THIS...

80 KG = 176 POUNDS

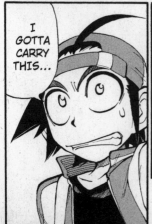

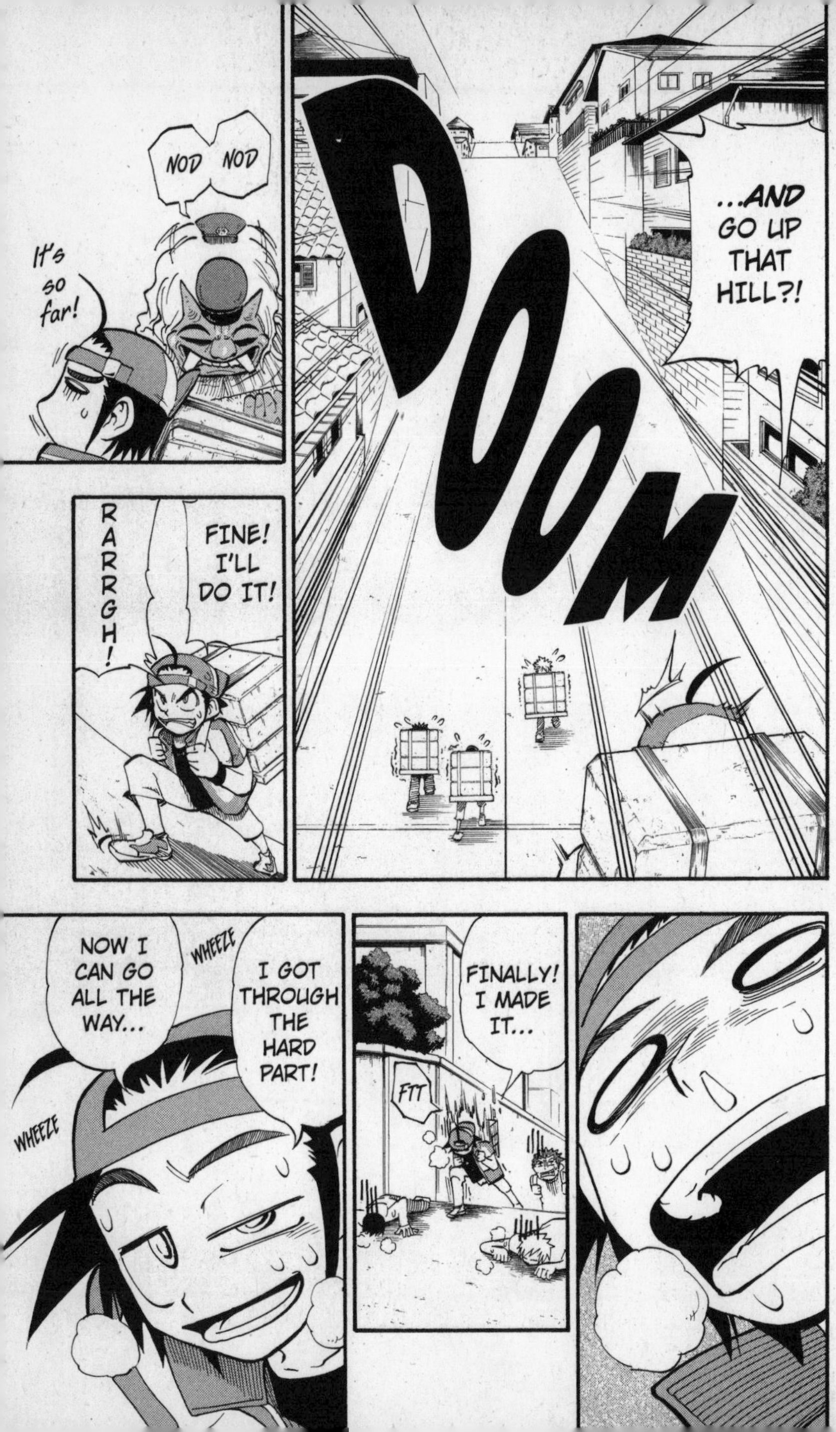
DOOM
...AND GO UP THAT HILL?!
NOD NOD
It's so far!
FINE! I'LL DO IT!
RARRGH!
FINALLY! I MADE IT...
FTT
I GOT THROUGH THE HARD PART!
WHEEZE
NOW I CAN GO ALL THE WAY...
WHEEZE

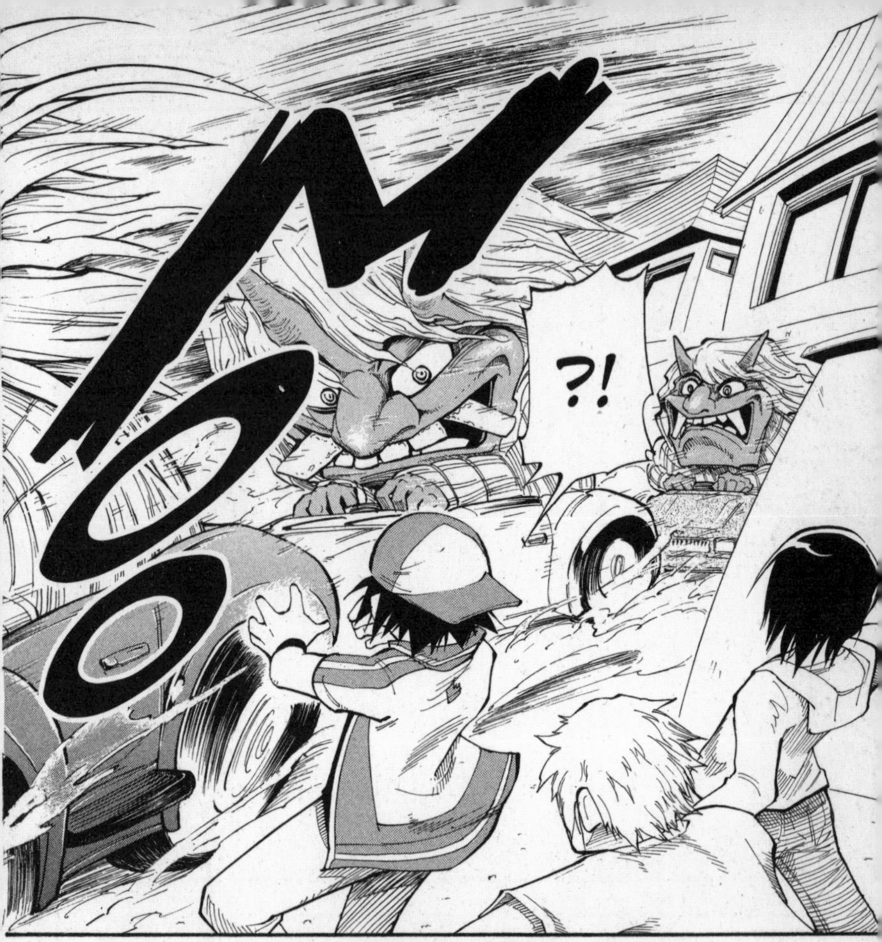
?!
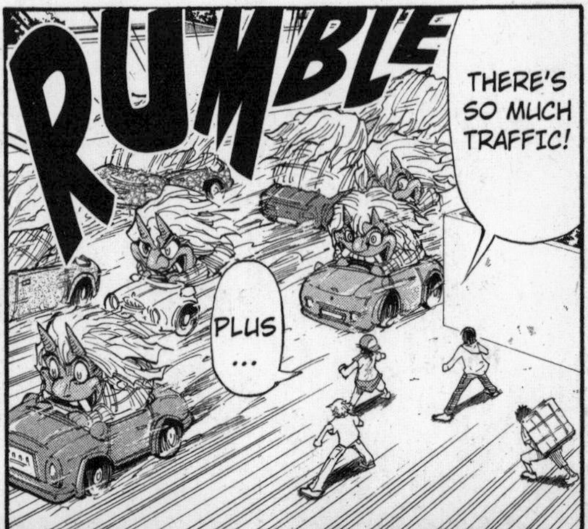
RUMBLE
THERE'S SO MUCH TRAFFIC!
PLUS ...
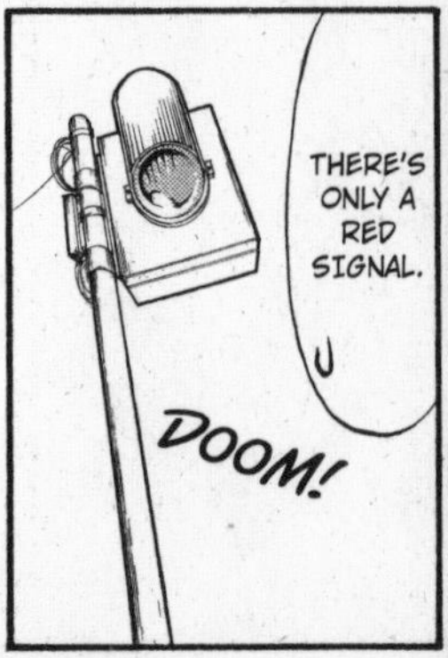
THERE'S ONLY A RED SIGNAL.
DOOM!

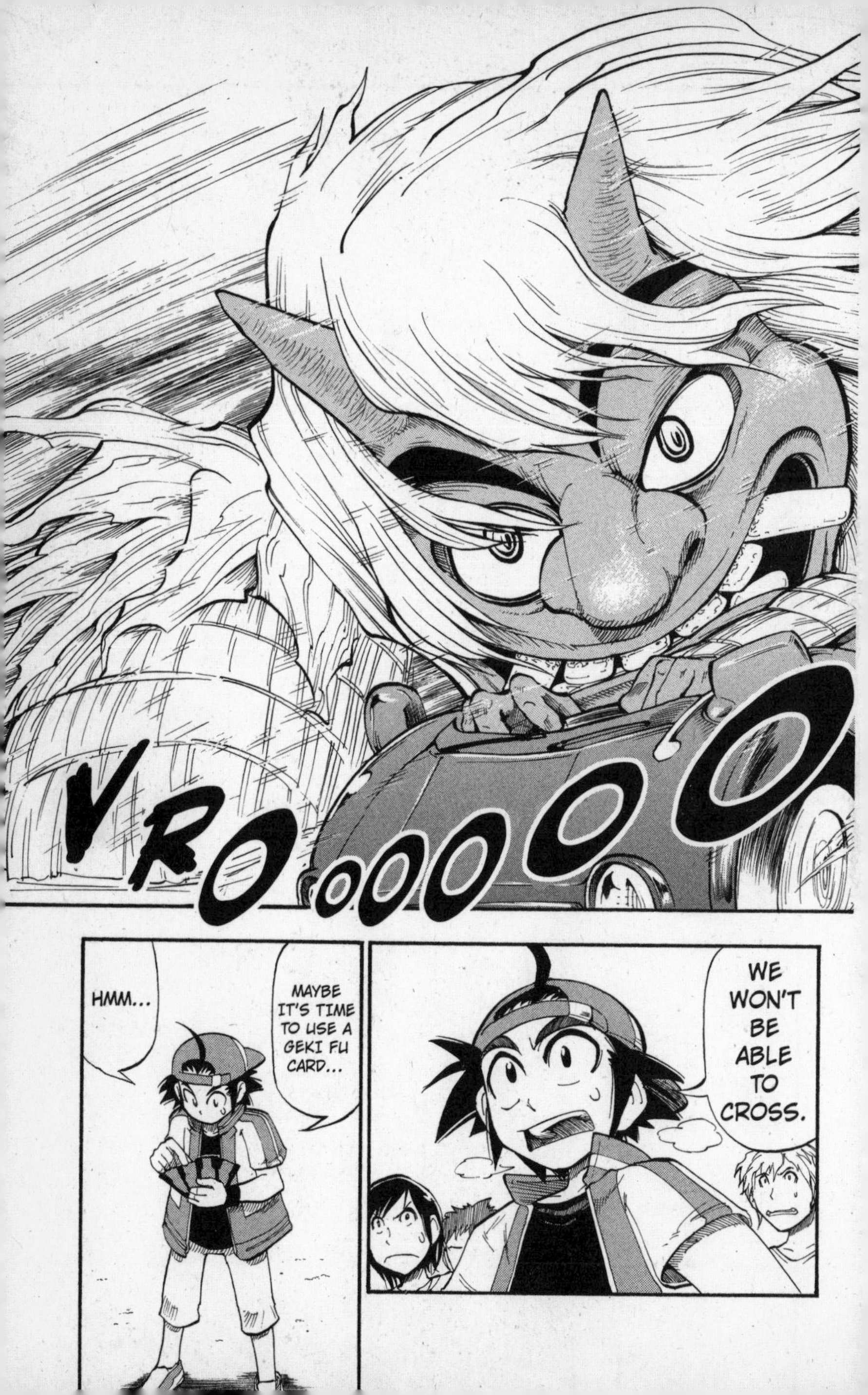
VROOOOOO
WE WON'T BE ABLE TO CROSS.
MAYBE IT'S TIME TO USE A GEKI FU CARD...
HMM...

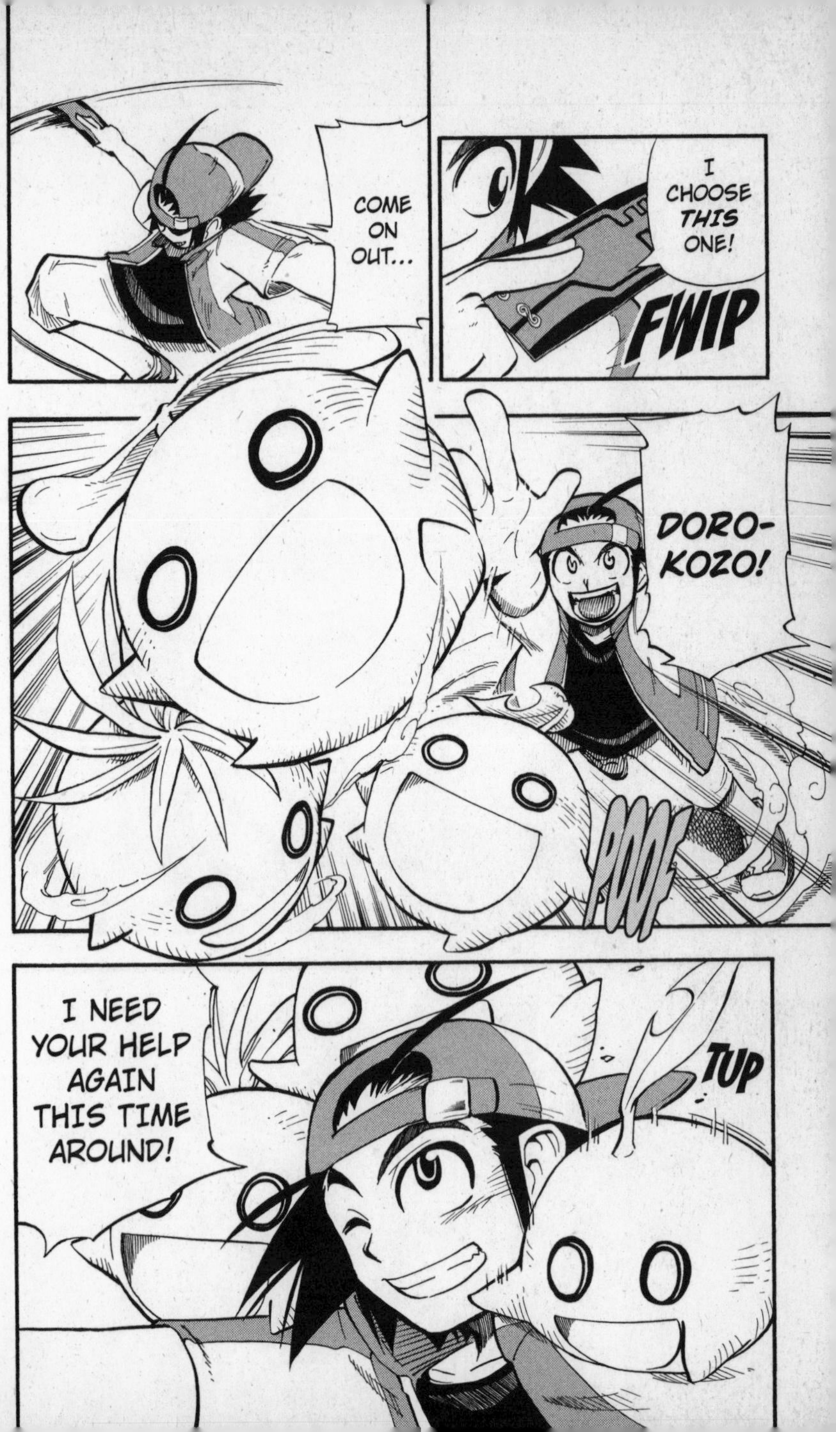
I CHOOSE THIS ONE!
FWIP
COME ON OUT...
DORO-KOZO!
POOF
I NEED YOUR HELP AGAIN THIS TIME AROUND!
TUP

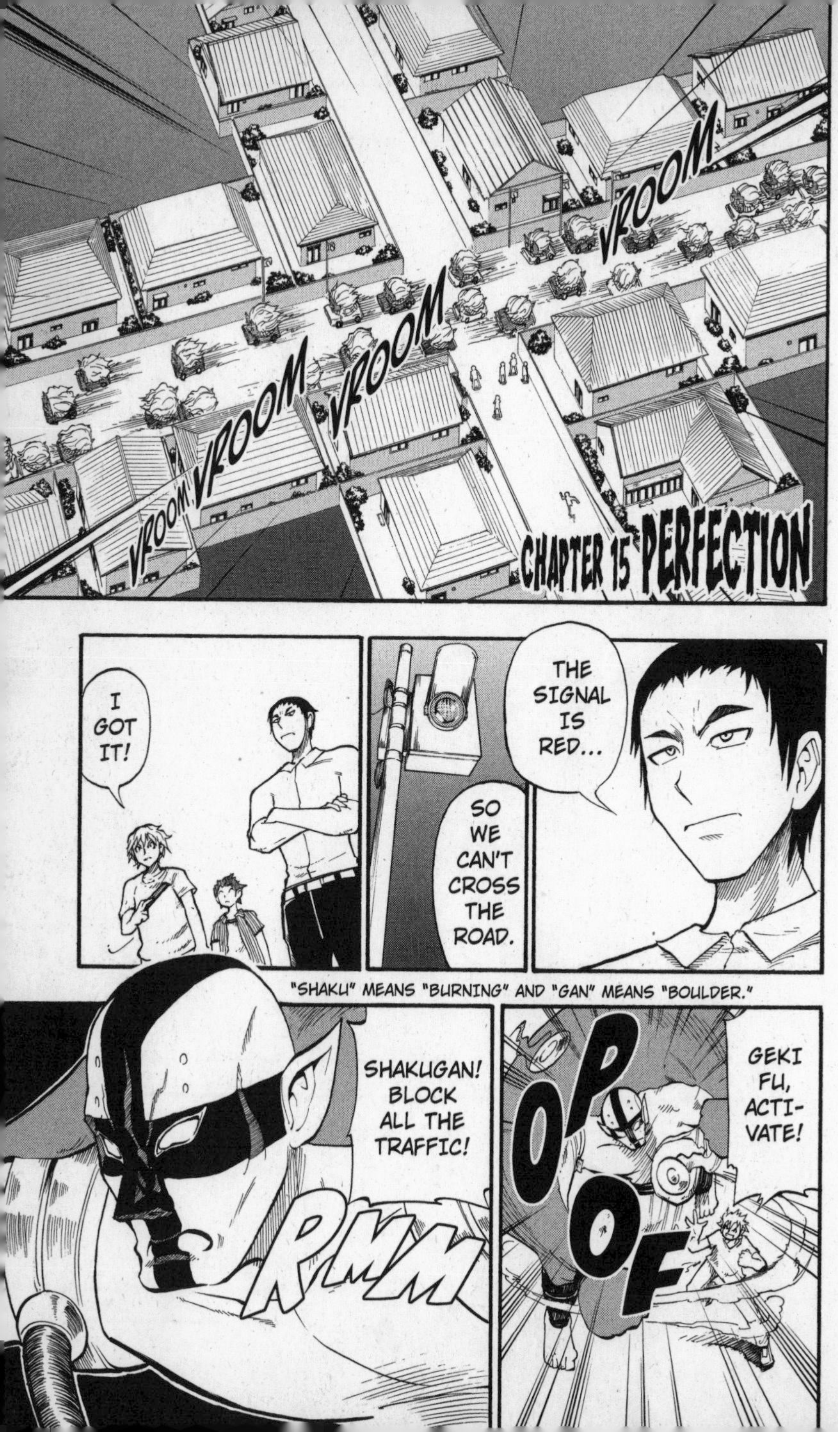
VROOM
VROOM
VROOM
VROOM
VROOM
CHAPTER 15 PERFECTION
THE SIGNAL IS RED...
SO WE CAN'T CROSS THE ROAD.
I GOT IT!
GEKI FU, ACTI-VATE!
POOF
SHAKUGAN! BLOCK ALL THE TRAFFIC!
RMM

"SHAKU" MEANS "BURNING" AND "GAN" MEANS "BOULDER."

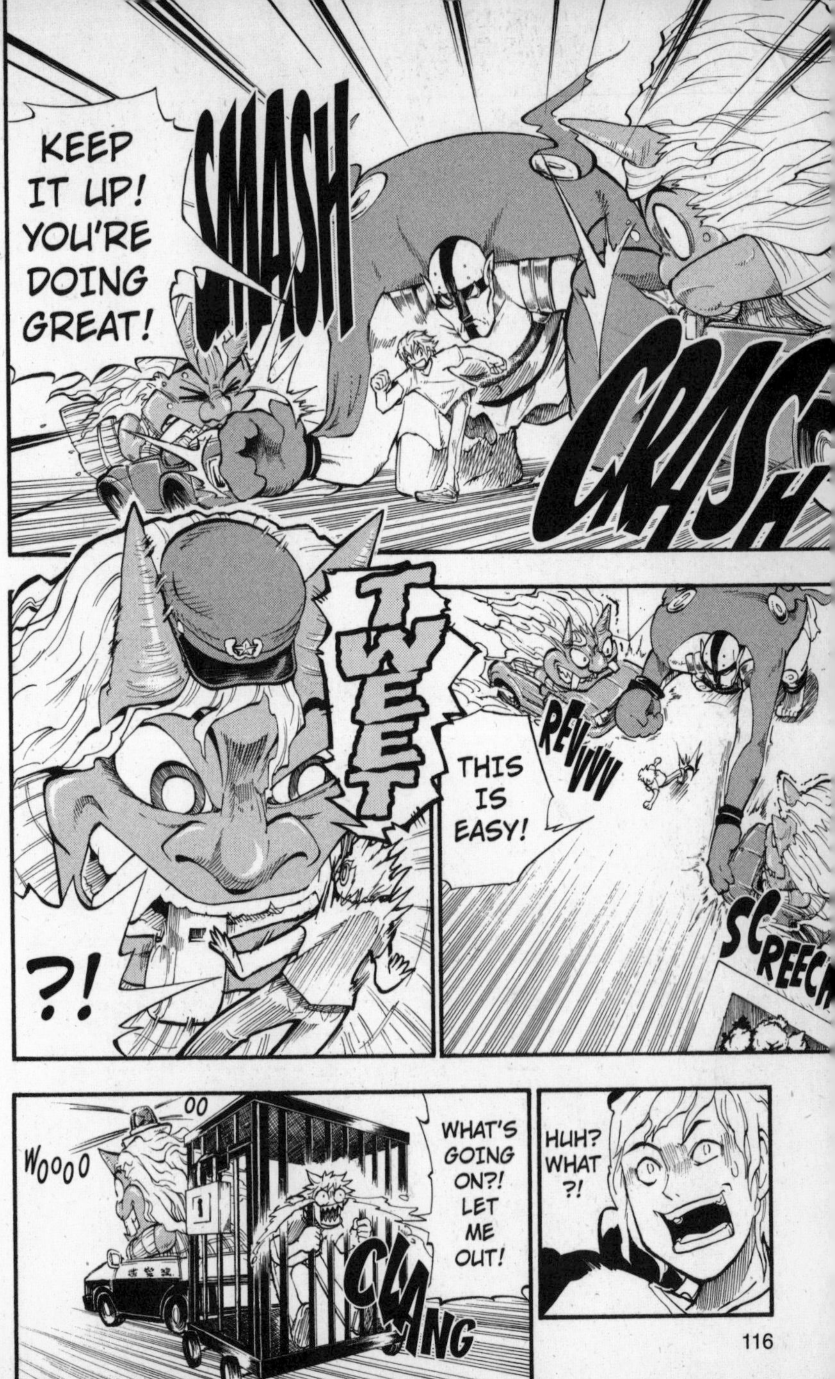
SMASH
KEEP IT UP! YOU'RE DOING GREAT!
CRASH
REVVVVV
THIS IS EASY!
SCREECH
TWEET
?!
HUH? WHAT?!
WHAT'S GOING ON?! LET ME OUT!
OO
WOOOO
CLANG

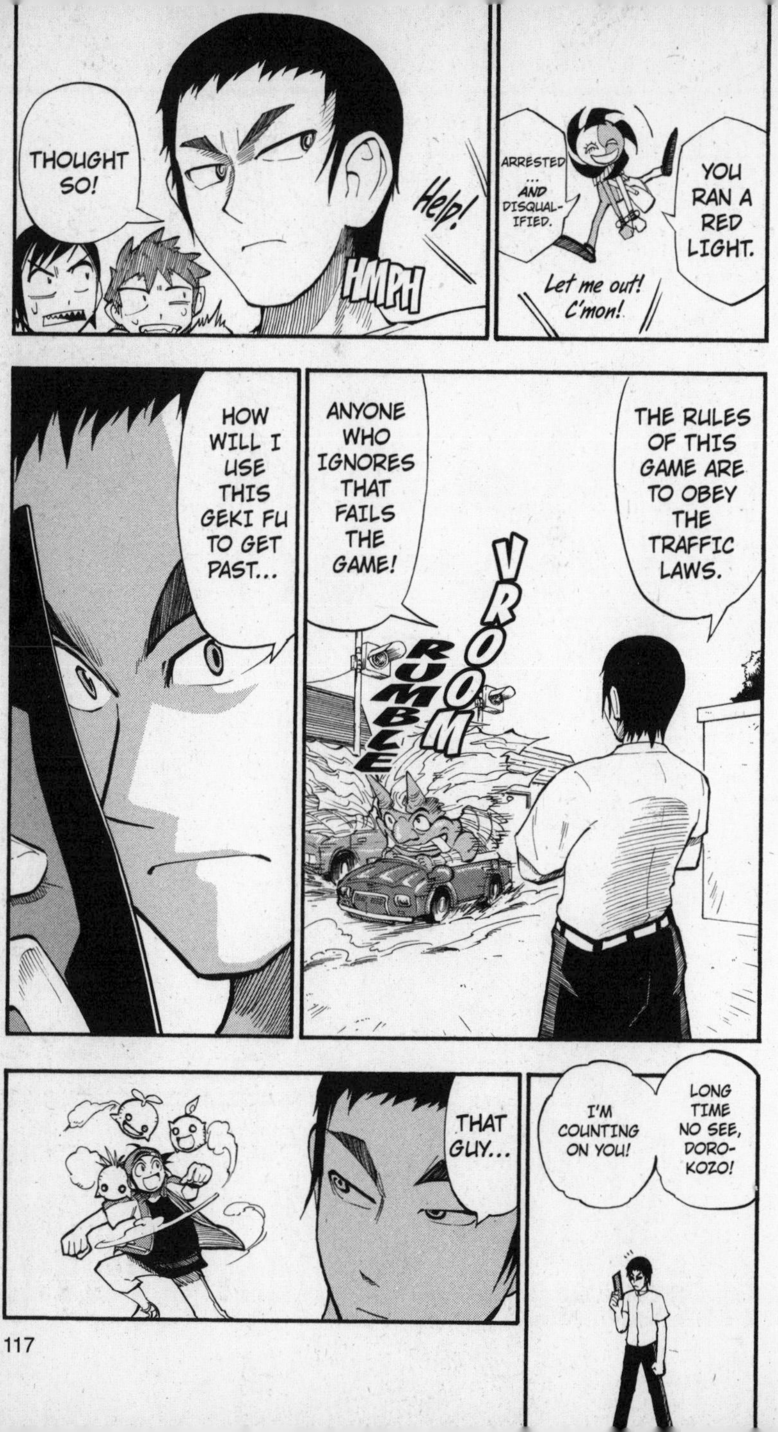
YOU RAN A RED LIGHT.
ARRESTED ... AND DISQUALIFIED.
Let me out! C'mon!
Help!
HMPH
THOUGHT SO!
THE RULES OF THIS GAME ARE TO OBEY THE TRAFFIC LAWS.
VROOOM
RUMBLE
ANYONE WHO IGNORES THAT FAILS THE GAME!
HOW WILL I USE THIS GEKI FU TO GET PAST...
LONG TIME NO SEE, DORO-KOZO!
I'M COUNTING ON YOU!
THAT GUY...

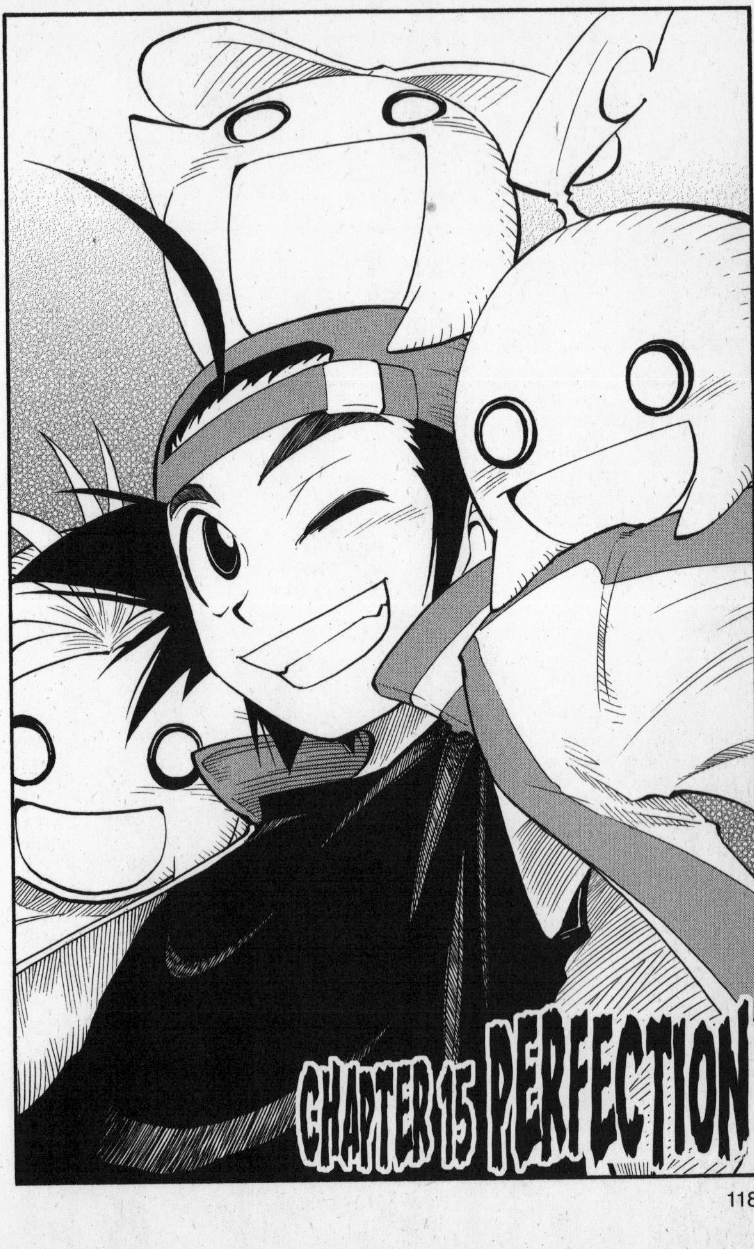
CHAPTER 15 PERFECTION

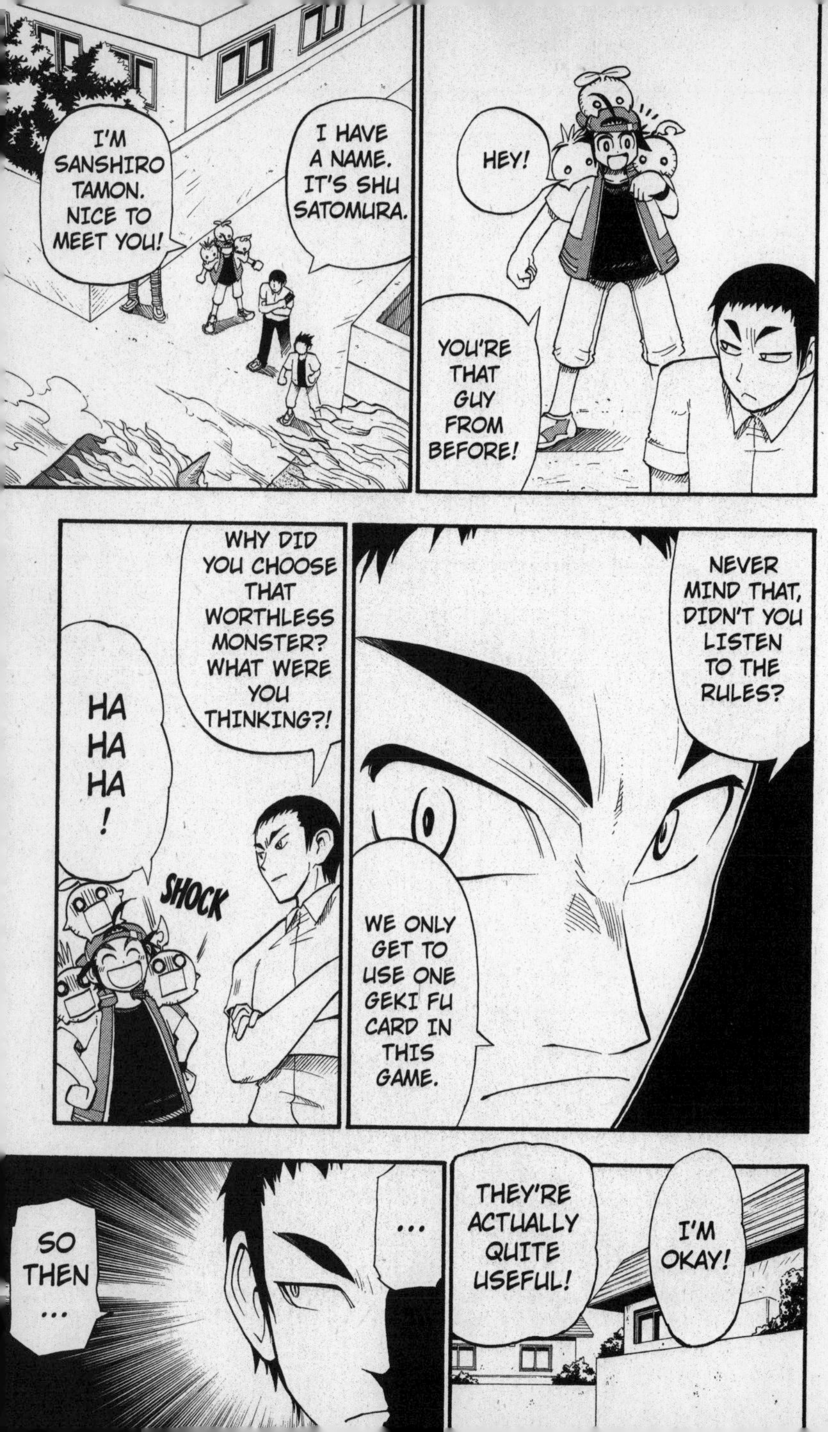
HEY!
YOU'RE THAT GUY FROM BEFORE!
I HAVE A NAME. IT'S SHU SATOMURA.
I'M SANSHIRO TAMON. NICE TO MEET YOU!
NEVER MIND THAT, DIDN'T YOU LISTEN TO THE RULES?
WE ONLY GET TO USE ONE GEKI FU CARD IN THIS GAME.
WHY DID YOU CHOOSE THAT WORTHLESS MONSTER? WHAT WERE YOU THINKING?!
HA HA HA!
SHOCK
I'M OKAY!
THEY'RE ACTUALLY QUITE USEFUL!
...
SO THEN ...

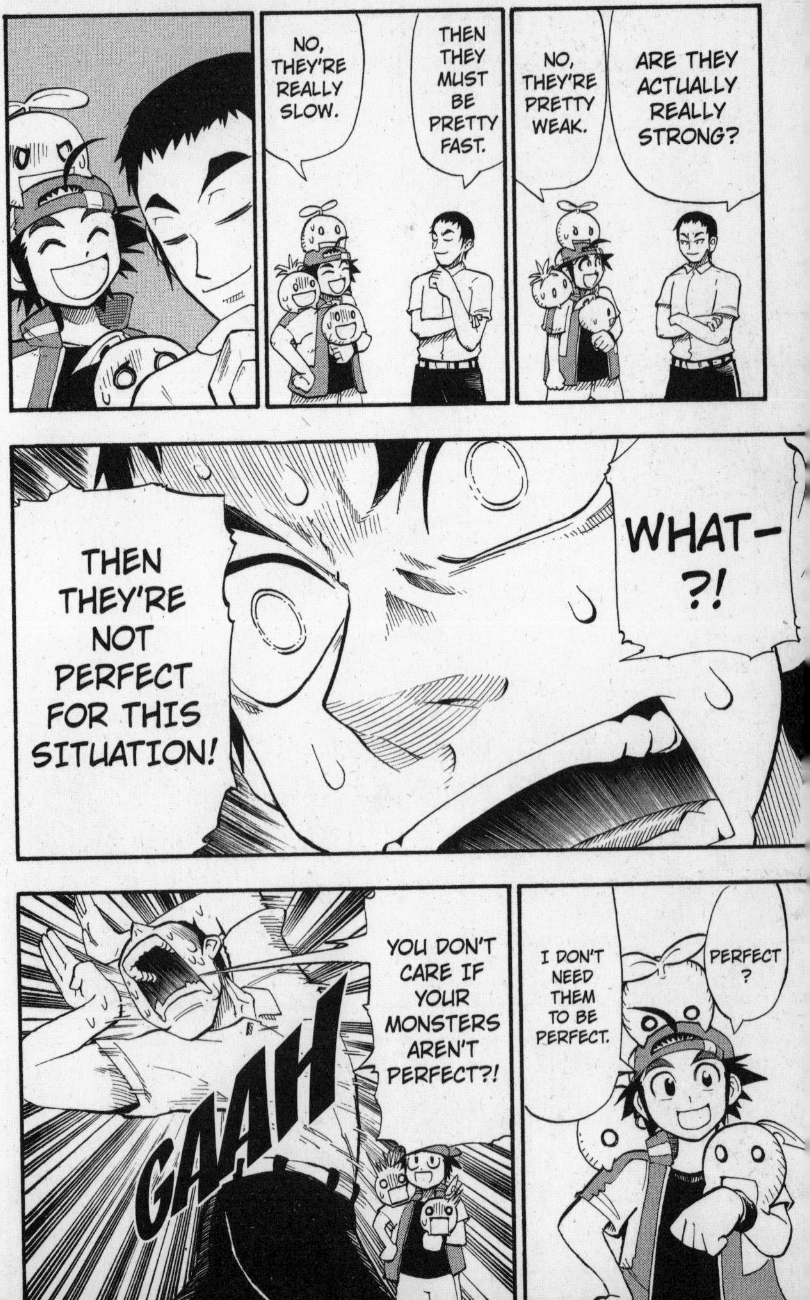
ARE THEY ACTUALLY REALLY STRONG?
NO, THEY'RE PRETTY WEAK.
THEN THEY MUST BE PRETTY FAST.
NO, THEY'RE REALLY SLOW.
WHAT-?!
THEN THEY'RE NOT PERFECT FOR THIS SITUATION!
PERFECT?
I DON'T NEED THEM TO BE PERFECT.
YOU DON'T CARE IF YOUR MONSTERS AREN'T PERFECT?!
GAAH

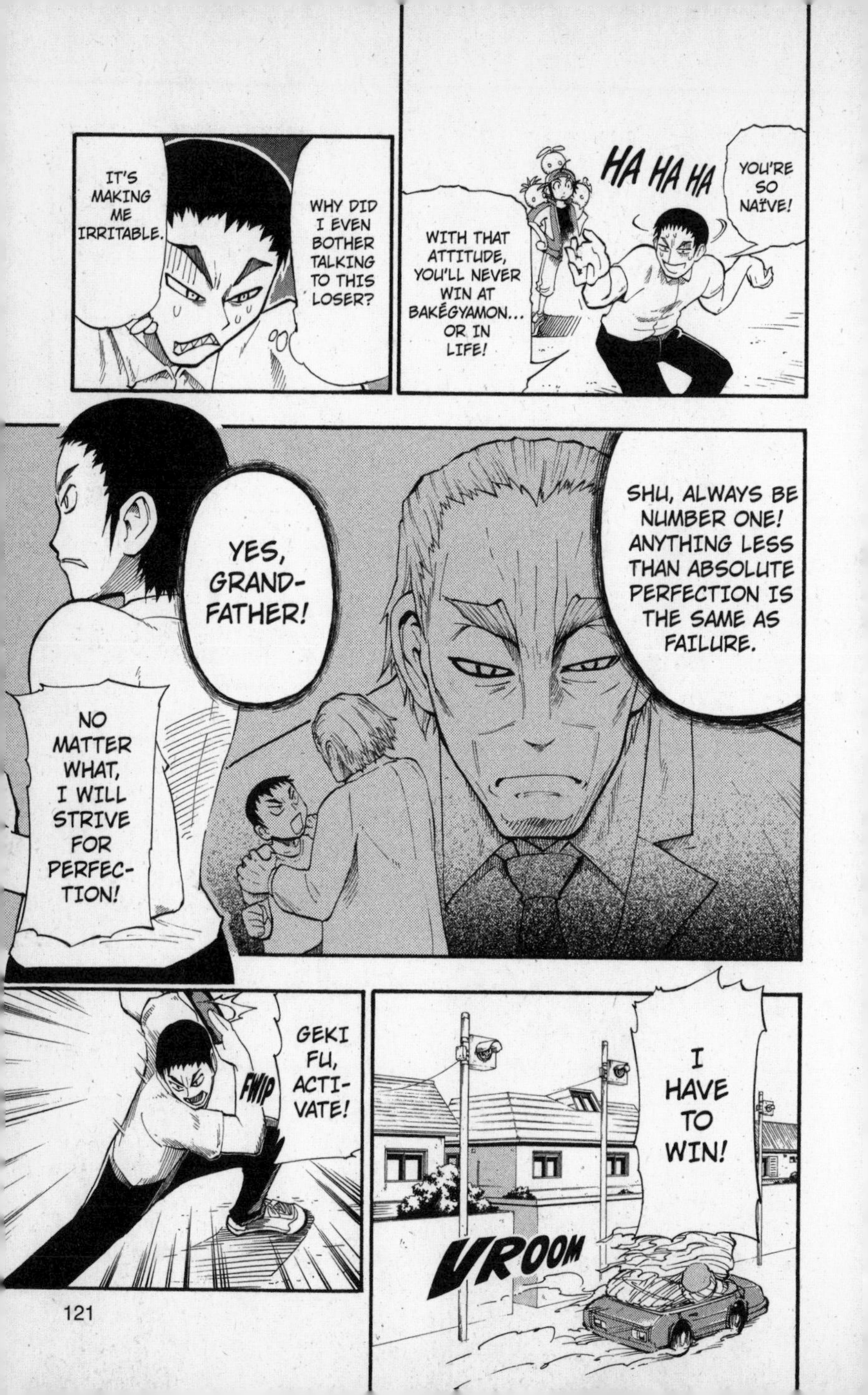
YOU'RE SO NAÏVE!
HA HA HA
WITH THAT ATTITUDE, YOU'LL NEVER WIN AT BAKÉGYAMON... OR IN LIFE!
WHY DID I EVEN BOTHER TALKING TO THIS LOSER?
IT'S MAKING ME IRRITABLE.
SHU, ALWAYS BE NUMBER ONE! ANYTHING LESS THAN ABSOLUTE PERFECTION IS THE SAME AS FAILURE.
YES, GRANDFATHER!
NO MATTER WHAT, I WILL STRIVE FOR PERFECTION!
I HAVE TO WIN!
VROOM
GEKI FU, ACTIVATE!
FWIP

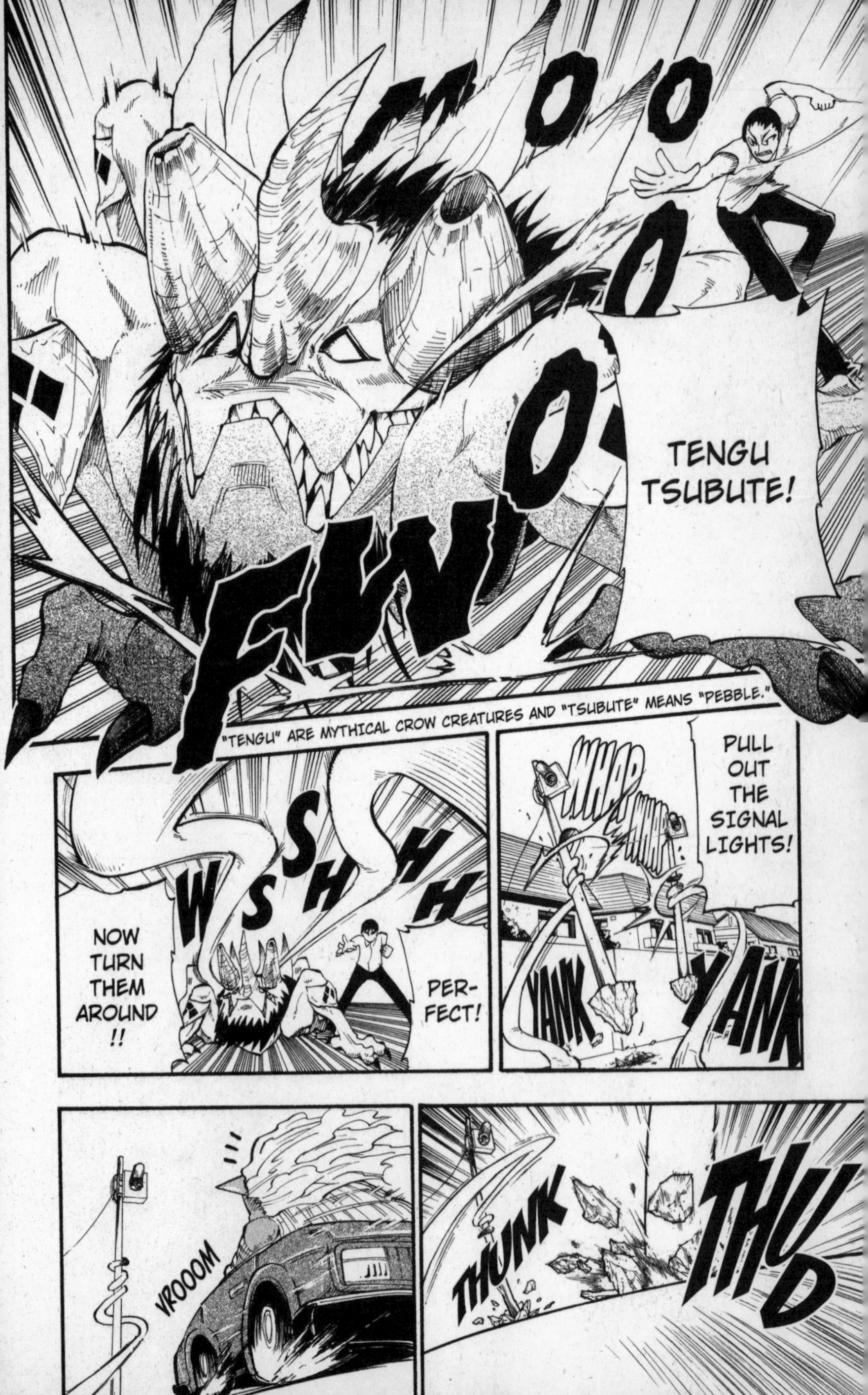
FWOOOOO
TENGU TSUBUTE!
"TENGU" ARE MYTHICAL CROW CREATURES AND "TSUBUTE" MEANS "PEBBLE."
PULL OUT THE SIGNAL LIGHTS!
WHIP
WHIP
YANK
YANK
WSHH
WSHH
PER-FECT!
NOW TURN THEM AROUND!!
THUD
THUNK
VROOOM

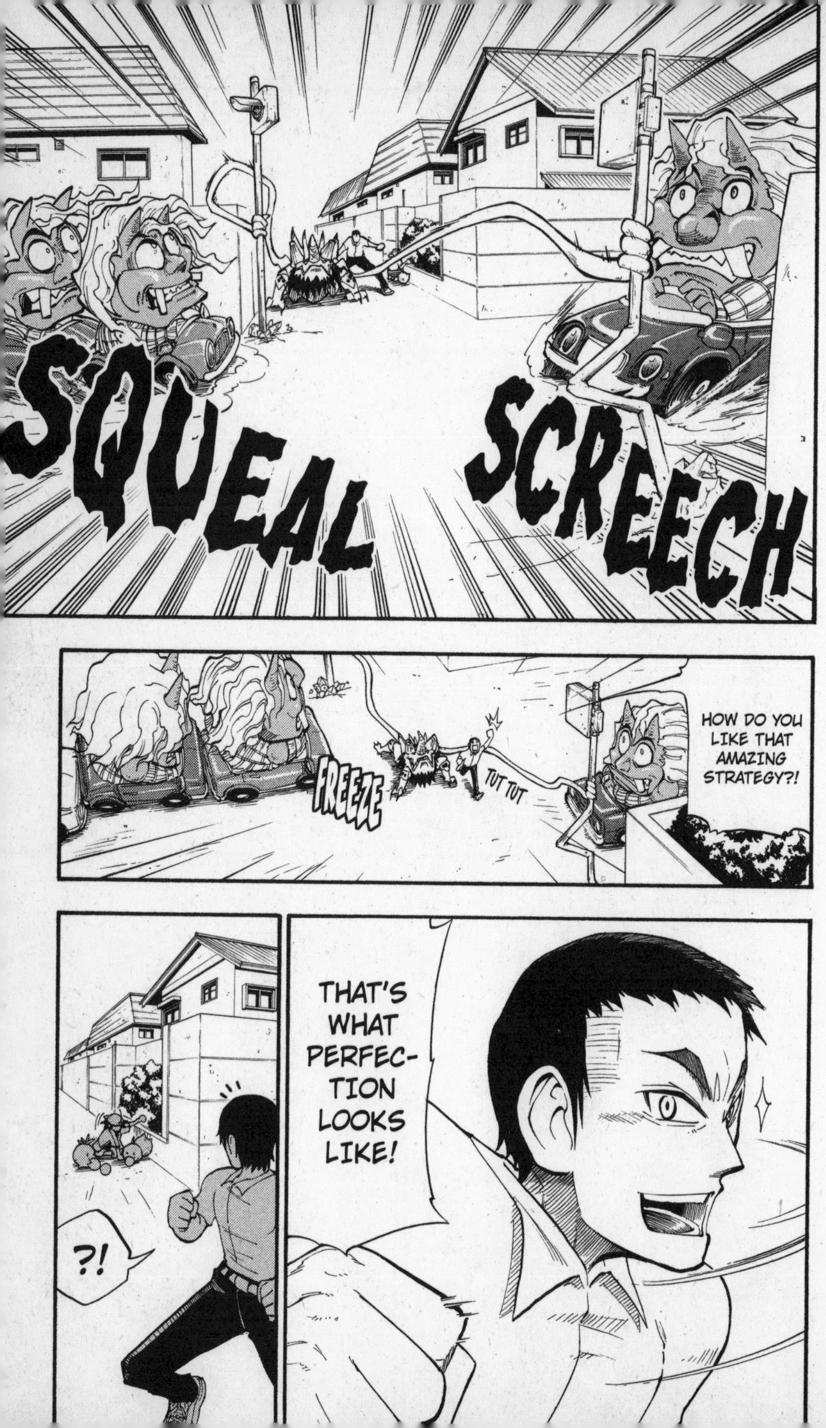
SCREECH
SQUEAL
HOW DO YOU LIKE THAT AMAZING STRATEGY?!
TUT TUT
FREEZE
THAT'S WHAT PERFEC-TION LOOKS LIKE!
?!

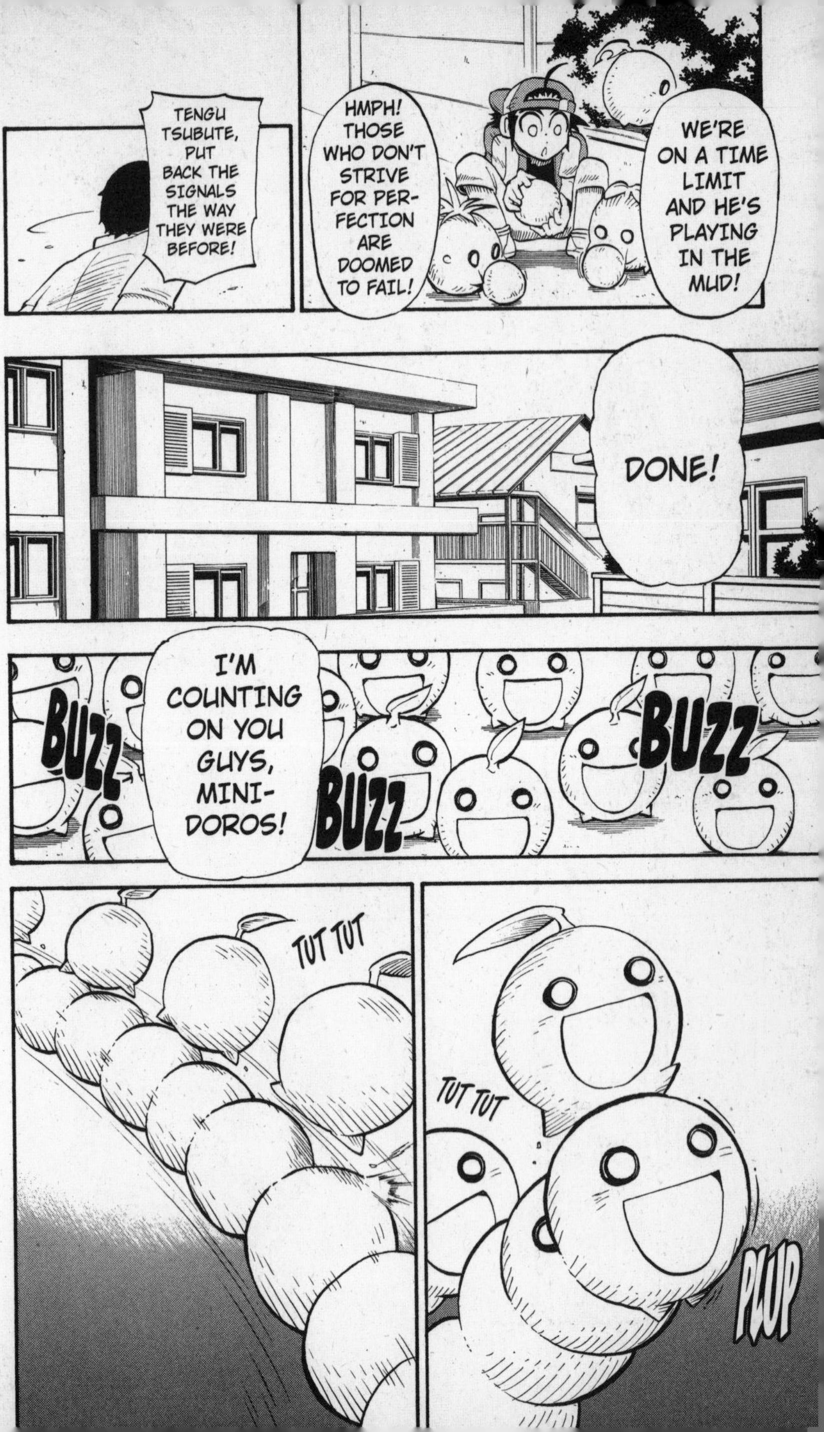
WE'RE ON A TIME LIMIT AND HE'S PLAYING IN THE MUD!
HMPH! THOSE WHO DON'T STRIVE FOR PER-FECTION ARE DOOMED TO FAIL!
TENGU TSUBUTE, PUT BACK THE SIGNALS THE WAY THEY WERE BEFORE!
DONE!
BUZZ
BUZZ
I'M COUNTING ON YOU GUYS, MINI-DOROS!
BUZZ
TUT TUT
PLUP
TUT TUT

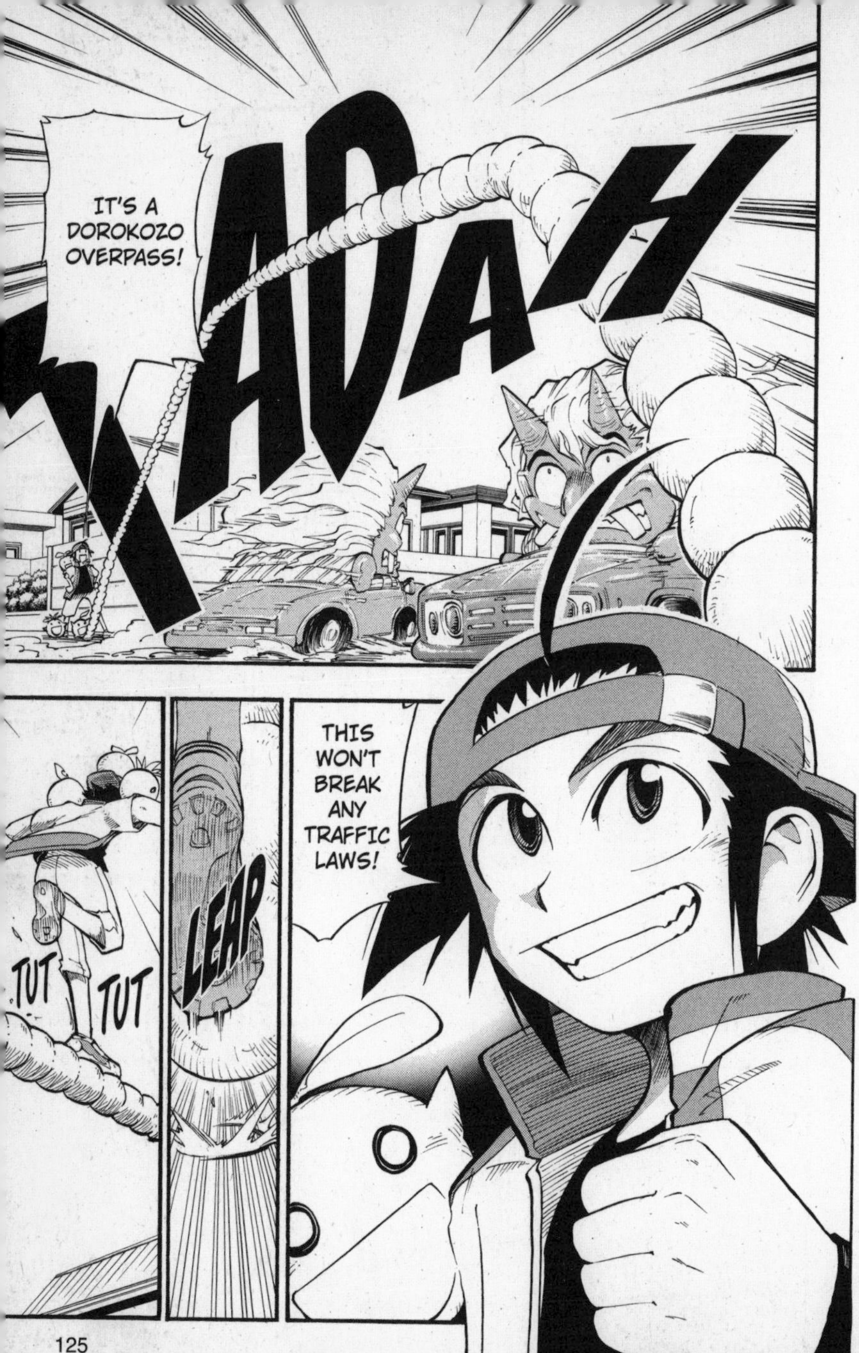
IT'S A DOROKOZO OVERPASS!
THIS WON'T BREAK ANY TRAFFIC LAWS!
LEAP
TUT
TUT

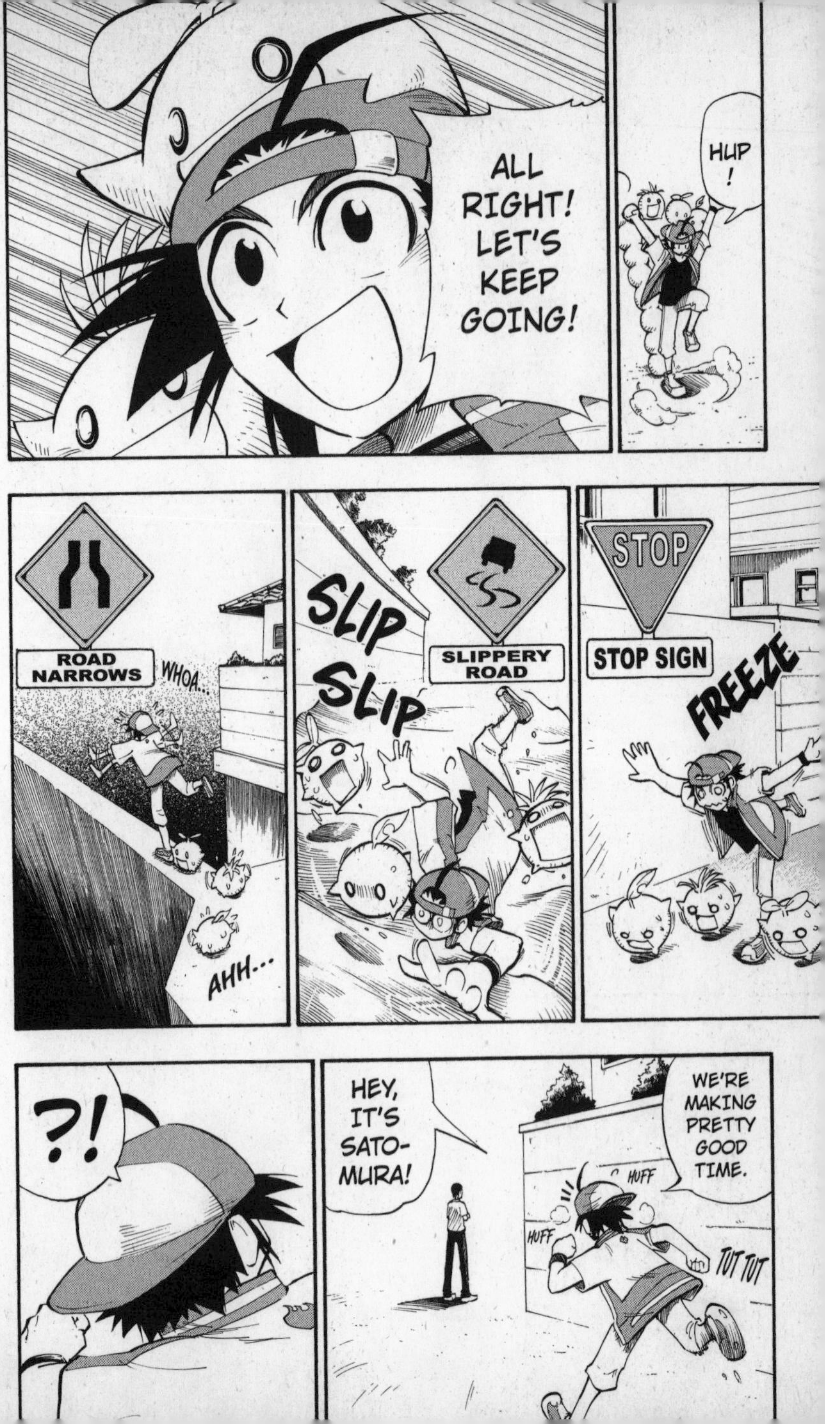
HUP!
ALL RIGHT! LET'S KEEP GOING!
STOP
STOP SIGN
FREEZE
SLIPPERY ROAD
SLIP SLIP
ROAD NARROWS
WHOA...
AHH...
WE'RE MAKING PRETTY GOOD TIME.
HEY, IT'S SATO-MURA!
HUFF
HUFF
TUT TUT
?!

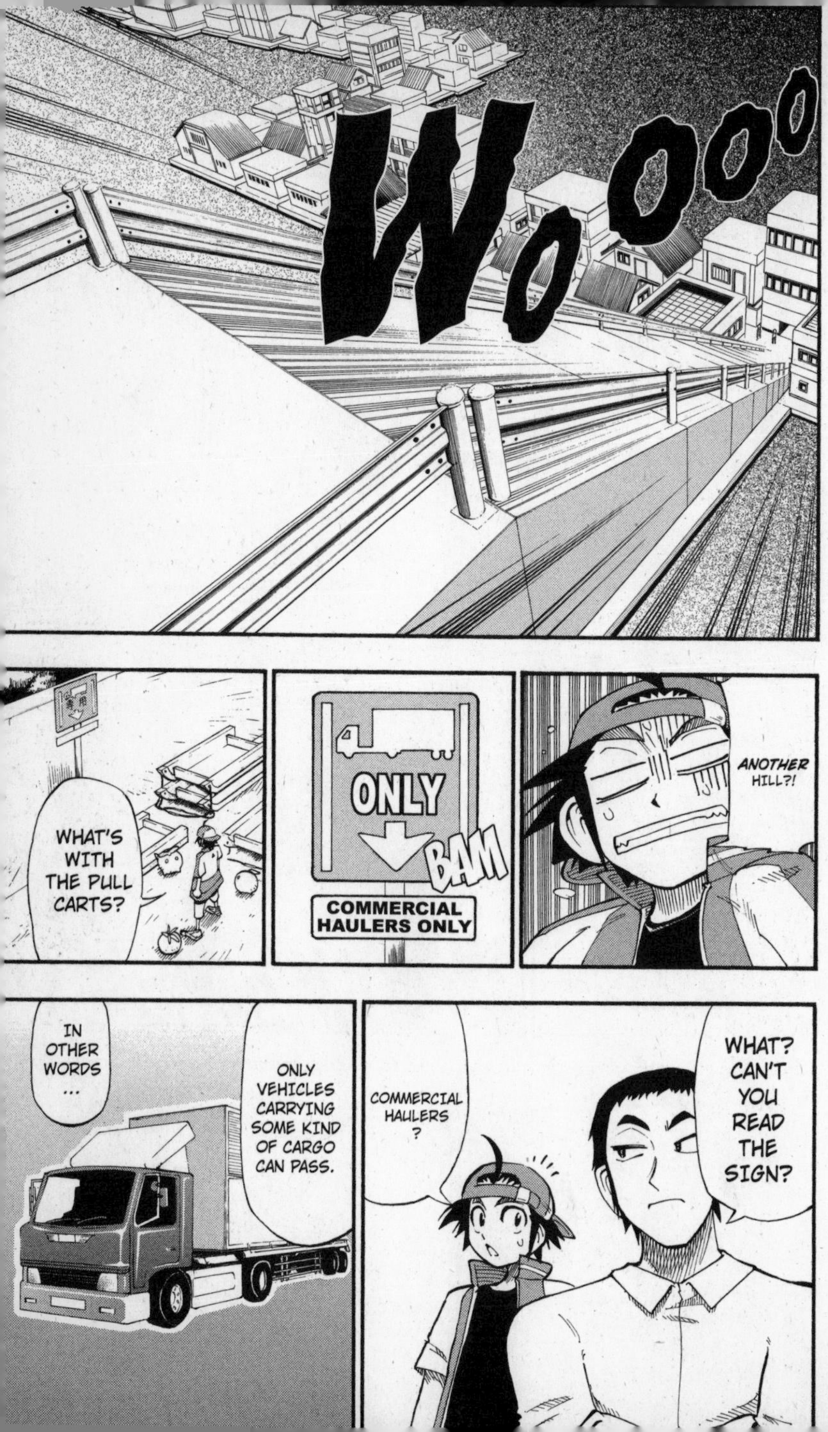
WOOOOO
ANOTHER HILL?!
ONLY
BAM
COMMERCIAL HAULERS ONLY
WHAT'S WITH THE PULL CARTS?
WHAT? CAN'T YOU READ THE SIGN?
COMMERCIAL HAULERS?
IN OTHER WORDS...
ONLY VEHICLES CARRYING SOME KIND OF CARGO CAN PASS.

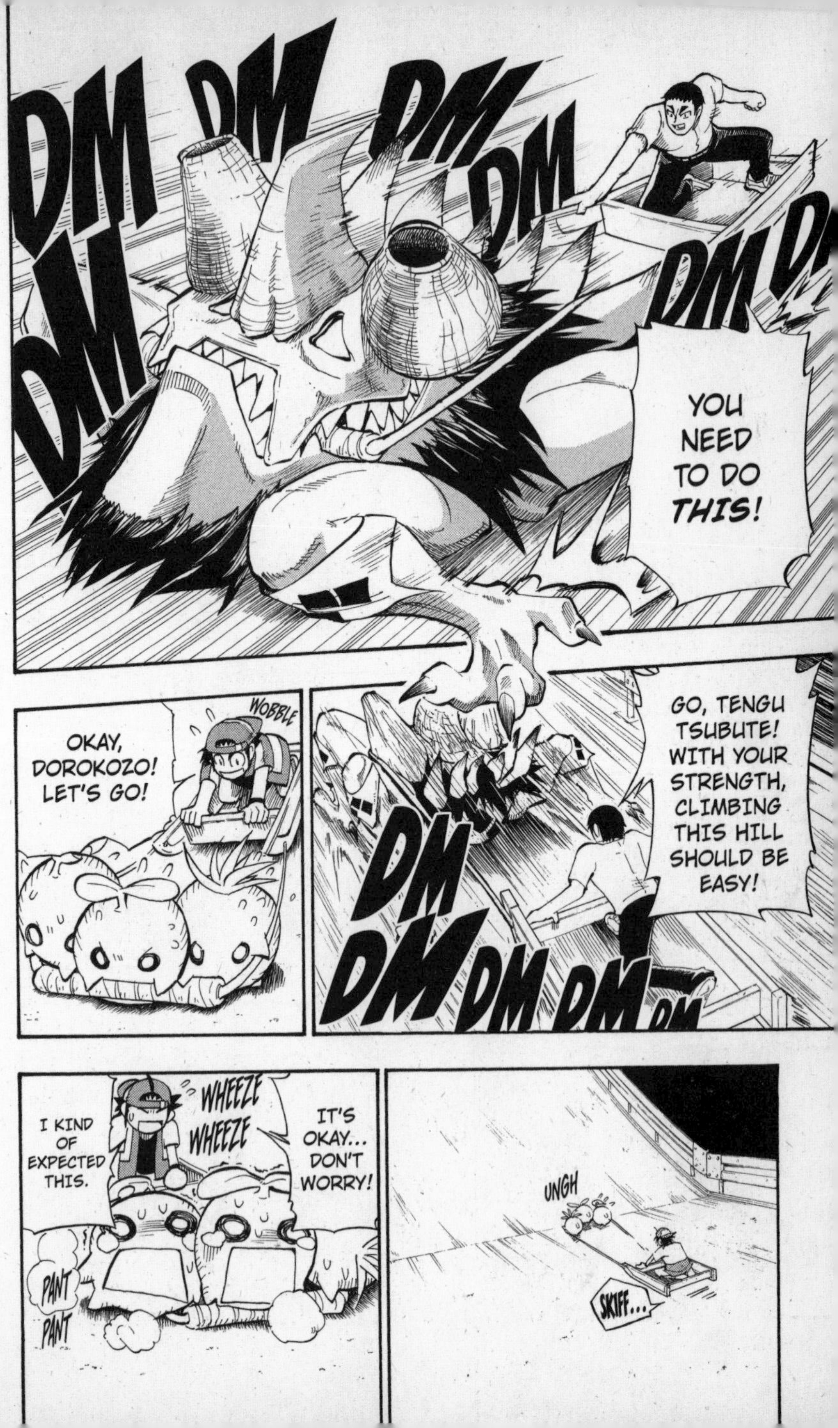
DM DM DM DM DM DM DM DM
YOU NEED TO DO THIS!
GO, TENGU TSUBUTE! WITH YOUR STRENGTH, CLIMBING THIS HILL SHOULD BE EASY!
DM DM DM DM DM DM
WOBBLE
OKAY, DOROKOZO! LET'S GO!
UNGH
SKIFF...
WHEEZE WHEEZE
IT'S OKAY... DON'T WORRY!
I KIND OF EXPECTED THIS.
PANT PANT

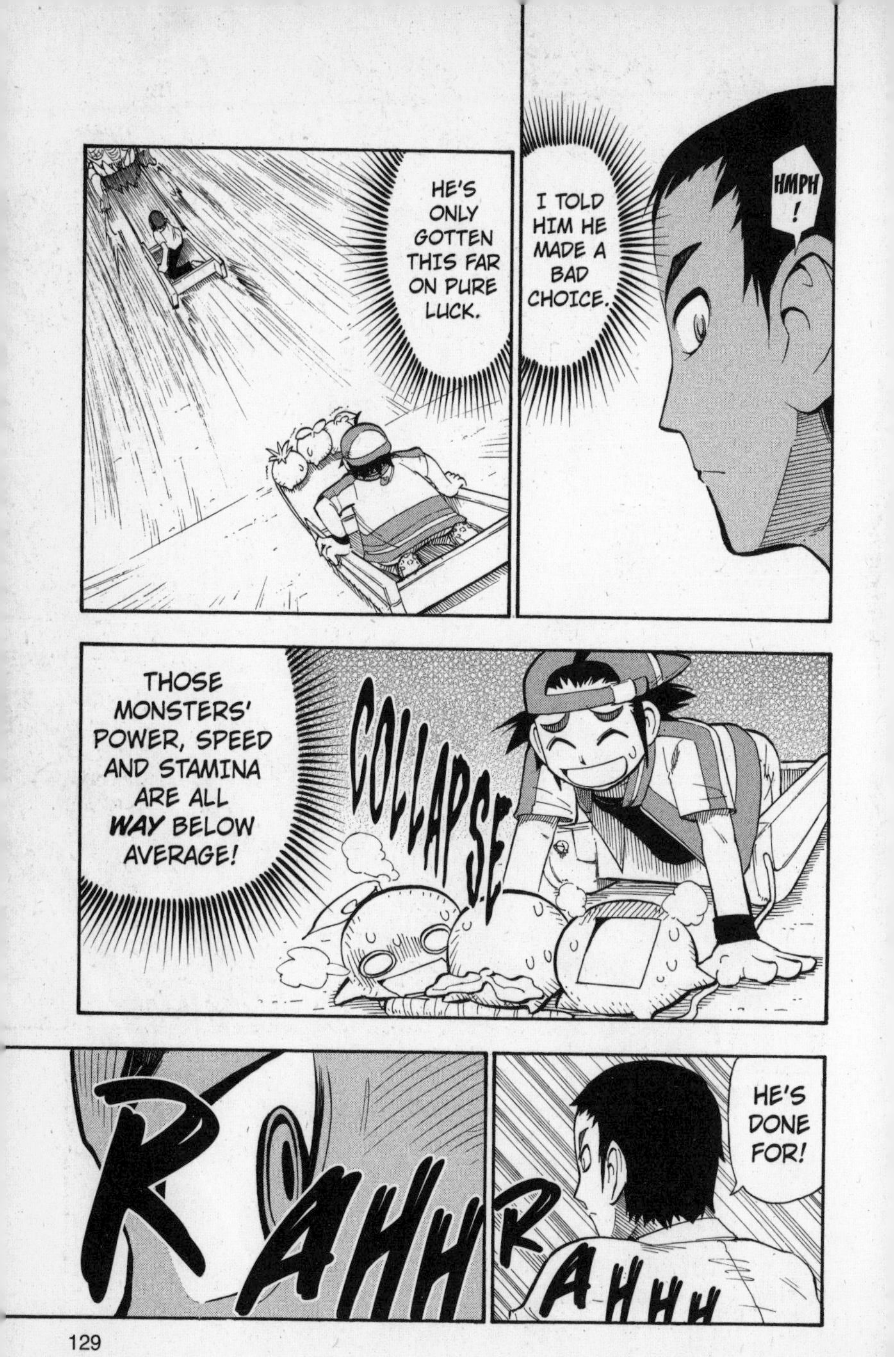
HMPH!
I TOLD HIM HE MADE A BAD CHOICE.
HE'S ONLY GOTTEN THIS FAR ON PURE LUCK.
THOSE MONSTERS' POWER, SPEED AND STAMINA ARE ALL **WAY** BELOW AVERAGE!
COLLAPSE
HE'S DONE FOR!
RAHHH
RAHHR

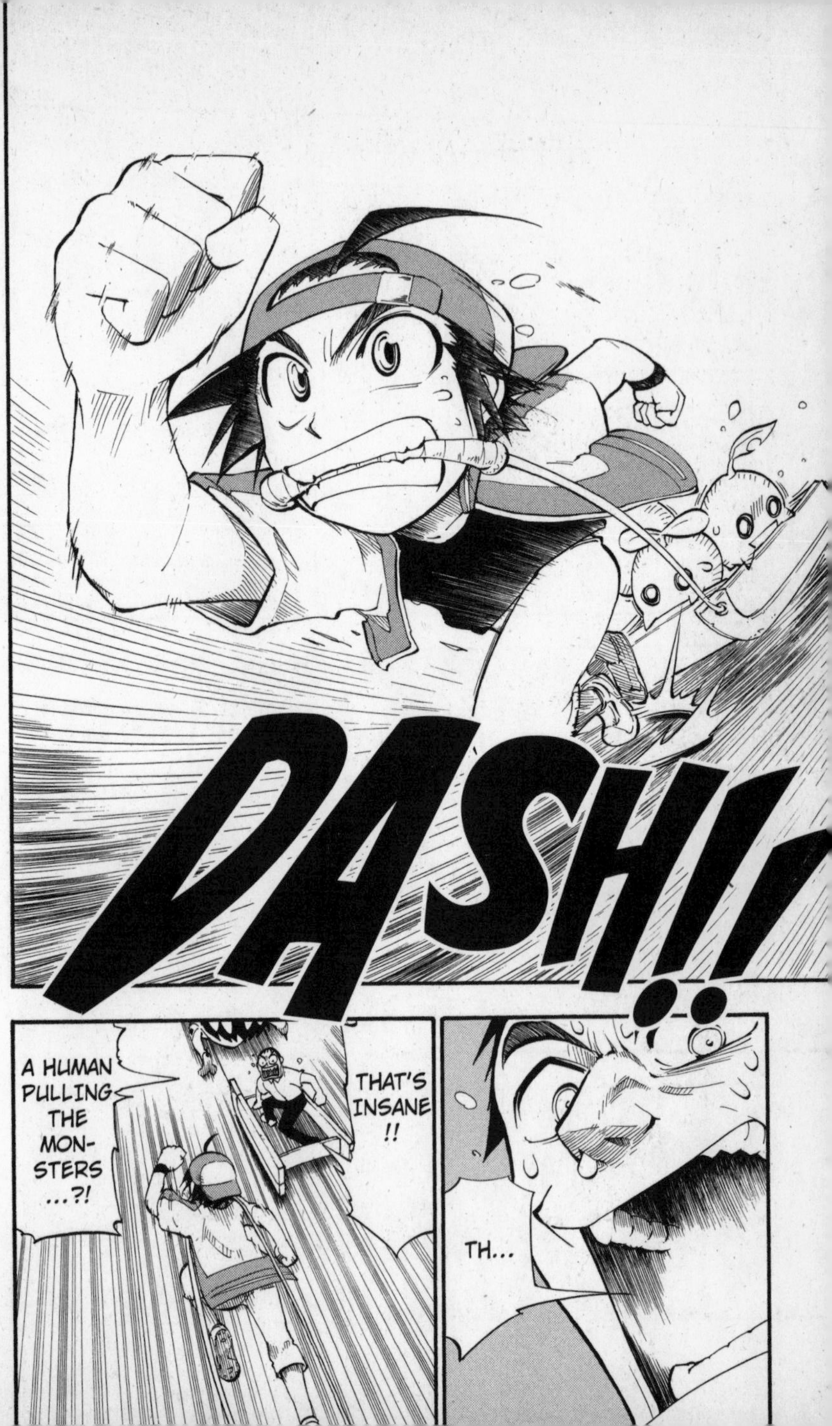
DASH!!
TH...
THAT'S INSANE!!
A HUMAN PULLING THE MON-STERS...?!

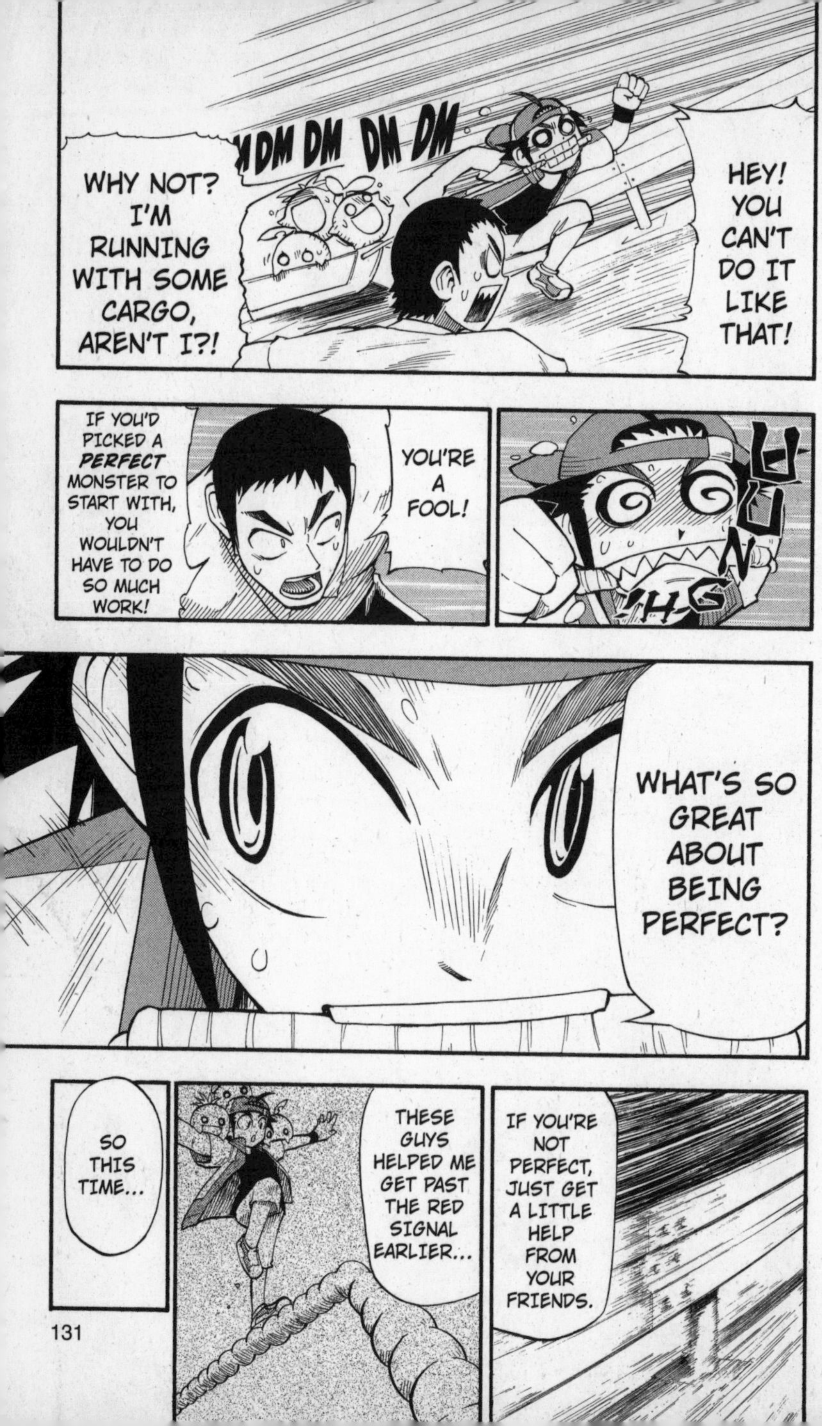
HEY! YOU CAN'T DO IT LIKE THAT!
DM DM DM DM
WHY NOT? I'M RUNNING WITH SOME CARGO, AREN'T I?!
UUNGH!
YOU'RE A FOOL!
IF YOU'D PICKED A *PERFECT* MONSTER TO START WITH, YOU WOULDN'T HAVE TO DO SO MUCH WORK!
WHAT'S SO GREAT ABOUT BEING PERFECT?
IF YOU'RE NOT PERFECT, JUST GET A LITTLE HELP FROM YOUR FRIENDS.
THESE GUYS HELPED ME GET PAST THE RED SIGNAL EARLIER...
SO THIS TIME...

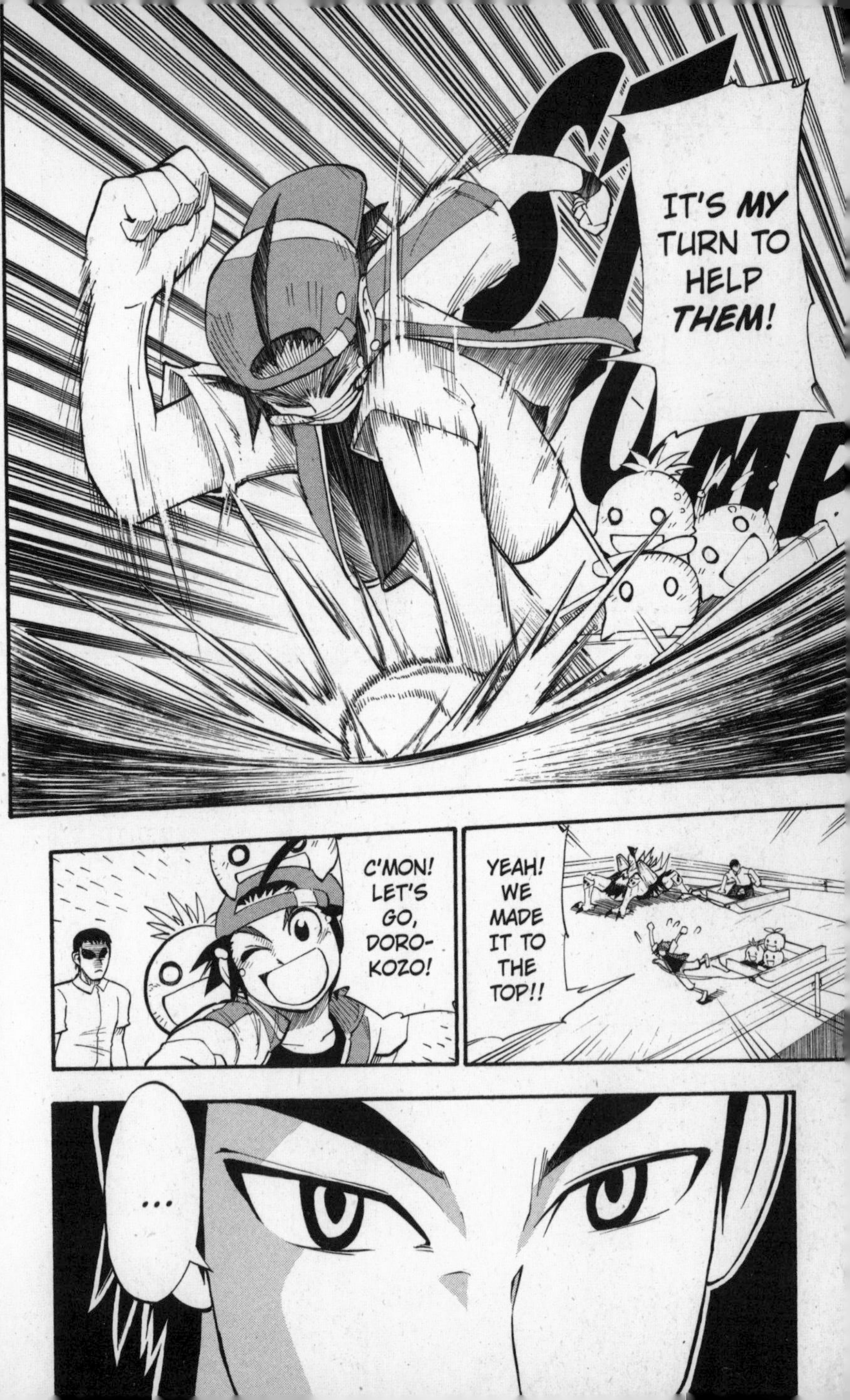
IT'S *MY* TURN TO HELP *THEM!*
YEAH! WE MADE IT TO THE TOP!!
C'MON! LET'S GO, DORO-KOZO!
...

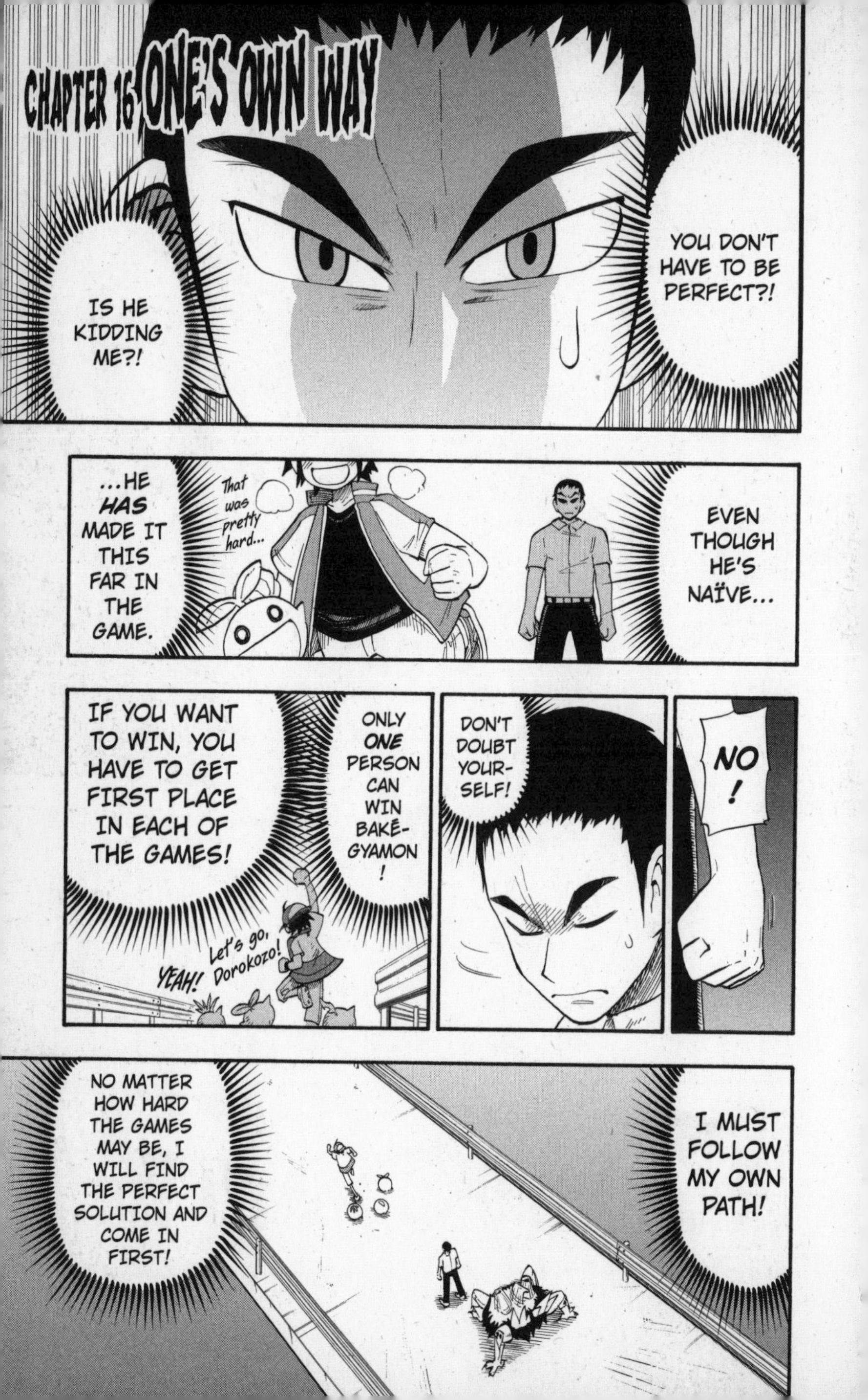
CHAPTER 16 ONE'S OWN WAY
YOU DON'T HAVE TO BE PERFECT?!
IS HE KIDDING ME?!
EVEN THOUGH HE'S NAÏVE...
...HE HAS MADE IT THIS FAR IN THE GAME.
That was pretty hard...
NO!
DON'T DOUBT YOURSELF!
ONLY ONE PERSON CAN WIN BAKÉ-GYAMON!
IF YOU WANT TO WIN, YOU HAVE TO GET FIRST PLACE IN EACH OF THE GAMES!
Let's go, Dorokozo!
YEAH!
I MUST FOLLOW MY OWN PATH!
NO MATTER HOW HARD THE GAMES MAY BE, I WILL FIND THE PERFECT SOLUTION AND COME IN FIRST!

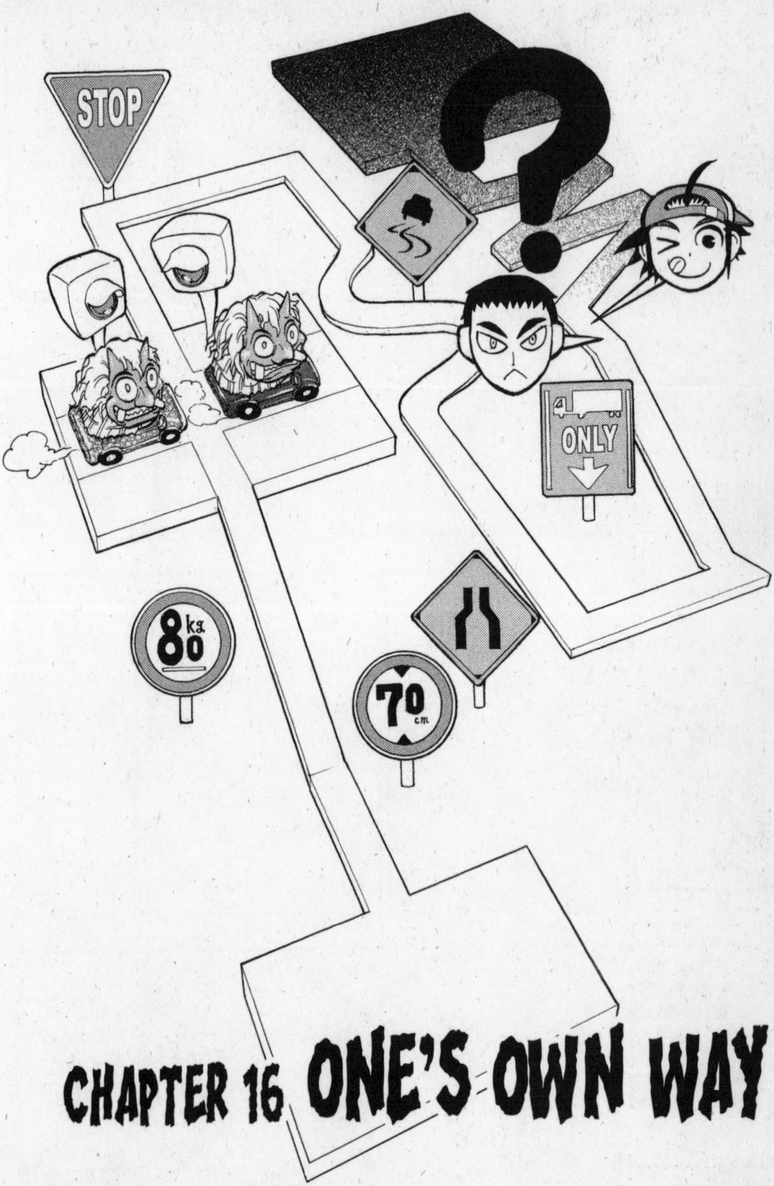
STOP
ONLY
80 kg
70 cm

CHAPTER 16 ONE'S OWN WAY

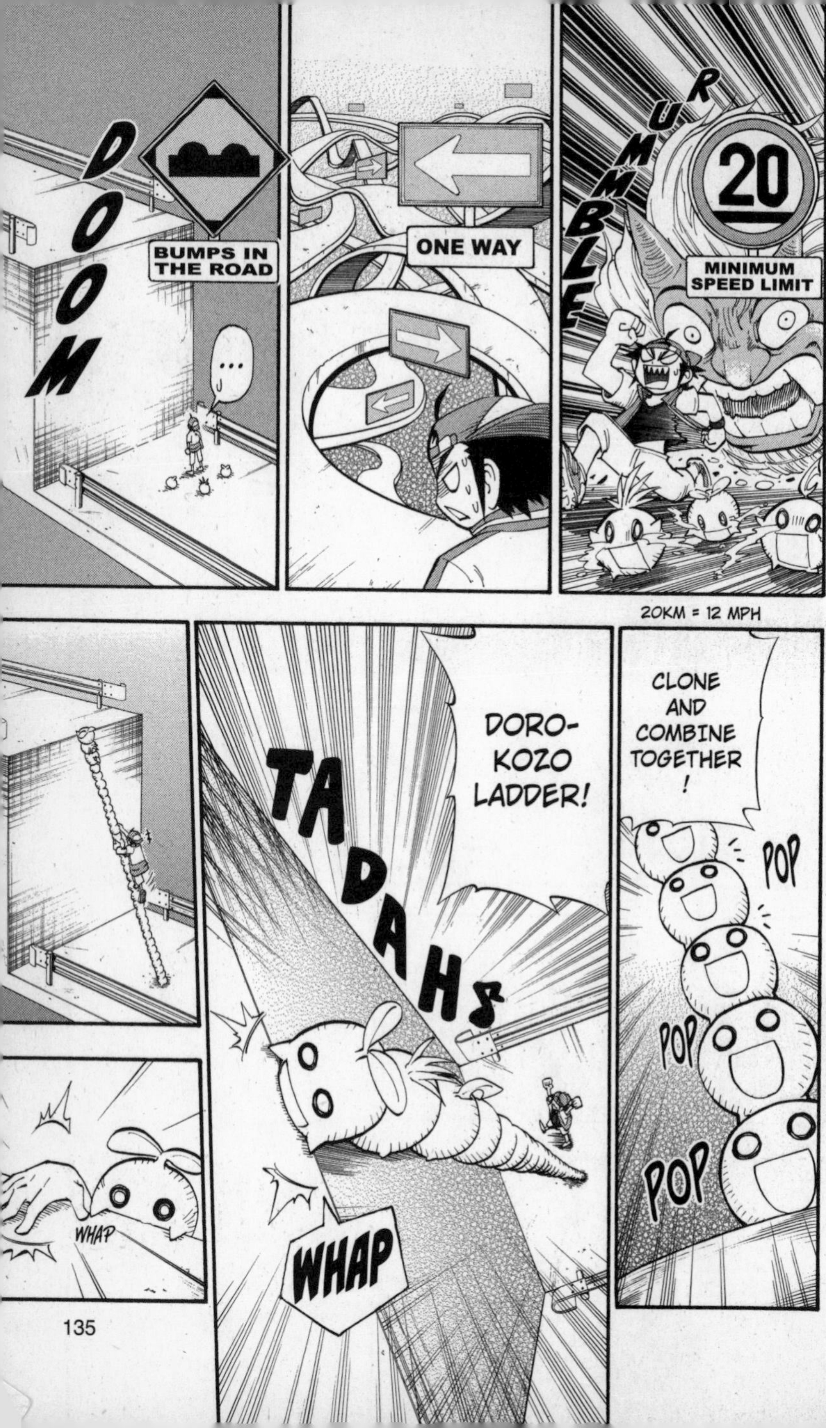
RUMMMBLE
20
MINIMUM SPEED LIMIT
20KM = 12 MPH
ONE WAY
DOOM
BUMPS IN THE ROAD
...
CLONE AND COMBINE TOGETHER!
POP
POP
POP
DORO-KOZO LADDER!
TADAHS
WHAP
WHAP

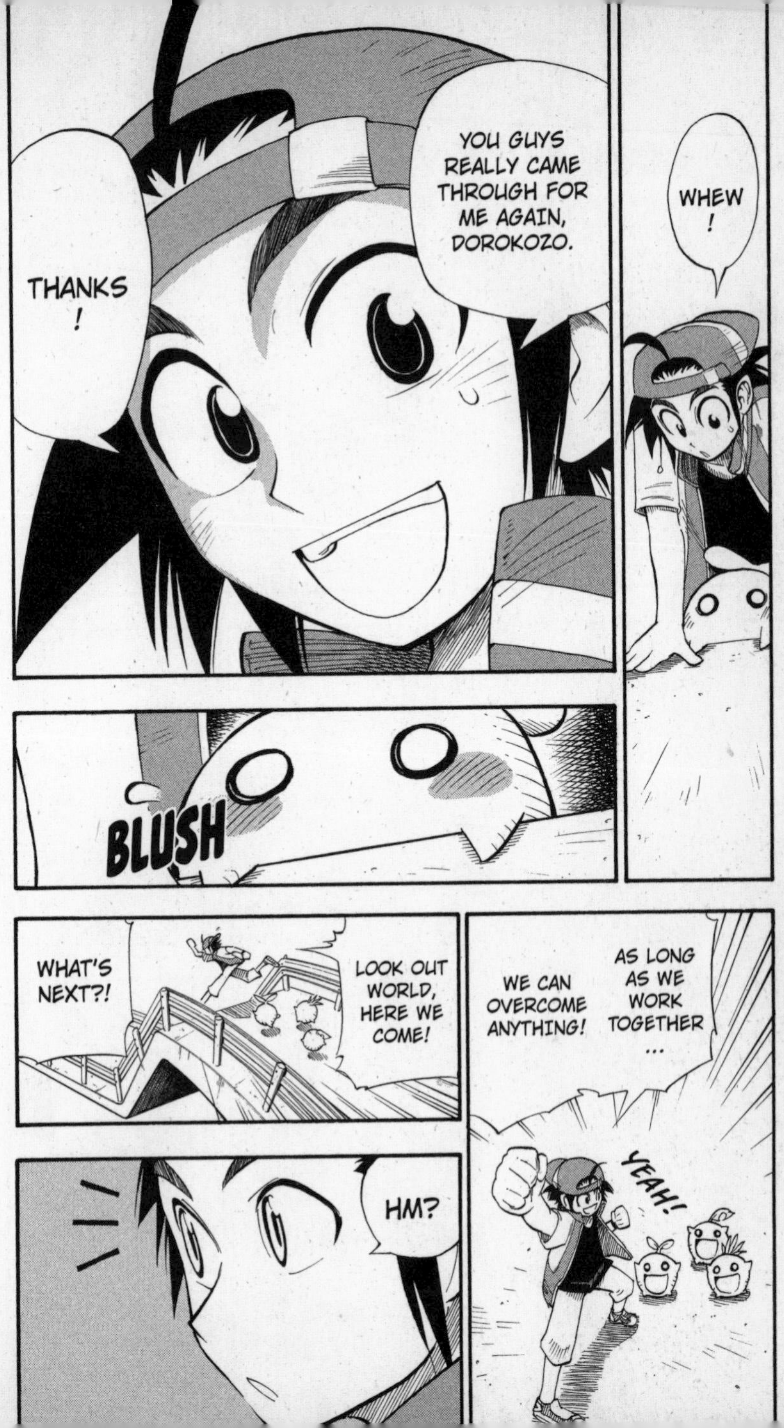
WHEW!
YOU GUYS REALLY CAME THROUGH FOR ME AGAIN, DOROKOZO.
THANKS!
BLUSH
AS LONG AS WE WORK TOGETHER...
WE CAN OVERCOME ANYTHING!
YEAH!
LOOK OUT WORLD, HERE WE COME!
WHAT'S NEXT?!
HM?

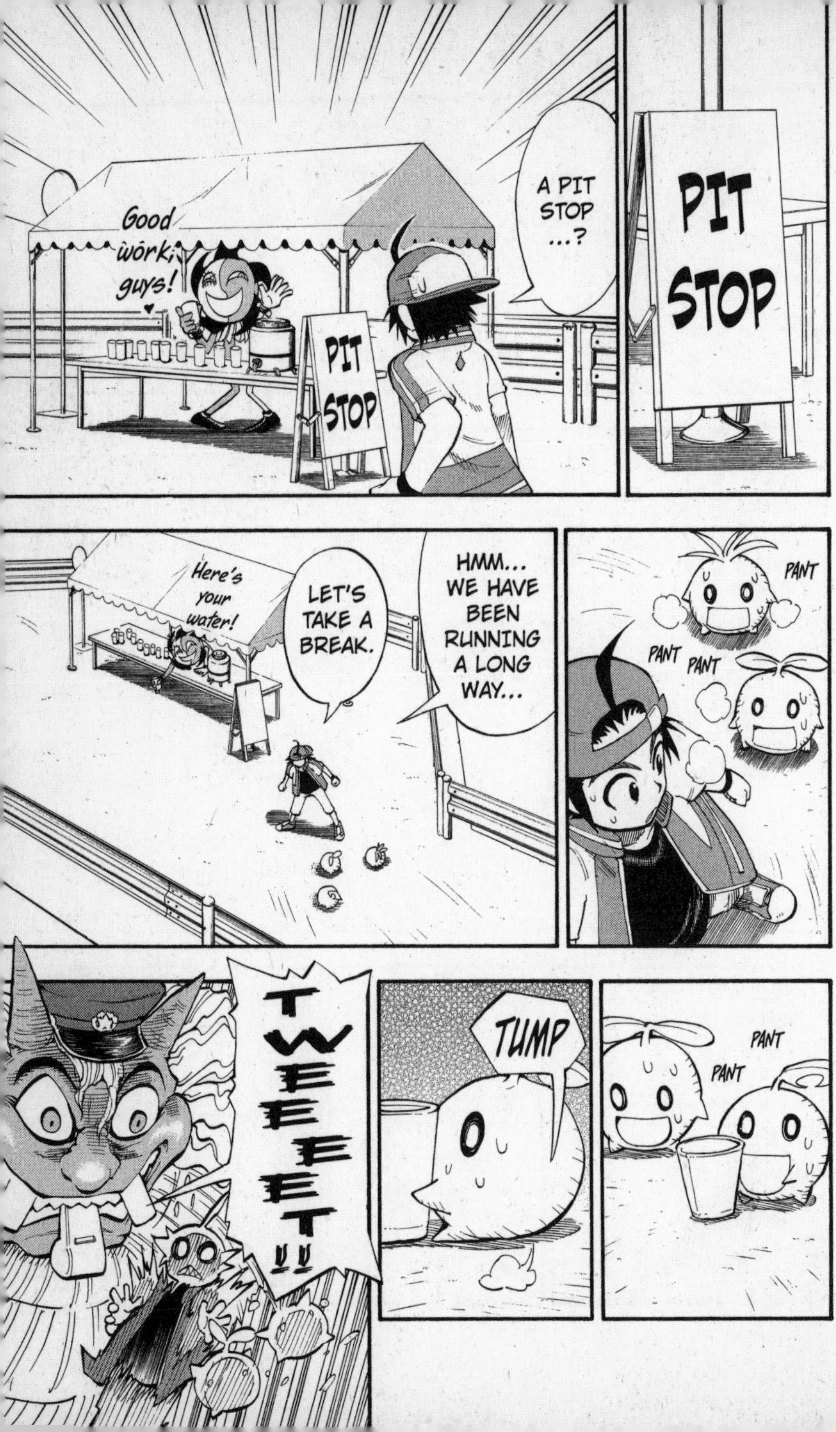
PIT STOP
A PIT STOP ...?
Good work, guys!
PIT STOP
PANT
PANT PANT
HMM... WE HAVE BEEN RUNNING A LONG WAY...
LET'S TAKE A BREAK.
Here's your water!
PANT
PANT
TUMP
TWEEEEET!!

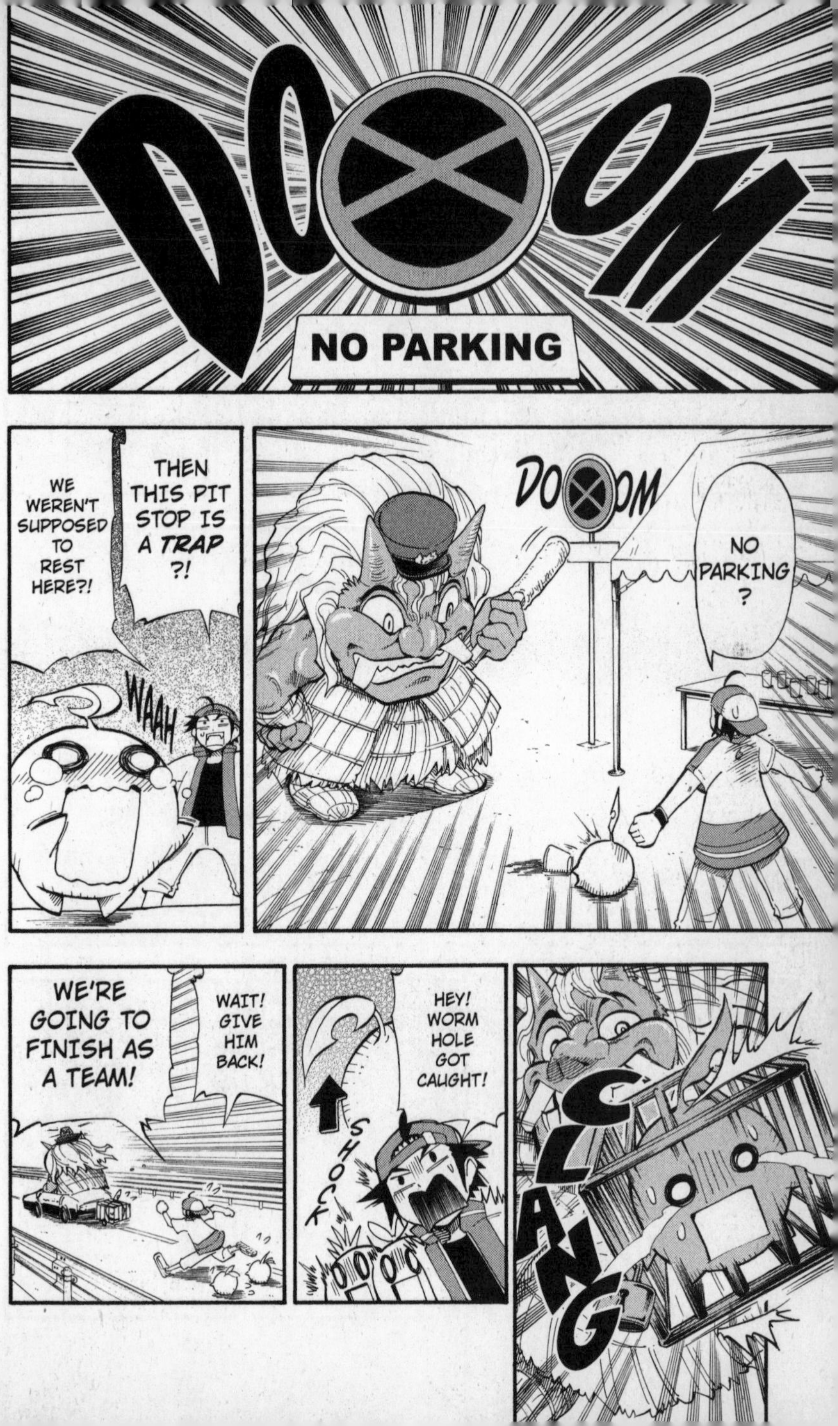
DOOOM
NO PARKING
DOOOM
NO PARKING?
THEN THIS PIT STOP IS A TRAP?!
WE WEREN'T SUPPOSED TO REST HERE?!
WAAH
CLANG
HEY! WORM HOLE GOT CAUGHT!
SHOCK
WAIT! GIVE HIM BACK!
WE'RE GOING TO FINISH AS A TEAM!

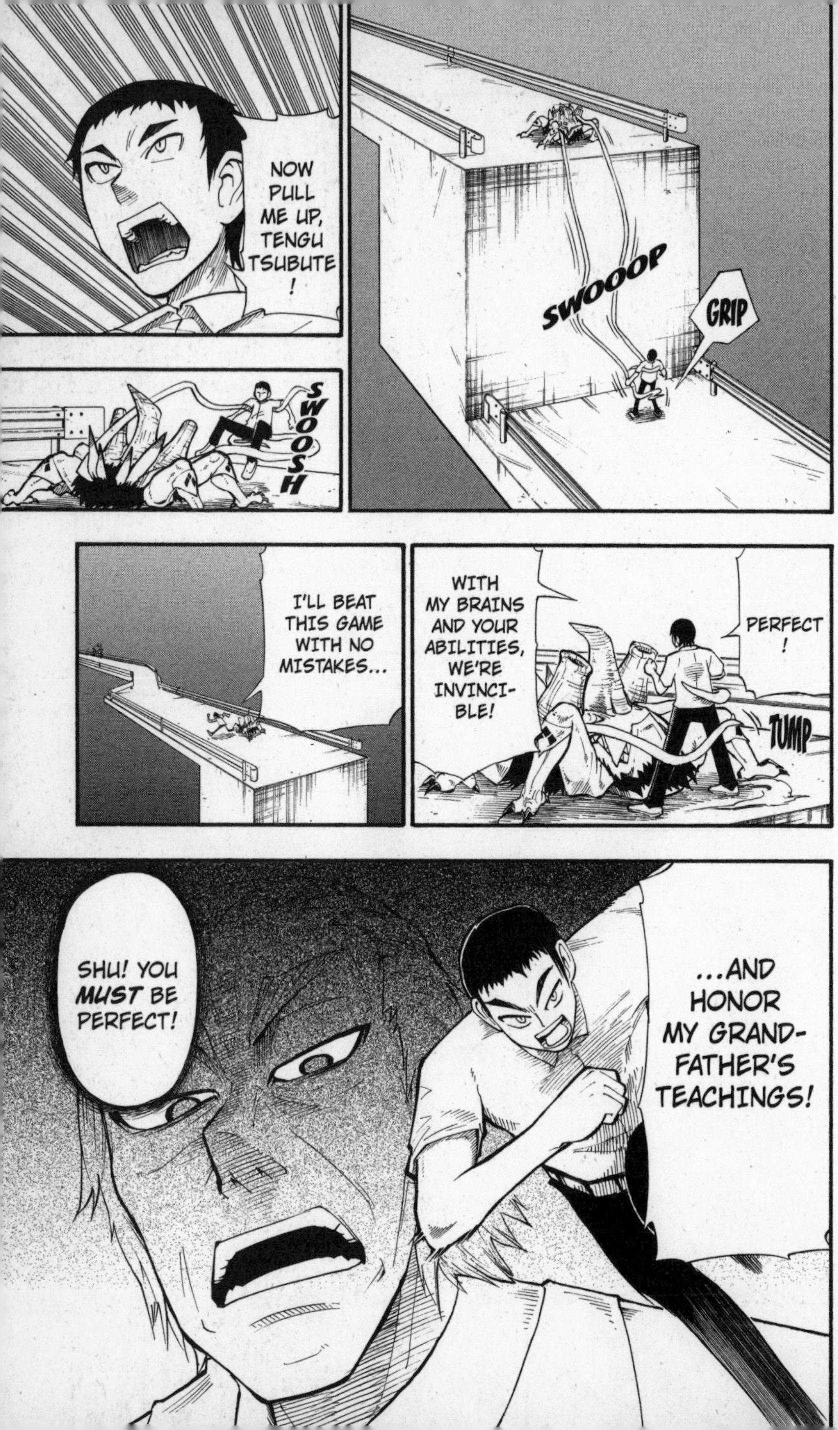
SWOOOP
GRIP
NOW PULL ME UP, TENGU TSUBUTE!
SWOOSH
PERFECT!
WITH MY BRAINS AND YOUR ABILITIES, WE'RE INVINCIBLE!
TUMP
I'LL BEAT THIS GAME WITH NO MISTAKES...
...AND HONOR MY GRANDFATHER'S TEACHINGS!
SHU! YOU *MUST* BE PERFECT!

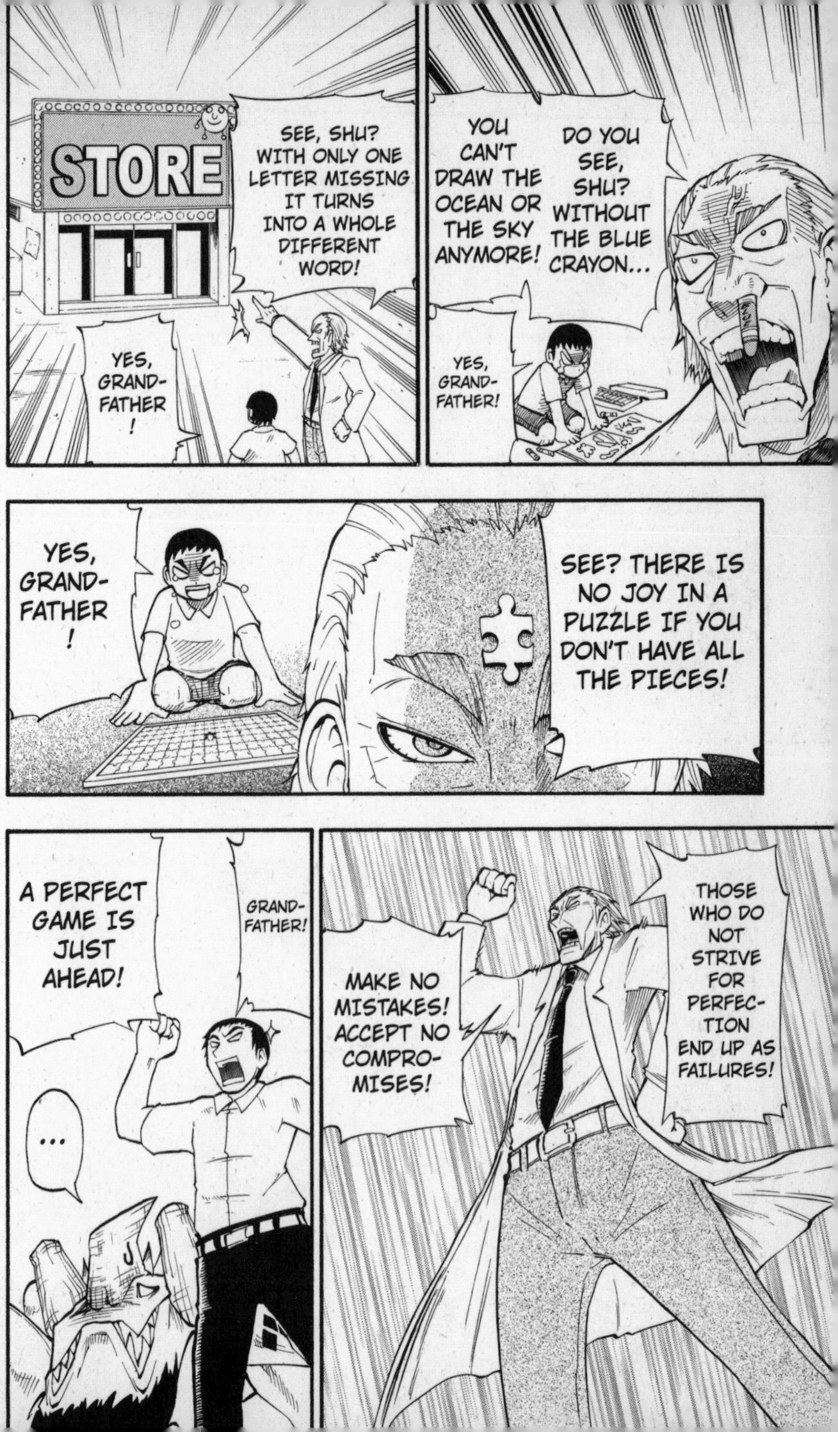
DO YOU SEE, SHU? WITHOUT THE BLUE CRAYON...
YOU CAN'T DRAW THE OCEAN OR THE SKY ANYMORE!
YES, GRAND-FATHER!
SEE, SHU? WITH ONLY ONE LETTER MISSING IT TURNS INTO A WHOLE DIFFERENT WORD!
STORE
YES, GRAND-FATHER!
SEE? THERE IS NO JOY IN A PUZZLE IF YOU DON'T HAVE ALL THE PIECES!
YES, GRAND-FATHER!
THOSE WHO DO NOT STRIVE FOR PERFEC-TION END UP AS FAILURES!
MAKE NO MISTAKES! ACCEPT NO COMPRO-MISES!
GRAND-FATHER!
A PERFECT GAME IS JUST AHEAD!
...

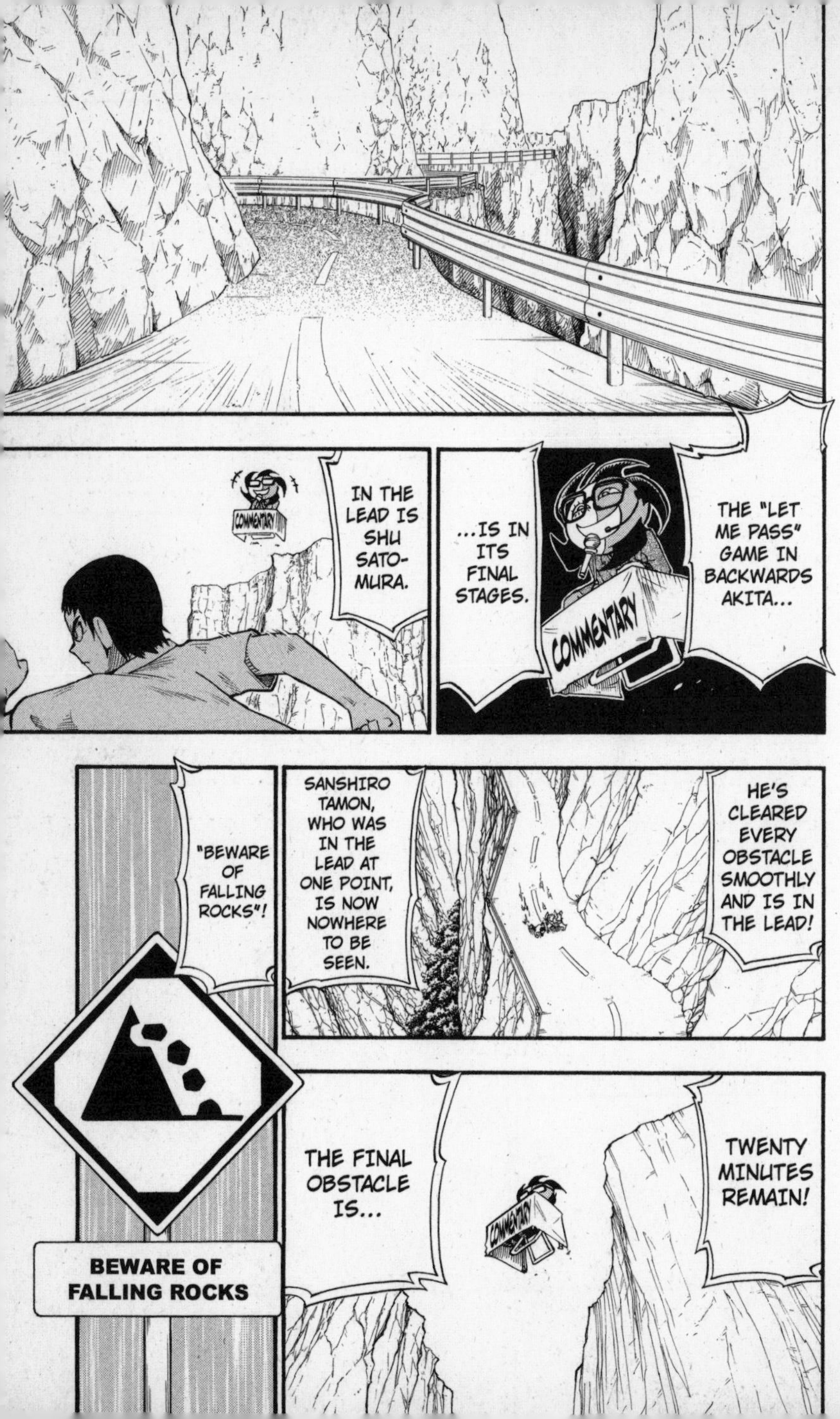
THE "LET ME PASS" GAME IN BACKWARDS AKITA...
...IS IN ITS FINAL STAGES.
COMMENTARY
IN THE LEAD IS SHU SATO-MURA.
COMMENTARY
HE'S CLEARED EVERY OBSTACLE SMOOTHLY AND IS IN THE LEAD!
SANSHIRO TAMON, WHO WAS IN THE LEAD AT ONE POINT, IS NOW NOWHERE TO BE SEEN.
TWENTY MINUTES REMAIN!
THE FINAL OBSTACLE IS...
COMMENTARY
"BEWARE OF FALLING ROCKS"!
BEWARE OF FALLING ROCKS

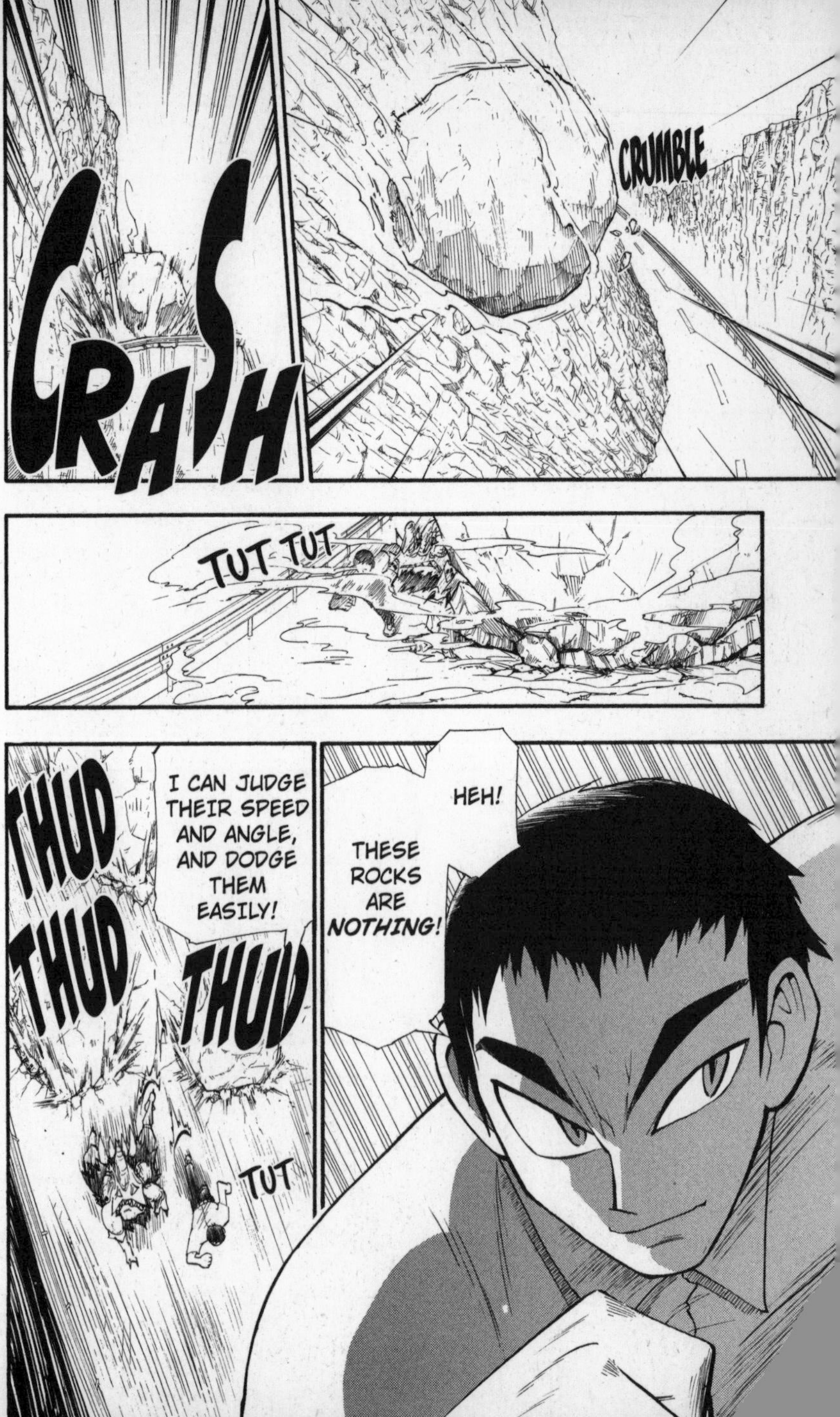
CRUMBLE
CRASH
TUT TUT
HEH!
THESE ROCKS ARE *NOTHING!*
I CAN JUDGE THEIR SPEED AND ANGLE, AND DODGE THEM EASILY!
THUD
THUD
THUD
TUT

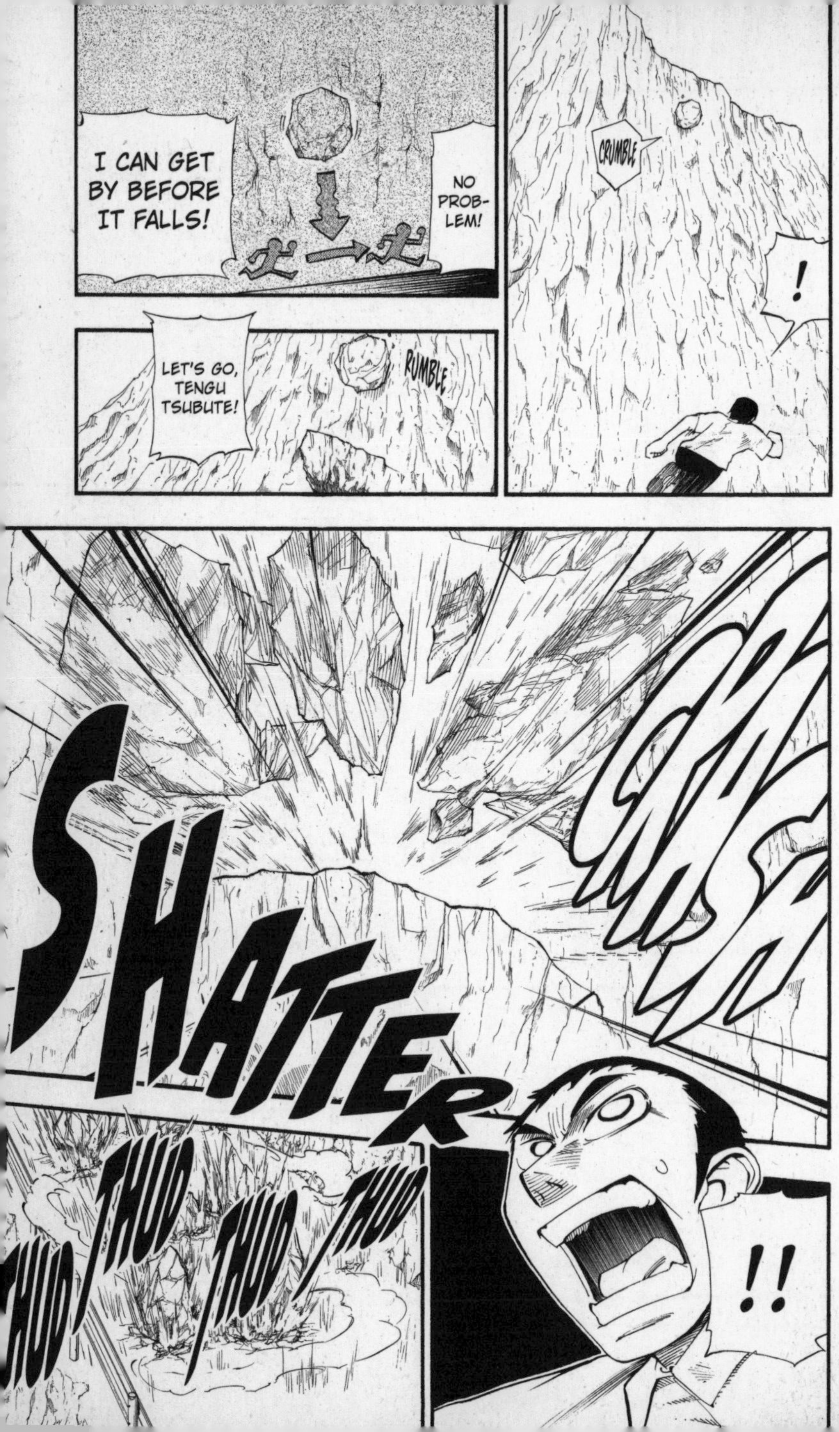
CRUMBLE
!
I CAN GET BY BEFORE IT FALLS!
NO PROB-LEM!
LET'S GO, TENGU TSUBUTE!
RUMBLE
CRASH
SHATTER
!!
THUD! THUD! THUD! THUD! THUD!

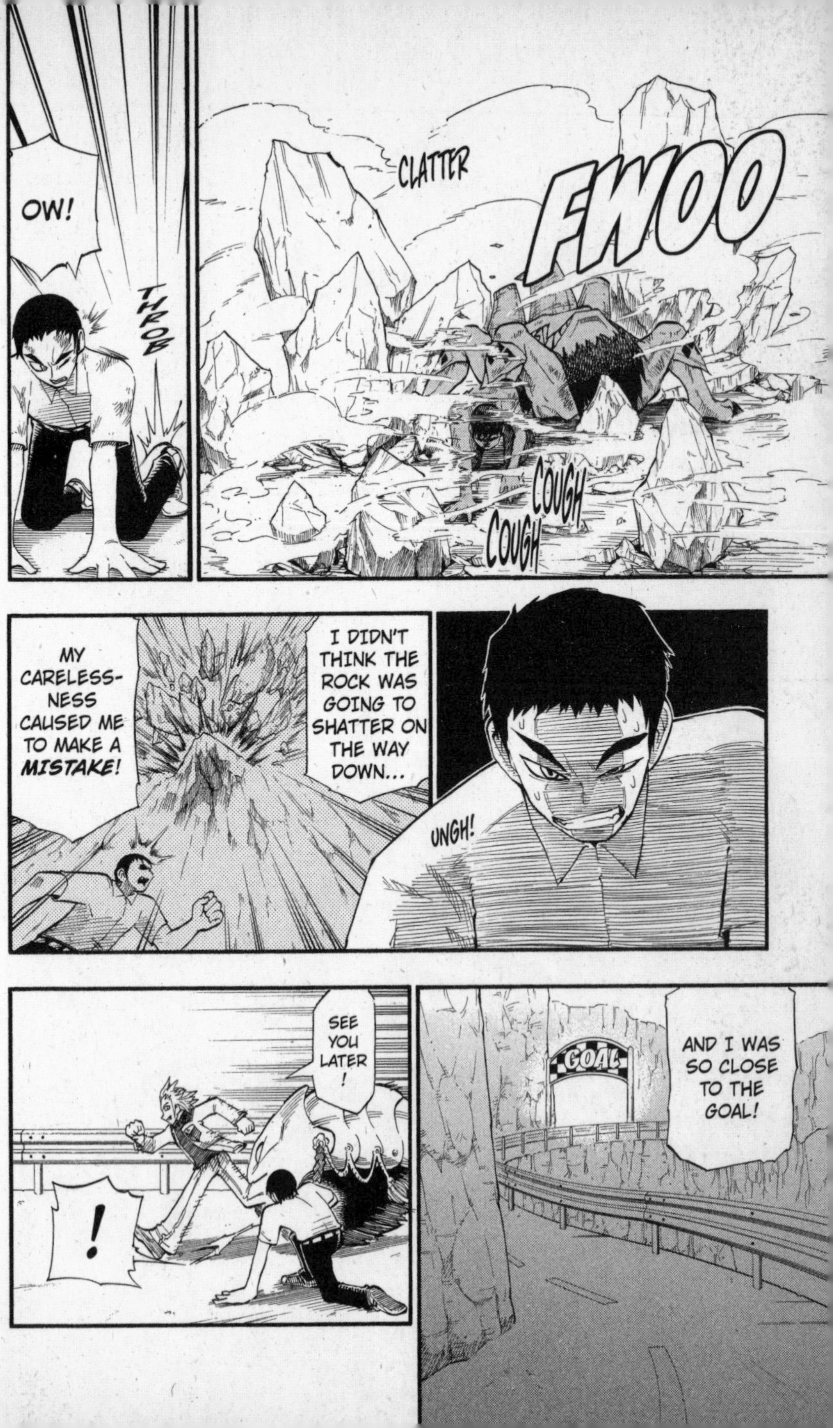
FWOO
CLATTER
COUGH
COUGH
OW!
THROB
UNGH!
I DIDN'T THINK THE ROCK WAS GOING TO SHATTER ON THE WAY DOWN...
MY CARELESS-NESS CAUSED ME TO MAKE A MISTAKE!
AND I WAS SO CLOSE TO THE GOAL!
GOAL
SEE YOU LATER!
!

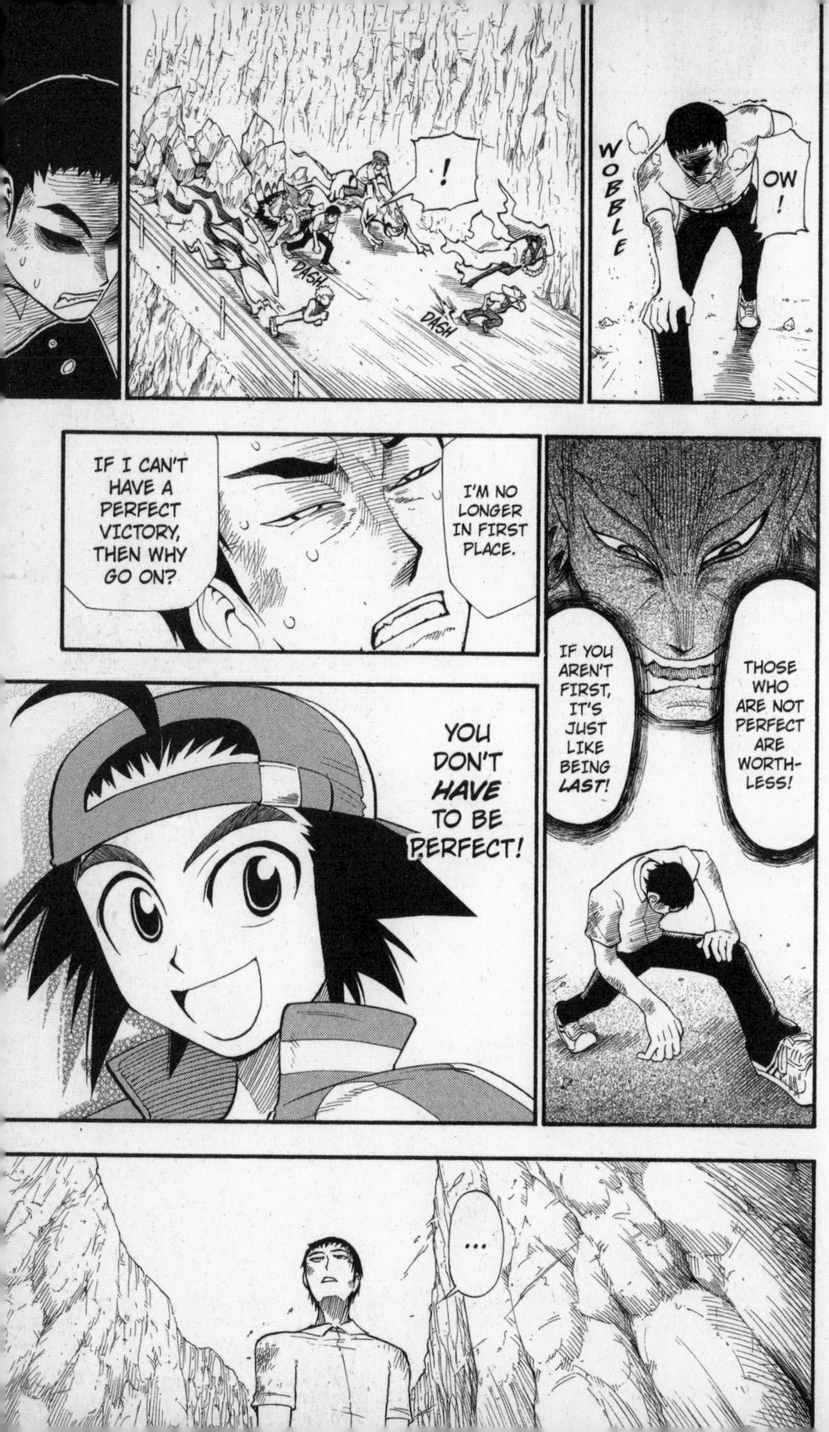

WOBBLE
OW!
!
DASH
DASH
THOSE WHO ARE NOT PERFECT ARE WORTH-LESS!
IF YOU AREN'T FIRST, IT'S JUST LIKE BEING *LAST*!
I'M NO LONGER IN FIRST PLACE.
IF I CAN'T HAVE A PERFECT VICTORY, THEN WHY GO ON?
YOU DON'T *HAVE* TO BE PERFECT!
...

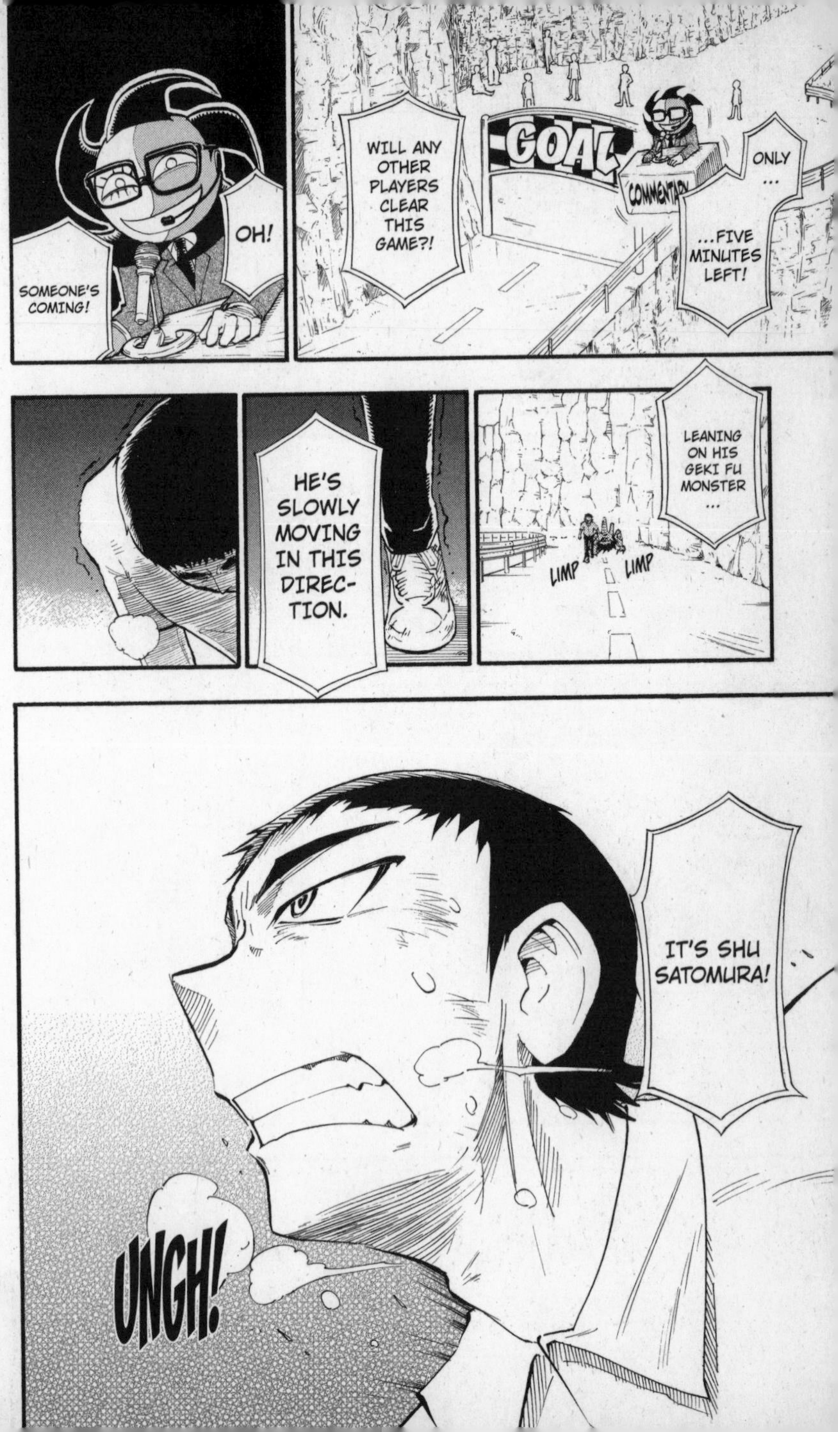
GOAL
ONLY ...
...FIVE MINUTES LEFT!
WILL ANY OTHER PLAYERS CLEAR THIS GAME?!
OH!
SOMEONE'S COMING!
LEANING ON HIS GEKI FU MONSTER ...
LIMP
LIMP
HE'S SLOWLY MOVING IN THIS DIREC-TION.
IT'S SHU SATOMURA!
UNGH!

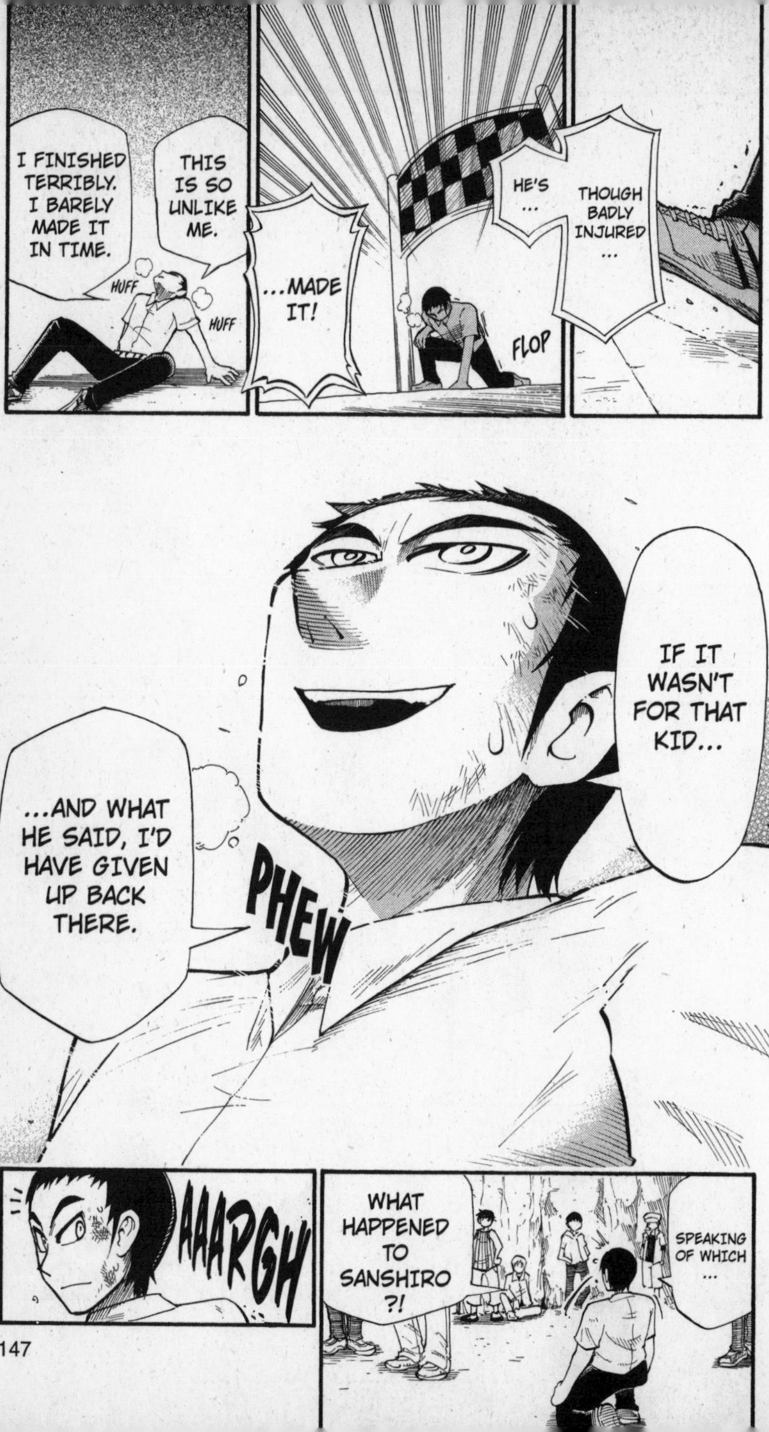
THOUGH BADLY INJURED ...
HE'S ...
FLOP
...MADE IT!
THIS IS SO UNLIKE ME.
I FINISHED TERRIBLY. I BARELY MADE IT IN TIME.
HUFF
HUFF
IF IT WASN'T FOR THAT KID...
...AND WHAT HE SAID, I'D HAVE GIVEN UP BACK THERE.
PHEW
SPEAKING OF WHICH ...
WHAT HAPPENED TO SANSHIRO ?!
AAARGH

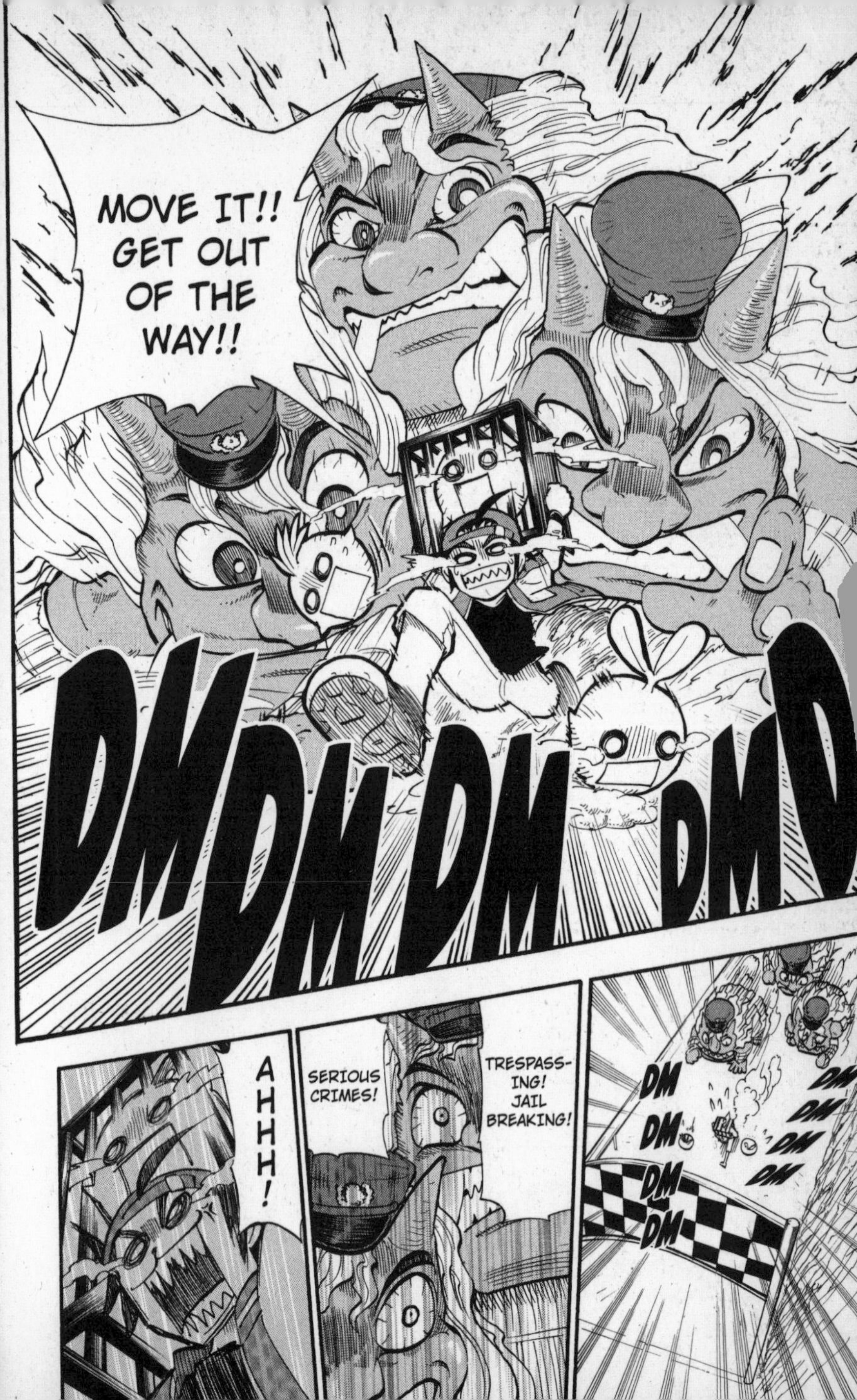
MOVE IT!! GET OUT OF THE WAY!!
DM DM DM DM DMD
DM DM DM DM
DM DM DM DM
TRESPASSING! JAIL BREAKING!
SERIOUS CRIMES!
AHHH!

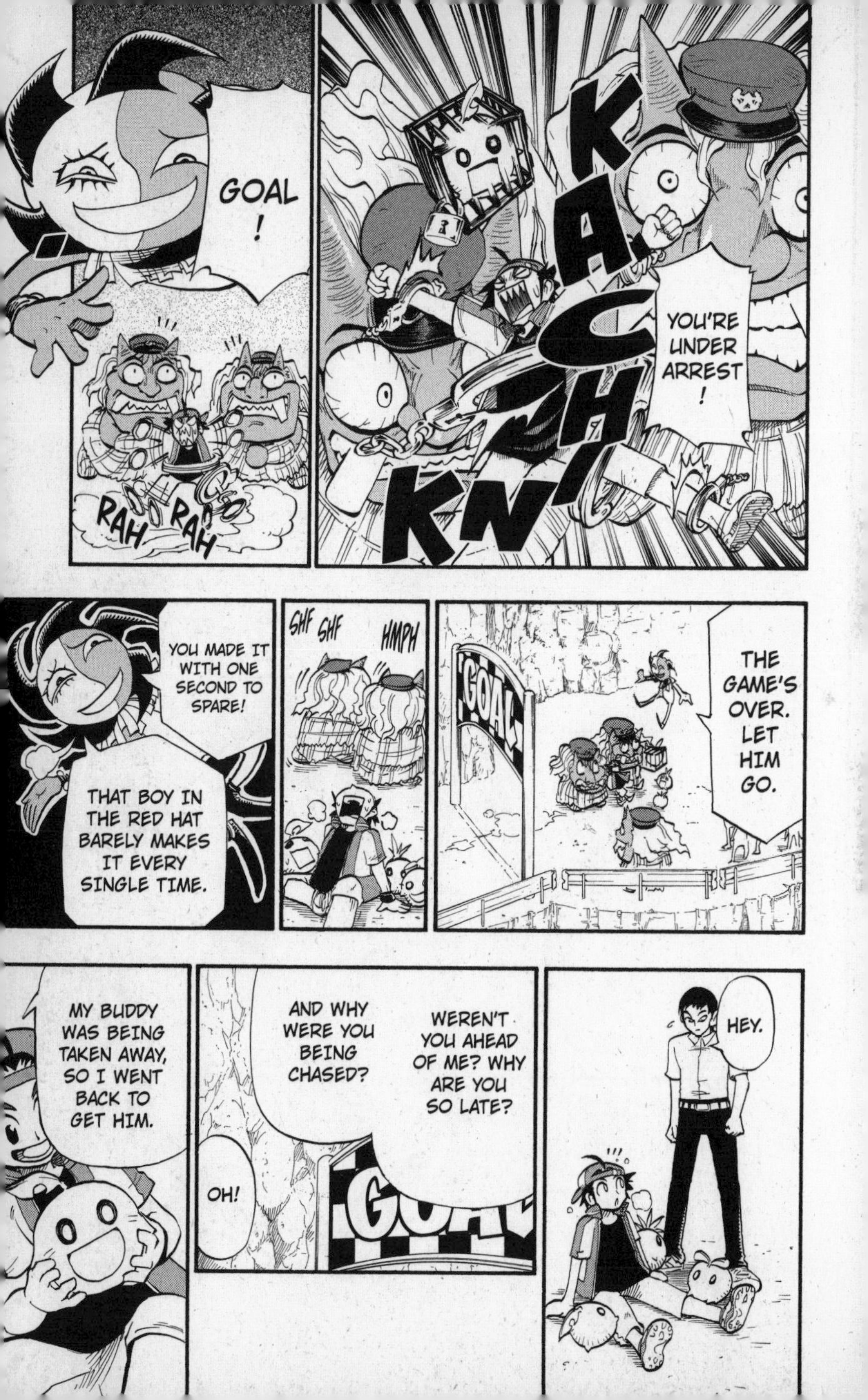
YOU'RE UNDER ARREST!
KACHNK
GOAL!
RAH RAH
THE GAME'S OVER. LET HIM GO.
SHF SHF
HMPH
YOU MADE IT WITH ONE SECOND TO SPARE!
THAT BOY IN THE RED HAT BARELY MAKES IT EVERY SINGLE TIME.
HEY.
WEREN'T YOU AHEAD OF ME? WHY ARE YOU SO LATE?
AND WHY WERE YOU BEING CHASED?
OH!
MY BUDDY WAS BEING TAKEN AWAY, SO I WENT BACK TO GET HIM.

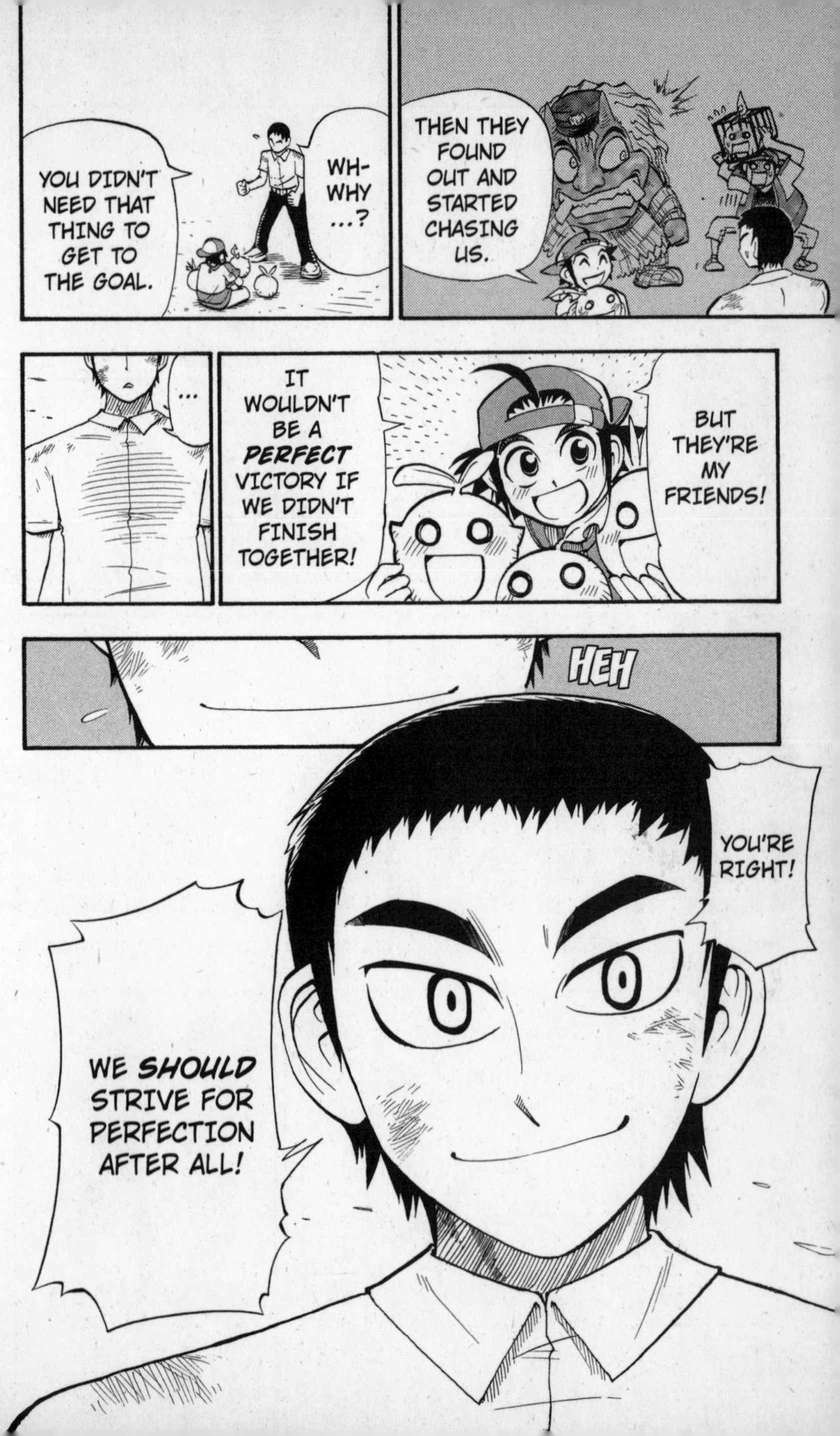
THEN THEY FOUND OUT AND STARTED CHASING US.
WH-WHY ...?
YOU DIDN'T NEED THAT THING TO GET TO THE GOAL.
BUT THEY'RE MY FRIENDS!
IT WOULDN'T BE A PERFECT VICTORY IF WE DIDN'T FINISH TOGETHER!
...
HEH
YOU'RE RIGHT!
WE SHOULD STRIVE FOR PERFECTION AFTER ALL!

BAKÉGYAMON DIARY 1

AUTOGRAPH EVENT

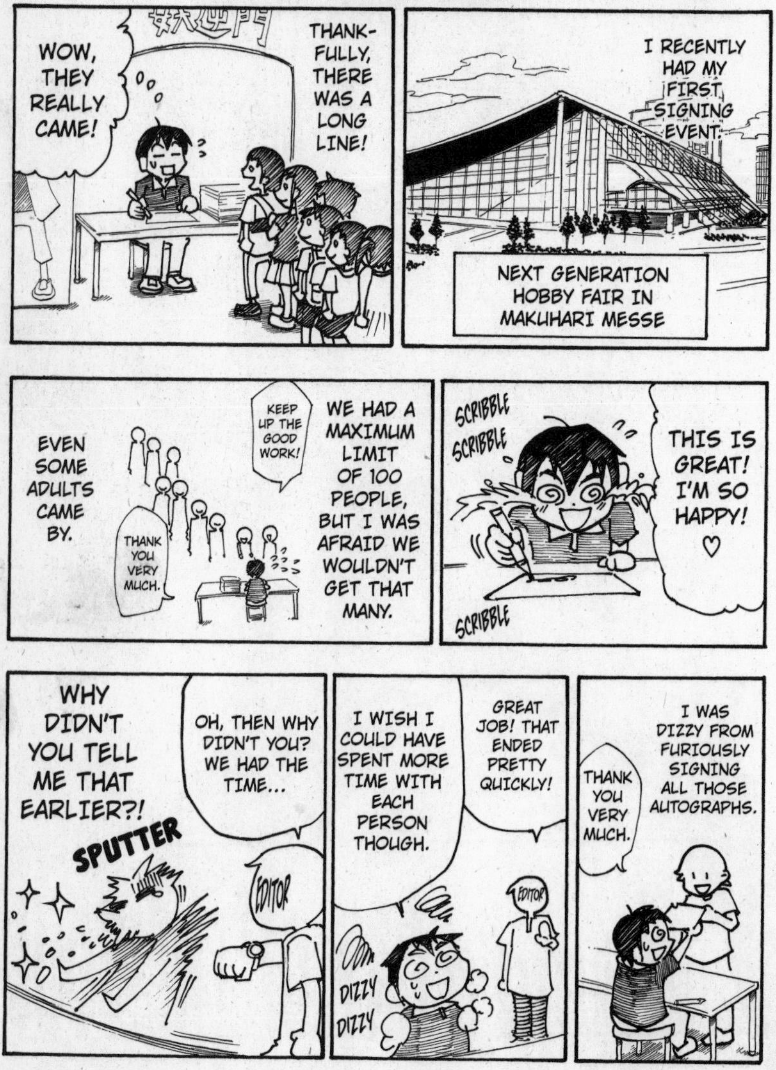
I RECENTLY HAD MY FIRST SIGNING EVENT.
NEXT GENERATION HOBBY FAIR IN MAKUHARI MESSE
THANKFULLY, THERE WAS A LONG LINE!
WOW, THEY REALLY CAME!
THIS IS GREAT! I'M SO HAPPY! ♡
SCRIBBLE
SCRIBBLE
SCRIBBLE
WE HAD A MAXIMUM LIMIT OF 100 PEOPLE, BUT I WAS AFRAID WE WOULDN'T GET THAT MANY.
KEEP UP THE GOOD WORK!
THANK YOU VERY MUCH.
EVEN SOME ADULTS CAME BY.
I WAS DIZZY FROM FURIOUSLY SIGNING ALL THOSE AUTOGRAPHS.
THANK YOU VERY MUCH.
GREAT JOB! THAT ENDED PRETTY QUICKLY!
EDITOR
I WISH I COULD HAVE SPENT MORE TIME WITH EACH PERSON THOUGH.
DIZZY
DIZZY
OH, THEN WHY DIDN'T YOU? WE HAD THE TIME...
EDITOR
WHY DIDN'T YOU TELL ME THAT EARLIER?!
SPUTTER

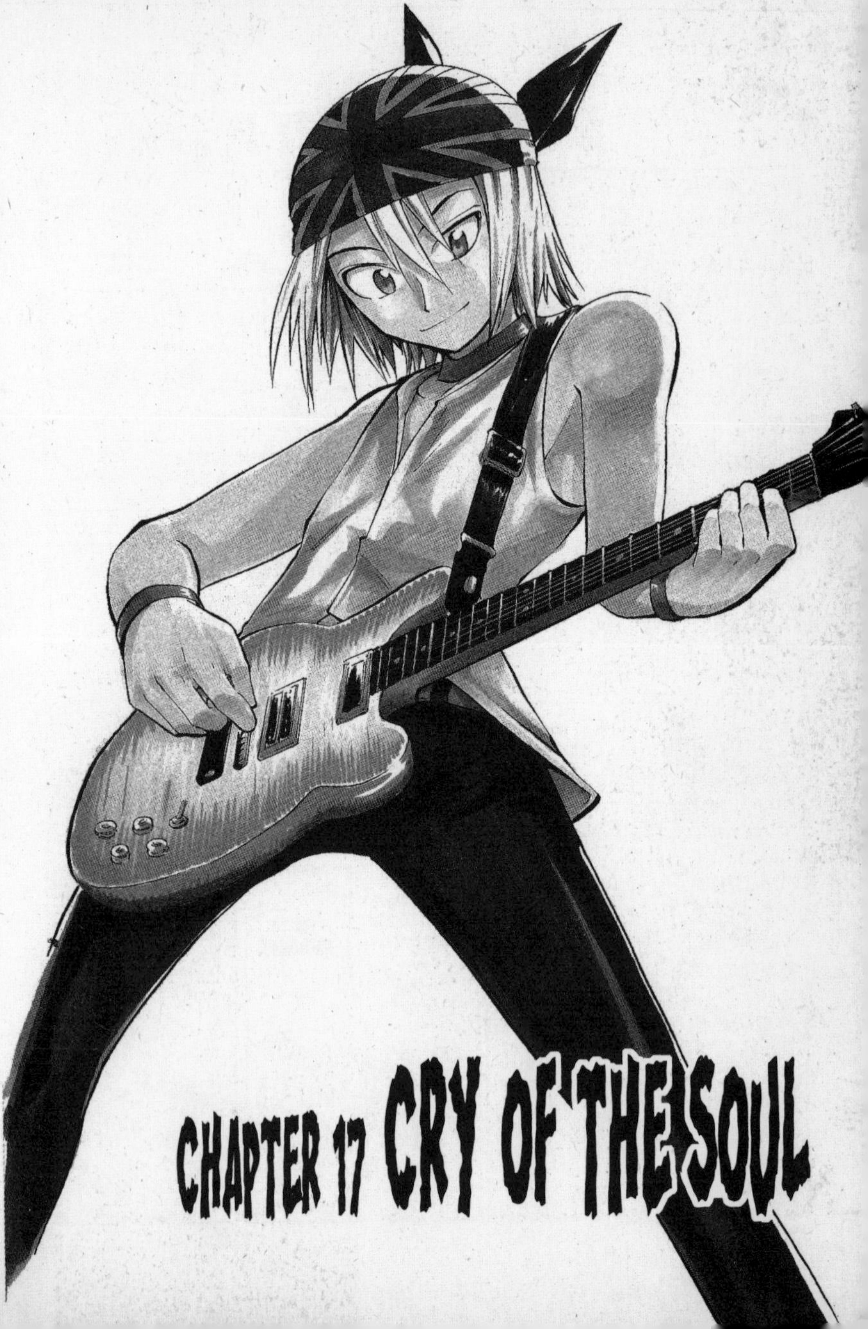
CHAPTER 17 CRY OF THE SOUL

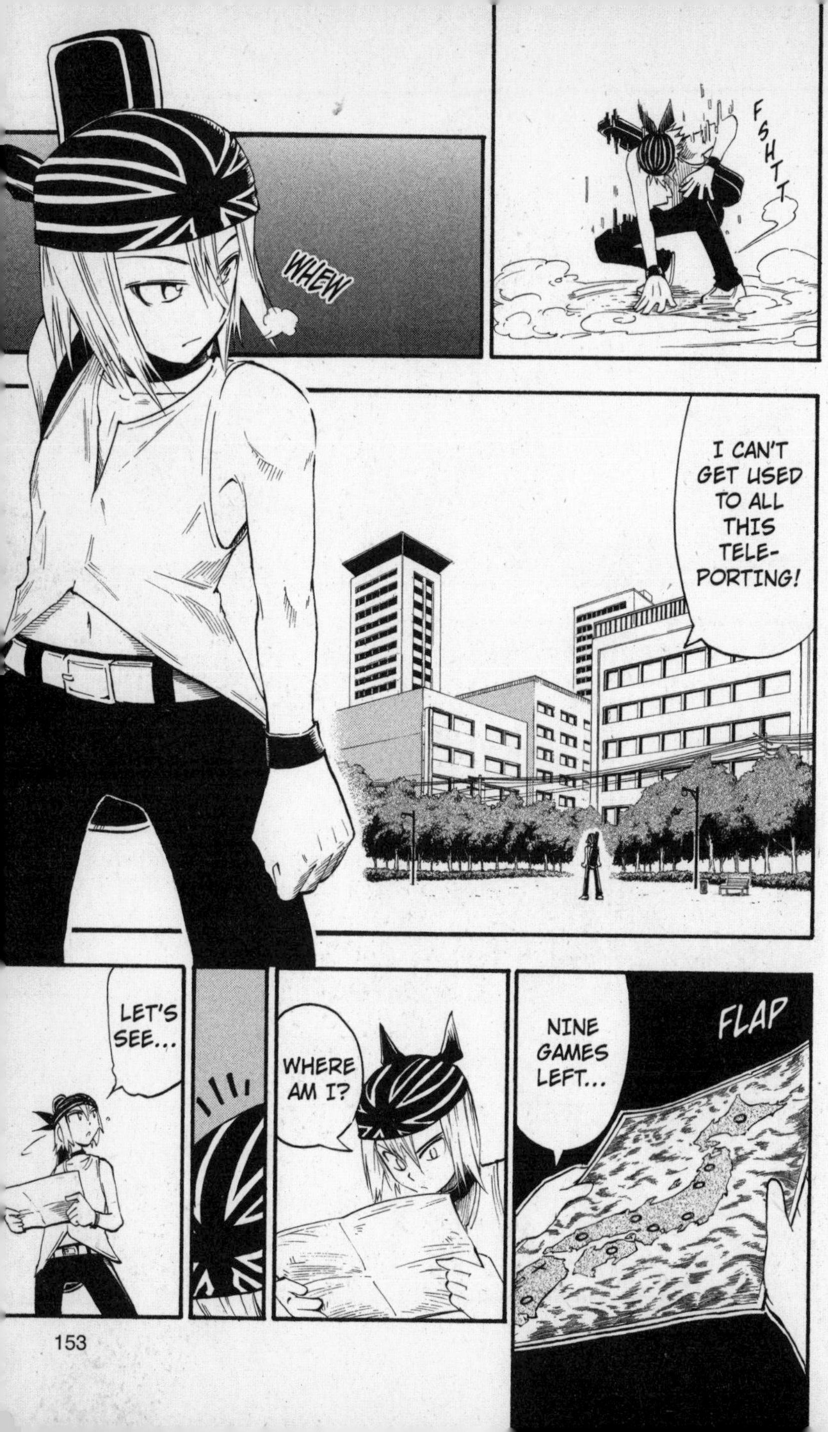
FSHTT
WHEW
I CAN'T GET USED TO ALL THIS TELE-PORTING!
FLAP
NINE GAMES LEFT...
WHERE AM I?
LET'S SEE...

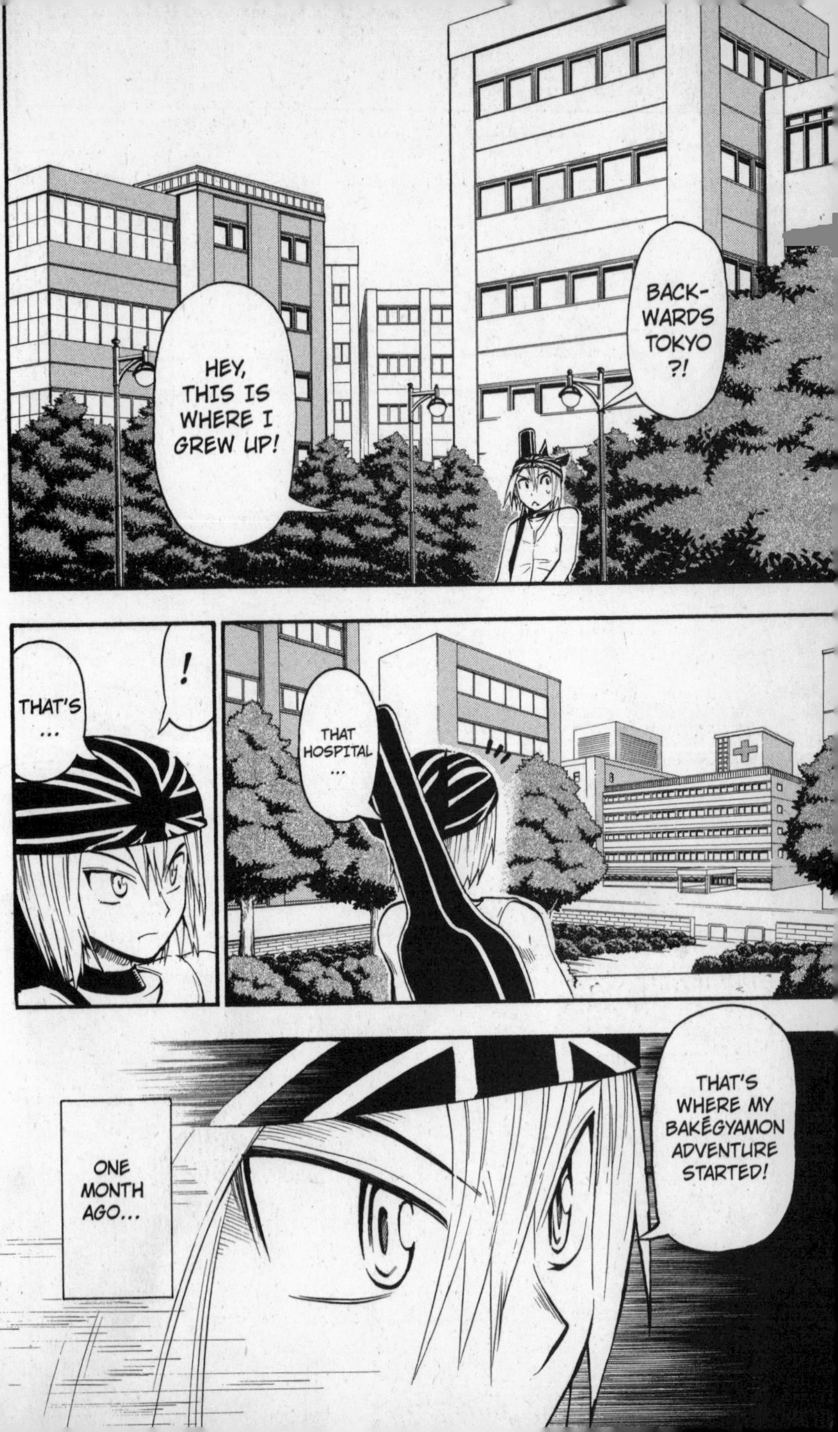
BACK-WARDS TOKYO ?!
HEY, THIS IS WHERE I GREW UP!
THAT HOSPITAL ...
!
THAT'S ...
THAT'S WHERE MY BAKĒGYAMON ADVENTURE STARTED!
ONE MONTH AGO...

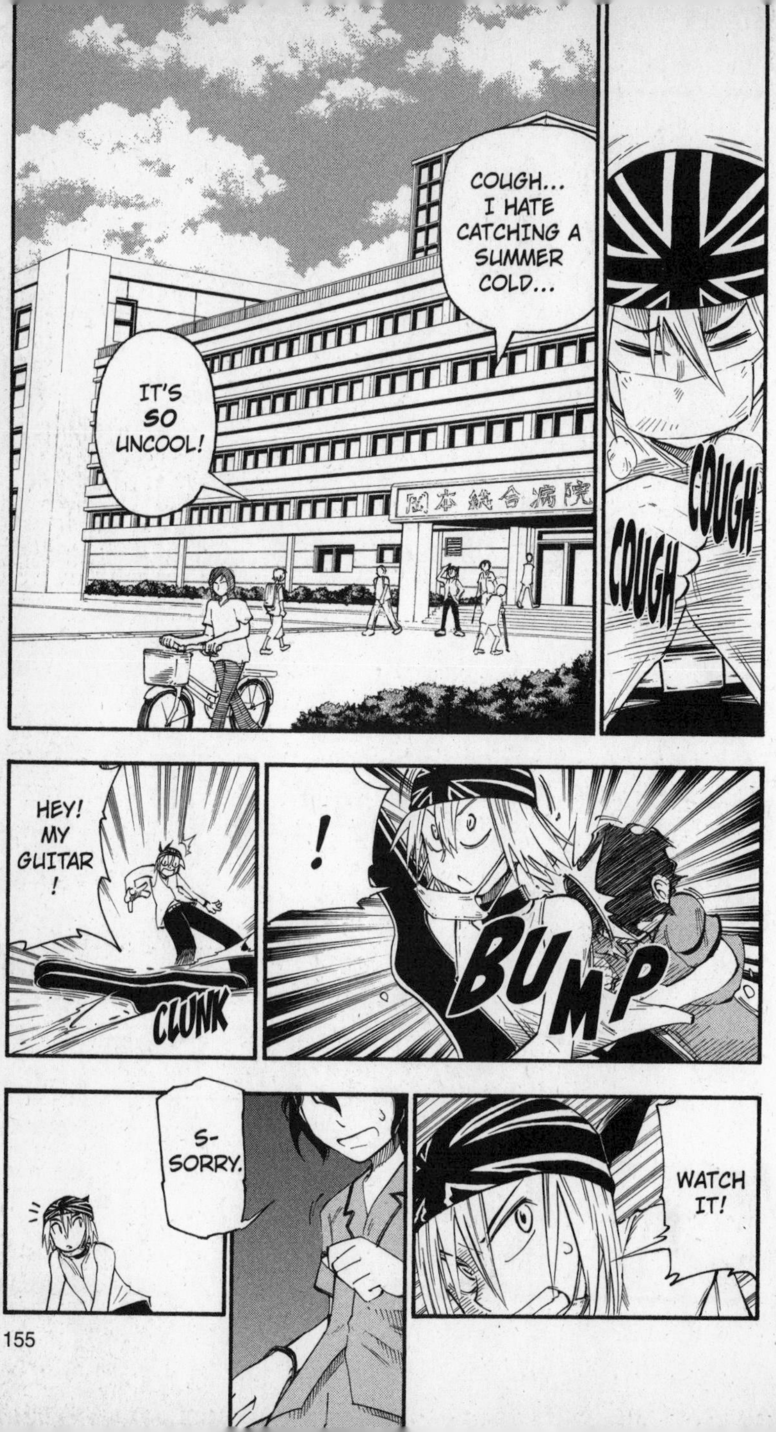
COUGH
COUGH
COUGH... I HATE CATCHING A SUMMER COLD...
IT'S SO UNCOOL!
!
BUMP
HEY! MY GUITAR!
CLUNK
WATCH IT!
S-SORRY.

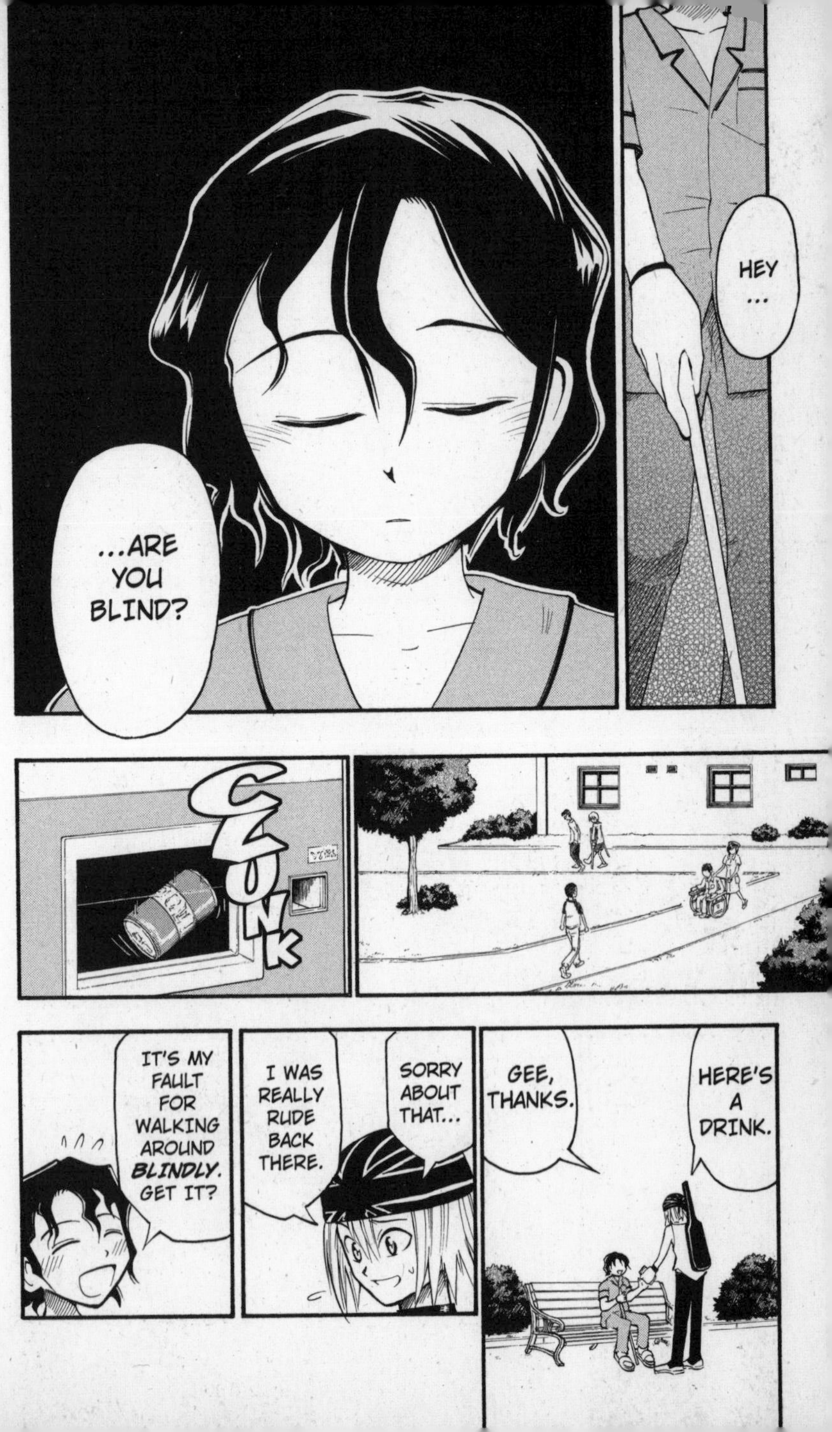
HEY ...
...ARE YOU BLIND?
CLUNK
HERE'S A DRINK.
GEE, THANKS.
SORRY ABOUT THAT...
I WAS REALLY RUDE BACK THERE.
IT'S MY FAULT FOR WALKING AROUND *BLINDLY*. GET IT?

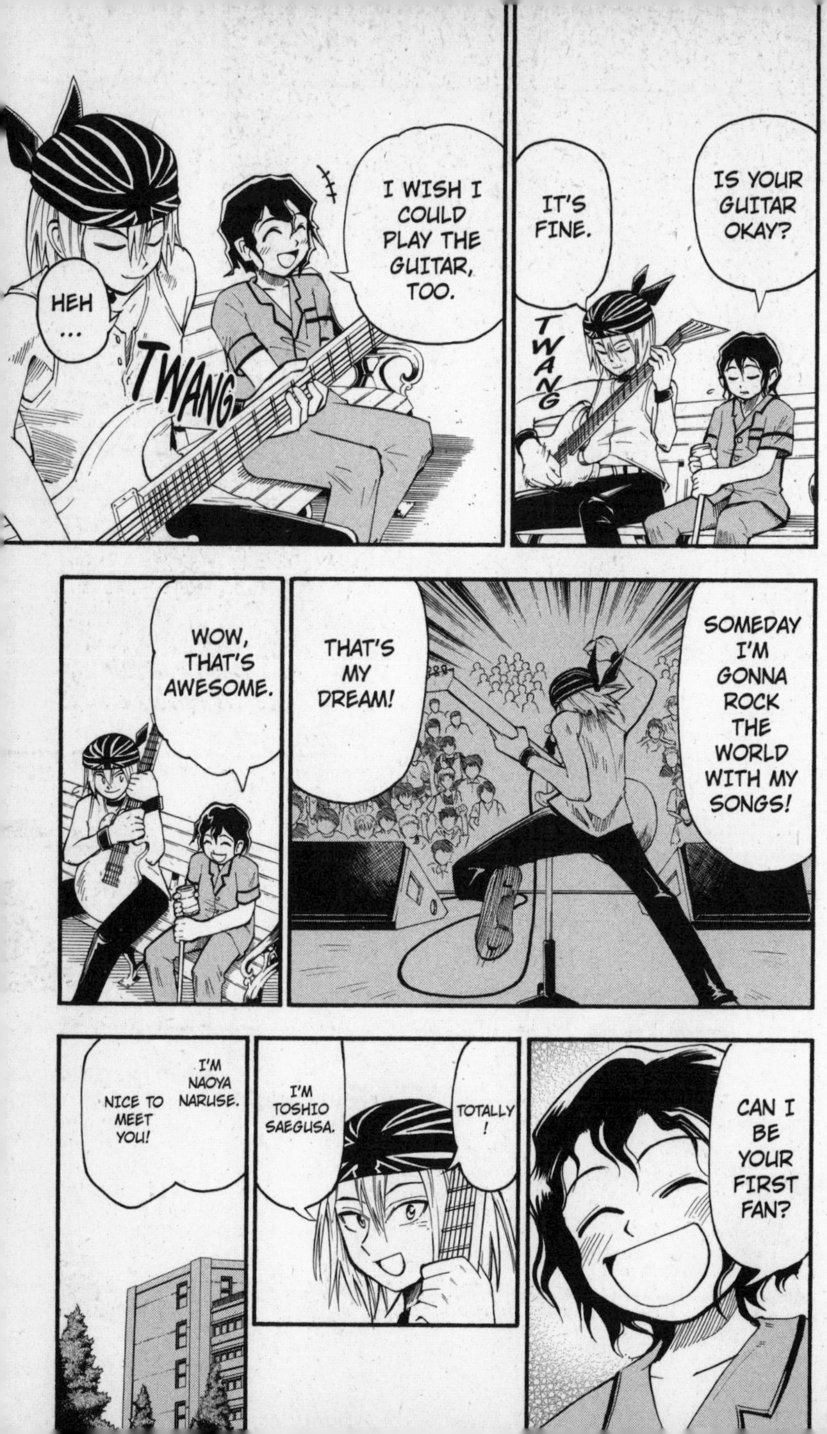
IS YOUR GUITAR OKAY?
IT'S FINE.
TWANG
I WISH I COULD PLAY THE GUITAR, TOO.
TWANG
HEH ...
SOMEDAY I'M GONNA ROCK THE WORLD WITH MY SONGS!
THAT'S MY DREAM!
WOW, THAT'S AWESOME.
CAN I BE YOUR FIRST FAN?
TOTALLY!
I'M TOSHIO SAEGUSA.
I'M NAOYA NARUSE.
NICE TO MEET YOU!

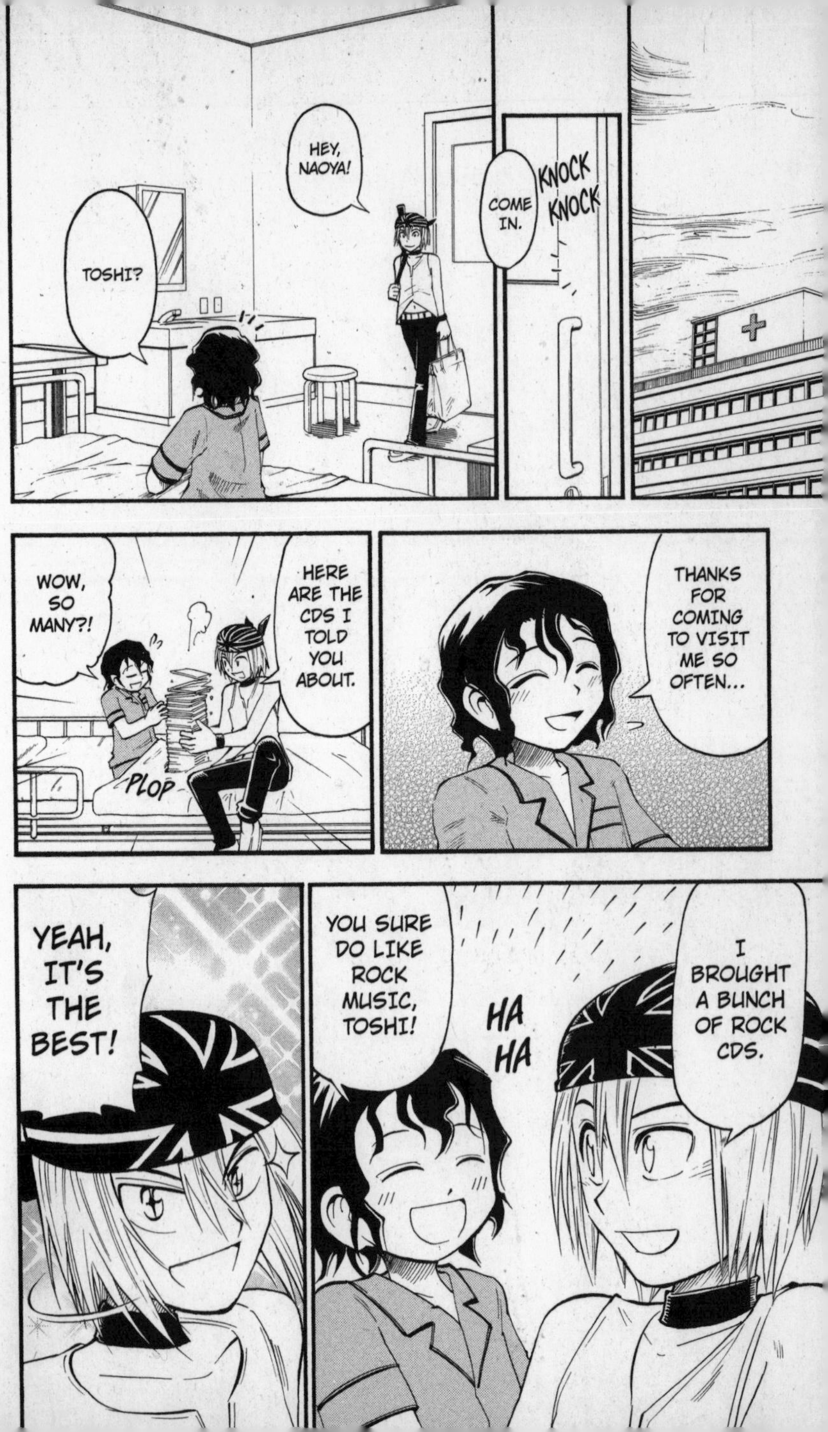
KNOCK KNOCK
COME IN.
HEY, NAOYA!
TOSHI?
THANKS FOR COMING TO VISIT ME SO OFTEN...
HERE ARE THE CDS I TOLD YOU ABOUT.
WOW, SO MANY?!
PLOP
I BROUGHT A BUNCH OF ROCK CDS.
HA HA
YOU SURE DO LIKE ROCK MUSIC, TOSHI!
YEAH, IT'S THE BEST!

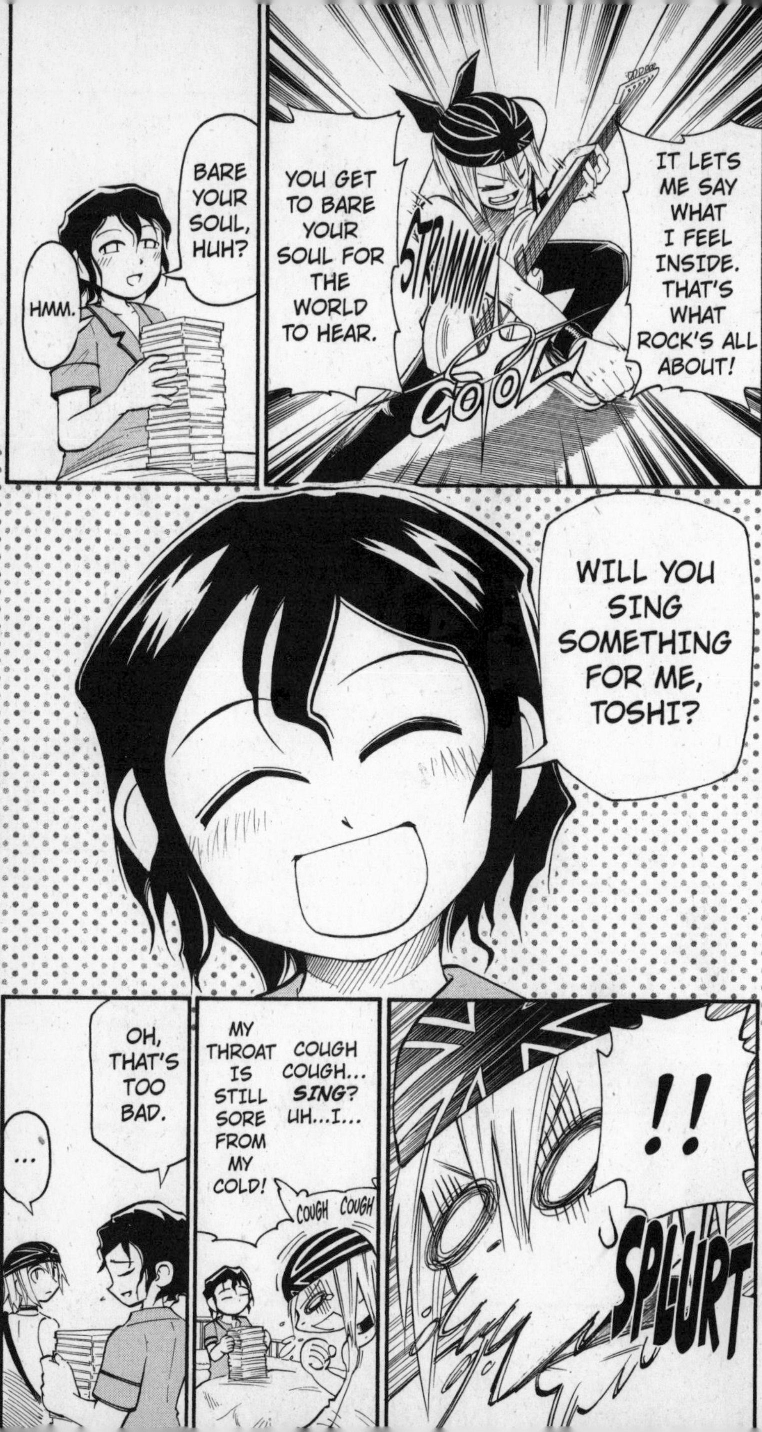
IT LETS ME SAY WHAT I FEEL INSIDE. THAT'S WHAT ROCK'S ALL ABOUT!
YOU GET TO BARE YOUR SOUL FOR THE WORLD TO HEAR.
BARE YOUR SOUL, HUH?
HMM.
WILL YOU SING SOMETHING FOR ME, TOSHI?
!!
SPLURT
COUGH COUGH... SING? UH...I...
MY THROAT IS STILL SORE FROM MY COLD!
COUGH COUGH
OH, THAT'S TOO BAD.
...

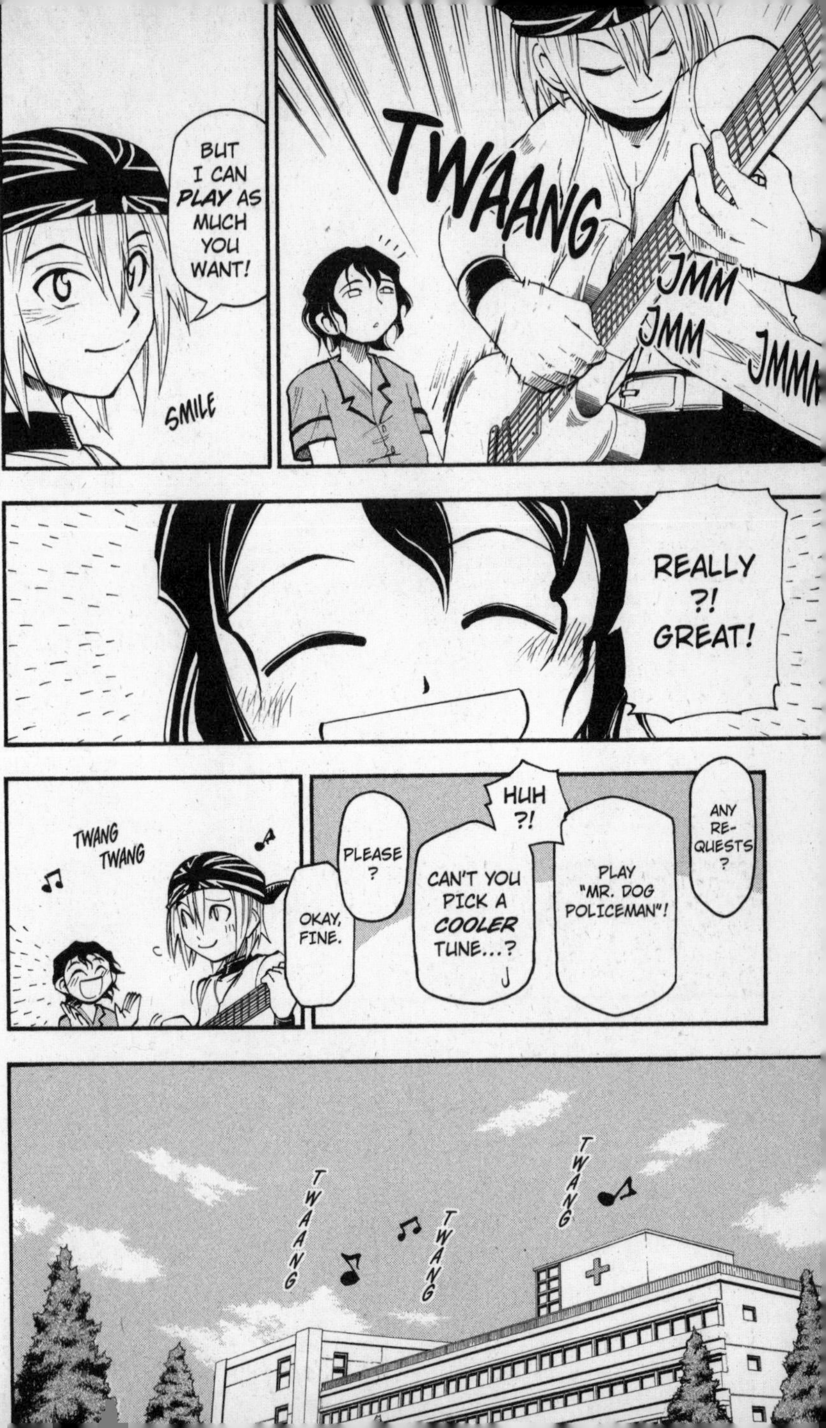
TWAANG
JMM
JMM
JMMM
BUT I CAN *PLAY* AS MUCH YOU WANT!
SMILE
REALLY ?! GREAT!
ANY RE-QUESTS ?
PLAY "MR. DOG POLICEMAN"!
HUH ?!
CAN'T YOU PICK A *COOLER* TUNE...?
PLEASE ?
OKAY, FINE.
TWANG TWANG
TWANG
TWANG
TWAANG

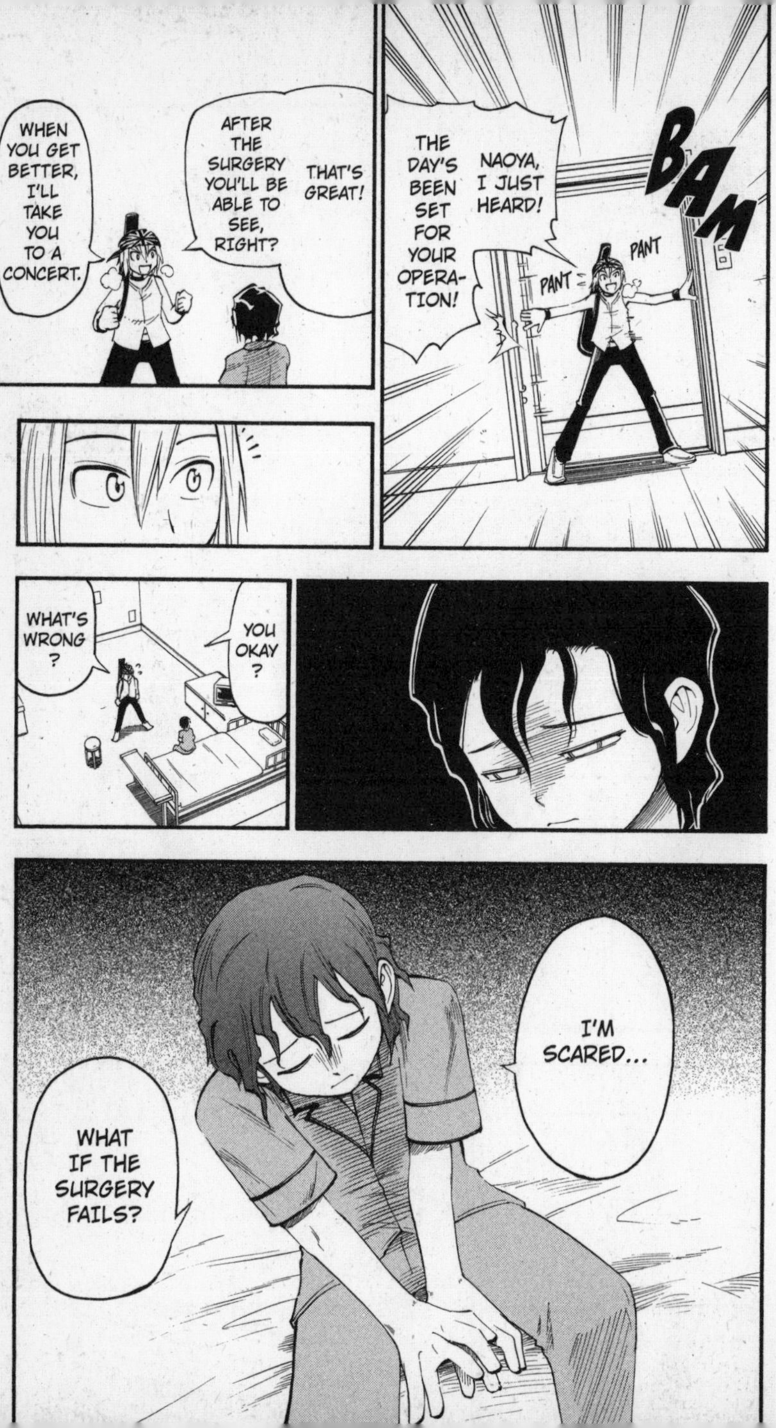
BAM
PANT
PANT
NAOYA, I JUST HEARD!
THE DAY'S BEEN SET FOR YOUR OPERATION!
THAT'S GREAT!
AFTER THE SURGERY YOU'LL BE ABLE TO SEE, RIGHT?
WHEN YOU GET BETTER, I'LL TAKE YOU TO A CONCERT.
YOU OKAY?
WHAT'S WRONG?
I'M SCARED...
WHAT IF THE SURGERY FAILS?

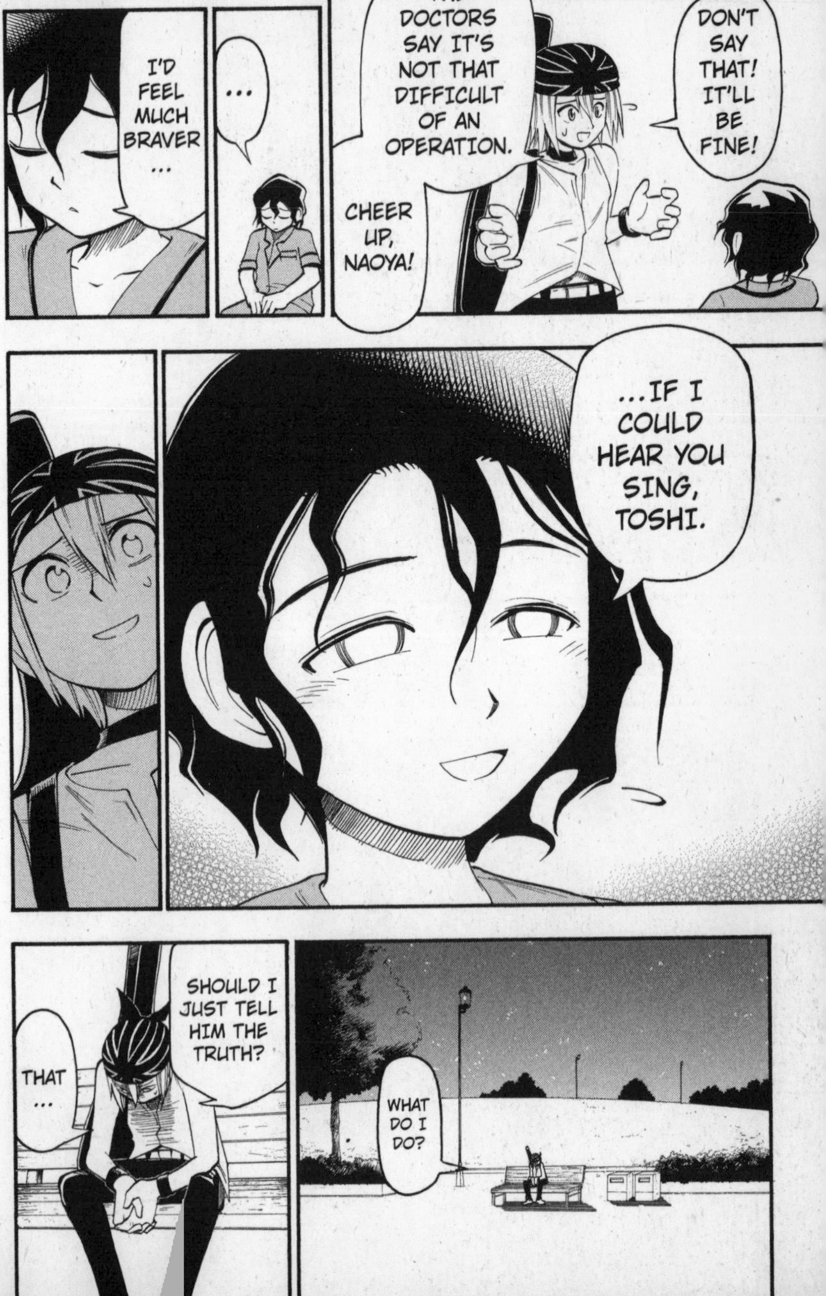
DON'T SAY THAT! IT'LL BE FINE!
THE DOCTORS SAY IT'S NOT THAT DIFFICULT OF AN OPERATION.
CHEER UP, NAOYA!
...
I'D FEEL MUCH BRAVER ...
...IF I COULD HEAR YOU SING, TOSHI.
WHAT DO I DO?
SHOULD I JUST TELL HIM THE TRUTH?
THAT ...

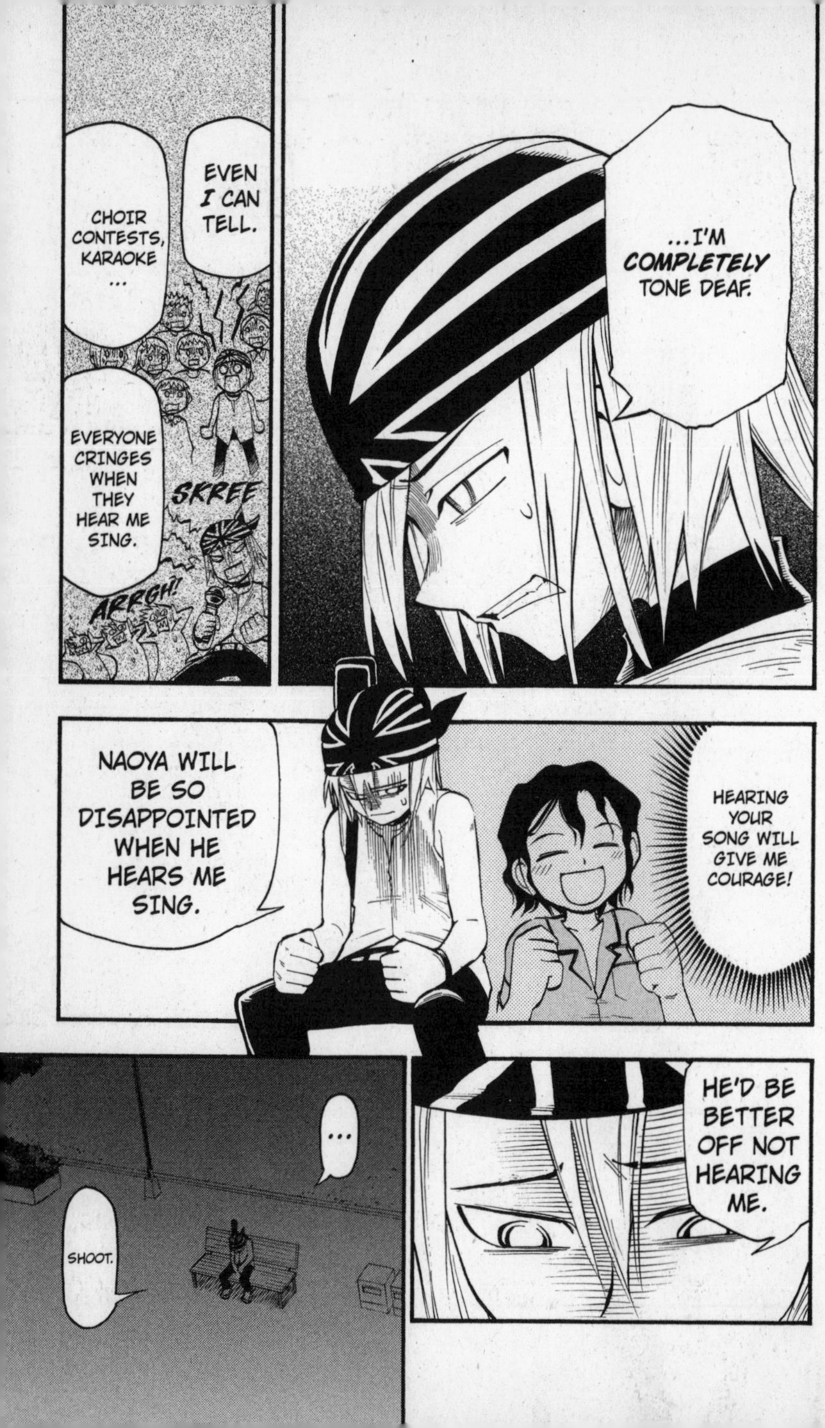
...I'M COMPLETELY TONE DEAF.
EVEN I CAN TELL.
CHOIR CONTESTS, KARAOKE ...
EVERYONE CRINGES WHEN THEY HEAR ME SING.
SKREE
ARRGH!
HEARING YOUR SONG WILL GIVE ME COURAGE!
NAOYA WILL BE SO DISAPPOINTED WHEN HE HEARS ME SING.
HE'D BE BETTER OFF NOT HEARING ME.
...
SHOOT.

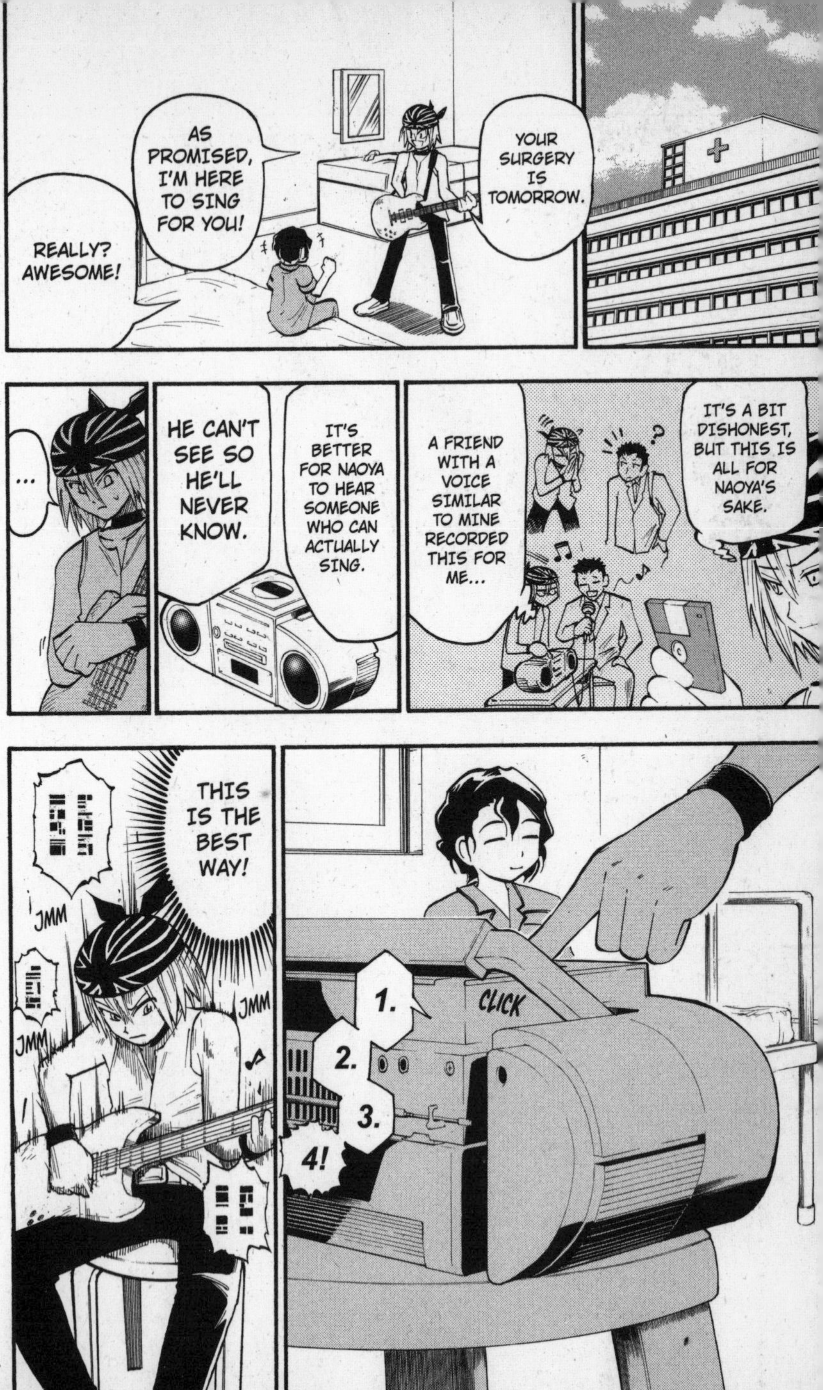
YOUR SURGERY IS TOMORROW.
AS PROMISED, I'M HERE TO SING FOR YOU!
REALLY? AWESOME!
IT'S A BIT DISHONEST, BUT THIS IS ALL FOR NAOYA'S SAKE.
A FRIEND WITH A VOICE SIMILAR TO MINE RECORDED THIS FOR ME...
IT'S BETTER FOR NAOYA TO HEAR SOMEONE WHO CAN ACTUALLY SING.
HE CAN'T SEE SO HE'LL NEVER KNOW.
...
CLICK
1.
2.
3.
4!
THIS IS THE BEST WAY!
JMM
JMM
JMM

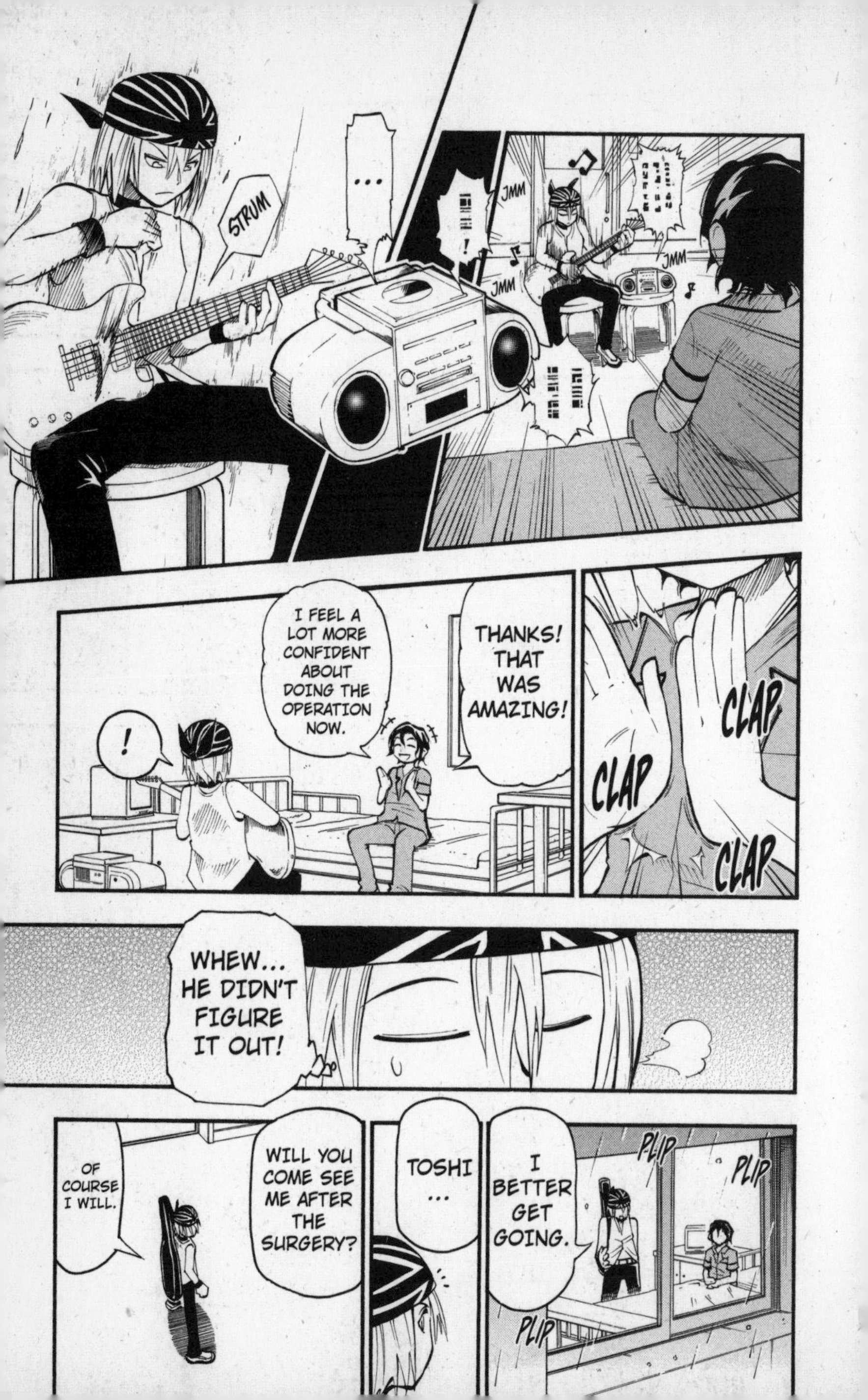
JMM
JMM
JMM
STRUM
...
CLAP
CLAP
CLAP
THANKS! THAT WAS AMAZING!
I FEEL A LOT MORE CONFIDENT ABOUT DOING THE OPERATION NOW.
!
WHEW... HE DIDN'T FIGURE IT OUT!
PLIP
PLIP
I BETTER GET GOING.
PLIP
TOSHI...
WILL YOU COME SEE ME AFTER THE SURGERY?
OF COURSE I WILL.

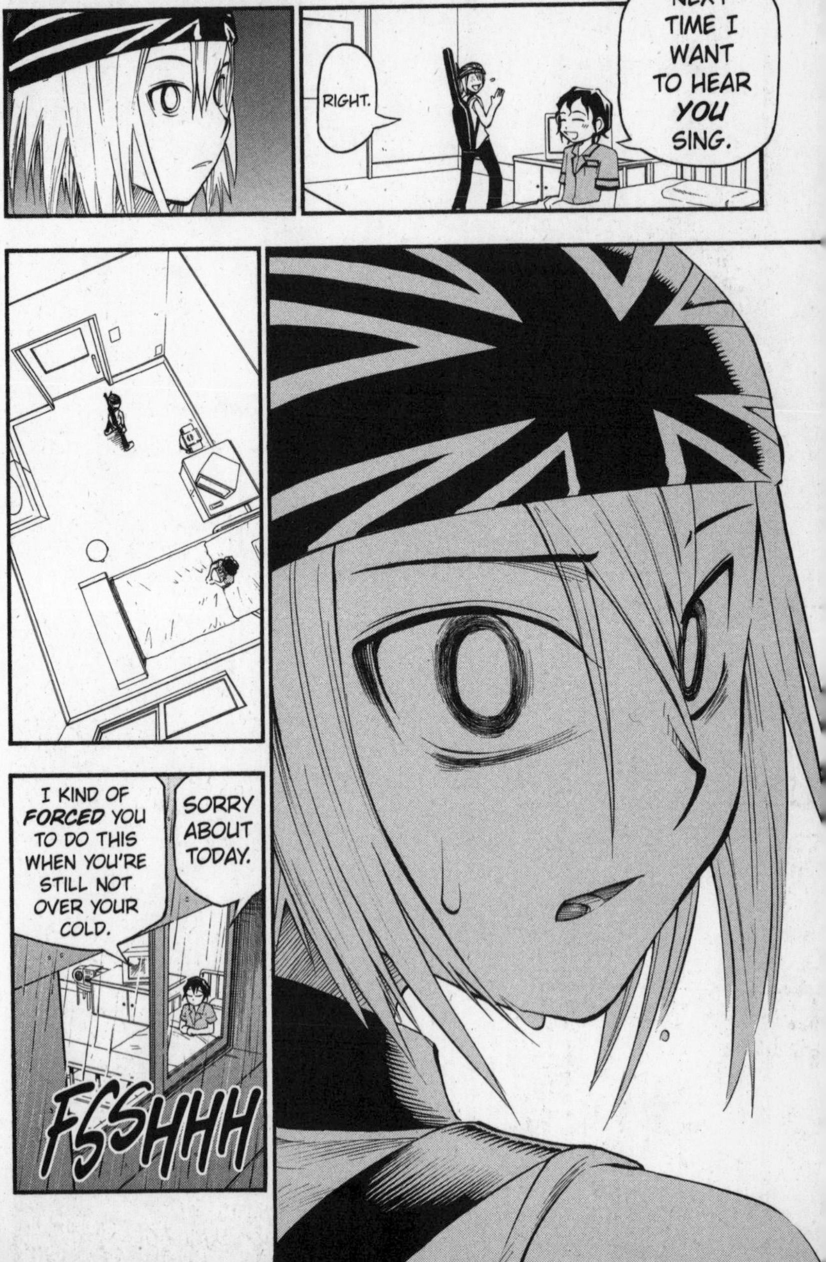
NEXT TIME I WANT TO HEAR *YOU* SING.
RIGHT.
SORRY ABOUT TODAY.
I KIND OF *FORCED* YOU TO DO THIS WHEN YOU'RE STILL NOT OVER YOUR COLD.
FSSHHH

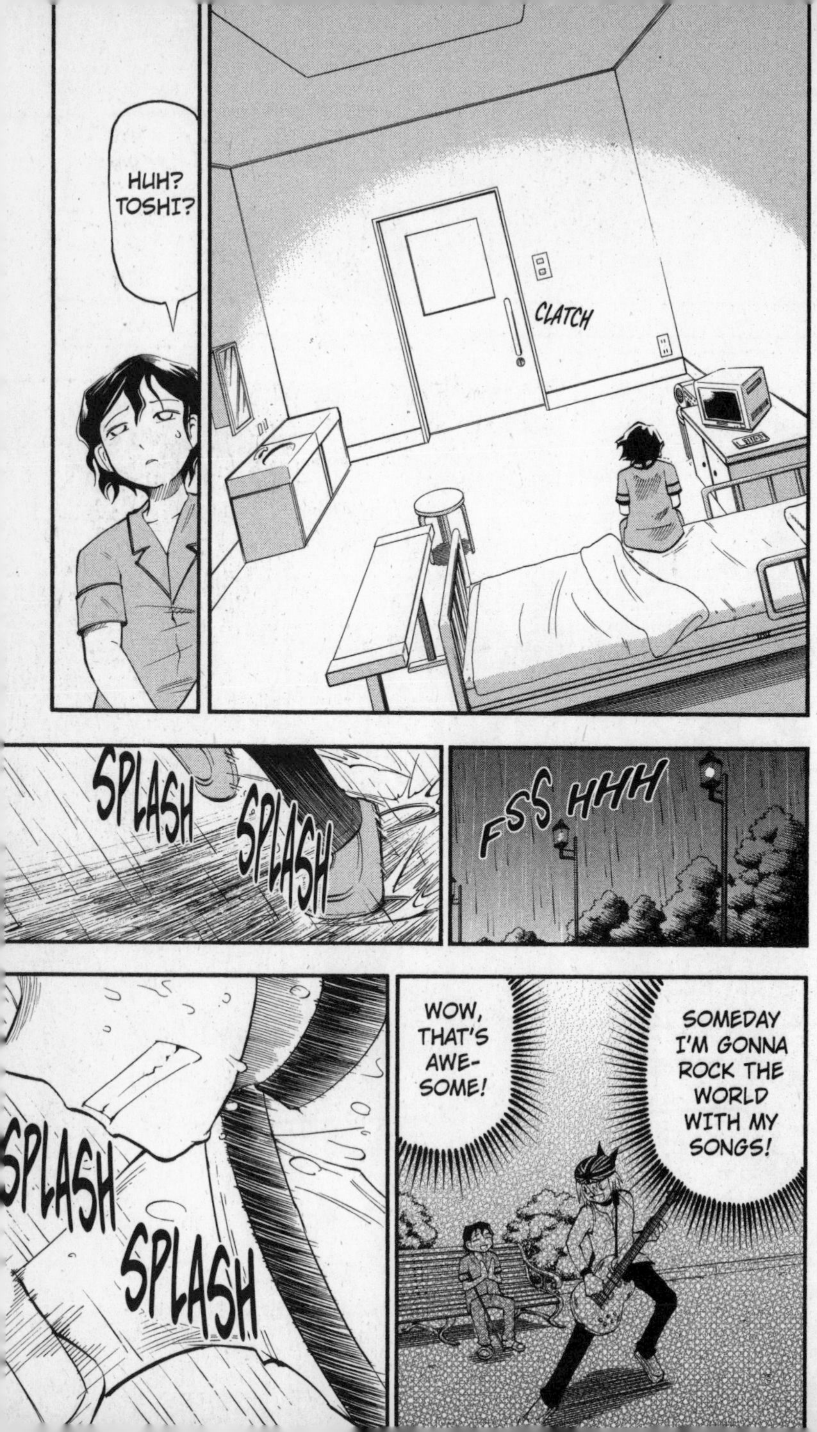
CLATCH
HUH? TOSHI?
FSS HHH
SPLASH
SPLASH
SOMEDAY I'M GONNA ROCK THE WORLD WITH MY SONGS!
WOW, THAT'S AWE-SOME!
SPLASH
SPLASH

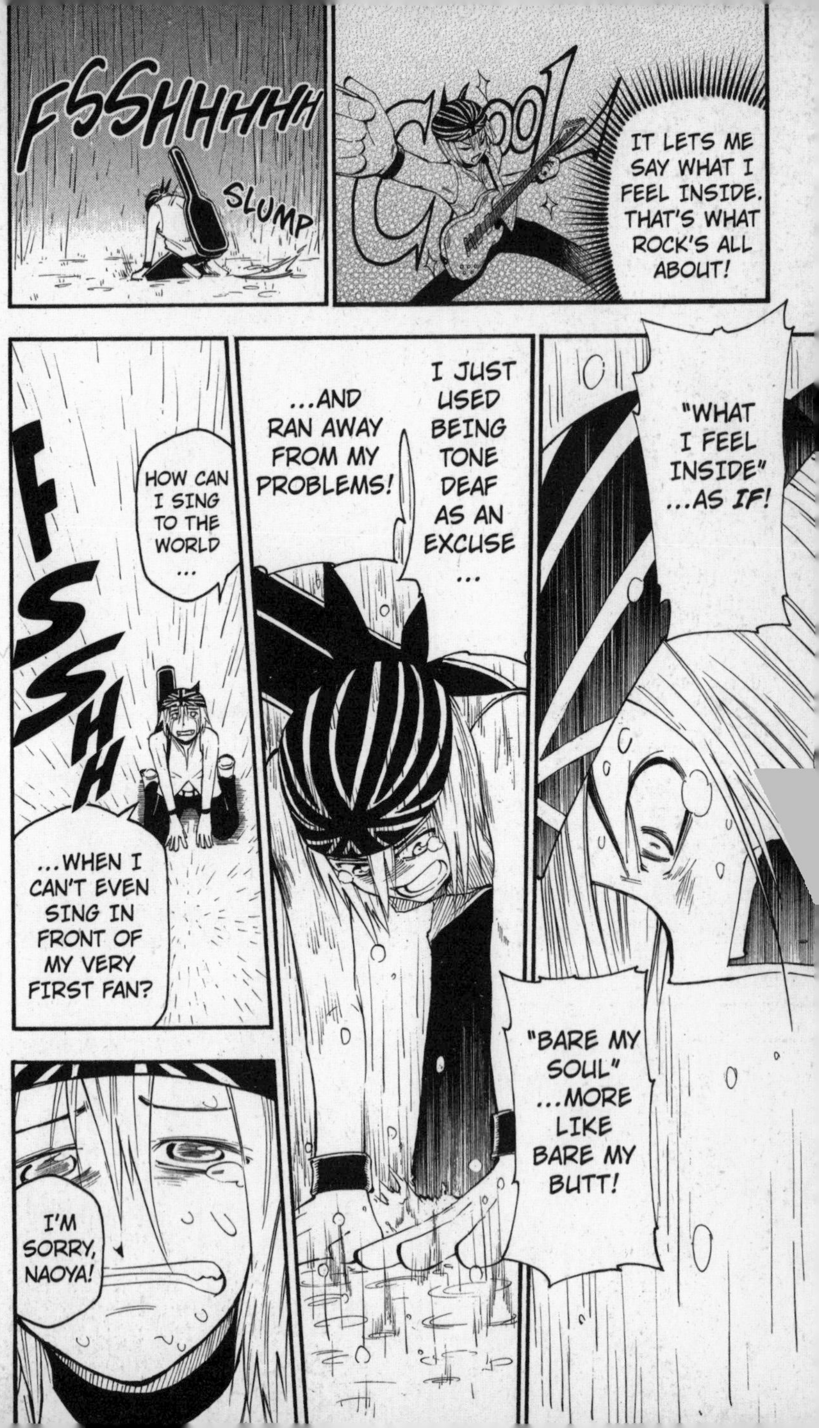
IT LETS ME SAY WHAT I FEEL INSIDE. THAT'S WHAT ROCK'S ALL ABOUT!
FSSHHHHH
SLUMP
"WHAT I FEEL INSIDE" ...AS IF!
"BARE MY SOUL" ...MORE LIKE BARE MY BUTT!
I JUST USED BEING TONE DEAF AS AN EXCUSE ...
...AND RAN AWAY FROM MY PROBLEMS!
HOW CAN I SING TO THE WORLD ...
FSSHH
...WHEN I CAN'T EVEN SING IN FRONT OF MY VERY FIRST FAN?
I'M SORRY, NAOYA!

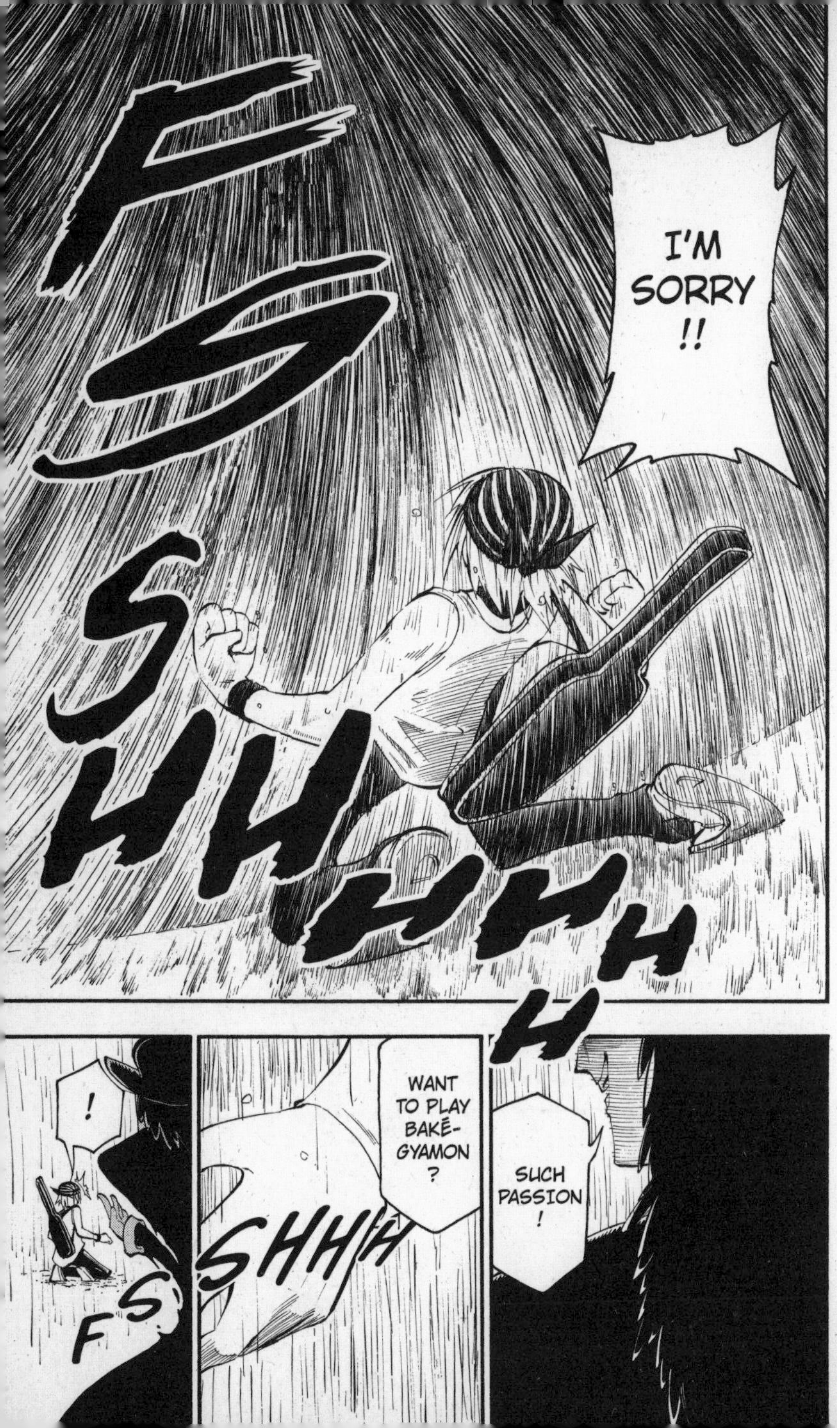
I'M SORRY!!
FSSHHHHHHHH
SUCH PASSION!
WANT TO PLAY BAKĒ-GYAMON?
!
FSSHHH

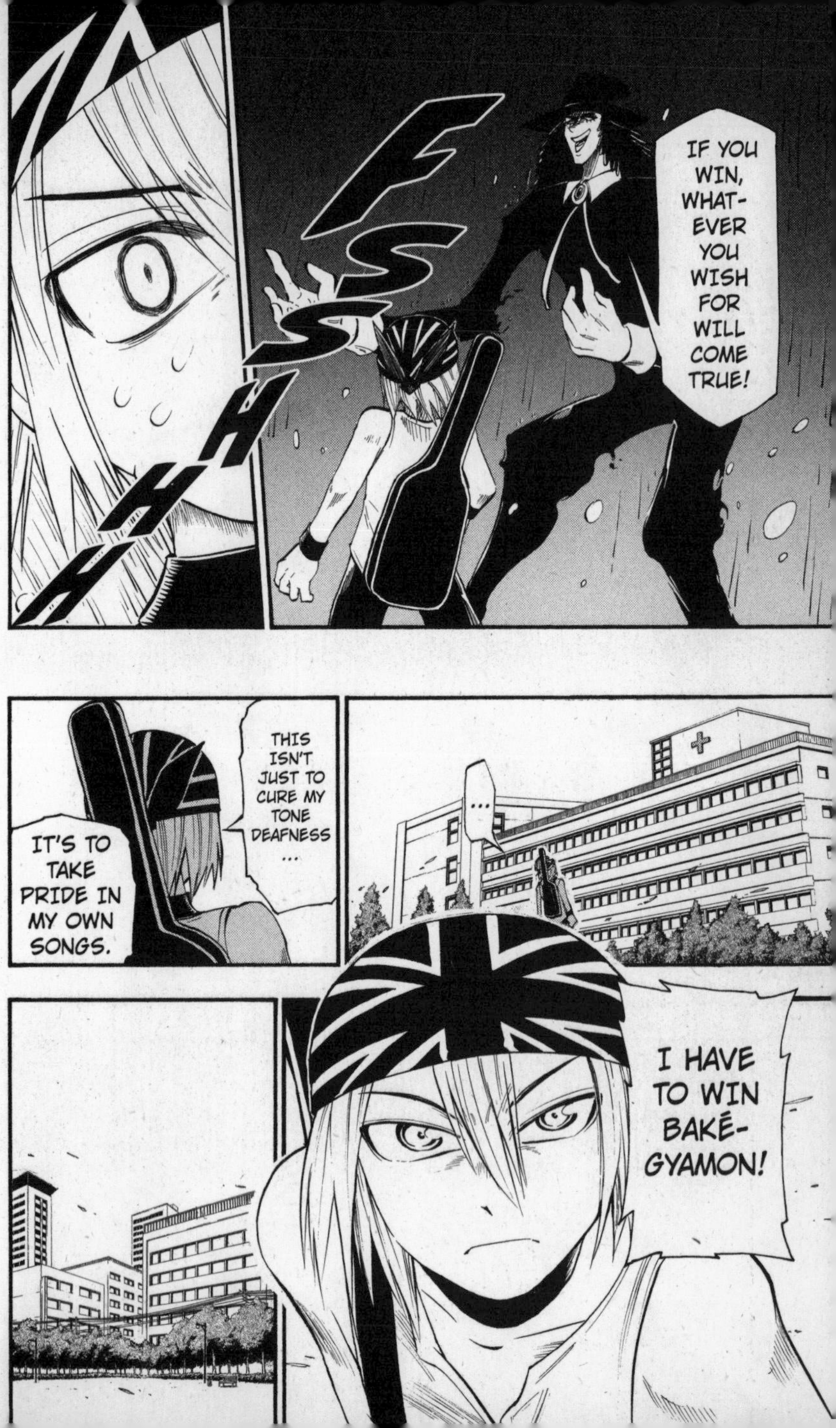
IF YOU WIN, WHAT-EVER YOU WISH FOR WILL COME TRUE!
FSSHHH
...
THIS ISN'T JUST TO CURE MY TONE DEAFNESS ...
IT'S TO TAKE PRIDE IN MY OWN SONGS.
I HAVE TO WIN BAKÉ-GYAMON!

CHAPTER 18 FIERCE BATTLE

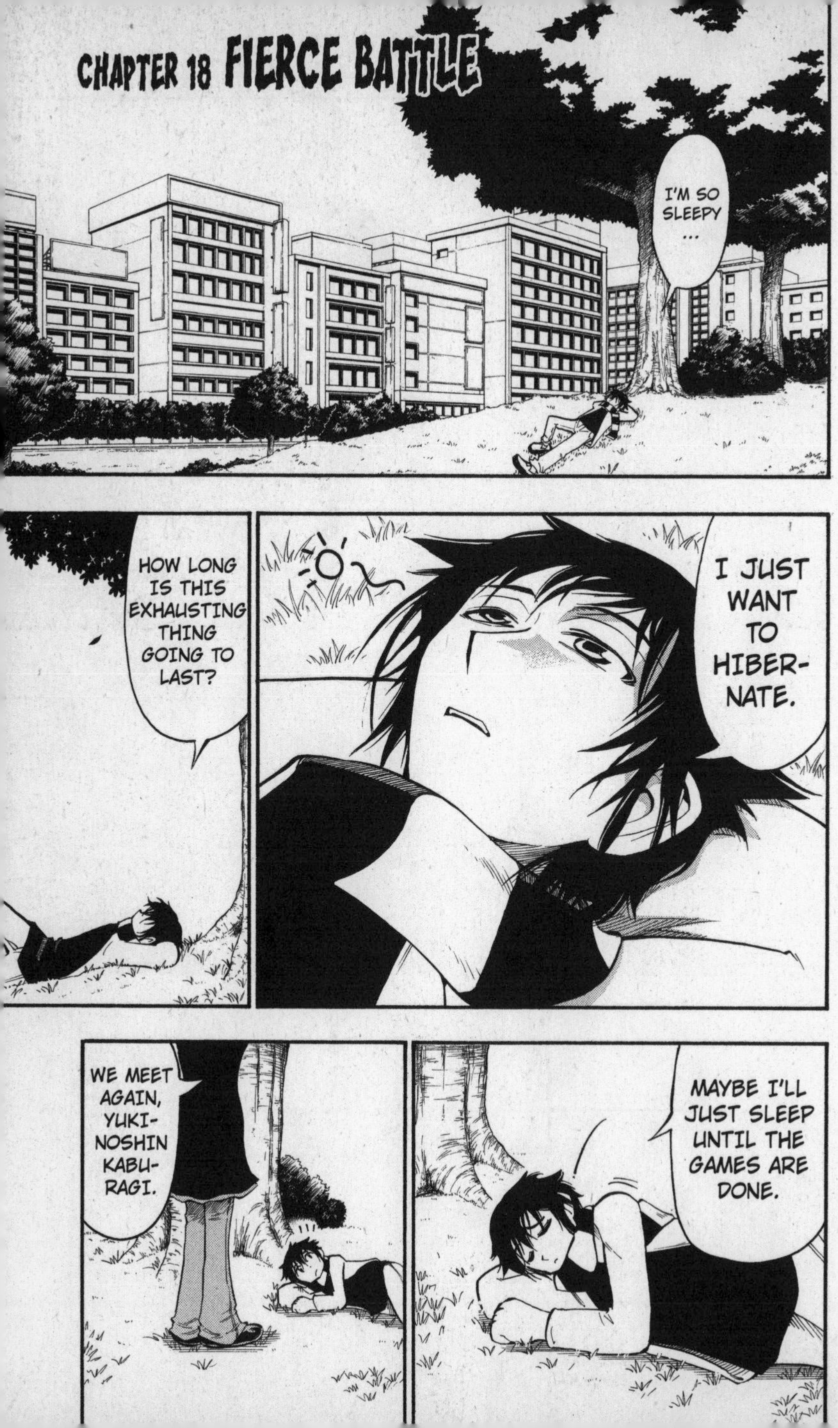
I'M SO SLEEPY ...
I JUST WANT TO HIBER-NATE.
HOW LONG IS THIS EXHAUSTING THING GOING TO LAST?
MAYBE I'LL JUST SLEEP UNTIL THE GAMES ARE DONE.
WE MEET AGAIN, YUKI-NOSHIN KABU-RAGI.

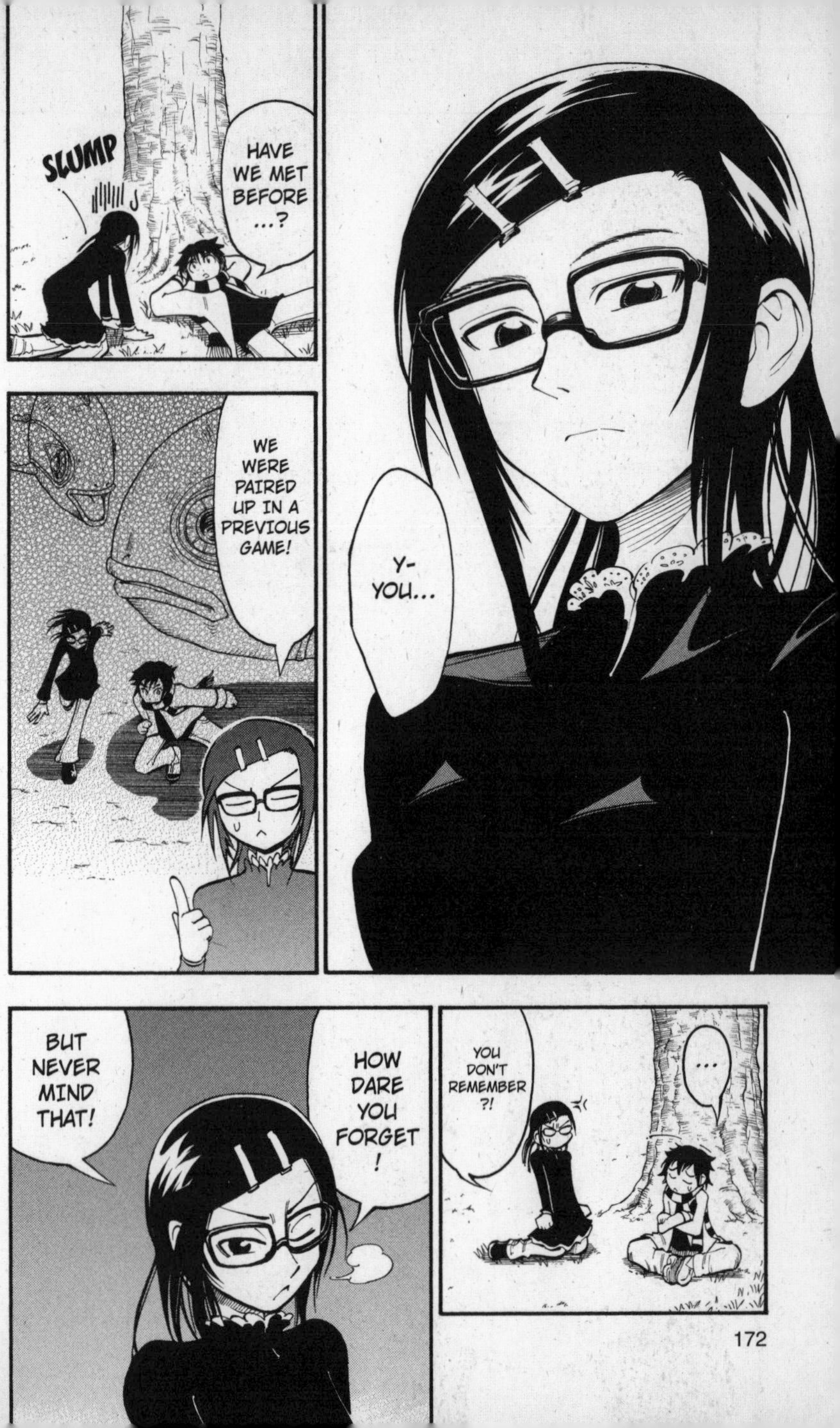
Y-YOU...
SLUMP
HAVE WE MET BEFORE ...?
WE WERE PAIRED UP IN A PREVIOUS GAME!
YOU DON'T REMEMBER?!
...
HOW DARE YOU FORGET!
BUT NEVER MIND THAT!

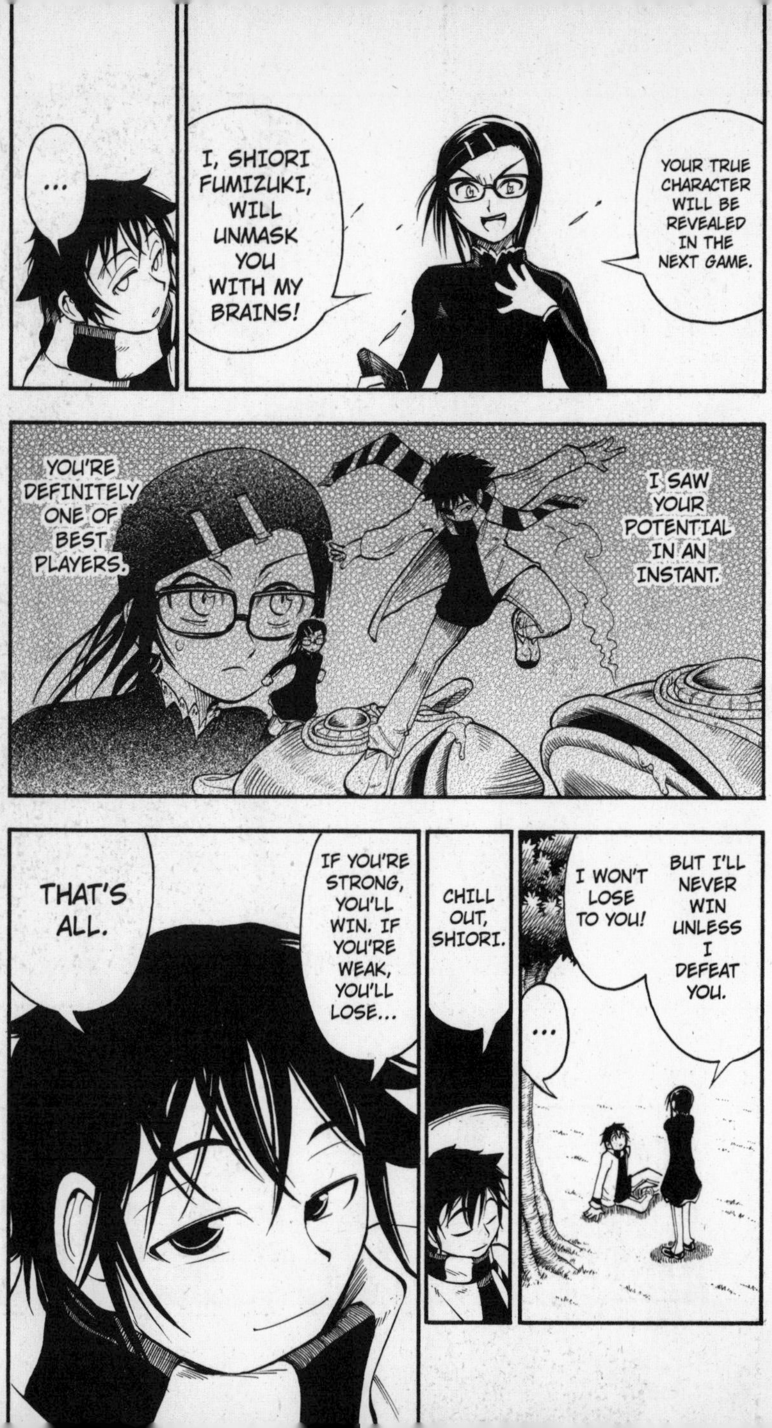
YOUR TRUE CHARACTER WILL BE REVEALED IN THE NEXT GAME.
I, SHIORI FUMIZUKI, WILL UNMASK YOU WITH MY BRAINS!
...
I SAW YOUR POTENTIAL IN AN INSTANT.
YOU'RE DEFINITELY ONE OF BEST PLAYERS.
BUT I'LL NEVER WIN UNLESS I DEFEAT YOU.
I WON'T LOSE TO YOU!
...
CHILL OUT, SHIORI.
IF YOU'RE STRONG, YOU'LL WIN. IF YOU'RE WEAK, YOU'LL LOSE...
THAT'S ALL.

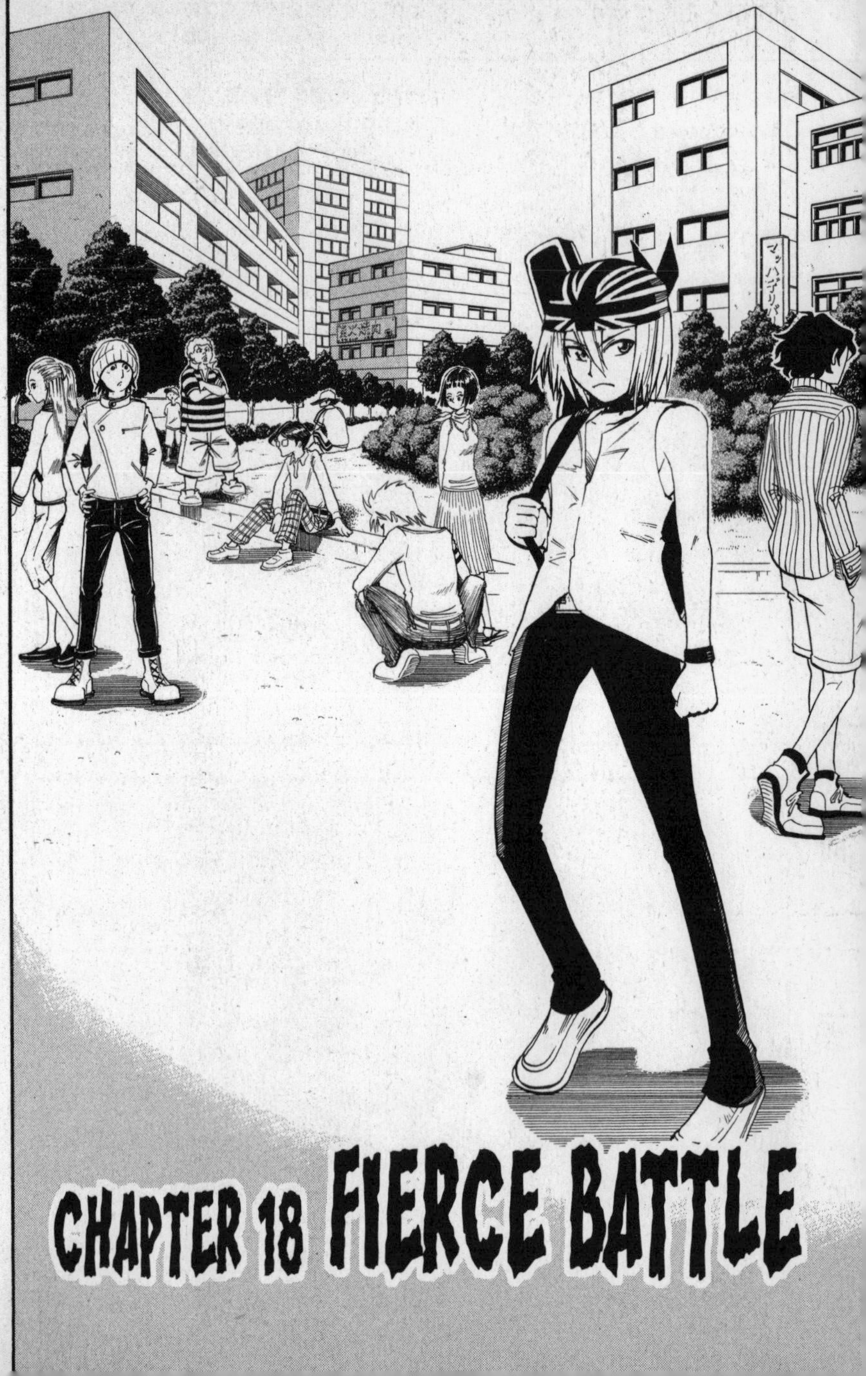

CHAPTER 18 FIERCE BATTLE

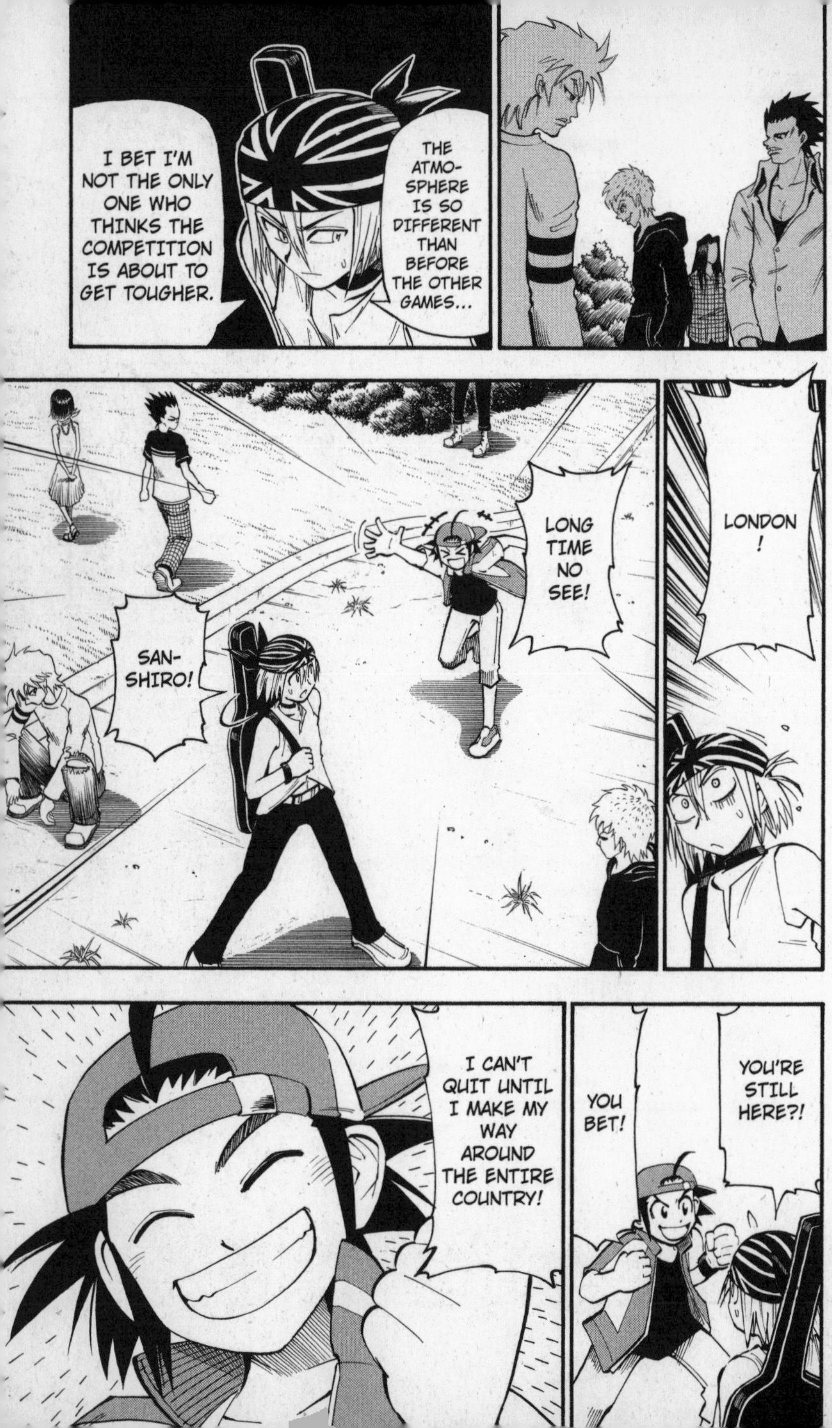
THE ATMOSPHERE IS SO DIFFERENT THAN BEFORE THE OTHER GAMES...
I BET I'M NOT THE ONLY ONE WHO THINKS THE COMPETITION IS ABOUT TO GET TOUGHER.
LONDON!
LONG TIME NO SEE!
SAN-SHIRO!
YOU'RE STILL HERE?!
YOU BET!
I CAN'T QUIT UNTIL I MAKE MY WAY AROUND THE ENTIRE COUNTRY!

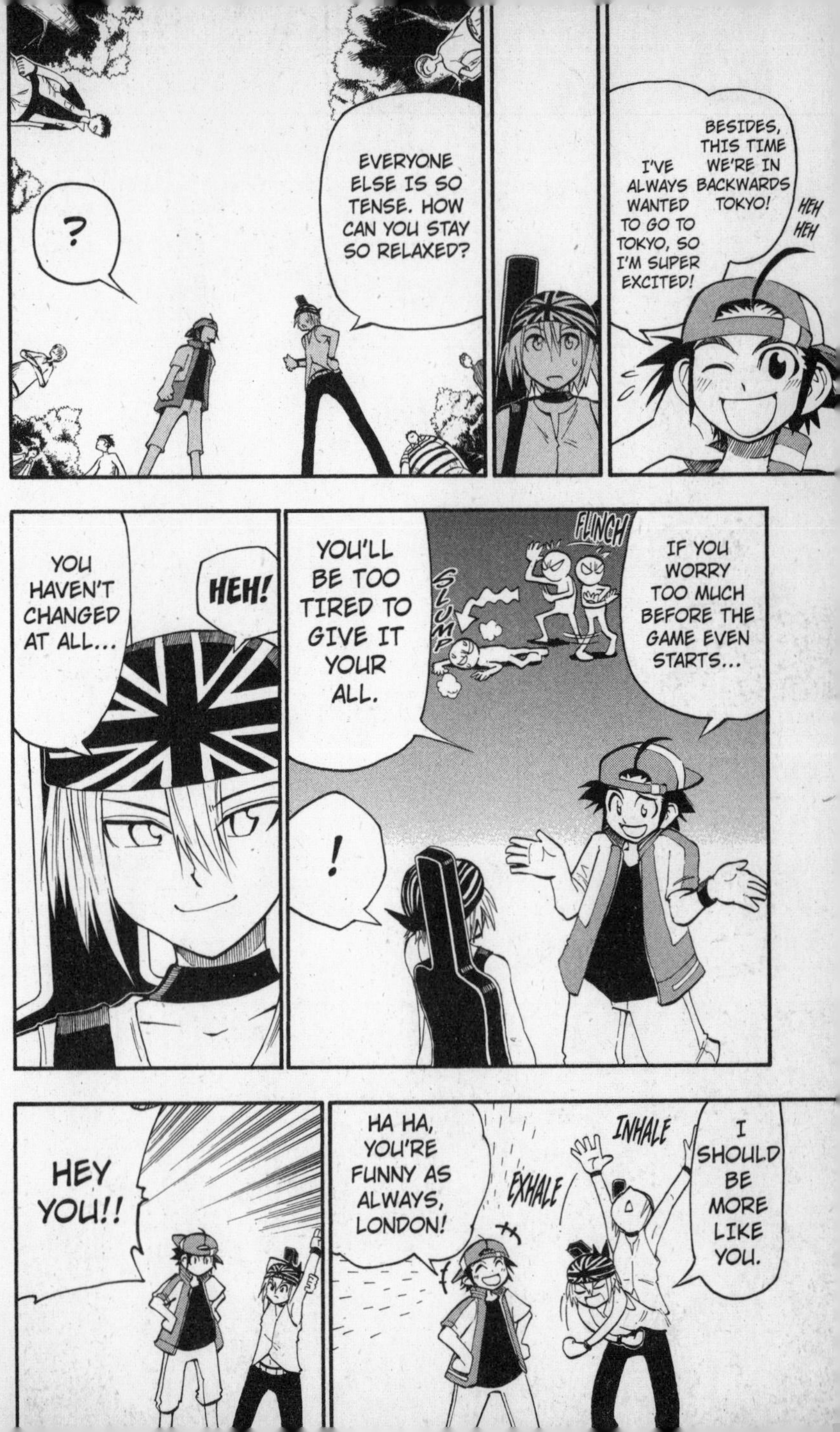

I'VE ALWAYS WANTED TO GO TO TOKYO, SO I'M SUPER EXCITED!
BESIDES, THIS TIME WE'RE IN BACKWARDS TOKYO!
HEH HEH
EVERYONE ELSE IS SO TENSE. HOW CAN YOU STAY SO RELAXED?
?
IF YOU WORRY TOO MUCH BEFORE THE GAME EVEN STARTS...
FLINCH
SLUMP
YOU'LL BE TOO TIRED TO GIVE IT YOUR ALL.
!
HEH!
YOU HAVEN'T CHANGED AT ALL...
I SHOULD BE MORE LIKE YOU.
INHALE
EXHALE
HA HA, YOU'RE FUNNY AS ALWAYS, LONDON!
HEY YOU!!

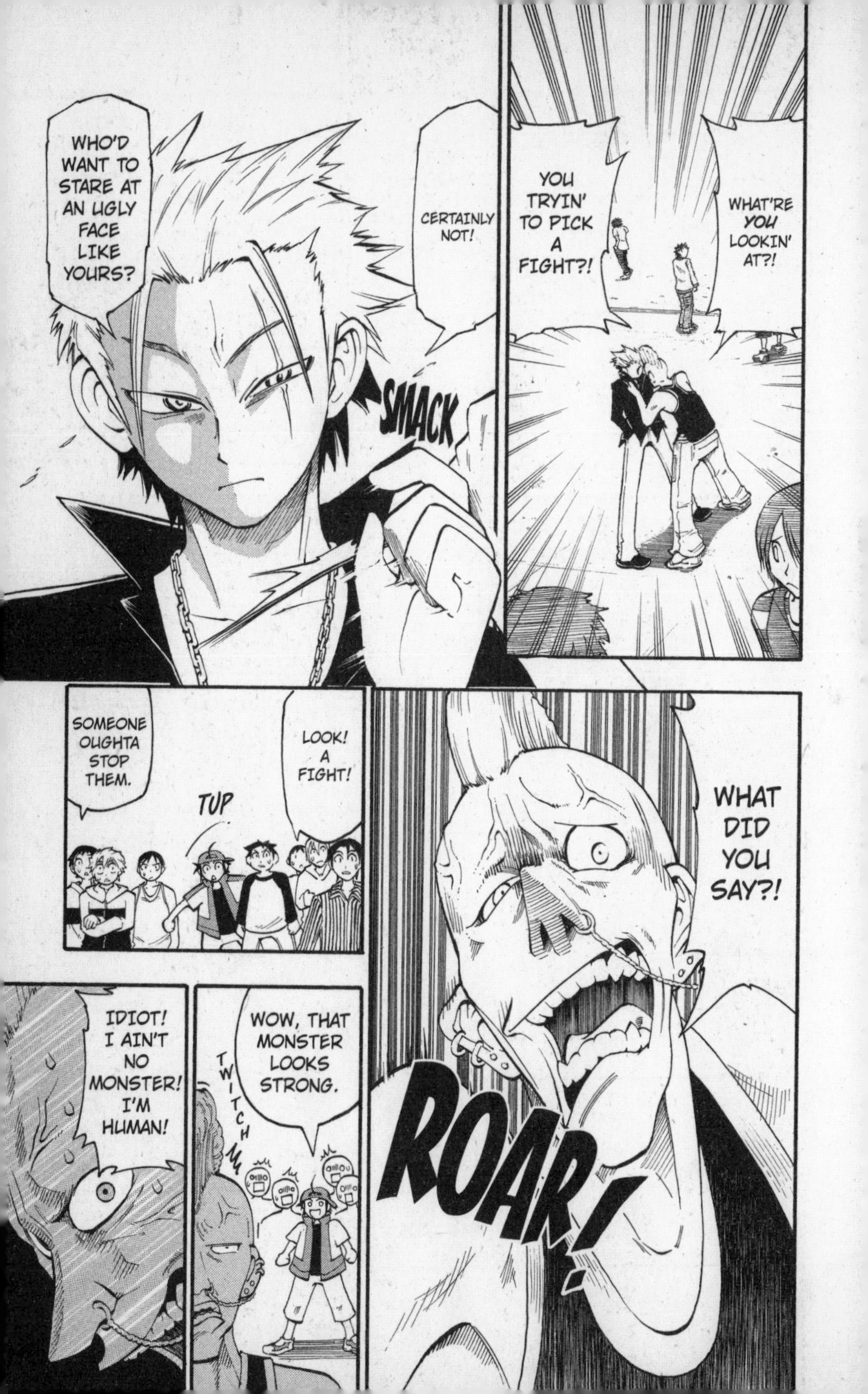
WHAT'RE YOU LOOKIN' AT?!
YOU TRYIN' TO PICK A FIGHT?!
CERTAINLY NOT!
SMACK
WHO'D WANT TO STARE AT AN UGLY FACE LIKE YOURS?
WHAT DID YOU SAY?!
ROAR!
LOOK! A FIGHT!
TUP
SOMEONE OUGHTA STOP THEM.
WOW, THAT MONSTER LOOKS STRONG.
TWITCH
IDIOT! I AIN'T NO MONSTER! I'M HUMAN!

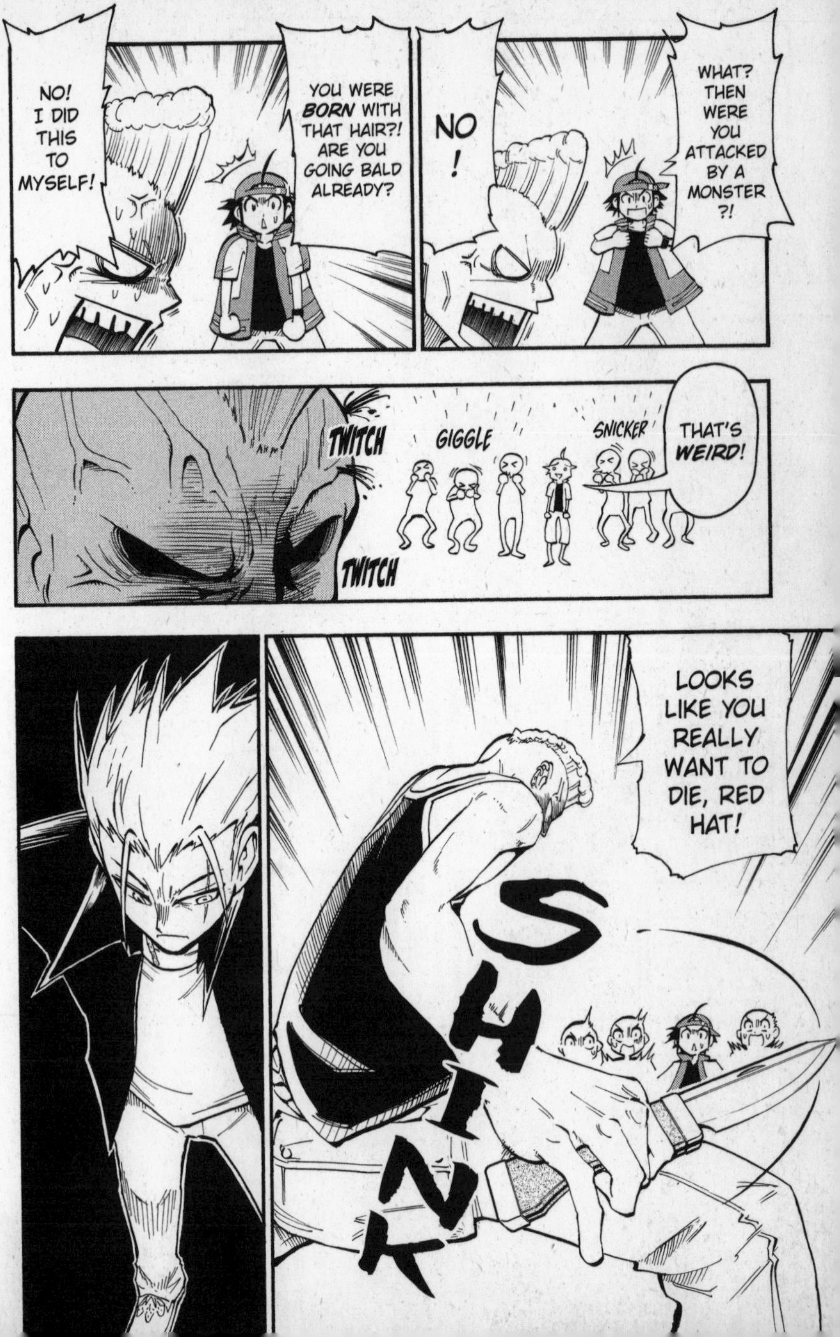
WHAT? THEN WERE YOU ATTACKED BY A MONSTER?!
NO!
YOU WERE **BORN** WITH THAT HAIR?! ARE YOU GOING BALD ALREADY?
NO! I DID THIS TO MYSELF!
THAT'S **WEIRD!**
SNICKER
GIGGLE
TWITCH
TWITCH
LOOKS LIKE YOU REALLY WANT TO DIE, RED HAT!
SHINK

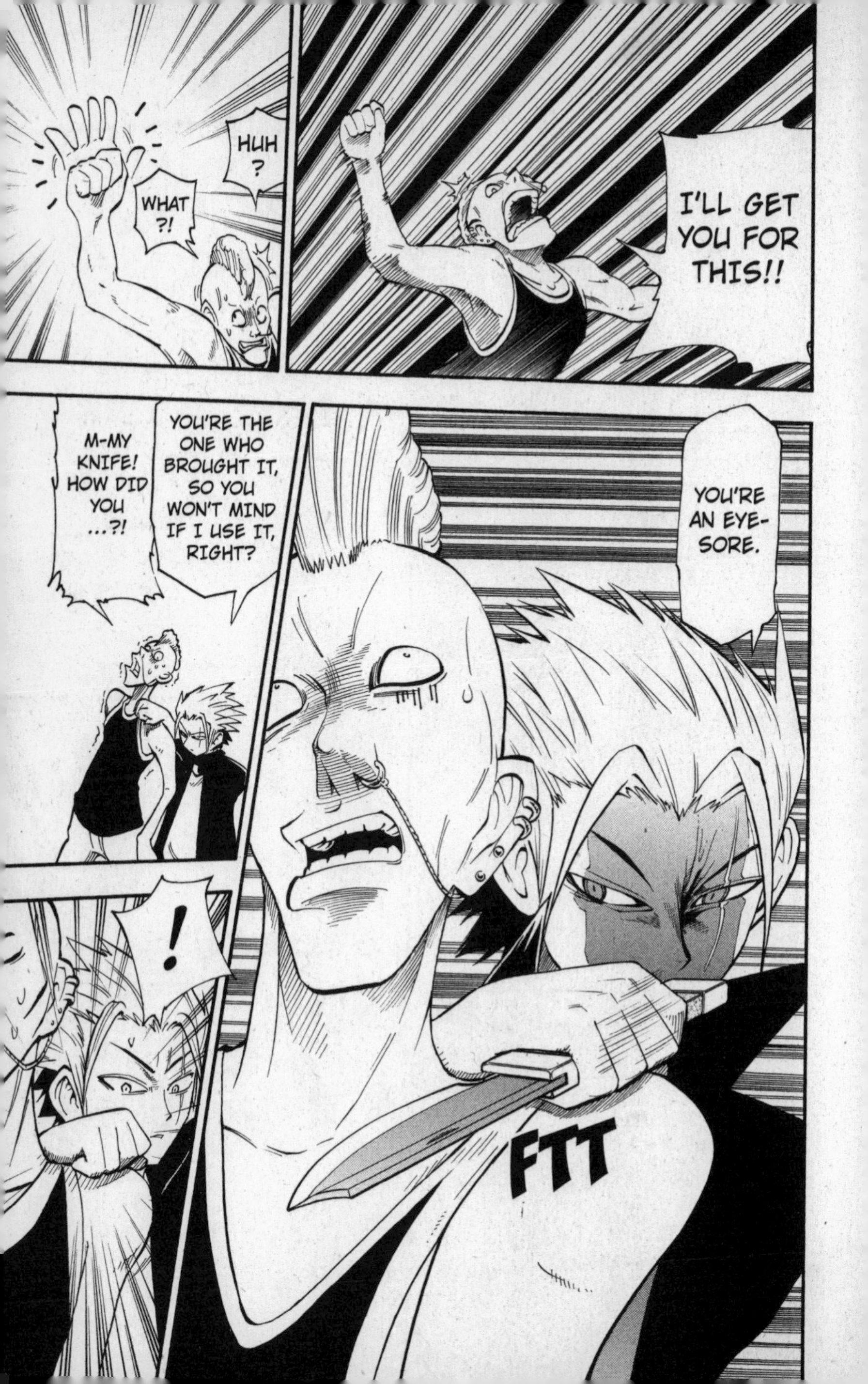
I'LL GET YOU FOR THIS!!
HUH?
WHAT?!
YOU'RE AN EYE-SORE.
FTT
YOU'RE THE ONE WHO BROUGHT IT, SO YOU WON'T MIND IF I USE IT, RIGHT?
M-MY KNIFE! HOW DID YOU ...?!
!

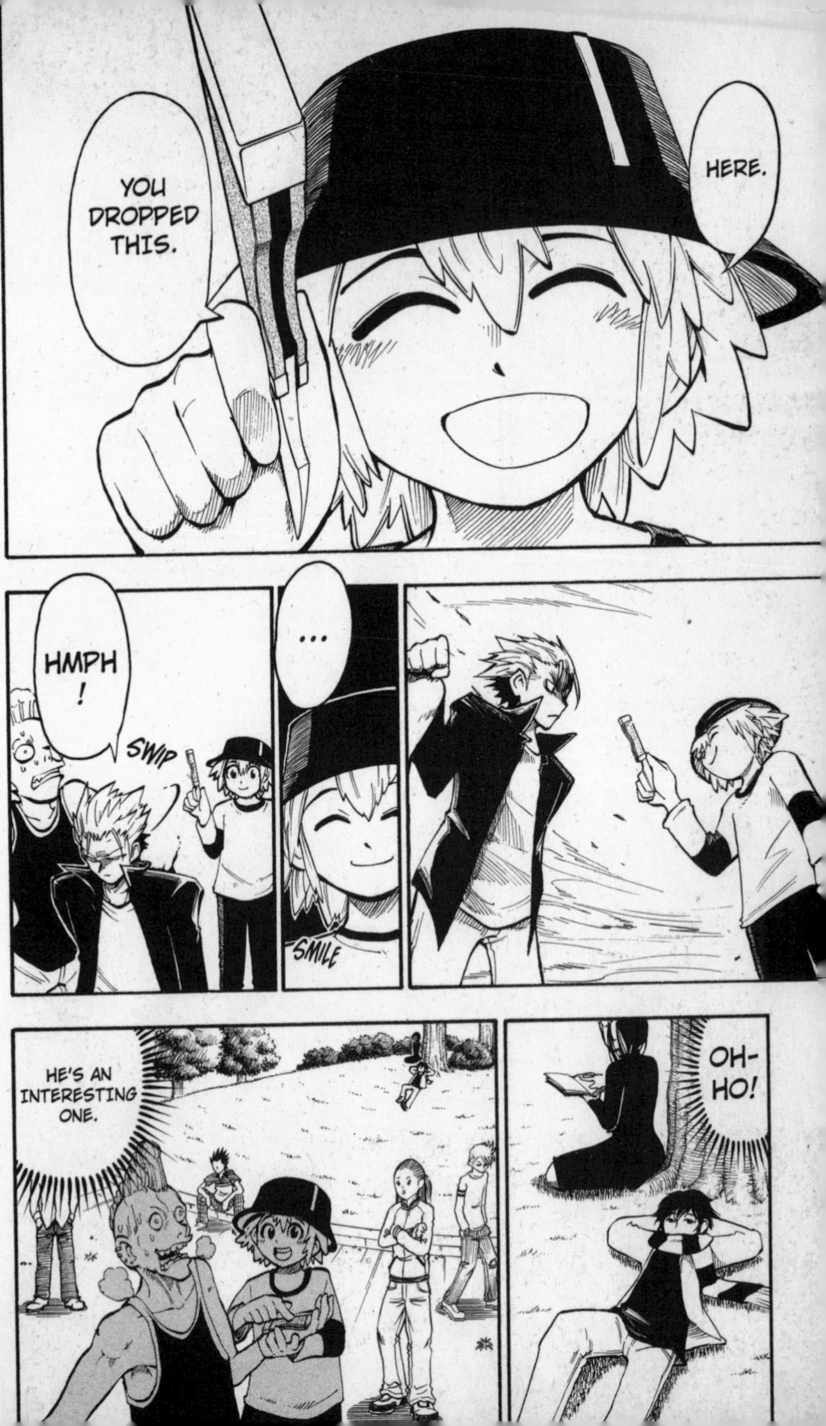
HERE.
YOU DROPPED THIS.
...
SMILE
HMPH!
SWIP
OH-HO!
HE'S AN INTERESTING ONE.

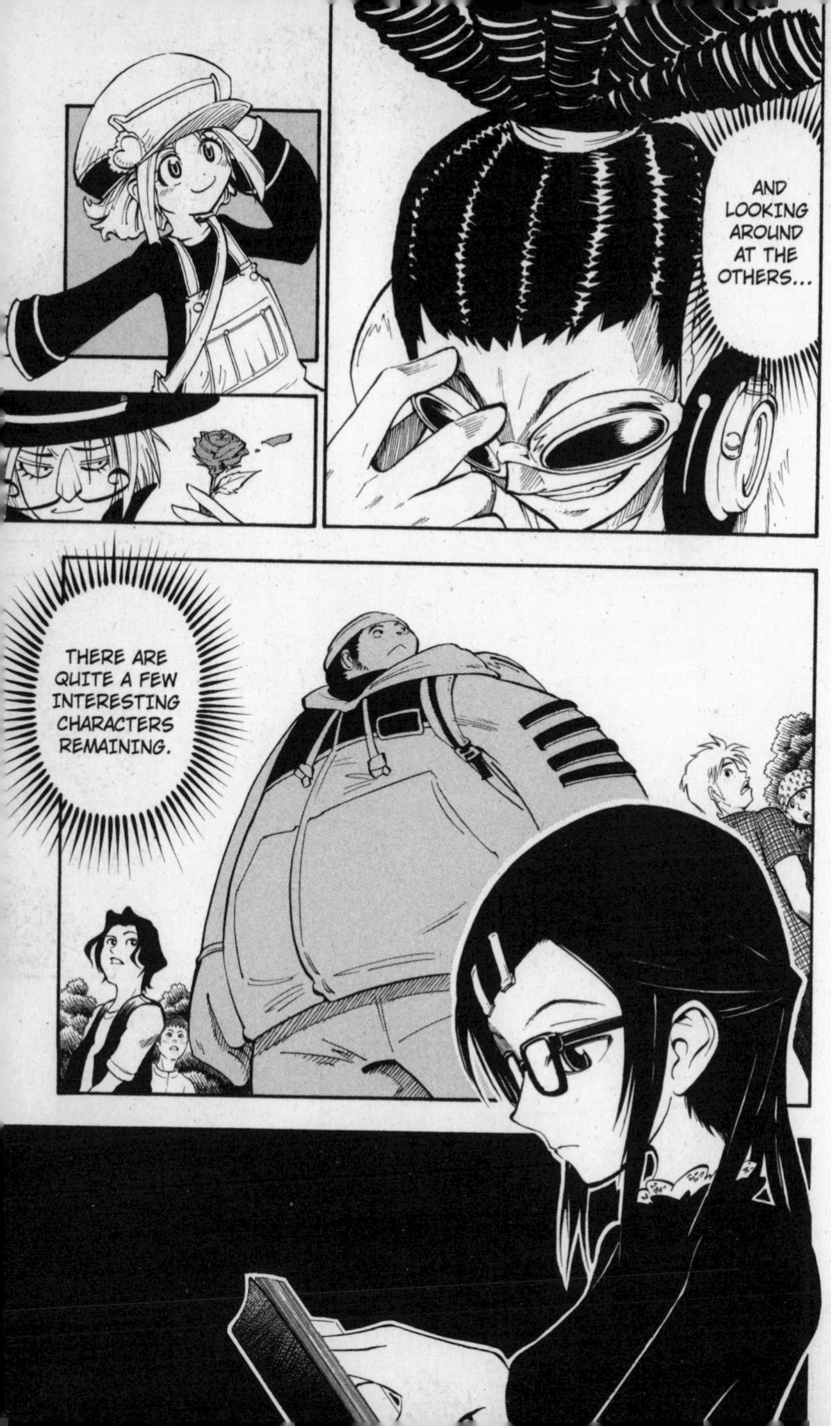
AND LOOKING AROUND AT THE OTHERS...
THERE ARE QUITE A FEW INTERESTING CHARACTERS REMAINING.

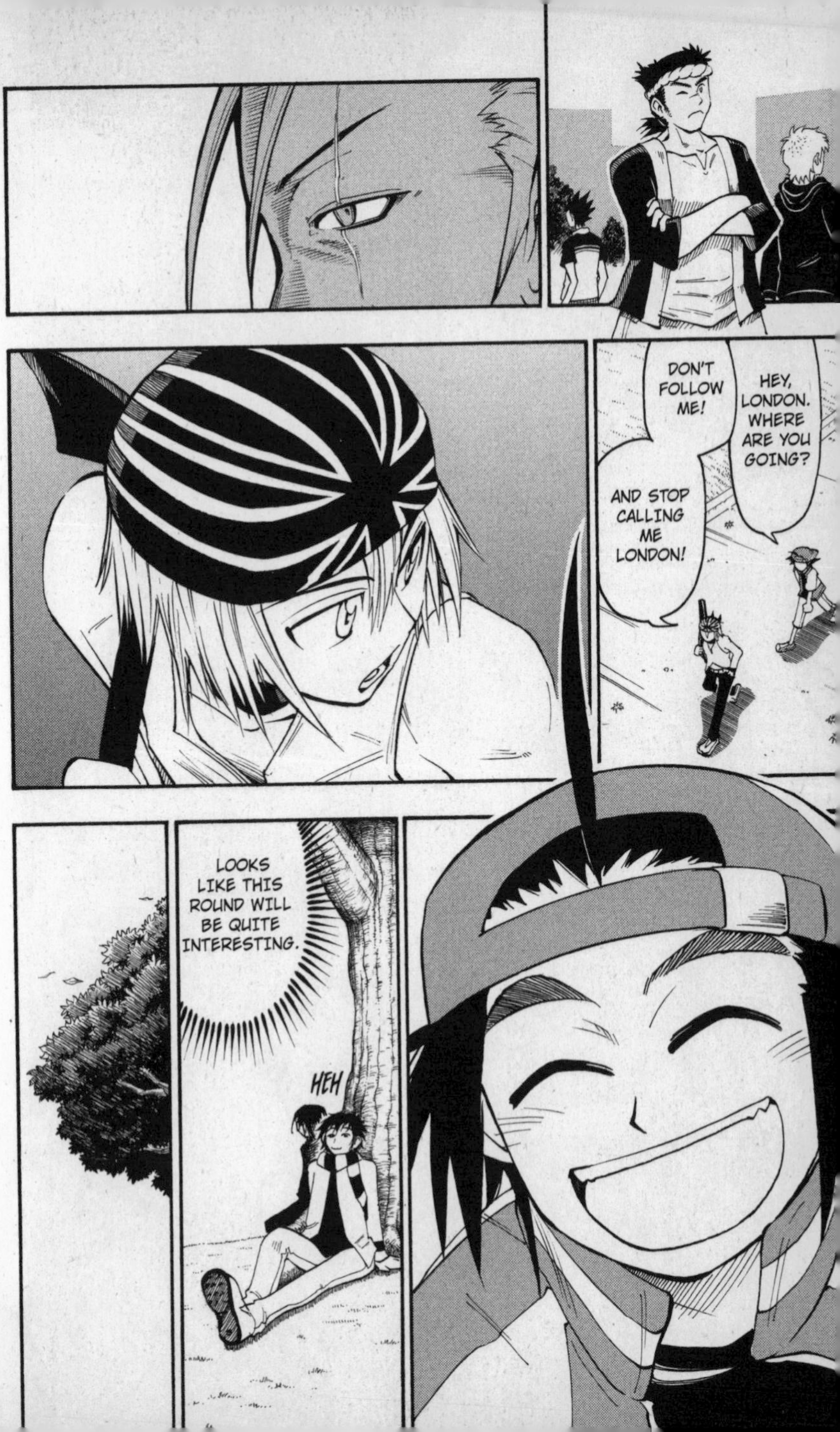
HEY, LONDON. WHERE ARE YOU GOING?
DON'T FOLLOW ME!
AND STOP CALLING ME LONDON!
LOOKS LIKE THIS ROUND WILL BE QUITE INTERESTING.
HEH

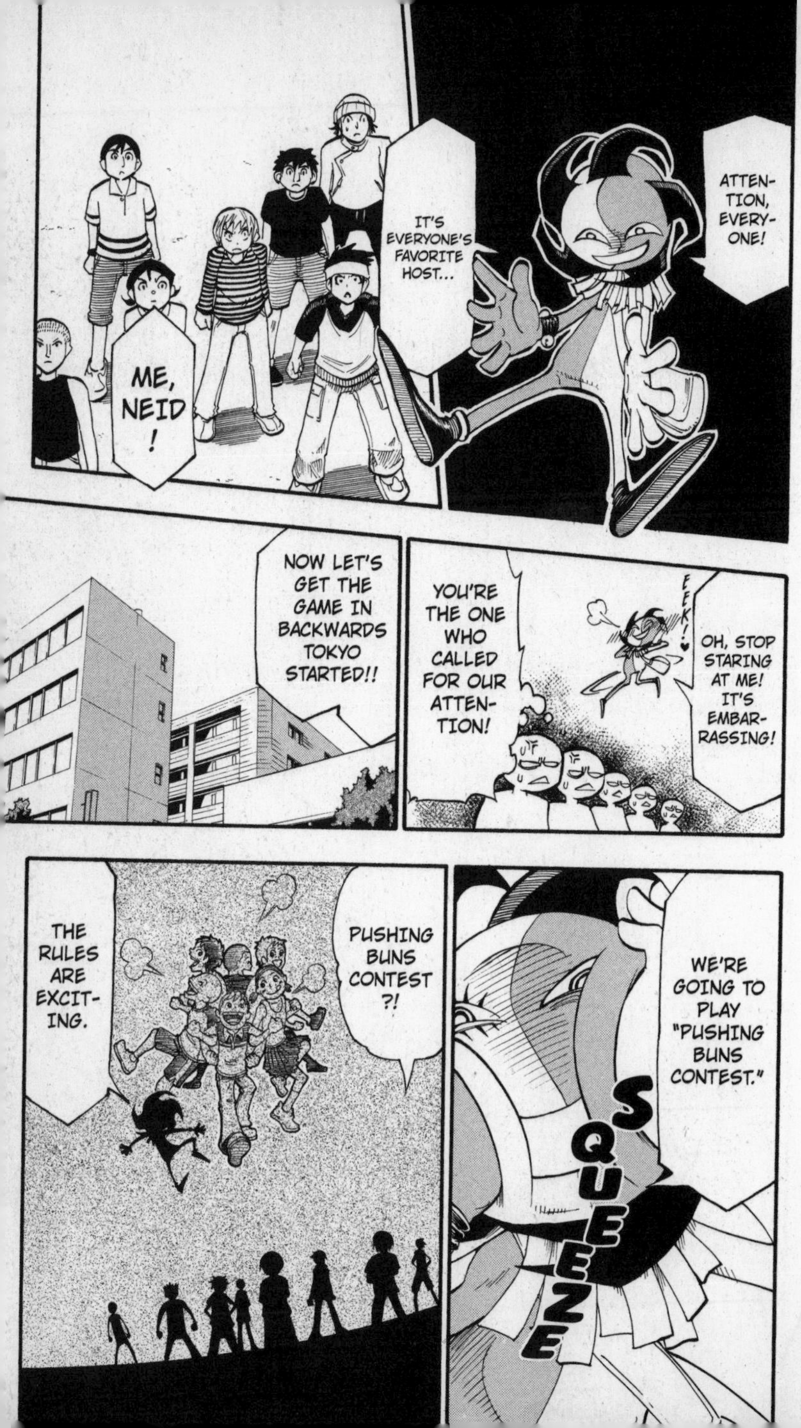
ATTENTION, EVERYONE!
IT'S EVERYONE'S FAVORITE HOST...
ME, NEID!
OH, STOP STARING AT ME! IT'S EMBARRASSING!
EEK!♥
YOU'RE THE ONE WHO CALLED FOR OUR ATTENTION!
NOW LET'S GET THE GAME IN BACKWARDS TOKYO STARTED!!
WE'RE GOING TO PLAY "PUSHING BUNS CONTEST."
SQUEEZE
PUSHING BUNS CONTEST?!
THE RULES ARE EXCITING.

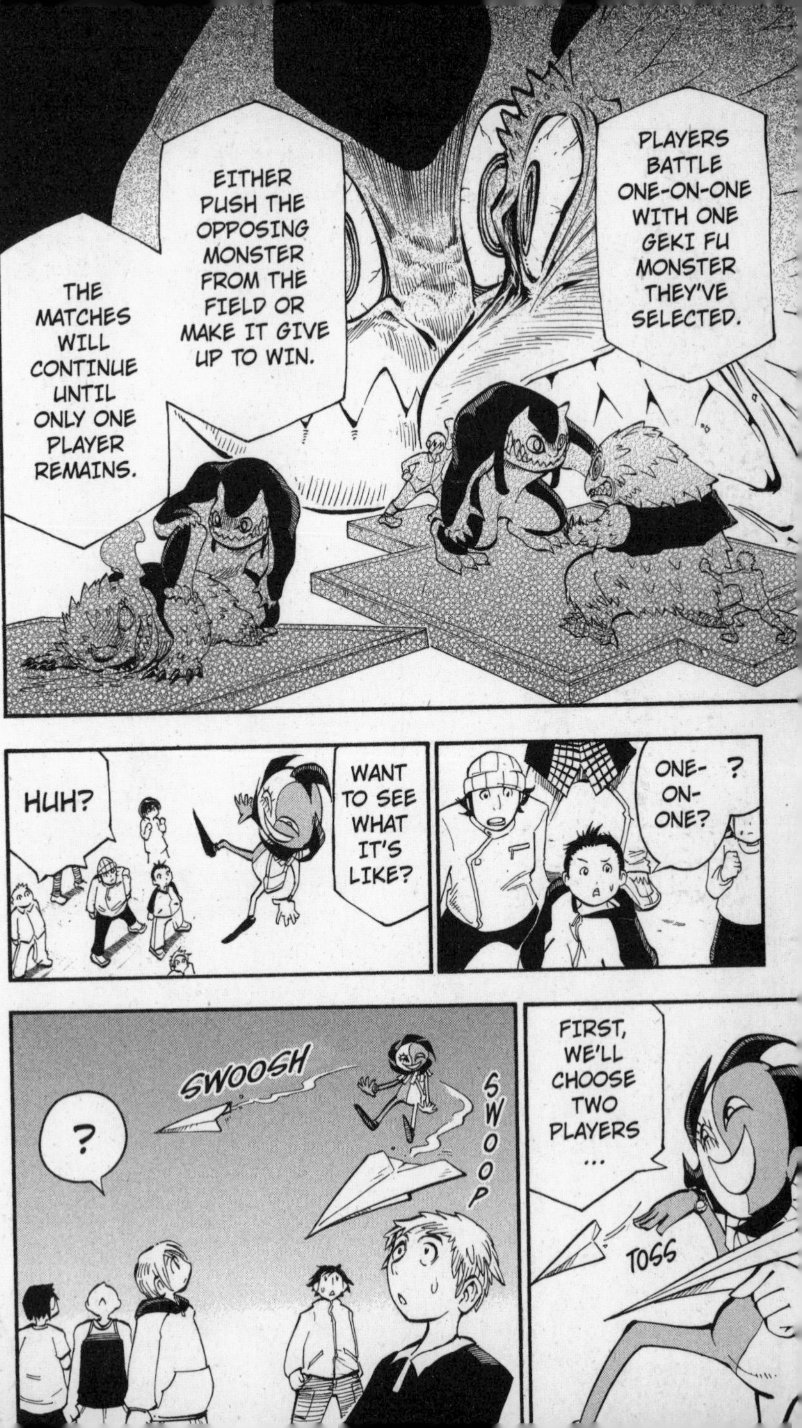
PLAYERS BATTLE ONE-ON-ONE WITH ONE GEKI FU MONSTER THEY'VE SELECTED.
EITHER PUSH THE OPPOSING MONSTER FROM THE FIELD OR MAKE IT GIVE UP TO WIN.
THE MATCHES WILL CONTINUE UNTIL ONLY ONE PLAYER REMAINS.
ONE-ON-ONE?
?
WANT TO SEE WHAT IT'S LIKE?
HUH?
FIRST, WE'LL CHOOSE TWO PLAYERS...
TOSS
SWOOP
SWOOSH
?

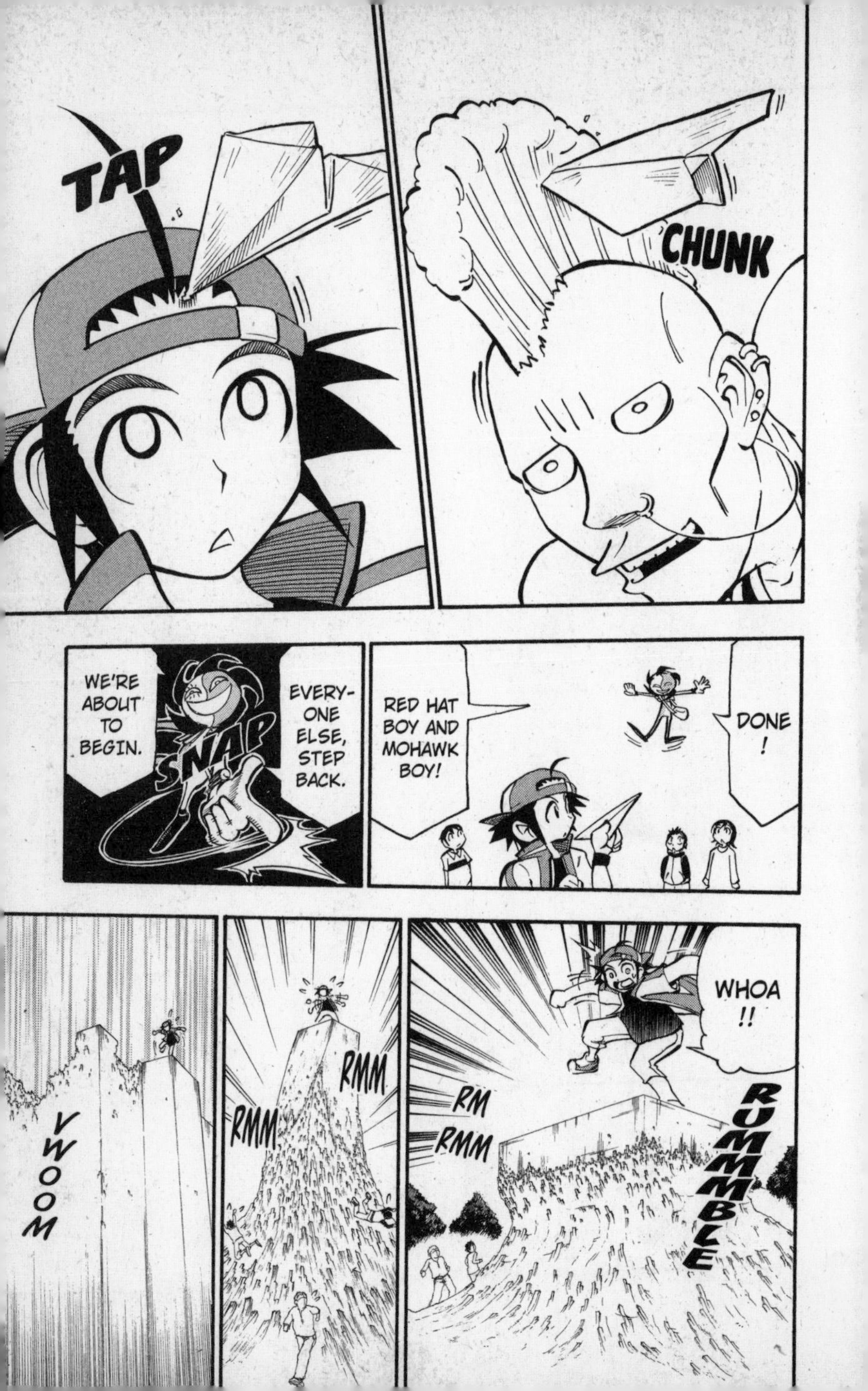
CHUNK
TAP
DONE!
RED HAT BOY AND MOHAWK BOY!
EVERY-ONE ELSE, STEP BACK.
WE'RE ABOUT TO BEGIN.
SNAP
WHOA!!
RUMMBLE
RM
RMM
RMM
RMM
VWOOM

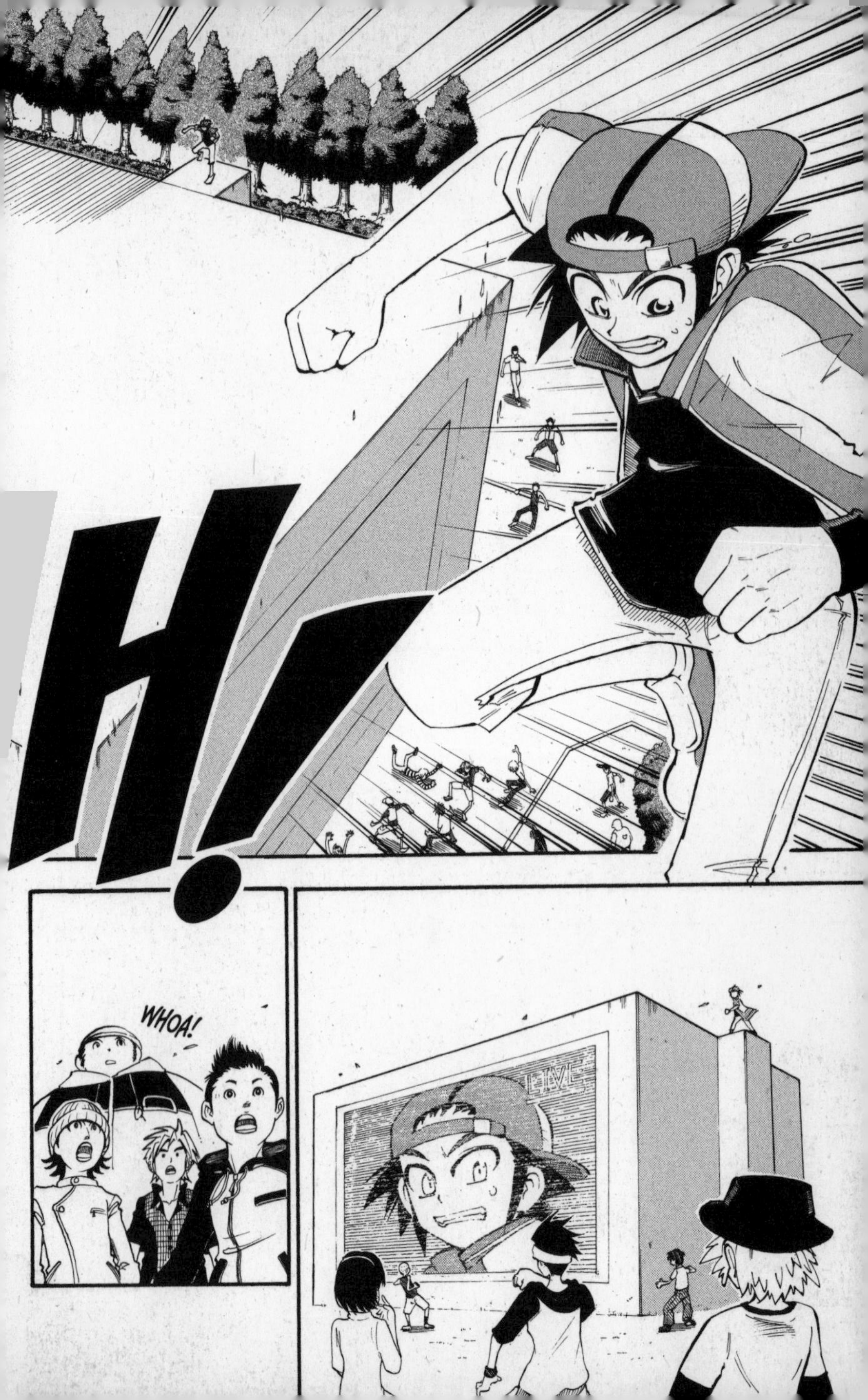
H!
LIVE
WHOA!

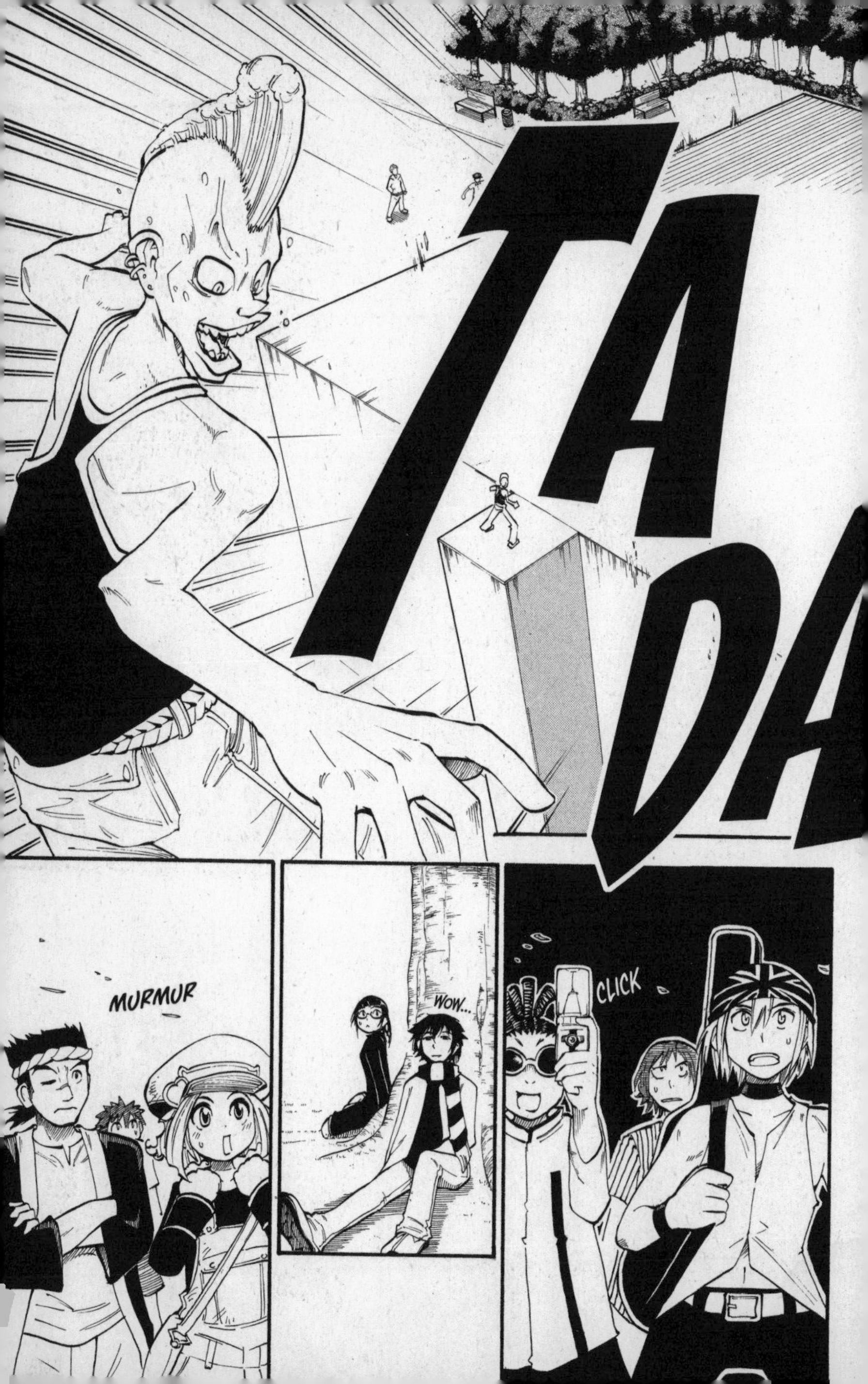
TA DA
CLICK
WOW...
MURMUR

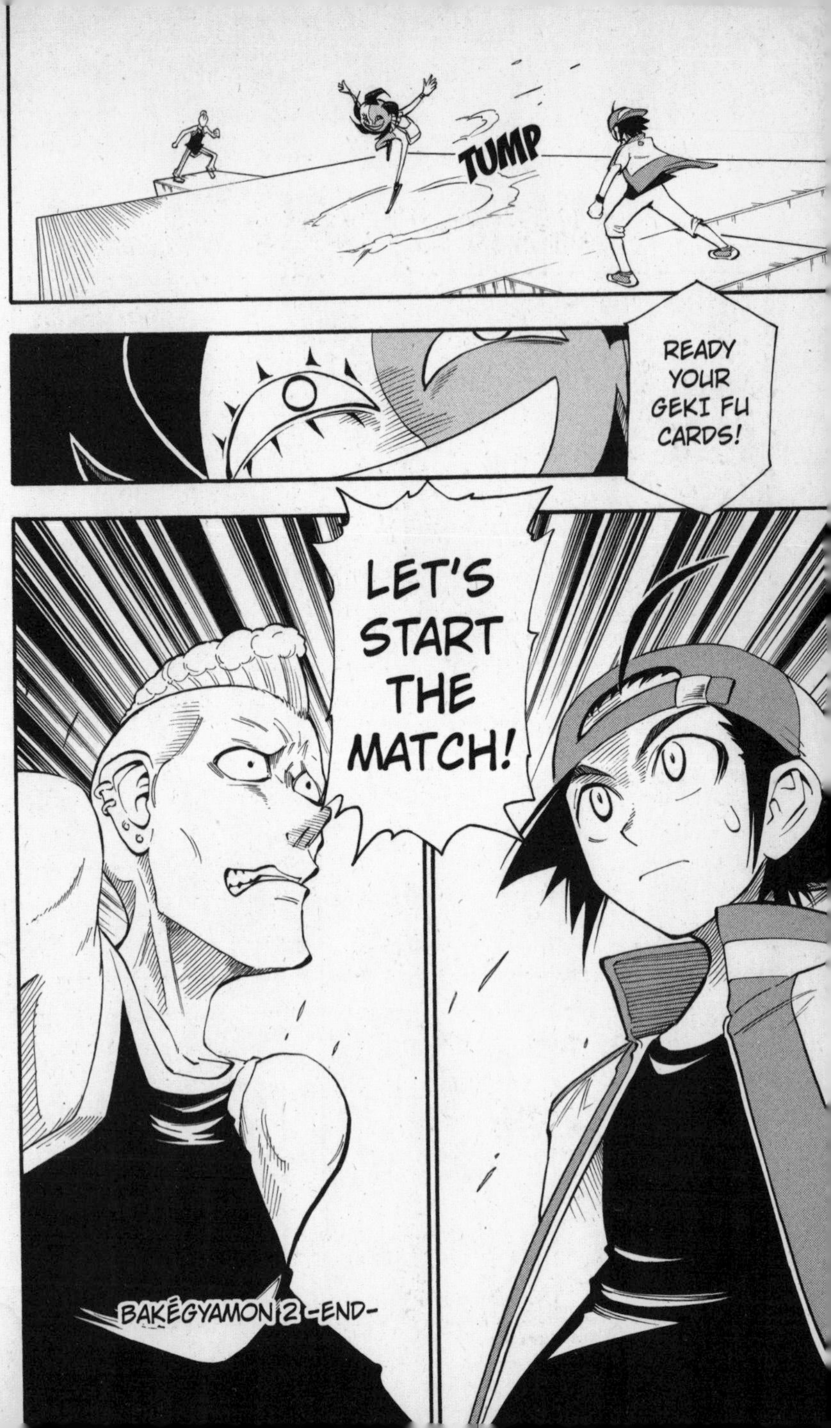
TUMP
READY YOUR GEKI FU CARDS!
LET'S START THE MATCH!
BAKÉGYAMON 2 -END-

BAKÉGYAMON DIARY 2

RECORDING STUDIO

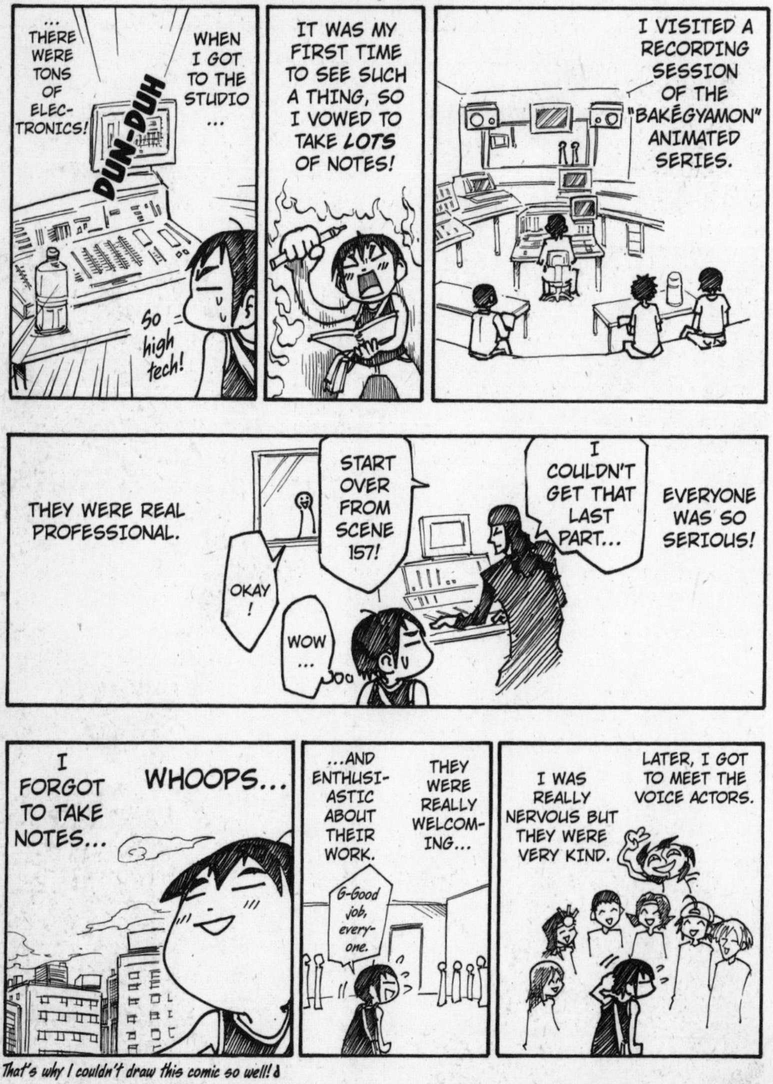

I VISITED A RECORDING SESSION OF THE "BAKÉGYAMON" ANIMATED SERIES.
IT WAS MY FIRST TIME TO SEE SUCH A THING, SO I VOWED TO TAKE LOTS OF NOTES!
WHEN I GOT TO THE STUDIO ...
... THERE WERE TONS OF ELEC-TRONICS!
DUN-DUH
So high tech!
EVERYONE WAS SO SERIOUS!
I COULDN'T GET THAT LAST PART...
START OVER FROM SCENE 157!
OKAY!
WOW...
THEY WERE REAL PROFESSIONAL.
LATER, I GOT TO MEET THE VOICE ACTORS.
I WAS REALLY NERVOUS BUT THEY WERE VERY KIND.
THEY WERE REALLY WELCOM-ING...
...AND ENTHUSI-ASTIC ABOUT THEIR WORK.
G-Good job, every-one.
WHOOPS...
I FORGOT TO TAKE NOTES...

That's why I couldn't draw this comic so well!

The Real Game Guide

The games that Sanshiro must clear in the preliminary rounds are based on actual games in Japan. Some may be familiar and some may be completely foreign to you. But since this all takes place in Backwards Japan, not everything is the way it should be!

Hide-and-Seek (かくれんぼう: Kakurenbo)

Played the same way in Japan and in America, whoever is "it" must find the other players who are hiding. But in Sanshiro's case, it looks like the hidden Geki Fu found him!

Let Me Pass (とおりゃんせ: Tôryanse)

Tôryanse is a popular nursery rhyme from Japan's Edo period (1603AD-1867AD). It is similar to the game "London Bridge is Falling Down" where two players hold their hands up high while the other players walk underneath. Once the song is finished, their hands will trap whoever is walking underneath, blocking their path.

But in Backwards Japan, Sanshiro can get past the roadblocks if he follows all the traffic rules!

Another fun fact: Today, the tune for Tôryanse can be heard playing at street intersections in Japan, letting people know when it's okay to cross.

Pushing Buns Contest (おしくらまんじゅう: Oshikura Manju)

This game is usually played in the wintertime when children want to get warm. Getting a group together, children interlock their arms, forming a circle looking out. Then everyone just pushes against each other, making the group sway this way and that. (A similar experience can be had on a jam-packed commuter train in Tokyo.) In Backwards Japan, instead of pushing in towards each other, the Monsters are trying to push each other off the platform!

Another fun fact: The "buns" in the game's title are actually the sweet buns you eat (manju). Manju expand on the baking sheet while in the oven and push against one another.

Backwards Game

BAKÉGYAMON

SHORT COMIC

?!
THUD
SLIP
I'M SO SORRY ...
OWW
Boxers? Really?!

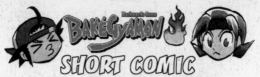

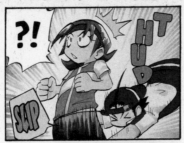

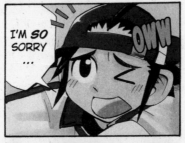

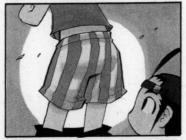

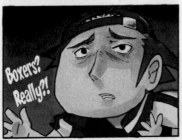

I like wandering around the neighborhood in the middle of the night. Walking around when everyone else is fast asleep, I keep hoping that I'll run into something or someone that isn't quite human.

–Mitsuhisa Tamura, 2006

Mitsuhisa Tamura debuted in 2004 with "Comical Magical," a one-shot manga in *Shonen Sunday R. BakéGyamon* is his first serialized manga. His favorite foods are cutlet curry and chocolate snacks.

BakéGyamon Vol. 2
Backwards Game

The VIZ Kids Manga Edition

STORY AND ART BY MITSUHISA TAMURA
Original Concept by Kazuhiro Fujita

Translation/Labaaman, HC Language Solutions, Inc.
English Adaptation/Stan!
Touch-up Art & Lettering/Primary Graphix
Cover Design/Sean Lee
Interior Design/Kevin Watson-Graff
Editor/Yuki Murashige

Editor in Chief, Books/Alvin Lu
Editor in Chief, Magazines/Marc Weidenbaum
VP, Publishing Licensing/Rika Inouye
VP, Sales & Product Marketing/Gonzalo Ferreyra
VP, Creative/Linda Espinosa
Publisher/Hyoe Narita

Printed in the U.S.A.

Published by VIZ Media, LLC
P.O. Box 77010
San Francisco, CA 94107

VIZ Kids Manga Edition
10 9 8 7 6 5 4 3 2 1
First printing, May 2009

www.viz.com

RATED
PARENTAL ADVISORY
BAKÉGYAMON is rated
A and is suitable for
readers of all ages.
ratings.viz.com

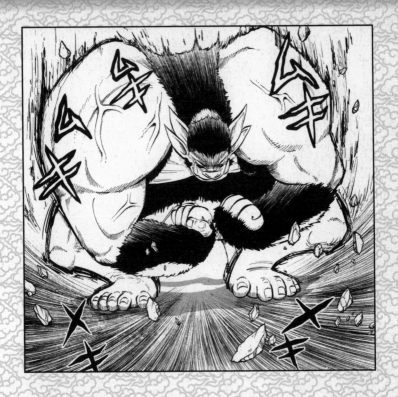

Coming Next Volume

BakéGyamon is no longer fun and games as the battle begins in earnest with the final 32 paired up tournament-style. With the new playing field a mock Tokyo Tower, there's only one way to go… *up*! Sanshiro will now have to use his battle skills against the very people he wants to be friends with!

Coming July 2009!

Legend tells of The Sea Temple, which contains a treasure with the power to take over the world. But its location remains hidden and requires a mysterious key. Can Ash, Pikachu and their friends prevent the unveiling of these powerful secrets?

Pokémon Ranger and the Temple of the Sea

Own it on DVD today!

COWA!

WHO'S GOT THE CURE FOR THE MONSTER FLU?

From AKIRA TORIYAMA, creator of *Dragon Ball, Dr. Slump,* and *Sand Land*

MANGA SERIES ON SALE NOW!

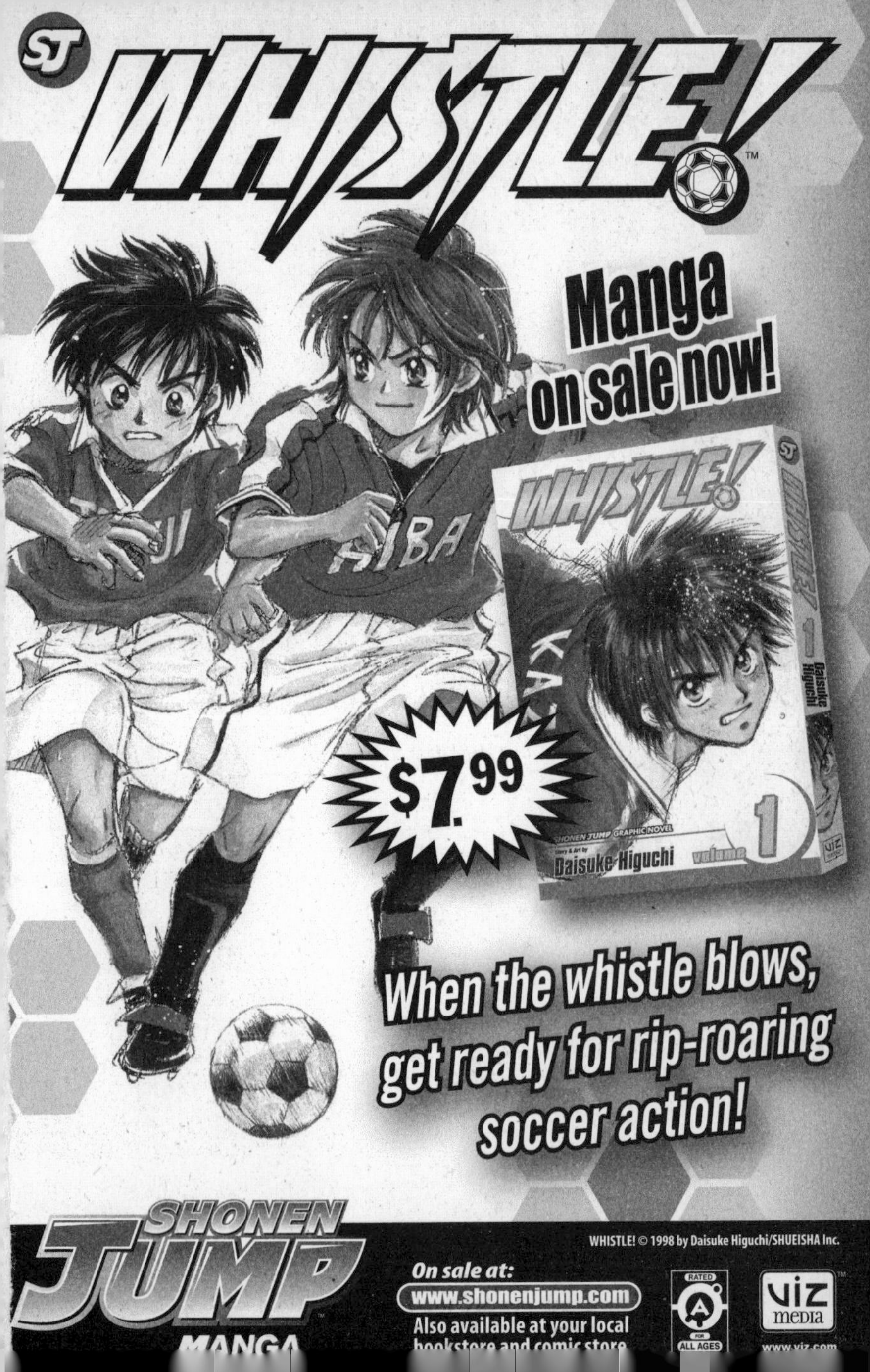
SJ
WHISTLE!™
Manga on sale now!
WHISTLE!
SJ
WHISTLE! 1 Daisuke Higuchi
SHONEN JUMP GRAPHIC NOVEL
Story & Art by
Daisuke Higuchi
volume 1
$7.99
When the whistle blows, get ready for rip-roaring soccer action!
SHONEN JUMP MANGA
WHISTLE! © 1998 by Daisuke Higuchi/SHUEISHA Inc.
On sale at:
www.shonenjump.com
Also available at your local bookstore and comic store.
RATED A FOR ALL AGES
VIZ media
www.viz.com